"In this breakthrough investigation, Kai Hafez and Anne Grüne place globalization, one of the most popular keywords of our times, under renewed critical scrutiny. In a powerful conceptual language, they develop an original account of the asymmetries and tensions of our interconnected world and offer a novel understanding of how its various communicative actors and their systemic relations, at once, bind us together and keep up apart. The outcome is a compelling narrative that sheds light on some of the most urgent challenges of our time, including the rise of global fundamentalisms and illiberal populisms. A must-read."

Prof. Lilie Chouliaraki, London School of Economics and Political Science

"This is a wide-ranging, sophisticated yet critical discussion of the globalization of communication. Telescoping from the systemic to the individual, and encompassing politics, commercial networks and media systems, the book provides a multi-faceted assessment of the potential and limitations of global communications."

Prof. Herman Wasserman, University of Cape Town, South Africa

"Hafez and Grüne's book offers much needed insight into the challenges of today's diversity of globalized interconnections. It is an excellent source for scholars and students alike when aiming to assess globalized communication in its concrete current formations. Through combining conceptual debates and empirical insights, the book is a key read to understand the multifacted interactions of our digital world."

Prof. Ingrid Volkmer, University of Melbourne, Australia

«Von der Erforschung vielschichtiger Interdependenzen (...) bis zur nötigen Verantwortung der Global Player ist hier anspruchsvoll nachzulesen. M.E. alternativlos.»
"The deep structure (of the handbook) enables users targeted entries. Readers receive complex and sophisticated information about multi-layered interdependencies (nation state vs. transnationalization, global elites vs. local majorities, role of the media) and the relevant responsibilty of global players. There is not alternative to this book."

Annette Rugen, ekz.bibliotheksservice (https://www.ekz-group.com)

«Hafez und Grüne gelingt es mit ihrem Handbuch, die Kommunikationstheorie prominent zu platzieren. (...) (Sie) tragen zu einer soliden Fundierung und fruchtbaren Diskussion zur Globalisierungsdebatte aus kommunikationswissenschaftlicher Sicht bei. (...) Nehmen Sie dieses Handbuch auch wirklich physisch oder virtuell „in die Hand". Das Lesen ist ein Gewinn.»
"Hafez und Grüne successfully and prominently position communication theory in the globalization debate. (...) They contribute to a solid foundation and fruitful discussion of globalization from the perspective of communication studies. (...) Make sure that you take this handbook really "into your hands". You will definitely profit from reading it." (own translation)

Prof. Dr. Thomas Herdin, Univ. of Salzburg, Publizistik 2021

"This extremely useful and timely translation of the original German publication by Hafez and Grüne is a great resource for students and researchers alike, as it deeply enriches – both theoretically and methodologically – the burgeoning literature on global communication."

Prof. Daya Thussu, Baptist University, Hong Kong

FOUNDATIONS OF GLOBAL COMMUNICATION

This book provides a wide-ranging theoretical and empirical overview of the disparate achievements and shortcomings of global communication.

This exceptionally ambitious and systematic project takes a critical perspective on the globalization of communication. Uniquely, it sets media globalization alongside a plethora of other globalized forms of communication, ranging from the individual to groups, civil society groupings, commercial enterprises and political formations. The result is a sophisticated and impressive overview of globalized communication across various facets, assessing the phenomena for the extent to which they live up to the much-hyped claims of globalization's potential to create a globally interdependent society. The setbacks of globalization, such as right-wing populism and religious fundamentalism, can only be understood if the shortcomings of global communication are taken more seriously.

Covering all types of cross-border global communication in media, political and economic systems, civil societies, social media and lifeworlds of the individual, this unique book is invaluable for students and researchers in media, communication, globalization and related areas.

Kai Hafez is a Chair Professor of International and Comparative Media and Communication Studies at the University of Erfurt, Germany. His research specializations are global and political communication, media and democracy and Islamic–Western relations. He is the author of *The Myth of Media Globalization* (2007).

Anne Grüne is a Senior Lecturer in the Department of Media and Communication Studies at the University of Erfurt, Germany. Her research specializations are globalization and social communication, comparative communication cultures and global popular culture. She is the author of *Formatted World Culture? On the Theory and Practice of Global Entertainment Television* (in German) (2016).

FOUNDATIONS OF GLOBAL COMMUNICATION

A Conceptual Handbook

Kai Hafez and Anne Grüne

TRANSLATED BY ALEX SKINNER

LONDON AND NEW YORK

Cover image: Getty Images

First published 2022
by Routledge
4 Park Square, Milton Park, Abingdon, Oxon OX14 4RN

and by Routledge
605 Third Avenue, New York, NY 10158

Routledge is an imprint of the Taylor & Francis Group, an informa business

© 2022 Kai Hafez and Anne Grüne

The right of Kai Hafez and Anne Grüne to be identified as authors of this work
has been asserted in accordance with sections 77 and 78 of the Copyright,
Designs and Patents Act 1988.

Translated by Alex Skinner

All rights reserved. No part of this book may be reprinted or reproduced or utilised
in any form or by any electronic, mechanical, or other means, now known or
hereafter invented, including photocopying and recording, or in any information
storage or retrieval system, without permission in writing from the publishers.

Trademark notice: Product or corporate names may be trademarks or registered trademarks,
and are used only for identification and explanation without intent to infringe.

Published in German by UVK Verlag 2021

British Library Cataloguing-in-Publication Data
A catalogue record for this book is available from the British Library

Library of Congress Cataloging-in-Publication Data
Names: Hafez, Kai, 1964– author. | Grüne, Anne, author. | Skinner, Alex, translator.
Title: Foundations of global communication / Kai Hafez and Anne Grüne;
translated by Alex Skinner.
Other titles: Grundlagen der globalen Kommunikation. English.
Description: Abingdon, Oxon ; New York, NY : Routledge, 2022. |
Translation of: Grundlagen der globalen Kommunikation : Medien – Systeme – Lebenswelten. |
Includes bibliographical references and index.
Identifiers: LCCN 2021054912 (print) | LCCN 2021054913 (ebook) |
ISBN 9781032185781 (hardback) | ISBN 9781032185828 (paperback) |
ISBN 9781003255239 (ebook)
Subjects: LCSH: Communication, International.
Classification: LCC P96.I5 H26 2022 (print) |
LCC P96.I5 (ebook) | DDC 302.2–dc23/eng/20220225
LC record available at https://lccn.loc.gov/2021054912
LC ebook record available at https://lccn.loc.gov/2021054913

ISBN: 978-1-032-18578-1 (hbk)
ISBN: 978-1-032-18582-8 (pbk)
ISBN: 978-1-003-25523-9 (ebk)

DOI: 10.4324/9781003255239

Typeset in Bembo
by Newgen Publishing UK

CONTENTS

List of figures	*xv*
Note on translation	*xvi*
Acknowledgements	*xvii*

	Introduction	1
	Two-speed globalization 1	
	Media, systems and lifeworlds in global communication 3	
	Phases of globalization research 5	
1	Theory of global communication	8
	1.1 General modes of global communication 8	
	Global public sphere and global community: synchronization and integration 8	
	Perception of distance and cosmopolitanism 10	
	Interaction, co-orientation and global synchrony 11	
	Discursive global society/dialogic global community: theories of communication 13	
	Integrationist systems theories 15	
	Dialogue between "cultures" in an extended lifeworld 17	
	1.2 Communicative systems, lifeworlds and their transformation 17	
	Systems and lifeworlds 17	
	System-lifeworld-network approach 18	
	Global centres and peripheries 20	
	Taking stock: globally communicating social systems and lifeworlds 21	
	Media, politics and economy as (trans)national systems 21	
	Global civil society and large communities 23	
	Global lifeworlds: a desideratum for "intercultural communication" 24	

viii Contents

Glocalization and hybridization of everyday action 25
Old and new global "elites" within systems and lifeworlds 26

1.3 Specific modes of communication (system connections) of systems and lifeworlds 27

Actors' modes of global communication: a continuum 27
Global interactivity beyond the mass media? 29
Synchronization of the global public sphere: the problem of the mass media 29
Local-global multi-level media-based public sphere(s) 31
Global organizational communication between discourse and interaction 31
Informality and mediatization of organizational communication 33
Global internal and external hybridity 34
Potential for global interaction of non-organized social systems 35
Global lifeworlds and group communication 37
Mobility, expanded space of interaction and the role problem 37
Social media and global monologue/dialogue 38
Global society, global community and global communication as a multiple phenomenon 39

1.4 System dependencies and lifeworld relations 39

Communication and inter-state relations 39
Media and national/international systemic relations 40
Relationships between mass media, systems of action and lifeworlds 43
Conclusion: horizontal and vertical interdependencies in the dominant and accidental mode 46

2 Mass media and the global public sphere 48

2.1 Systems and system change 50

A basic model of global mass communication 50
(Trans)national media ethics and professionalism 53
(G)local media production 54
The global reception gap: informational masses and elites 55
The environmental system of politics: the hegemony of the nation state 56
The environmental system of the economy: the limits of transnationalization 57
Non-traditional mass media: extended hypermediality 59
Interdependence gaps and two-speed globalization 60

2.2 Communicative system connections 61

2.2.1 Discourse analysis 61

Fundamentals: interdiscursivity, convergence and the domestication of media discourses 61
A fragmented news agenda: the tip of the globalization iceberg 62
Global framing or domesticated discourses? 64
Visual globalization and stereotypes 67
Transnational media: contraflows without cosmopolitanism 67
Incomplete synchronization of global media discourses 68

2.2.2 Public sphere theory 69

Theoretical perspectives on the "global public sphere" 69

Contents **ix**

The role of the global public sphere in global society 70
Alternative theories of the public sphere: dialogic, constructive and
cosmopolitan journalism 71
Global public sphere and global governance: the case of Europe 72
Conclusion: global public sphere, global society and lagging structural
change of the mass media 74

3 Politics: the state's global communication 75

3.1 Systems and system change 76
Actors, target audiences and "third spaces" of global
communication 76
Diplomacy: realism versus constructivism 77
Second-track diplomacy and global governance 78
Target audiences of public diplomacy 80
New communicator roles in foreign policy 81
Inconsistent shifts towards a "global domestic policy" 81

3.2 Communicative system connections 82

3.2.1 Interaction and dialogue 82
Interests, values and communication 82
Diplomatic process stages and metacommunication 83
Agenda-setting and framing in political negotiations 84
Diplomatic mediation: from interaction to dialogue 85
Signalling as non-verbal global communication 86
Global governance as a diplomatic "hotline"? 87

3.2.2 Interaction and organizational communication 88
Informality at the relational level of global communication 88
Trends in informality: networks of associated states rather than cultural
boundaries 89
Diplomatic protocol as global symbolic communication 90
Cyber-diplomacy: new dynamics, old substance 91
Global spaces of interpretation through the text-speech
relationship 92
Continuities within changing global diplomatic communication 93

3.2.3 Observation and diffusion 93
The state's communicative multi-competence 93
Ambassadors and secret services as information gatherers 94
Media monitoring as the global observation of observation 94
Knowledge management between rationality and power politics 95

3.2.4 Discursive (external) communication 96
The non-transparency of action systems 96
Public diplomacy/propaganda 96
"Understanding"-based persuasion 97
Foreign cultural policy: "dialogue" between "cultures"? 99
War communication: the return of global disinformation 101
State international broadcasting: more than persuasion? 102
Public diplomacy 2.0 104
Conclusion: the state's global communication between integration
and isolation 104

x Contents

4 Economy: global corporate communication   106

4.1 Systems and system change 107

Shift of perspective: global institutionalism 107
Power and communication in global companies 108
Technological gaps and cosmopolitan lifeworld capital 110
A critique of essentialism in the discipline of economics 111
The ethical unpredictability of global capitalism 112

4.2 Communicative system connections 112

4.2.1 Interaction and dialogue 113

New dialogic action and negotiation in global enterprises 113
Corporate culture and global storytelling 114
Of "chains" and "stars": network structures as communicative
   channels 116
Global teams as reconfigured global communities 117
Is the network the global message? 118
The dimensions of global economic interaction 119

4.2.2 Interaction and organizational communication 119

Informality as a research desideratum 119
Oral communication and global language skills 121
Mediatization of global economic communication 121
Face-to-face communication in global virtual teams 123
"Global cities" rather than "the death of distance" 124

4.2.3 Observation and diffusion 124

Economic knowledge gaps 124
Global knowledge diffusion and local adaptation 124
Limits to global circulation and global observation 125
Knowledge capitalism rather than a global knowledge society 126
"Semi-modernity" amid the global flow of knowledge 128

4.2.4 Discursive (external) communication 128

Direct marketing as global micro-contact 128
Advertising and PR: dominant culturalism 129
"Glocal marketing" without cosmopolitan codes 130
Conclusion: capitalists are (not) internationalists after all 131

5 Civil society and global movement communication   133

5.1 Systems and system change 134

International NGOs: grassroots or self-interest? 134
Social movements: the politics of information and mobilization 135
A crisis of global movements? 136
Tenuous ideology, fragmentation and global networks 136
North–South divide and sociospatial ties 137
Weak ties and low risk in global civil society 138

5.2 Communicative system connections 139

5.2.1 Interaction and dialogue 139

INGOs and global interaction 139
Face-to-face communication in social movements 140
Boomerang effects and domestication 141

Contents **xi**

Interaction and global scale shifts 141
Networks and North–South elites 142
Mass media as internal system environment 144
A hybrid interaction-media system 146

5.2.2 Interaction and organizational communication 147
The Internet: mediatization as resource 147
The Internet is increasing weak ties involving meagre
interaction 148
New forms of activism, old (North–South) rifts 149
Global text-conversation cycles? 150
Informality as incivility: who is a member of global civil society? 151
Weak-tie globalization through digitization 152

5.2.3 Observation and diffusion 152
Alternative information policy 152
INGO expertise versus symbolic TAN resources? 153
Informational quality and circulatory limits 154
New global knowledge elites 155

5.2.4 Discursive (external) communication 155
Professionalization of public relations 155
Cosmopolitan PR? 156
Conclusion: civil society as an expanded global public sphere 158

6 Large communities: global online communication   160
  6.1 Systems and system change 161
Community and society 161
Virtual community and the constructivism of placelessness 161
Structuralist social co-presence and "re-tribalization" 162
The reciprocity model of the global online community 164
Global social capital: cosmopolitanism or cultural battle between
communities? 166
Global community or global society? 167

  6.2 Communicative system connections 168
6.2.1 Interaction and dialogue 168
The cascade model of global online communication 168
Connectivity: Internet geography and online territories 169
Digital divides and the multilingualization of the Internet 170
Relationality: asynchrony and community density 172
Dialogicity 1: global echo chambers 173
Dialogicity 2: pop cosmopolitanism, gaming and "global
metropolis" 175
Dialogicity 3: digital (trans)cultural salons 176
Discursive community through media use 178
Interactive global community? 179

6.2.2 Observation and diffusion 180
Global wiki-knowledge community? 180
Wikipedia: Eurocentrism of worldview 180
Separation and quality of knowledge 181
A global knowledge community? 182

xii Contents

6.2.3 Discursive (external) communication 183
Intercultural dialogue versus online global war 183
Antinomy between internal and external capital 184
Conclusion: social networks as global communities, plural 186

7   Small groups: global lifeworldly communication I   187

7.1   Lifeworldly structures of global group communication 188
Neglected research on groups 188
Global action contexts of stationary groups 189
The geopolitical positioning of urbanity 190
Mobile horizons of action 191
Digital spatial shifts in group structures 192
Temporal structures of global group communication 193
Contact as a symbolic resource of group communication 194
Transformation and persistence of the small group in a
    globalizing world 195

7.2   Communicative connections in the lifeworld 195

7.2.1 Interaction and dialogue 195
Transnational connectivity of the lifeworld 195
The interaction paradox of global group communication 197
A theoretical fallacy in intercultural communication research 198
Interaction patterns of global group communication: three
    case analyses 200
Interactivity 1: circular interaction – the dialogic model of the
    global community 200
Global education and "intimate tourism" 201
Family/peer communication and circular global community 202
Interactivity 2: reciprocal interaction – the hegemonic model
    of the global community 204
Migration and tourism communication 204
Interactivity 3: reciprocal discourses – the discursive model of an
    imagined global community 207
Interactive group communication and participatory global
    community 208

7.2.2 Observation 208
Collective observation and medial keyhole 208
Local small groups and the media's conception of other countries 211
Self-referentiality and we-identity through media observation 212
Integration through the culture-connecting interpretation of global
    media events 214
Conclusion: the small group as norm or disruptive element in global
    communication? 215

8   The individual: global lifeworldly communication II   216

8.1   Lifeworldly structures of individual global communication 216
Individualization as a meta-tendency of globalization? 216
Cosmopolitans and the paradox of knowledge 217
Cosmopolitanism as social capital 218
Levels of action of cosmopolitanism 220

Contents **xiii**

Stereotypes and individual relationships to the world 221
Conditions for stereotype change 222
Global socialization through family and education 224
Individual lifeworlds' ambivalent relations to the world 226

8.2 Communicative connections in the lifeworld 226
    8.2.1 Interaction and dialogue 227
        Interpersonal dialogue and global community/society 227
        Dynamics and imponderables of global dialogue 228
        Structural variants of global dialogue 230
        Overlap between observation and dialogue 232
        Influences of digital media 233
        The power and impotence of individual interaction 233

    8.2.2 Observation and diffusion 234
        The individual's discursive global knowledge processing 234
        A critical worldview through media appropriation? 235
        Filters for the processing of global knowledge (or ignorance) 236
        Ignorance as a risk in global society 238
        The individual en route to global knowledge optimization 239

    8.2.3 Discursive (external) communication and global actions 239
        Cosmopolitan action and role adaptation 239
        Synchronizing "internal" and "external" globalization 240
        Conclusion: the global individual between "genius" and
          "madness" 240

9   Interdependencies of systems and lifeworlds   242

9.1 Foundations of interdependence 242
        The research primacy of local (inter)dependence 242
        Dimensions and levels of interdependence 243

9.2 Global horizontal interdependence 245
        Global communication as a necessary condition 245
        Global regulatory coupling as a sufficient condition 247

9.3 Global and local vertical interdependence 248
        Politics, media and the public sphere: globally extended
          indexing 248
        Civil society, media and politics: the inversion of
          dependence 251
        Lifeworlds, media and politics: decolonization through
          globalization? 254
        Conclusion: interdependence – diverse but incomplete and
          reversible 255

Conclusion and future prospects   257
        Overall assessment 257
        Future prospects 260

Bibliography   *265*
Index   *313*

FIGURES

1.1	Global communication: public spheres and interactions	10
1.2	Actor-specific modes of communication	28
1.3	Local–global multilevel media-based public sphere(s)	32
1.4	Global communicative interdependencies	47
2.1	Dimensions of global mass communication	52
3.1	Actors and target audiences of international political communication	76
4.1	Dimensions of global economic interaction in transnational companies	120
5.1	Discursive and interactive arenas of transnational social movements	146
6.1	The cascade model of interaction in the global online community	169
6.2	Diasporic digital networks	177
7.1	Variants of global inter- and intragroup communication	209

NOTE ON TRANSLATION

All direct quotes from German texts appearing in the bibliography of this book have been translated by Alex Skinner.

ACKNOWLEDGEMENTS

We would like to thank a number of people without whom this book would never have seen the light of day. A debt of gratitude is owed to those involved in the production of the original German book and this English edition, especially Alex Skinner (translation), Dan Lohmeyer (final editing), Uta Preimesser and Tina Kaiser (at our German publisher UVK/UTB), Natalie Foster, Jennifer Vennall, Thara Kanaga and Susan Dunsmore (at our English publisher Routledge), Annett Psurek, Kirsten Wünsche, Antonia Hafner and Maximilian Einhaus (literature acquisition and graphic support). Colleagues such as Joachim Höflich, Sven Jöckel (University of Erfurt) and Christian Stegbauer (University of Frankfurt) helped clarify certain issues. We discussed aspects of this book at a workshop featuring Friedrich Krotz, Hubert Knoblauch, Carola Richter, Christine Horz, Sabrina Schmidt and others.

Our thanks also to those who invited us to give keynote addresses and lectures on the topic of globalization over the past years and decades. In Kai Hafez's case, these included the Institut für Auslandsbeziehungen, the Federal Foreign Office, the Federal Office of Administration, Netzwerk Recherche, the Toda Institute for Global Peace and Policy Research (Honolulu), the Goethe-Institut Karachi and the universities of Oxford, Westminster, Oslo, Kalmar, Pelita Harapan (Jakarta), the London School of Economics and Political Science and expert bodies including the International Association of Media and Communication Research, the German Communication Association, the International Communication Association, the Global Communication Association and the German Sociological Association. Anne Grüne spoke at the International Association of Media and Communication Research, the German Communication Association and the Global Communication Association.

We would also like to thank the international Working Group of German Communication Studies Scholars, of which we are members, which seeks to foster the "deep internationalization" of communication research in Germany. The other

xviii Acknowledgements

members of the group are Hanan Badr, Markus Behmer, Susanne Fengler, Anke Fiedler, Oliver Hahn, Kefa Hamidi, Thomas Hanitzsch, Christine Horz, Beate Illg, Anna Litvinenko, Martin Löffelholz, Melanie Radue, Carola Richter, Barbara Thomaß and Florian Töpfl.

We warmly acknowledge all our students at the University of Erfurt, whether they are taking the bachelor's degree in communication studies or the English-language master's degree in "Global Communication: Politics and Society", which we founded (together with Patrick Rössler). For many years, our students, from almost every continent, have been our interlocutors on all issues of global communication. Colleagues from all over the world provided us with support when we established the master's degree course, particularly Lilie Chouliaraki (London School of Economics and Political Science), Daniel Hallin (University of California, San Diego), Yahya Kamalipour (North Carolina A&T State University, Greensboro), Deddy Mulyana (Universitas Padjadjaran, Bandung), Daya Thussu (Baptist University, Hong Kong), Stephen Reese (University of Texas at Austin), Karina Horsti (Academy of Finland, Helsinki) and Naila Hamdy (American University in Cairo). Without our lecturers Sabrina Schmidt, Regina Cazzamatta, Sarah Elmaghraby, Danny Schmidt, Anja Wollenberg, Imad Mustafa, our colleague Alexander Thumfart, with whom Kai Hafez taught a joint seminar on globalization, and our Indonesian university cooperation partner Subekti Priyadharma, our efforts to synthesize research and teaching would surely have been less successful.

A signal contribution has also been made by the once again international team of doctoral students with whom we have been working intensively for many years on topics in international and comparative media and communication studies – such as foreign coverage, media ethics, and migration and media – and in the fields of media systems and media conflict. Many of these former students are now lecturers and professors at universities.

We would like to express our sincere thanks to the German Academic Exchange Service and the International Office of the University of Erfurt – as represented not least by Ms Manuela Linde – for their wonderful, long-standing support.

INTRODUCTION

In today's market of ideas, globalization has few rivals. Like no other phenomenon, it shapes our thinking and engenders a vision of simultaneity, connectedness and even togetherness uniting all of humanity. Beyond the horizon of globalization only the stars await, though as yet we can make no sociological statements about them. On this planet, however, all significant visions of progress are connected to globalization because all other social formations – from the family through the village to the nation state – already exist. While localization is in some sense the antithesis of globalization, it has no great significance as a notion of human progress. Globalization has thus taken on a unique intellectual appeal, although it still seems unfinished and is projected into the future, which explains why it has become a tendentious political term. Political rifts have opened up between advocates and opponents of globalization. After the euphoria surrounding globalization came disillusionment, triggering opposition. Vision, chimera, chameleon – globalization is all these things.

Two-speed globalization

For these reasons, over the last few decades the term globalization has become one of the leading explanatory models in the academy, one with considerable social relevance. It refers to nothing less than a fundamental reordering of political, economic and social relations with a view to eliminating or overcoming existing national and cultural-linguistic boundaries. But despite this widely shared quotidian understanding of globalization, there is no clear definition of the term, even within the bounds of scholarly discourse.

The concept of globalization, as used in this book, does not simply mean "universality", the idea that people around the world now live within similar forms of modernity (in terms of technology, for example), a modernity that has mysteriously

DOI: 10.4324/9781003255239-1

2 Introduction

spread across the globe. Instead, we understand globalization explicitly as "connectivity" (Axford 2013, p. 22). The key question here is how media, systems and lifeworld actors cross borders through diverse types of human communication, and whether, and, if so, how, this communicative dissolution of boundaries across the world relates to new forms of an integrative global and epistemic community and society.

In a sense, globalization has remained a myth in the fullest sense of the term, not because it has not been realized at all, but because the phenomena associated with it remain ambivalent. We find setbacks to globalization and countervailing trends at every turn. German sociologist Richard Münch has clearly identified the challenges posed by globalization. He assumes that, often, the growing interdependence between states is not immediately understood by national populations, that political, economic and social elites find themselves in a mediating role, on the basis of which they open the nation state to the outside world, while at the same time having to appeal for trust in this policy domestically (1998, p. 350ff.). Münch refers to a split between the "avant-garde" of a "modernizing elite that thinks in global terms and the masses, who insist on national solidarity all the more vehemently" (ibid., p. 352). He sees the creation of a community of global citizens as the crucial task for the present era.

While the concepts of the "elite" and the "masses" make us a little uneasy, Münch's analysis recalls earlier distinctions, such as that put forward by Richard K. Merton between "cosmopolitans" and "locals" (1968, p. 441ff.) and the concept of the "globalization of the two velocities" proposed by Kai Hafez (2010a, p. 6ff.). The non-simultaneity of globalization affects not only social groups, but also organized social systems such as the mass media, which has undergone a "tectonic shift" in the past few decades because technological and economic aspects of media globalization have often progressed more rapidly than content and because, in the supposed age of globalization, reports about other parts of the world are neither greater in number nor more varied than before (Hafez 1999). On the contrary, there are now fewer resources available for journalism with an international focus, meaning that (structural) political and economic interdependencies between states have increased but societies' dialogic and discursive understanding has not automatically grown in tandem with this process, giving rise to hackneyed visions of "the enemy" and fuelling conflicts both within countries and internationally (ibid.; see also Stone and Rizova 2014).

The internal development of the purported global elites is similarly uneven. Even the liberal sector of society often thinks and acts in an anything but cosmopolitan manner and remains deeply rooted in the national habitus (Müller 2019a, 2019b). With their ambivalent attitude towards globalization, political and economic systems contribute to the hostility to globalization displayed by certain political currents, even if these systems' rate of globalization is higher overall than that of most people's lifeworlds. At the very least, upon close examination, the "globalization of everyday life", as experienced by individuals, groups and communities, though heterogeneous, appears to be more sluggish than that of politics and the economy. Despite numerous "global injections" through goods, mass media and occasional global mobility in people's private worlds, these are still strongly localized. The "globalization of the two velocities", the "gap between the avant-garde and the masses", a "tectonic shift" or "ambivalences": these are all more or less apt terms describing the heterogeneous position of systems and lifeworlds within the process of globalization.

We can fairly interpret the renaissance of far-right politics worldwide, whose symptoms include the election of Donald Trump in the United States, Brexit in the United Kingdom and right-wing populist governments in countries as diverse as Hungary, Poland, Brazil and India – not to mention Islamism – as an anti-globalist rebellion. The fact that right-wing populists have managed to win elections is clear evidence of how out of synch with globalization the world's societies are and demonstrates that much of the internationalization that has occurred in recent decades has been superficial and culturally undigested, amounting to little more than the circulation of goods.

Even a global and, as one might have thought, unifying event such as the COVID-19 pandemic that began in early 2020 has featured global discrepancies in perception. Views of this global health crisis seem to depend on the form taken by the communication about it at the local level. By no means do the associated media and public constructions automatically generate global narratives of solidarity. Local clichés about different countries have been reheated, racist responses have intensified and globalization has been interpreted as a high-risk venture. The overemphasis on the negative in distant places is not a new or unusual phenomenon, but a well-known accompaniment to global modernity. Within and through their communicative mediation, "far-off lands" remain distant indeed.

Media, systems and lifeworlds in global communication

Contemporary debates have featured numerous attempts to analyse the reasons for the populist backlash: racism and cultural overload, social deprivation or a combination of these factors (Geiselberger 2017). So far, however, no approach has sought to identify who or what might be responsible for communicative shortcomings, that is, for the failure of the "feats of mediation" that Münch describes as vital. But the idea that we can presuppose global communication as a more or less fixed variable, while all other motives for global social action fluctuate, is fundamentally wrong. Worldwide connectivity is also a heterogeneous phenomenon – one that this book seeks to take stock of.

Till now, no text has dealt in a truly comprehensive way with the cross-border communication processes within, or between, social systems and lifeworlds. Yet it seems obvious that the organized systems of politics, economy and society, that is, the state, businesses, organizations and social movements, are better placed to engage in global communication than many citizens. Global communication entails dealing with spatial distance and also involves cross-border contacts. To interact with high intensity and on an enduring basis, and to follow local discourses in

4 Introduction

other parts of the world in different languages, can be a costly undertaking for which many organizations and the global avant-garde of civil society are better equipped than most private individuals, despite mass tourism and cultural exchange programmes. If we also take into account the prosperity gap between industrialized, emerging and developing countries, it becomes clear that global tourism is in fact only possible for a small part of humanity. From a statistical point of view, even migration does little to change this fact, because only around 3 per cent of people worldwide live outside the country in which they were born (IOM UN Migration 2018, p. 18). On the other hand, global social movements and international online communities show the fascinating speed with which at least some sections of the population can overcome vast distances communicatively. Global "understanding of the other" and a "global civil society" are no longer pipe dreams – but this does not make them an all-encompassing reality.

This book sets out to provide a theoretical and empirical overview of the disparate achievements and shortcomings of global communication. For a study of such communication, our decision to organize chapters on the basis of social actors (mass media, the state, businesses, civil society, large communities, small groups and individuals) rather than communication processes (such as interactions, discourses and observations) might seem to require some explanation. First of all, communication processes are obviously co-present in that they shape the internal arrangement of the individual chapters. But the deeper reason for the book's core structure lies in our conceptual framework, which seeks to tread a middle path between the structuralist and constructivist perspectives. In our theoretical introduction we present a system-lifeworld-network approach, which works on the assumption that communication is no free-floating epiphenomenon and can only be understood if we reflect upon communicators' specific prerequisites and capacities.

The authors of this book agree that today's globalization research is bedevilled by a "lack of actor- and practice-centred studies" (Schmitt and Vonderau 2014, p. 11) and that the acting subject must be reintegrated into our analyses if we are to produce convincing theories (Hay and Marsh 2000, p. 13). To mention one example: the ego-centred global network of an individual is completely different from a corporate network, such that the prominent concept of global "networking" (Castells 2010, among others) becomes meaningful only if we include consideration of the specific way it is used within social theory. In other words, we can grasp global communication only if we combine the process theories offered by the discipline of communication studies with social scientific theories of structure. In the present work, at the level of process, we deploy theories of discourse, interaction, organizational communication and diffusion, approaches centred on intergroup, intragroup and interpersonal communication, and stereotype theory. At the structural level we draw on media systems research, theories of the public sphere, general theories of systems, organizations and civil society, concepts of the lifeworld and action theory. Since there is no unified globalization theory currently available, we have tried to fit the different approaches in modular theory building into an analytical framework that is as rigorous as possible, one that explains global communication in a holistic way.

Despite the breadth of our overview of different parts of society, there are some gaps in this book due to the exclusion of certain areas. We have not, for example, dedicated chapters either to the global system of scholarship nor to the art and culture sector in the narrower sense. In the social systems we have examined, we have scrutinized the state rather than parties and organizations in the field of politics, transnational companies rather than trade within the economy, and non-governmental organizations (NGOs) and social movements in civil society rather than associations or organizations. Our account of large communities is limited to online communities and in reflecting on the small group, we have not taken every single type into account. But we believe this book provides a systematic overview of most of the key fields of global communication, from the mass media through organized systems of action to crucial areas of the lifeworld, and, perhaps for the first time, brings these elements together to paint an overall picture. Nonetheless, we regard the present text as part of a long-term project in the field of communication-oriented globalization research, which should be followed by further studies.

Phases of globalization research

Globalization, understood as a theory centred on the crossing of national borders, is one of the most significant scholarly concepts, though it has been beset by conceptual crisis in the twenty-first century. The "strange death of 'globalization'" (Rosenberg 2005) has left many of the main protagonists in the globalization debate at a loss. How did perhaps the most scintillating intellectual paradigm of the present era undergo such rapid decline? One reason was surely that the early "hyperglobalism" of authors such as Anthony Giddens (2000), Ulrich Beck (2000), David Held and Anthony McGrew (2000, 2002), and Manuel Castells (2010), a perspective informed by the idea of globalization as a virtually all-powerful phenomenon, had simply been too audacious to be empirically tenable. The end of the nation state, the transnationalization of the economy and the complete deterritorialization of social relations were visions too extensive and too demanding to be realizable.

A sceptical "second wave" of globalization research soon emerged to challenge this rampant normativism. As befits any revisionism worth its salt, this turned the basic assumptions of the field upside down (Martell 2007). From the perspective of critics such as Paul Hirst and Graham Thompson (1999), Colin Hay and David Marsh (2000), Terry Flew (2007) and Kai Hafez (2007a), the nation state was alive and kicking, economic globalization was of limited scope and, in particular, the notion of the comprehensive networking of the world through media and communication was largely a myth.

But there is reason to believe that the "post-mortem" (Rosenberg 2005) on the globalization approach is as premature as the old hyperglobalism and that we are now

6 Introduction

experiencing a more realistic "third wave" of globalization theory (Martell 2007). Strangely enough, it is the former weaknesses of globalization research that are now ensuring its survival. The reality is that globalization has always been a catchphrase that, while invoking a new spatial concept for scholars, has never become a coherent social scientific theory. If classical approaches such as neo-institutionalism, functionalism or even actor-network theory seem so vital today (see Chapter 1, Section 1.2), it is partly because globalization theory has failed to exhaust its potential. The transformation of older concepts generated by social theory, such as "nation", "society", "public sphere", "organization" or "community" has rarely been truly successful in the globalization debate. Key terms such as "transnationalization", "global public sphere", "global society", the "virtual community" or the "global village" (McLuhan 1962) imply the straightforward deterritorialization of familiar social concepts without really taking into account that a condition of spacelessness changes things substantially. At the global level, what used to be "society" is no longer a society, just as the public sphere or community do not operate according to familiar rules. This, however, implies pushing scholars well beyond their current capabilities, because it requires a shift away from the compartmentalizing of academic subjects and theories (Axford 2013, p. 3) and an interdisciplinary approach that has yet to be realized.

One of the main reasons for the stagnation described above may be that the pioneering thinkers never really took communication processes into account in a consistent way. The sociologists and philosophers who dominated the debate relegated the discipline of communication studies, which ought to have played a leading role in it, to the status of an auxiliary field, one whose processual logics were often obscured by nebulous terms such as "networking". For leading intellectuals such as Giddens or Held, the acceleration and deterritorialization of technology-based communication became the unquestioned premise of a research that subsequently considered only when the nation state would fall victim to the pressures of cross-border communication (Hafez 2007a, p. 57ff.). The marginalization of communication theory pushed one of the three great resources of theory building – power, capital and communication – to the periphery, for decades guaranteeing the primacy of the other two (and that of the associated academic disciplines).

We can only speculate about the reasons for this marginalization of communication theory. Was it due to "technophilia", an excessive fascination with the new possibilities opened up by digital technology? Similar to earlier theoretical debates between modernization and dependency theorists, the fixation on digital technology and the undervaluation of social communication have always been partly an expression of Eurocentrism. It is not surprising, then, that the globalization debate originated primarily in the Anglo-American countries – and also came to grief there. Still, the discipline of communication studies is certainly guilty of a form of self-marginalization as well: at present, comprehensive macro-theories seem less important in the field than partial theorems developed by media researchers or limited ideas focused on interpersonal communication. A subject that borrows the macro-theory of the public sphere or systems theory (Habermas, Luhmann, and so on) from other social sciences and humanities disciplines or fails entirely to reflect on them is in no position to complain about its marginal contribution to major intellectual issues.

The fact that one of this book's authors (Hafez) expressed views sceptical of globalization at an early stage does not mean that the analysis we present here can simply be considered part of the second wave of the globalization debate. Numerous revisionist facts and arguments certainly flow into this book and above all into our attempt to take empirical stock of global communication as it currently exists. At the same time, however, on the basis of a well-founded communication theory, what we attempt to do here is in fact associated with the "third wave" of research on globalization. Although this strand of scholarship no longer assumes a general, all-pervasive and all-transforming species of globalization, it recognizes global "patterns of stratification across and within societies involving some becoming enmeshed and some marginalised" (Martell 2007, p. 189). On the basis of a sceptical, revisionist view of things, then, we simultaneously highlight transformative potential pointing to a genuinely new quality of globalization, though its effects on the world are still far from clear. This book can thus be viewed as a realist's attempt to "ride" the "third wave" of globalization research.

1

THEORY OF GLOBAL COMMUNICATION

The following theoretical outline begins with an introduction to basic modes of communication in Section 1.1, which is necessary because the present book is not only about global mass media communication, but also takes into account the processes of political and social communication of various kinds. In Section 1.2, we then present the actors involved in communication – organized and non-organized social systems and lifeworlds – and consider their relationship to modes of communication. This is followed in Section 1.3 by an introductory look at the specific forms of communication characteristic of social systems and lifeworlds within the global realm. The final section, Section 1.4, provides a basic overview of the global exchanges and interdependencies between actors' various ways of communicating.

1.1 General modes of global communication

Global public sphere and global community: synchronization and integration

A variety of concepts are of significance when it comes to global and cross-border communication. The best known is probably that of the "global public sphere" (Sparks 1998; Volkmer 2014). In the case of the mass media, we are used to asking whether a global public sphere in fact exists. Are discourses and thus topics, frames, concepts, symbols and images dealt with at the same time in different national media systems or even transnationally, that is, through media that operate in several media systems? We can call this a question of synchronization or even co-orientation and express it in simple terms as follows. Do people across the globe observe the world, with the help of media, in a similar way? Does journalistic self-observation really lead to the "synchronization of global society" (Blöbaum 1994, p. 261) by providing us with similar knowledge? While the concept of the "public sphere"

DOI: 10.4324/9781003255239-2

is widely known, sociological concepts such as the "global society" or the "global community" (Richter 1990; Beck 2000) play virtually no role in communication research. Historically, the term "society" has been closely linked with the emergence of a media-based public sphere. In a society, people observe their environment with the help of media (Kunczik and Zipfel 2001, p. 47ff.). The concept of a "global community", meanwhile, is problematic for communication research. It evokes a problem different from that of synchronization, namely the interaction problem, which is also a problem of integration. While direct interaction is not absolutely necessary in societies, and observation through the use of mass media is of central importance, communities are created when people interact with one another rather than merely communicating or learning about others. For a community, especially a local and relatively static one, interpersonal dialogue is virtually indispensable. Through dialogue, we optimize our knowledge and create a shared sense of togetherness as a key value.

We have thus established two basic definitions: (1) networking as interpretive information processing without interaction is *observation*; and (2) networking as cooperative and integrative information processing is *interaction* or *dialogue*. Both forms of communication are important in human life.

It is true that it is difficult to draw a clear defining line between society and community, given that "nations" (in contrast to the state) are also surrogate communities in the form of large groups, which can develop a sense of unity even if there is no direct interaction between all the members of the community. Here we might introduce the term "discursive communities", which are not held together by direct interaction, but rather by a broadly synchronized public sphere: language, history and culture are hegemonically defined via storage media, and this may determine prevailing notions of communality. But like "virtual communities" (Rheingold 2000), national communities are not fully developed ones characterized by intense interaction, a pronounced sense of togetherness and clear horizons of action. If a strong sense of unity prevails, as is often the case with nations (patriotism, nationalism), then this usually implies a fusion of a discursive and an interactive community. Identification is inculcated through direct contact with a small number of community members, but is otherwise based on the shared experiences of a discursive community (one facilitated by the media). The concept of the "global community" can also be imagined as a combination of this kind. Cosmopolitanism, in other words, a worldview that goes beyond the concept of the "nation" to encompass humanity as a whole, arises through (1) direct cross-border interactions between human beings; (2) (representative) direct interaction between certain social systems across borders (such as with politics and diplomacy); and (3) globally synchronized knowledge, values and perspectives conveyed by the mass media.

The key proposition expounded in this book is that mass media alone can at most generate a "global public sphere", but not a "global community". The latter emerges, if at all, only with the help of other social systems and in people's lifeworlds. As we shall see, in its current state, global mass communication is quite unable to synchronize public spheres and knowledge of the world, because national

10 Theory of global communication

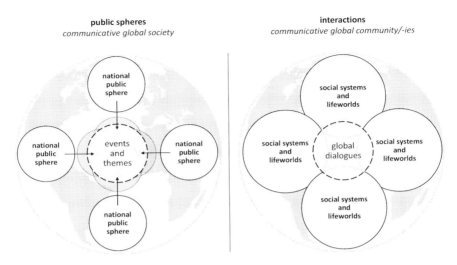

FIGURE 1.1 Global communication: public spheres and interactions

media systems are still largely isolated from one another. Furthermore, due to the monologic structure of the media – one-to-many rather than face-to-face, person-to-person or group-to-group – global mass communication is *fundamentally* incapable of generating community-building dialogues. Figure 1.1 illustrates the observational and public sphere-generating structure of the media system, as well as the interactive and community-generating character of other social systems and lifeworlds.

Perception of distance and cosmopolitanism

Why do we need an expanded conceptual model? Why do we emphasize the aspects of interaction, dialogue and the participatory community? There are, of course, instances in which the media and the public sphere generate empathy and a sense of togetherness. Media-based discursive communities may, under special conditions, create a feeling of solidarity and connectedness among people that goes far beyond the usual social coexistence within the nation and the coexistence of parallel lifeworlds. Particularly in situations of war and crisis, however, these feelings clash with an underlying patriotism. In this context, media discourses help to separate countries and populations from one another by disseminating simplistic concepts of the enemy (Hafez 2007a, p. 46ff.).

Positive facets of the global public sphere – such as media-induced cosmopolitan solidarity with refugees – are extremely unstable in nature. Lilie Chouliaraki has shown that media narratives about "distant" suffering are most successful in helping build a consciousness of community (cosmopolitanism) when they humanize and individualize suffering and create a sense of closeness by highlighting shared responsibilities and opportunities for action (2006). How unstable such phenomena

Theory of global communication **11**

are, however, was apparent in European reporting on refugees and German public opinion on this topic in 2015–16 (Hafez 2016; Georgiou and Zaborowski 2017). Public discourses are fleeting, fickle and erratic.

If we adapt the co-orientation approaches focused on interpersonal communication to the media, we come to understand that observation is a complex process in which misinterpretations quickly arise, such as so-called "pluralistic ignorance", which is generated by assumptions about how others interpret a given phenomenon (Hafez 2002a, vol. 1, p. 171ff., vol. 2, p. 253ff.). What do non-Muslim Germans believe, based on media information, regarding what Muslims think about terror? And are they correct? Chouliaraki has been interpreted to the effect that, even under the conditions of international media reportage, as a rule, the state of tension between a universal consciousness and people's specific (local) involvements impedes global communality, with the self-assignment to a particular community (nation, "cultural area" or religion) remaining unaffected (Yilmaz and Trandafoiu 2014, p. 7f.). Transcultural, long-distance communication through media-based observation is, therefore, not community-building or is so only to a limited extent.

Interaction, co-orientation and global synchrony

Hence, the question is: is there a need for the observation and synchronization performed by national public spheres to be joined by a true cross-border dialogue, one that better integrates national systems and allows the individual to act beyond the local level? It is true that traditional societies, the highly interactive tribes and clans that dominated social life in earlier times, were highly racist and xenophobic and that their propensity for war was quite similar to that of modern societies (Diamond 2013, p. 142ff.). The question we have to ask, then, is: why should we favour more interaction, if it is modern society, with its institutions such as the state, media and the public sphere, that has created rules for the enduring survival of human beings in the territories of other groups? The answer is that it is the cross-border interaction that began in the modern age – interaction with out-groups rather than only the in-group as in the past – that has advanced the networking of the world. It is not so much observation by the media as direct interaction between states that, to remain with the above example, has created a system of rights of residence and citizenship under international law. Like exchange at other levels of society, direct interaction between political systems and states must therefore be an indispensable part of any survey of global communicative relationships. Certainly, not every form of interaction leads to a positive, cosmopolitan sense of togetherness, because a variety of motives may play a role in any interaction and divisions may come to light. At the same time, however, in line with the claims of symbolic interactionism, it is only through direct interaction that there is any chance at all of establishing a feeling of togetherness in the form of individual, experience-based knowledge.

As yet, there is no even remotely coherent theory of the international community that also foregrounds issues of communication. However, there are numerous

12 Theory of global communication

strands that fill in part of the picture, such as the classic research anchored in socio-logical communication theory, though this is geared essentially towards small groups. In symbolic interactionism, George Herbert Mead and Herbert Blumer underlined that the meanings of the world arise through mutual interactions (Mead 1934). Here, interaction with oneself plays as important a role as social interaction (dia-logue). Blumer describes the fundamentals of symbolic interactionism as follows:

> It [symbolic interactionism] does not regard meaning as emanating from the intrinsic makeup of the thing that has meaning, nor does it see meaning as arising through a coalescence of psychological elements in the person. Instead, it sees meaning as arising in the process of interaction between people. The meaning of a thing for a person grows out of the ways in which other persons act toward the person with regard to that thing.
>
> *(1986, p. 4)*

This interactionist perspective differs from the co-orientation approach, which describes communicative processes through a three-step procedure. If several actors ("a" and "b", and so on for Newcomb) are oriented towards a certain symbol ("x" for Newcomb), they are considered to be "co-oriented", their respective interpret-ations of meaning can be compared and the degree of "agreement" can be measured. The next step is to determine to what extent the actors themselves assume that their interpretation of meaning corresponds to that of the others, which allows us to establish the degree of "congruency". Finally, "agreement" and "congruency" are compared in terms of their "accuracy" (Newcomb 1953).

Direct social interaction differs from social co-orientation, which is based on observations in everyday life or may occur through media. Both objects in the environment and media may be viewed as x-objects to which people (a and b, and so on) are oriented. In contrast to the interpretation of the observable environment, media provide a kind of observation of observation, such that we gain access to the observation of others. We might also refer to direct and indirect observation. Here, media are resources for negotiating the world. They may create knowledge, but interpretations of meaning must be constantly renegotiated interactively, even within a collective framework, in order to ensure the stability of society. Both forms of observation are also significant to the process of global communication.

Direct observation of the world occurs through the physical process of individ-uals crossing borders (in the context of tourism, diplomacy, and so on). A perception of the world co-oriented towards media also imparts knowledge, and occasionally even cosmopolitan sentiments. But the direct interaction of people – whether in the private lifeworld or in the case of individuals performing specific roles in polit-ical and social systems – is an additional meaningful phenomenon that is important to the emotional cementing of the global community. Hence, simultaneity through observation and through mass media (as well as universal human orientations and cosmopolitan values) are important prerequisites for understanding the world. But in themselves they do not constitute understanding, because these communication processes still do not impart a stable awareness of global commonality (Axford 2013, p. 32), which can only arise through direct interaction and experiential knowledge. Successful co-orientation through mass media is a necessary prerequisite for integration into a global community, but it is not sufficient as long as re-negotiation or further processing takes place exclusively in separate social systems and lifeworlds (Hafez 2002a, vol. 1, p. 171ff.; Grüne 2016, p. 421ff.).

It is tempting at this point to apply to the global community the famous metaphor of the orchestra, as used by Alfred Schütz to illuminate symbolic interaction. Schütz contends that in order to play good music, you not only have to be able to read the right notes, but always have to pay attention to how your colleagues play as well (1951, p. 94ff.). If you see the world as an orchestra, then it is not enough to co-orient yourself within a global framework, and synchronize yourself with the world, through observation and with the help of the media. You also have to enter into direct communication with the world. Cosmopolitanism as a value is good, but global communication as a practice is better.

Discursive global society/dialogic global community: theories of communication

In contrast to global society, a global community entails more than the development of a common ethics, such as human rights and cosmopolitanism (Albert et al. 1996, p. 19, see also Etzioni 2004). These ethics can only arise through interactive action at every level, making the transition from global society to global community an intrinsically communication- and dialogue-based project. To quote Emanuel Richter:

> [This project] finds expression in those ideas that may be classified as a 'communicative' model of global unity. This model elevates the near-revolutionary spread of communicative exchange processes within every area of life to the status of new, determining element of the global context … Expressed at the highest level of abstraction, this global community appears as a kind of 'cognitive global society', which glimpses nothing less than a new form of global unity in the universalization of communication. This system-theoretical take on notions of global unity thus throws into sharp relief that aspect of global society relating to the globalization of processes of communicative exchange.
> *(1990, p. 277)*

Philosophers such as Immanuel Kant, Richard Rorty, Jürgen Habermas and Nancy Fraser have all articulated visions of a dialogic global community (see Linklater 1998, p. 85ff.). But the associated concepts have never been fleshed out with theoretical precision, not least because of the fragmentation of the humanities and social sciences (Albert 2009). In addition to theorists of social communication, international relations and political philosophy, media philosophers also offer valuable insights, as do theorists of communication and networks who seek to illuminate

14 Theory of global communication

the modern information and communication society, although they too have rarely referred to global conditions. One of the best-known media philosophers is Vilém Flusser, whose cardinal distinction between discursive and dialogic communication lies at the root of our own theory building, which separates observation and interaction in a similar way:

> To produce information, people exchange various existing pieces of information in the hope of synthesizing new information out of this exchange. This is the dialogic form of communication. To preserve information, people distribute existing pieces of information in the hope that the information thus distributed will be better able to resist the entropic effect of nature. This is the discursive form of communication.
>
> *(2000, p. 16)*

Jürgen Habermas too takes his lead from this fundamental distinction between interaction (or "communicative action") and discourse, ascribing to interaction direct consequences for action, while discourse is a system of "*possibly* existing facts" in which the individual can understand and interpret information without any direct social consequences (1971, p. 21f.).

In his media theory, Flusser described the existing imbalance in the modes of communication characteristic of modernity and called for an end to the primacy of text-based discursive communication. What human beings need, he contended, is a "communicative revolution", the "shielding of humanity's interests from the discourses that programme it" (ibid., p. 47). The spread of literacy in the modern era, the development of the printing press, the emergence of linear historiography and the great ideological narratives, including modern ideas of the nation state and modern wars, are closely connected in Flusser's work (ibid., p. 56). In this process, the population becomes the "masses", while the lifeworld is colonized. We might think Flusser's language a little melodramatic and his emphasis on the repressive character of media discourses contradictory, given the indispensability, which he himself affirmed, of dialogue *and* discourse (ibid., p. 16). But the dualism of discursive and dialogic communication, as the basis of a theory of social communication, is evident in the work of numerous authors.

Michael Giesecke is one of the most interesting scholars developing this intellectual agenda by tackling questions of media, dialogues, communication processes and communitization. Giesecke's thinking is fundamentally anchored in the concept of communicative ecology as the interplay of different forms of communication (2002). Human communication is based on observation that is made possible by media as well as on direct interaction in the lifeworld. Disturbances and pathologies arise from imbalances that cause the interaction between the various types of communication to go awry (ibid., p. 35). His "myths of book culture" are a well-known case in point. Giesecke describes the modern culture of the West and the Enlightenment as overly text- and observation-centred. Had Columbus relied on the prevailing discourse of his time, Giesecke states, he would never have set off in search of new worlds. Only direct observation – of the dead bodies of indigenous North Americans and bamboo stems washed up on the coast of Western Europe – and interaction with like-minded people encouraged him to embark on his adventures (ibid., p. 114ff.).

Giesecke sees the Internet in particular as an opportunity for a new vision of the information society, one that can restore the balance in the ecology of communication destroyed by monologic book and press cultures. This is not just a matter of reviving interpersonal dialogue, but above all of revitalizing group and multi-person dialogues. However, if we think through Giesecke's proposal, it is open to question what the theoretical position of the group discussion ought to be, given the dichotomy of discourse and dialogue. Is group dialogue essentially an instance of the "repressive" distribution of medial knowledge that disseminates media agendas and discourses? Or does it facilitate creative appropriation and the interactive-dialogic interpretation of meaning?

What is particularly interesting about Giesecke is that he includes the long-distance intercultural relationship in his analysis (ibid., p. 145ff.). He affirms that, in intercultural communication, the communicative mode of media observation has dominated for centuries, in other words, writing *about* and visualizing "others" rather than interacting *with* them. Observation rather than dialogic exchange was, of course, also the predominant mode in the colonial era, whose repercussions continue to be felt today. According to Giesecke, in the Enlightenment we established a culture of curiosity but without real dialogue. By contrast, he describes dialogue as a medium capable of bringing out that which is "common to humankind", and he considers the new digital media an effective remedy for our communicative failings, though he adds:

> Whatever the *global village* is supposed to be, it is not based solely on the Internet. We are connected not just by cables but by other media as well. The "global village" requires a range of media of interaction, cooperation and communication if it is to hold together and function.
>
> *(ibid., p. 376)*

Integrationist systems theories

There is comparatively little literature dealing specifically with international communication and communitization. A number of pioneers have, however, investigated the effects of world-spanning interaction on global communitization. The key authors here are those categorized by Howard Frederick as "integrationist systems theorists", such as Karl W. Deutsch, Claudio Cioffi-Revilla, Richard L. Merritt, Francis A. Beer, Philip E. Jacob and James V. Toscano (1993, p. 202ff.). The focus of their studies, some of which were published as early as the 1960s, are the dynamics highlighted by the orchestra metaphor. International integration theory primarily measures the extent of interactions between units such as states and relates this to the volume of communication within society. The empirical basis for these early

16 Theory of global communication

investigations is usually the exchange of letters and contact by telephone, along with data on cultural exchange, as in the case of periods of study abroad. The hypotheses associated with this highly quantitative form of research are variations on the basic assumption that only an interactive rather than merely co-oriented and observing world can provide a stable framework for a world community. Karl W. Deutsch argues that the absence of communication between states does not necessarily lead to conflicts, but that the means of social communication must keep pace with the requirements of political, economic and social transactions in other fields (1970, p. 58).

In other words, a lack of cross-border interaction does not automatically lead to conflicts (see also Rosecrance 1973, p. 136ff.; Beer 1981, p. 133) but Deutsch considers integration into larger communities, for example within the framework of the European Union or other international security-based communities unthinkable under such conditions of non-interaction. Deutsch is emphatic that political or economic integration of any kind will only be accepted if people experience this integration themselves; this is the only way to create a we-feeling (1970, p. 36). He underlines that such experiences are significant with respect to both political elites and society as a whole (he refers to a "favorite societal climate", 1964a, p. 51). Integration theorists emphasize the connection between the image of another country conveyed by the media and human relationships between countries arising from interactions, such as the exchange of letters and telephone calls – today we would include the Internet and novel forms of travel (ibid., p. 54, 1964b, p. 75ff.).

The integrationist systems theorists recognized early on that it is mostly wishful thinking to imagine that there is congruence between international political and economic relationships, on the one hand, and social interactions, on the other. To quote the work of one of the present authors, they acknowledged that "tectonic shifts" (Hafez 1999, p. 54ff.) between relational levels are the norm: "Human relations are ... far more nationally bounded than movements of goods" (Deutsch 1964b, p. 84). We can understand secession, as with the end of British rule in the American colonies and the emergence of the United States in the eighteenth century, partly in light of communicative connections. Initially, the postal traffic between Great Britain and the individual colonies predominated. A few decades later, the picture had changed. The colonies were communicating more intensively with each other and social contacts with Britain were becoming increasingly sparse; the American Revolutionary War broke out shortly afterwards (Deutsch 1964a, p. 51). The integrationist systems theorists were also able to show that the multinational merger of European states after the Second World War increased the quantity of postal traffic and other interactions between countries, which in turn allowed the European idea to take its place at the heart of societies and enabled the elites to become increasingly integrated (Clark and Merritt 1987, p. 230ff.). Up to the present day, despite increased criticism of the European Union and the rise of neonationalist movements and right-wing populism, the European idea still commands majority support, even in Europe. Hypothetically, we could ask whether possible tendencies

Theory of global communication **17**

towards disengagement or withdrawal from the EU might partly be due to the fact that there is still too little cross-border communication between certain areas (Northern and Southern Europe or Eastern and Western Europe) – quite apart from the lack of a shared European media-based public sphere.

Dialogue between "cultures" in an extended lifeworld

Regardless of whether we can always relate to the quantitative methods of earlier research (is the quality of some interactions not more important than the sheer number of letters, phone calls and e-mails?) or whether we wish to expand systems theory into a theory of action in the lifeworld, as in this book (see Section 1.2), the school of integrative systems theorists points us in the right direction. The fact that ideas about global integration emerged in social research of a political science hue shows that it is not so much the mass media as other social systems in politics, economy and society, as well as individuals and groups within lifeworlds, that are responsible for dialogic relations. The assumption that social communication is as important as political and economic exchange entails a revolutionary theoretical interpretation that makes communication a central resource of social science theory building on a par with economic relationships and power relations.

Subsequent research in communication studies, such as that concerned with the "dialogue of cultures" or "Islamic-Western dialogue", has focused chiefly on global media communication, notions of the enemy and images – strands of research that are undoubtedly legitimate in light of Flusser's division of communicative modes into discourse and dialogue, but that tend to consider interactions at the margins (Quandt and Gast 1998; Hafez 2003b). Recent works of political philosophy on the global community do use the term "dialogue" in an interactive sense but ignore those dimensions of the problem identified by communication studies (Linklater 1998; Etzioni 2004). What we want to underscore explicitly at this point is that the "dialogue of cultures" has never been a satisfactory notion in theoretical terms because the synthesis of analyses of society and communication, as originally found in the work of systems theorists such as Deutsch, has been lost.

1.2 Communicative systems, lifeworlds and their transformation

Systems and lifeworlds

Having established a dual model – informed by theories of communication – of both an observing global public sphere and an interactive global community, we now ask which actors within international relations might serve as communicators. Before going into more detail about types of actor, however, we need to make a number of metatheoretical observations in order to prevent misunderstandings in the course of theory building. James N. Rosenau has described it as the task of globalization theory to keep in mind the micro- and macro-interactions of individuals

18 Theory of global communication

or states and organizations (2007). Saskia Sassen goes a step further and considers overlapping and reciprocal processes between actors to be crucial (2007). Not all theorists are so open to different actors, systems and the variety of interactions between them. There are, for example, radical theories of action such as that of Bruno Latour, who starts from the premise that the global is always local, since no matter where you are, you act locally, and we can portray even long-distance journeys as the sum of local stages, whose reconstruction he describes as the task of his specific form of actor-network theory (2014; see also Gerstenberger and Glasman 2016). Here the influence of observational systems, such as the mass media or other social systems, as mediating agents of (supposed) knowledge of the world that shape our actions, takes a back seat. From this perspective, then, global communication is nothing but interaction between acting individuals.

Such ideas recall the old dispute between systems and action theorists, though in this book we try to resolve this through an integrative perspective akin to that of Rosenau or Sassen, which takes account of different systemic logics and actors' logics in systems and lifeworlds. The individual is never completely dominated by systems, even if their life requires them to take on roles that structure their life, but which they constantly breach or interpret independently, at both the formal and informal levels. Systems also influence people's lifeworlds, yet they are influenced by them as well; or both these actors' spaces may remain unconnected. In our analysis, we take into account the basic concepts of social theory, such as social action/interaction, norms, roles, structures and systems (for an introduction, see Bahrdt 1997). Finally, Habermas's dualism of system and lifeworld is important here (1995), though one would have to clarify who is "colonizing" whom. In our view, however, a nuanced view of the communicative modes of systems and individuals (see Section 1.3) and their interdependencies (see Section 1.4) is indispensable.

System-lifeworld-network approach

A second preliminary remark is necessary. The concept of system used here is not a strictly functionalist one. While we confidently introduce communication processes as elements of theory building, we eschew a purely process-oriented form of theory building that turns actors, as communicators, into mere "objects" of abstract phenomena such as "networking", "connectivities" and "communication flows". Modern network theory tends to shift the emphasis from social actors to networks, with the internal logic of systems (such as organizations and businesses, but also individuals' psychological systems) or lifeworlds receiving less attention than the networks and exchange relations that exist between systems or lifeworlds. The internal structures collapse, as it were, under the weight of networking. To quote Jan van Dijk: "Traditional internal structures of organizations are crumbling and external structures of communication are added to them" (2012, p. 33). George Ritzer makes similar observations with reference to the process sociology of Norbert Elias: "[F]ollowing Elias, in thinking about globalization, it is important that we privilege process over structure (just as we have privileged flows over barriers)" (2010, p. 25).

We certainly foreground communicative processes in this book, but we pay attention to systems and lifeworlds as well. Networks are relationships within or between social systems (Endruweit 2004, p. 26), but they are not social systems themselves, which must therefore be taken into account. Our perspective is neither that of Latour's actor-network theory nor that of Castells's network theory but can best be described as a *system-lifeworld-network* approach. This is similar to the perspective introduced by Roger Silverstone and developed further by Nick Couldry at the London School of Economics and Political Science (LSE). Here the network metaphor is regarded as too theoretically unsophisticated for social theory, since it ignores actors' interpretations of networks (Couldry 2006, p. 104). Couldry rightly refers to a "problematic functionalism", to "acting as if media were the social and natural channels of social life and social debate, rather than a highly specific and institutionally focused means of representing social life" (ibid., p. 104). He rejects the "myth of the mediatized centre" and criticizes the tendency in communication studies to equate media with society (ibid., p. 105). German communication theorist Manfred Rühl articulates similar views:

> Global communicative systems are embedded in psychological, organic, chemical, physical, in short, in non-communicative environments that ... contribute to the realization of communication without being part of it. Communicative systems must be clearly delimited, but not separated, from their environment.
>
> *(2006, p. 362)*

The structural-functionalist systems theory rooted in the work of Talcott Parsons relates fast-moving functional processes to stable structures, on the "assumption of a system-immanent need for self-preservation, that is, for integration and continuity" (Kunczik and Zipfel 2001, p. 69). Even Niklas Luhmann does not ultimately deny the existence of such structures, though his "functional-structural systems theory" emphasizes the dynamism of processes and moves away from a Parsonian approach (Kneer and Nassehi 1997, p. 116). In the work of Parsons in particular, then, actors do not dissolve into networks, but remain recognizable as autonomous structures, even if they adapt functionally and can be influenced by (communicative) processes. Sociologist and Luhmann interpreter Armin Nassehi also takes his lead from a similar basic idea when he emphasizes the astonishing tenacity of social structures but also recognizes the growing complexity of modern (digital) communication, explicitly leaving open the question of changes in social structure resulting from such communication (2019). Network theorists, in contrast, assert the primacy of "relationism" over "substantialism" (Nexon 1999); they contend that processes *are* structures.

20 Theory of global communication

By contrast, we take the view that a meaningful analysis should assume the co-presence of systemic and lifeworld structures, on the one hand, and processes of communication, on the other, but must also be open to:

- the possible interleaving of systemic and lifeworld structures (informal lifeworlds are also found in organizations, just as systems may be influential in lifeworlds) (Kneer and Nassehi 1997, p. 142f.);
- the possibly dominant influence of structures with regard to processes of communication (strategic action);
- the possibly dominant influence of processes of communication with respect to structures (communicative action).

This whole debate is reminiscent of the dispute in the theory of international relations between neo-institutionalists (such as Robert O. Keohane and Joseph Nye) and functionalists (such as David Mitrany). Our system-lifeworld-network approach aims to drop the dualism of actors and functions in favour of a pragmatic perspective that leaves room for the possibility that functional (including technological) aspects of global mediatization processes may exercise a major influence, while remaining alive to the possibility that systems and lifeworlds, as the two poles of global discourses and dialogues, may make a constitutive impact. Hence, the system-lifeworld-network conception chimes with our approach to a greater degree than pure neo-institutionalism or functionalism. Crucially, network theory can be combined with other theories, such as systems or lifeworld theory (Häußling 2005, p. 269ff.). We consider this form of "modular theory" a useful way of dealing creatively with the contradiction between structuralism and functionalism.

Global centres and peripheries

We need to make one final preliminary remark concerning postcolonialism. Anyone who emphasizes structures in their analysis must inevitably deal with the question of whether these structures require yet further differentiation, with regard, for example, to the relationship between industrialized and developing countries or between formerly colonized and colonizing states. Johan Galtung's idea of a structural imperialism characteristic of global society, which forms (power) centres and (power) peripheries (1973), functions as a latent perspective in this book, for example, when it comes to the forms taken by discursive and dialogic structures in the context of specific formations, such as the OECD, the European Union, or geolinguistic entities, such as the Spanish-speaking or Arabic-speaking world.

Nevertheless, we believe that such structural variables ought to be interpreted as universal rather than particular and certainly not as culture-specific. Both the internal communicative processes in systems and lifeworlds and the relations of interdependence between systems and/or lifeworlds as environments (see p. 39ff.) reveal striking global similarities across the boundaries of political and cultural systems, whenever cross-cultural structural constructs such as nation states, transnational companies, social movements, communities and lifeworlds are present. On this one point, then, we are on the same page as the proponents of relationism. Global structural differences reflect real disparities of power. But they are not absolute cultural differences: they are in fact subject to constant change as a result of the processes of global observation and interaction.

Taking stock: globally communicating social systems and lifeworlds

Following these preliminary remarks, we now seek to take stock of the actors engaged in global communication. Before attempting to describe complex lifeworlds, we can discern a variety of systemic entities: individuals as psychological systems as well as organized and non-organized social systems. Cross-border communication can arise between equal as well as unequal poles, that is, between political systems or between individuals and organized social systems, and so on. Depending on their specific modes of communication, such communication may primarily take the form of observation or interaction. Alternatively, and this will be of signal importance when we seek to define functions more precisely, cross-border communication may engender hybrid forms, since very few systems and actors *only* observe *or* interact. There are, however, system-specific logics, the elaboration of which is one of this book's key objectives.

To provide a more detailed definition of actor-specific global modes of communication, it is important to distinguish between individuals and both organized and non-organized social systems. Organized social systems not only have an organizational idea, but also an organizational structure (Hauriou 1965), which distinguishes them from non-organized systems. Non-organized social systems are, for example, "communities" that feature an idea but no structure or organization (organizations can develop out of communities, but then we can no longer view them solely as communities, but also as organizations). Conversely, organizations always feature a notion of community, an informing template and an identity. In addition, organized social systems are action-oriented. Politics, as the dominant supersystem of society (Gerhards and Neidhardt 1990), is primarily responsible for establishing security and order, the economy is meant to secure material resources, while the media is tasked with the autonomous observation of all other systems, and so on.

Media, politics and economy as (trans)national systems

As a result of the specific logics of the individual systems, however, they form secondary transnational systems in very different ways (the United Nations, transnational firms, transnational media, and so on), whose rules of communication differ from the border-crossing of national systems. Mass media tend to act as national (local) media systems that use "other countries" as an information resource, while the information processing takes place within a local media system that is equipped with its own organizational structures, staff and resources. The communicative border-crossing of such national mass media is referred to as "foreign

22 Theory of global communication

coverage" (Hafez 2002a). So-called "international broadcasting" also consists of national media, but they reverse the flow of communication. BBC World, RT, Voice of America and many other such broadcasters produce content specifically for foreign audiences (which threatens their autonomy and often makes them a de facto part of the political system).

In contrast, the media have developed transnational structures only to a very meagre extent. Most broadcasters regarded as international are actually national products with global ambitions (such as CNN) (Hafez 2007a, p. 12f.). This applies even to broadcasters like Arab television network Al-Jazeera, which have established themselves across borders in large geolinguistic regions such as the Arab world. International news agencies are still the most transnational entities because they provide information from and for most of the world's countries. But because their input is subject to postproduction by the media, they should be viewed more as a media subsystem than as an independent media system. In the field of mass media, commercial structures may well be interwoven transnationally – but once the final stage of journalistic production has been reached, it is the nation state or at least the national language that predominates.

As far as the contours of the political system are concerned, we must distinguish between two levels: the transnational system (the UN, the EU, and so on), which exists in rudimentary form, and the nation state. In the political sphere, the state communicates within the framework of transnational organizations, but it also has a history of diplomacy, of exchange between states, that goes back thousands of years, and this form of internationality and foreign policy is still dominant in international relations today. In response to the world wars, transnationalization advanced in the twentieth century, for example, in the form of the United Nations and collective security alliances such as NATO. In the present day, interactions take place within these transnational organizations as well as directly between independent states, both bilaterally and multilaterally.

The dissolution of the nation state and the transnationalization of politics, as often anticipated in the early days of the globalization debate, did not occur, despite the existence of a number of multinational alliances (such as the EU) and international governance regimes (such as the Kyoto Protocol in the environmental field) (Frei 1985; Brand et al. 2000). The nation state is still the primary locus of global politics. Because of this, we are chiefly concerned with foreign policy communication in this book. It is important to understand diplomacy as a process of communication in which interaction and dialogue play a key role in negotiations, and in some cases we can refer to trilogue, given the role of mediators. Acts of violence or threatened acts of violence can also be a form of international communication – but such acts tend to be monologic and unilateral. In addition, the political system is a core component of public communication. It observes, is observed *by* other systems and *in* lifeworlds, and influences the synchrony of the mediatized global public sphere.

Much the same applies to the economic system. Here, too, incipient transnationalization has occurred, for example, in the form of major economic institutions such as the World Bank, the IMF, and international financial and trade agreements. There is also a well-advanced trend towards the establishment of transnational corporations (TNCs), which are commonly referred to as "global players". The second wave of globalization researchers, however, disputed the dominance of this development and the pre-eminence of the transnational in the economic system (Hirst and Thompson 1999).

It would thus be wrong to view politics or the economy as purely cross-border forces. We should instead refer to simultaneous trends of global homogenization (in the sense of the global governance of the transnationalization of economic areas or companies) and national heterogenization (national politics and protectionism). Existing transnational company structures, however, open up a field of research in its own right. In contrast to the general picture within the field of politics, the key phenomenon here is not communication between systems, but internal communication in cross-border systems, which proceeds according to special rules, since in principle the organizational goals and programmes no longer have to be negotiated and membership of a cross-border institution seems to be a settled matter. Here, the global integration that theorists such as Karl W. Deutsch sought to promote in the field of politics has already taken place. This might open up new horizons for multicultural communication and the idea of communality.

Global civil society and large communities

Beyond the political and economic systems, there are numerous organized social systems in society that may be globally networked. Global civil society has been much discussed since the 1990s (Anheier et al. 2001; Kaldor 2003). The main actors in the debate were initially international non-governmental organizations (INGOs) such as Amnesty International, Greenpeace, and so on, in other words, organizations with roots in civil society that had developed into global network organizations: a parallel to transnationalization in the political and economic spheres. With the mass spread of the Internet, a second basic type of global actor emerged in the realm of civil society, namely social movements, such as the anti-globalization movement. Social movements are not member organizations, but hybrids of organized and non-organized social systems with an organized core – the so-called "social movement organizations" (SMOs) – and a loose community structure that is formed around a central idea and symbols (della Porta and Diani 2006). As we shall see, this structural distinction has consequences for modes of communication. NGOs and SMOs, for example, have different preferences when making use of mass media or social media.

However, beyond their organized cores, social movements must be viewed as non-organized social systems/communities. They consist of voluntary sympathizers, are fundamentally weak in organizational terms, and are thus based all the more on a central idea and a strong sense of unity among members. The idea of intellectual and emotional connectedness is usually more pronounced in social movements than in organizations. Their action orientation and function, however, are often unclear. Communities exist on a variety of levels, with a distinction typically being

24 Theory of global communication

made between traditional communities, such as the family or the village, into which one is born, and new instances of communitization (nation, associations, groups of friends, and so on).

Communities function not just locally but also virtually, digitally, as online communities, ethnic communities, communities of solidarity, global communities, and so on. Large communities without an organization are primarily discursive communities and only to a very limited extent interactive ones. Not only do media help unify large communities by furnishing them with discursive resources, but there are also specific online communities whose (apparent or actual) interaction is becoming more and more dynamic. Thanks to the Internet, there is in fact a trend towards neo-communitization. Some commentators have referred, for example, to diaspora groups on the Internet, and every conceivable social difference can find expression in online communities. Virtual communities enable the individual to engage in the group dialogues highlighted by Giesecke (Rheingold 2000). Yet as we shall see, communicative behaviour in online communities should not be equated thoughtlessly with "dialogic interaction", since behaviour in global spaces is radically different than in the case of cross-border communication by individuals and in real-world groups.

Global lifeworlds: a desideratum for "intercultural communication"

To the systemic actors outlined above we must add actors and complex communicative processes in lifeworlds. Individuals and small groups too observe and interact across borders, even if they do not do so in the context of specific communities or organizations, but informally, and thus in a "real" space. The concept of the community is thus complemented by that of the small group, since the group members' personal contacts are absolutely necessary and – in contrast to the large community – identificatory and imagined assignations, chosen by oneself or others, do not determine membership. In the lifeworld, wherever we refer to "social life", encounters in non-community groups are in fact typical (at the cinema, on the street, at the supermarket, and so on). We can clearly separate large communities from communal or non-communal small groups in as much as large communities, apart from special situations such as online communities or certain forms of communication between assemblages of individuals, cannot be interactive communities, which small groups generally are.

With regard to the lifeworld contexts of individual, group- or community-based communication, the question we have to ask is whether a shift is taking place away from national/local to global, that is, inter- or transnational lifeworlds. In light of the arguments we have developed so far, one crucial prerequisite for the emergence of "global lifeworlds" – beyond the individual observation of the world, for example, through media offerings – is the presence of a range of "intercultural communicative situations" in everyday social worlds.

Due to conceptual disagreements, the research field of "intercultural communication", which might have seemed predestined to answer this question, has not yet

Theory of global communication **25**

provided us with reliable findings. This is because the idea of the individual as the bearer of a particular, objectified "culture" remains a widespread paradigm in this field (see, for example, Maletzke 1996; Hofstede et al. 2010). This, however, is highly problematic, as it allows the individual no room for independent feats of communication and affirms essentialist ideas about cultural areas, according to which individuals within a national or even supranational social order have identical sets of interpretations of the world and scarcely differ in their behavioural patterns. It is true that individuals in groups and communities share certain local experiential contexts that mould their action, and they may well be co-oriented as a result of their shared observation of national media discourses. But to straightforwardly identify fundamentally different, nationally determined forms of communication with various parts of the world is empirically and theoretically untenable in view of the diversity of human lifeways. In line with the integrationist ideas discussed above, it is in fact politically dangerous if we inadvertently adopt a problem-oriented perspective on cross-border understanding and assume that there are differences, sometimes of an insurmountable nature, hampering communication (Hansen 2011, pp. 179ff., 251ff., see also Chapter 7. Section 7.2.1). It is surely clear in principle that individuals with different cultural, social and geolinguistic socialization experiences can overcome differences in the context of global interaction. The question is, under what conditions, in what form and in association with which possible manifestations of change might this occur in everyday cross-border communication?

But even if the concept of the "cultural" is sometimes a source of misunderstandings, it should not and cannot be abandoned entirely. We deal with cultural influences at many points in this book, for example, when considering stereotypical media images, public diplomacy or the interplay of global interaction, media and prejudices about groups. But we examine "culture" not as detached from the actor or from the communicative construction of culture, but through our system-lifeworld-network approach. Our understanding of culture is essentially consonant with that of the discipline of cultural studies and centres on concrete problems entailed in the assignment of meaning and in systems of symbolic classification, as well as their everyday appropriation, production and deconstruction by specific social actors (Hall 1980). But these actors have to be reassessed in the context of global communicative relations in everyday life. Crucially, we will be distinguishing individuals with experience of global communication from those who lack it. This experience may in turn vary in many ways, in line with our classificatory scheme of communicative modes, such that it has variable consequences for processes of change in local lifeworlds.

Glocalization and hybridization of everyday action

In the field of cultural theory, the dynamics of cultural change under conditions of globalization – as a phenomenon complementary to systemic change – have been described as "glocalization" or "hybridization" (see, for example, Hall 1992a; Nederveen Pieterse 1994, Robertson 1995; 1998; Appadurai 1998; Kraidy 2005;

26 Theory of global communication

García Canclini 2005). While these authors adopt a range of perspectives within sociology, anthropology and cultural studies and their arguments vary, all highlight the fundamental heterogeneity of processes of cultural change under the influence of global developments. If people, ideas, symbols and goods can now circulate more and more easily at the global level, this does not imply a one-dimensional logic of change towards cultural alignment (homogenization) or a return to cultural traditions (heterogenization). These processes may well occur simultaneously.

Rather than the adoption or rejection of cultural practices, hybrid forms often arise as cultural actors appropriate aspects of global offerings, displaying creative autonomy as they develop new variants. These hybrid practices have been discussed chiefly with reference to local responses to global popular culture. In the tradition of cultural studies, the key question is what the power-dependent options for action are, that is, how free local individuals actually are in their appropriation of global offerings – against the background, for example, of postcolonial power relations that can influence the extent and direction of their dissemination or in connection with the role of hegemonic local and global interpretive models, which may determine modes of representation and thus circumscribe opportunities for individual engagement and positioning.

Research on cultural globalization, then, has clearly highlighted the everyday world of individuals, but it has not yet systematically explained their processes of communication. The appropriation of global media offerings describes just one, namely indirect or mediate, form of cross-border observation. Even if we sometimes allow ourselves to be influenced by global trends in our everyday actions, this results at most in the synchronization of lifestyles, but not in cross-border dialogues. Media coverage of distant worlds, entertainment programmes with a similar format around the world, and global pop culture only provide us with some initial starting points for a selective knowledge of the world. Individuals may also interact globally in their lifeworld, for example, during private or professional trips or in the multicultural contexts of modern societies. The form taken by these communicative situations depends in turn on whether individuals have these experiences alone or in groups, for example, with family, friends or colleagues, in which community context experiential knowledge is embedded and how enduring the global contacts are. It makes a difference whether global knowledge remains within an individual's professional role, as expert knowledge, or becomes an object of negotiation in a local community. What matters, therefore, is not just the roles entailed in, and the parameters of, individuals' global interactions, but also the local processing of global knowledge that arises from a variety of contact situations and may be essentially explicit (as in the case of factual knowledge) or implicit (as with experiential knowledge).

Old and new global "elites" within systems and lifeworlds

All of this culminates in the question of the role of today's global elites. An analysis of global communication must be about more than just identifying *strategic elites*

Theory of global communication **27**

(within organized social systems) who help shape global developments through the interactions of social systems (as in early integrationist systems theory; see p. 15ff.). We must also explore which *social elites* shape lifeworlds today. If we include in this category those who have had experience of global contact, then this has implications for the conventional understanding of elites. This is because "global capital", in the sense of knowledge that goes beyond the experience of reality within local lifeworlds, is a characteristic of groups and individuals who are rarely recognized as social opinion leaders. One example is migrants. While they are still exposed to social marginalization in the societies to which they immigrate, in principle, they have privileged experiences of border-crossing. "Old" and "new" elites must therefore be redefined under the conditions of global communication. As we proceed through the present book, our examination of global communication within the lifeworld will always include discussion of the positions of elites and "masses". It is the individual, group and community-based global experiences of global elites, both old and new, that influence the development of societies and it is the communicative negotiation of global experiences that determines their social role and relevance.

1.3 Specific modes of communication (system connections) of systems and lifeworlds

Actors' modes of global communication: a continuum

If we ask what forms of global communication are typical of actors, the first thing we will notice is that all relevant actors use a number of channels or media of communication simultaneously, including:

- mass media communication
- face-to-face communication
- assembly and group communication
- interpersonal mediatized communication.

Characteristically, however, at each of these levels the key communicative difference, discussed above, between observation and interaction/dialogue, is present to varying degrees. Subsystems and individuals within societies communicate in a variety of ways, but their capacity to observe and interact is more or less pronounced, as the continuum shown in Figure 1.2 attempts to illustrate.

With the help of the continuum set out above, we can now determine, with reference to the basic modes of communication, *specific primary and secondary communicative modes characteristic of individual actors* engaged in global communication, which are described in more detail in the course of this chapter. Mass media are good at observing, archiving and systematizing, and they are among the leading media engaged in the storing of collective memory. But they practise a monologic, one-to-many form of communication and are essentially non-interactive, even if

28 Theory of global communication

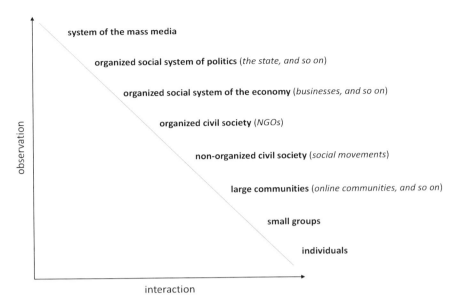

FIGURE 1.2 Actor-specific modes of communication

individual elements of mass media communication (research interviews, talk shows) are interactive in character – though this can be classified as a secondary mode of communication.

At the other end of the continuum are individuals and small groups, and to a limited extent also large communities (especially in the form of interactive online communities), which are good at interacting and at dialogue, but not as good at observation as organized social systems because they lack the resources for it. They are, however, primed for "genuine" dialogues and shared interpretations of meaning in the course of face-to-face interaction. For example, the potential for direct observation is limited during international travel: expert knowledge about the country a person is travelling in is generally only available with the help of social systems that provide systematized knowledge about the region through media and books. Conversely, despite language barriers there are opportunities for direct interaction without high transaction costs, and these opportunities are easier to realize than in the social systems that enable observation, such as the mass media, in which interaction is at best an element in the production of a journalistic text, but then gives way to a monologic form of communication as a result of the unambiguous producer-consumer relationship into which the text ultimately enters.

Other organized social systems, such as the political sphere, the economy and NGOs/social movements, are characterized by a high degree of hybridity with respect to their basic modes of communication. They have resources and competencies for world observation akin to those of the mass media. It makes sense that the ambassadorial system within the world of diplomacy and the system of correspondents within the world of journalism are structurally similar. Both institutions serve to obtain global information. International NGOs (INGOs) such as Amnesty International also produce reports around the world (for example, on the state of human rights). Furthermore, these social systems likewise engage in direct cross-border interaction as dedicated *systems of action* that not only observe but also seek to influence (diplomacy, foreign trade communication, and corporate and organizational communication in TNCs and INGOs).

Global interactivity beyond the mass media?

Overall, it is clear that among all actors observation and interaction are present in different forms, which can be traced back to the actors' specific functions and objectives. Of course, our list of systems is not complete and can certainly be expanded to include, for example, the subsystem of science with its unique mix of global discourses and interactions. The diverse interactions between individuals and social systems, which represent "environments" for one another, will by no means be ignored and will in fact be the subject of a further step in our theory building on interdependence (see Section 1.4). In the first instance, however, we put forward the following working hypothesis. When we refer to the formation of global communities (global communality) in today's world, what we have in mind is not so much the mass media, whose primary task is to create a discursive global public sphere, as other interactive social systems, as well as individuals and their lifeworlds, in which interactive communality may in principle come into effect.

It is probably no exaggeration to claim that, so far, globalization research has chiefly sought to analyse discourses, namely communication in the public sphere and media, while the analysis of interaction, especially when it comes to non-public communication in systems and lifeworlds, has rarely been the focus of theoretical or empirical studies. The fundamental question of whether social interaction can "migrate" within the process of globalization as discursive communication can thus remains unanswered. This means that the community dimension has also been ignored completely. A comprehensive assessment of globalization, however, must pay attention to all fields of communication.

Synchronization of the global public sphere: the problem of the mass media

How might we describe more precisely the processes of global communication characteristic of the three main types or dimensions of actors – mass media, organized social systems and lifeworlds? The main task of the mass media is to create non-interactive discourses. There are of course exceptions, such as talk shows, corporate media blogs, and so on, but the core function of the mass media is still to structure topics and organize discourse, otherwise journalism would mutate into public/civic journalism, that is, into media (co-)designed by citizens (Merritt 1998; Rosen 1999), which tends to be the preserve of social media and online communities

30 Theory of global communication

(Forster 2006). Furthermore, as Tanjev Schultz has rightly stated with reference to Germany, major talk shows focused on specifically global topics account for a negligible proportion of media production, such that interactive formats are of minor importance in the context of foreign coverage as elsewhere (2006, p. 169). In mass media, the production of texts functions more discursively than dialogically due to the limited selection of propositions about society, some but not all of which are considered in relation to one another. This is inevitable, since the mere reproduction of the talk of billions of people across the world would result in a vast, unmanageable cacophony, such that so-called "gatekeeping" and selectivity are among the basic principles of editorial work. The media are not an arena in which everyone talks to everyone else. Instead, a small number of individuals observe a vastly larger number and communicate by means of and about texts.

In creating discourses, the mass media – at least under democratic parameters – pursues an autonomous agenda informed by a combination of media ethics and publishing programmes or broadcasting mandates. The roles ascribed to the media vary depending on whether, for example, we privilege democratic objectives (such as the creation of a deliberative, rational public sphere) or make functionalist assumptions (with respect, for example, to the structuring of themes, including through entertainment) (Hafez 2010b). The main task of the media, following Niklas Luhmann, is to create a difference between oneself and one's environment, which we might describe as the intrinsic function of a system (Hafez 2002a, vol. 1, p. 124ff.). At first sight, the autonomy of the mass media makes it look like a self-contained system that observes the world in an independent manner. Of course, the autonomy of the mass media does not mean autarky. Media are influenced at the micro-, meso- and macro-levels and by the political, economic and cultural environment (ibid.). They are embedded in a complex web of environmental influences and exist in a state of "dynamic equilibrium" in relation to their environment (Kunczik 1984, p. 205ff., 212ff.; Hafez 2002a, vol. 1, p. 124ff.), which repeatedly compels them to adapt, as we will be discussing later (see Section 1.4). First, though, this section scrutinizes the autonomous role of the media.

If autonomous observation is the primary mode of the mass media, then the key issue on a global scale is the "synchronization" of its feats of observation. The transnationalization of the media system must be the ultimate expression of a rational global public sphere that seeks to co-orient the world's citizens, a global public sphere whose participants are supposed to be provided with knowledge about the world. Luhmann's idea of autonomous systems between which we can differentiate related to social systems such as politics or the economy, not to other media in other countries. The mass media has to be independent of politics and the economy; but it does not necessarily have to come to different conclusions than other media in other countries. In principle, it seems to make sense to see the world as other people in the world and their media see it – the rational reconciliation of all meaningful frames and discourses is the hallmark of the "global village" thesis, which highlights intimate knowledge of the world. In fact, in the spirit of the first wave of globalization theory and the radical idea of a global public sphere, we must

Theory of global communication **31**

in principle be able to view the mass media of this world as a single system that no longer stops at national borders.

Yet this points us to the core problem of global media communication. Is it capable of a high degree of synchronization and globalization? In the second wave of globalization research, a number of scholars, including one of the authors of this book (Hafez), questioned whether discourses were being homogenized due to enhanced observation by the mass media. They pointed out that, even with respect to the same event, the attention paid to it and the journalistic treatment it receives often differ fundamentally in the individual national media systems, as we will examine in more detail later in this book. These scholars emphasized the prevailing domestication of foreign coverage across the world (Hafez 2002a, vol. 1, p. 24ff., 2007a; Flew 2007; Stanton 2007; Ulrich 2016; see also Williams 2011, p. 21ff.). In contrast, some studies have underlined synchrony as a result of medial border-crossing (Fraser 2014; Volkmer 2014).

Local-global multi-level media-based public sphere(s)

To avoid succumbing to the unproductive dogmatism often engendered by rival schools of thought, we now attempt to establish a transformative concept of local-global public sphere(s). The primary focus here remains on national foreign coverage, with its tendency towards domestication. Yet this foreign coverage within particular nations does feature a certain, albeit limited, degree of calibration with global discourses, an effect that has been described elsewhere as a tip-of-the-iceberg phenomenon (Hafez 2011, p. 484). This is still far from the ideal of the total synchronization of all discourses, topics and frames of the kind that might typify a world shaped by truly transnational media (Wessler et al. 2008, p. 15f.; Splichal 2012, p. 149).

In addition, an initial form of cross-border transnationalization of production contexts may occur in homogeneous linguistic areas (as exemplified by Al-Jazeera for many years now in the Arab world). Recently, technological access to foreign and foreign-language media has enabled consumers, above all, a multilingual informational elite, to enjoy comparative access to different national media systems, which allows the simulation problem to persist at the production level but solves it at the recipient level (see Figure 1.3). In Chapter 2 on mass media, we will examine the various levels of global mass communication in order to shed meaningful light on the synchrony of global media observation.

Global organizational communication between discourse and interaction

Communication processes in other organized and non-organized social systems must be investigated using different theories than in the case of the media. The theoretical challenges mount in tandem with the diversity of actors because there is no single theory capable of grasping their communicative action. In principle,

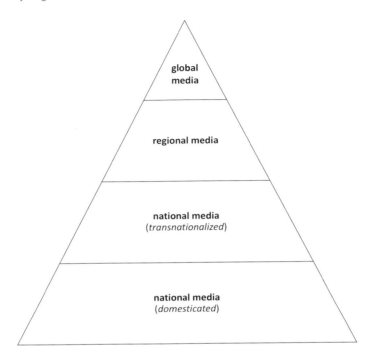

FIGURE 1.3 Local–global multilevel media-based public sphere(s)

a shift from the observational system of the mass media to organized systems of action (politics, economy, and so on) implies a shift away from discourse analysis and towards organizational analysis. One of the challenges for research is that many of the communication processes unfolding in these social systems are not publicly visible and are also difficult for researchers to access. If we are to understand non-mediatized communication, we require a good grasp of organizational structures and of the typical communicative processes associated with them. Drawing on organizational sociology, we can identify a number of "communicative structures" (see, for example, Endruweit 2004, p. 178ff.) found in all organized social systems, though, as we will see, we require additional input at various points from other theoretical strands such as negotiation communication, decision theory, network theory and deliberation research.

The first structure relates to the duality or hybridity, as outlined above, of feats of observation and interaction. We described it as characteristic of systems of action that they both observe (store, systematize and analyse) and interact. In Manfred Rühl's analysis of editorial teams, which is anchored in organizational theory and can be applied to other organizations, he makes it clear that goal-oriented programming (at the executive level) and conditional programming (employees' experiential knowledge and routines) are subject to repeated social renegotiation when conditions change (1979, 1980). Process models informed by decision theory show that in foreign policy the priority is to identify problems, collect information, work out alternative courses of action, and so on (Behrens and Noack 1984, p. 113). Nevertheless, we should not idealize the fundamental rationality of social system processes. Political, economic and social systems are often structured in such a way that – much like the media system – they include a variety of organizations that are only loosely held together by policy-making powers (the global communication of foreign policy is carried out, for example, by a number of ministries).

Further, within every organization, feats of observation and interaction are performed by various departments and at different hierarchical levels, and these are not always well coordinated. In foreign policy, for example, there is often a failure to sufficiently integrate in-house analyses and monitoring services into decision-making processes because decisions are made by ad-hoc teams, by ignoring established channels and procedures, under pressure of time or on ideological grounds. Global governance has also led to a new form of so-called "second track diplomacy", which extends to networks of NGOs, lobbies and external experts (Hafez 2002c, p. 138). Since economic, social and political systems also differ in their organizational goals, their organizational structures are not identical; this makes their communication structures so diverse that we can only refer to a small number of examples in this introductory context. The tension between the structures of observation and interaction in organized social systems engenders an increased need for communication, which has opened up a whole new field for communication consultancy in political and economic organizations (Hafez 2002c).

Informality and mediatization of organizational communication

This is further complicated by the fact that within organizations we have to differentiate between formal and informal communication, as manifest, for example, in the coexistence of departmental meetings and the "office grapevine". It has long been known that informal communication plays a significant role in bureaucracies, since it may generate innovative solutions but also obstruct formal communication processes. In the past, scholars often viewed informal communication as a disruptive factor, but at present there is an increasing tendency to emphasize its positive emotional and cognitive facets (Torjus 2014, p. 29ff.). In any case, successful informal communication is important in creating a sense of togetherness within a community. In our context, this raises the question of whether informality also comes into play in long-distance global relationships, for example, in transnational companies, and thus fosters interactive communality, in other words, a "global community", rather than just a "global public sphere". Further, the community dimension of informal communication not only plays a role in the internal communication of transnational organizations and systems, but also exists between systems, when businesspeople or diplomats interact across borders. As Jürgen Habermas might put it, this is not solely a matter of strategic but also of dialogic communication and thus of genuine communicative action (Habermas 1995, vol. 1, p. 126ff.). Hence, even

34 Theory of global communication

more than organizational communication and decision theory, negotiation communication is often at the heart of theories of global interaction.

A second important communicative structure is the distinction between speech and text. Texts may play a role in both observations and interactions, for example, in the case of international agreements or communiqués in which the perspectives of different international partners are set out. Interaction thus occurs in a variety of aggregate states, for example, as spoken or written dialogue. Each variant has specific advantages. Spoken dialogues have a high potential for participation and community. The written text, meanwhile, makes communities binding – we need only think of treaties under international law. In any case, we have to be aware of both forms of interaction in organized social systems and seek to grasp their internal dynamics and interplay.

The next significant communicative structure is the distinction between direct and mediatized social communication. Almost all communicative structures now have an additional dimension of mediatized interpersonal communication (e-mail, telephone, online services, and so on). This opens up new opportunities for deterritorialization but may also diminish the quality of observational activity and trigger a decline in participatory, interactive communitization. New types of text – such as the international online petition – and informal relationships are emerging in digital space. Technological changes in digitization are directly affecting global communication. New opportunities are opening up for the global community as well as novel dangers.

Global internal and external hybridity

Another structure is of key significance in assessing global communication: the internal and external relations of communication. The boundary between internal and external communication is identical to that between non-public and public communication. Once again, then, much as with the mass media, discourse analysis of published texts and political rhetoric may have a role to play here. Social systems' internal communication, including communication with other affiliated systems (such as diplomacy), is often interactive. External communication, conversely, is characterized by strategic communication (such as corporate PR and state PR/propaganda) and thus tends to be monologic and persuasive in nature rather than interactive and community-building. Hence, in this context the key question for the present book is: how much community-building potential is there in the interaction typical of non-public diplomacy if foreign policy propaganda ultimately prevails in the public realm? To what extent does strategic corporate PR, however dialogic companies' *internal* communication may be, unite our world into a "global community"? In terms of communication theory, we can explain the hybridity of social systems in the political-economic sector, their constant oscillation between egocentrism and a community orientation, in light of their location at the interface between discourse and dialogue. Discursive public relations and dialogic interaction

Theory of global communication **35**

across national borders form a complicated and often confusing mixture, one this book seeks to unpack and evaluate.

In the context of a system-lifeworld-network approach, however, we have to understand the intrinsic structures of systems as well as functional exchange processes. It is thus important to understand global communicative hybridity not only as a communicative contradiction or as a lack of simultaneity, but also as a structural problem. After all, the "hybridity" of discourse and dialogue does not in itself explain when and why which modes are used and why contradictions arise, for example, between internal and external communication. We immediately begin to understand this, however, if we factor in the idea of autonomous structural self-preservation, along with the environmental adaptation that is simultaneously required. Interaction then appears as a means of adaptation, whereas discursive communication serves to increase autonomy. Systems communicate with the modes they believe to be apt means of maintaining the basic functions of autonomy and adaptation. Communicative hybridity thus becomes a matter of the above-mentioned systemic "dynamic equilibrium", whereby systems constantly alternate between the search for autonomy and the need to adapt to their environments (see also Section 1.4). Robert S. Fortner pointed out decades ago that we need to think of international communication partly as a coherent global system and partly as an assemblage of separate systems (1993, p. 37f.). This applies to communication between similar systems (as in the interaction between states in diplomacy) as well as to the interdependence between dissimilar systems (such as media, politics or the economy), which we will deal with later.

Potential for global interaction of non-organized social systems

Non-organized social systems cannot simply be examined using the same tools that are applied to organizational communication. Here we find discursive or even dialogic structures rather than organizational ones, which means that online communities are investigated both in sociological studies of networks and in research on deliberation within the discipline of communication studies (Stegbauer and Rausch 2006; Stromer-Galley and Wichowski 2013). It is sociologically interesting that the flip side of organization-less and in principle hierarchy-free online communities is often the dominance of informal hegemonic opinion leaders and "informational elites". For the "mass" of people, language area boundaries and cultural hegemony are often serious obstacles in online communities. This may limit the supposedly dialogic character of the Internet, which is typically regarded as interactive, and this in turn has consequences for global communality. We will therefore be considering the quality of online discourses. How global are online communities in reality? Is the Internet ultimately a global or a local medium?

Another challenge lies in the systematic investigation of (global) communication within lifeworlds, which requires an augmented theoretical toolkit. When we scrutinize the global communicative relations characteristic of individuals, groups and

36 Theory of global communication

"small lifeworlds" (Luckmann 1970), there is a need for a greater focus on inter-personal communication, symbolic interactionism, social psychology and, above all, sociological theories of communication rooted in the tradition of the sociology of knowledge and culture (Schützeichel 2004; Averbeck-Lietz 2015). This is because these theories tackle the foundations of human communication and perception of the world, which are key to illuminating global communication from the micro-perspective of everyday life.

Drawing on the modes of communication introduced above and sociological theories of communication, we initially assume that the communicative action of the individual is mutually interactive. Through interaction with others, people learn to interpret and understand themselves and the world and to construct their own actions on the basis of this understanding of the world (Mead 1934; Blumer 2010). Our experiential knowledge, which we thus accumulate through ongoing communication, ultimately condenses into categories that Schütz and Luckmann described as social typification (2003, p. 313ff.; Schützeichel 2004, p. 128ff.). Hence, people develop everyday theories about communicative situations, anticipate the actions of others and fit new experiences into these classification systems. This also means that our individual knowledge systems, with whose help we gain access to the world, are shaped by our specific experiences of socialization and social contact. That is, our mutual orientation towards one another means that we become acquainted with communicative patterns, repertoires and routines that are institutionalized in certain social milieus as communicative conventions and are thus passed on to the next generation. Hence, the individual's experiential knowledge within the lifeworld is fed by an interplay of different social knowledge systems. But the "structures of the lifeworld" (Schütz and Luckmann 2003), in other words, the general conditions of spatially, socially and temporally structured interaction in the everyday social world, remain the same for all human beings, such that mutual understanding between "social others" should always be possible in principle.

This means, first of all, that cross-border understanding is characterized by a tension-filled dialectic. On the one hand, our communicative action is always a product of our social environments and socialization experiences. Even today, for many people these are still primarily of local origin and depend on local discourses. On the other hand, precisely because of its intrinsically social character, communicative action within the lifeworld is always subject to a dynamic process of change. If our experiences continuously lead to the (re)ordering of our typical schemes of action and communication, then theoretically it is always possible for these schemes to change in light of new experiences, thus altering our action-guiding knowledge systems.

This dialectic is of particular interest with regard to the crucial distinction between observation and interaction. We ascertained earlier that the mere observation of the world by individual actors is largely dependent on the performance of other social systems, since expert knowledge in modern societies is primarily provided by the media, educational and scientific systems. Far from everyday interactions in other, distant lifeworlds, however, these systems mainly allow us to observe the strategic actions of social systems within the political sphere (Hafez and Grüne 2015). Media communication, then, is a highly limited form of global communication within the lifeworld. In stark contrast, theoretically the lifeworld is the obvious locus of global dialogues, because, in line with our analysis so far, it is primarily face-to-face interaction that takes place here. In this context, through their interactions, individual actors can conduct indirect and direct cross-border dialogues and they can accumulate direct and mediated experience-based knowledge, that is, knowledge derived from their own global contact or from dialogues via third parties' global contact.

Global lifeworlds and group communication

The latter phenomenon highlights the complexity of global communication in the lifeworld. Even if people occasionally obtain knowledge from purely interpersonal communicative situations, this is often further negotiated through group contact. Families, peers, interest groups or hobby and fan groups rarely consist of just two people, usually entailing communitized group relations. This applies not only to informal roles in the private sphere, but also to social contexts in which actors act within their assigned formal roles. In educational contexts or at work, too, people usually find themselves in group contexts.

These various groups and communities in turn constitute the horizon of shared experiences and knowledge systems within the lifeworld. Hence, to achieve social integration through transactions, individual knowledge has to be linked back again and again to these group contexts and thus requires discursive compatibility. Individual lifeworlds, then, are always related to milieu-specific "small lifeworlds", as Benita Luckmann put it (1970). This relationship can in turn help us to understand processes of the reproduction or unsettling of socially ossified misinterpretations, stereotypes or ignorance of global "others" and their lifeworlds. In this book, we will therefore have more to say about the dynamics of change in actor-specific everyday knowledge and the prerequisites for the development of a genuine global community under the conditions of global contact.

Mobility, expanded space of interaction and the role problem

So far, data on tourism, transnational communitization and the use of social media indicates that the potential for a global expansion of communicative experiences, that is, social communication beyond the limits of everyday reality, is largely untapped (Zuckerman 2013; see also Mau 2007). This applies to both physical and digital mobility, which is interesting in as much as – in the context of direct and mediatized social communication in the lifeworld – indirect global dialogue has become much easier thanks to the tools of social media. But for now, the local boundaries of language and discursive communities seem to be holding sway in digital lifeworlds. Just a few individuals have shifted their interaction indirectly or directly beyond these local limits in such a way as to participate in both the

38 Theory of global communication

dialogues and discourses of other lifeworlds, thus negotiating knowledge systems in a truly cross-border way and developing global communities.

The knowledge of these "cosmopolitans" (Hannerz 1996, p. 102ff.) can only be passed on in select communicative scenarios. In this context it is helpful to include the theoretical distinction between formality and informality with respect to communicative lifeworlds as well. Analogous to the formal and informal contexts of organizational communication, we also find both modes in lifeworlds. At first glance, informal communication seems to dominate in the private sphere, but in the course of lifeworld communication individuals repeatedly slip into formalized roles in which they become agents of organizational goals. Depending on its focus, global experience may be linked either to formal roles (as in the case of external employees in global companies) or informal ones (as when private individuals travel). In the first case, both role functions may coincide. The passing on of global experience may then be of an essentially strategic or random nature and may influence local lifeworld contexts to varying degrees, potentially changing them on an enduring basis. Global community building is, therefore, not automatically fostered by cross-border, face-to-face interactions between individuals, but depends in part on communicative structures.

These include the varying internal and external relationships characteristic of global communication in the lifeworld. As intimated above, it is chiefly the internal communication of the small group that helps determine the nature of the collective compatibility of global experiences, since the private social renegotiation of these experiences mostly takes place in small-group contexts. Such groups, however, have no explicitly formulated strategic external communication of the kind familiar from social movements, organizations or large communities. The fact that small groups in particular strategically communicate global knowledge to larger publics is thus theoretically problematic. In the cultural "transit" space of the small group, however, a new everyday approach to globalization may well be negotiated and implemented by its members. While non-public direct or indirect global contact scenarios predominate in small groups, individuals may also interact globally in functional (partial) public spheres. They may do this strategically, for example, in representative roles within organized systems. In theory, individual actors may both help shape discourses (by publishing them, for example) and conduct direct global dialogues with others. Far more than the small group, then, they are the true actors in global, external communication within the lifeworld.

Social media and global monologue/dialogue

Finally, we have to address the speech/text distinction as characteristic of communicative action in the lifeworld. Here, too, the dominance of face-to-face interaction seems to suggest an analogous dominance of speech acts, which also implies that feats of communication in the lifeworld are fundamentally non-binding in nature – even the conventions of everyday action do not follow fixed rules of the kind found in diplomatic communication, but are instead a matter of tradition and implicit institutionalization. In the best-case scenario, global negotiations between social systems lead to secure global agreements, but global dialogues within the lifeworld may result in global knowledge, global experience and a sense of global solidarity, which may not immediately become manifest in a visible way, hampering attempts at empirical assessment.

Nevertheless, we can tentatively identify a shift towards textuality in global communication. Whenever people tap the potential for global interaction inherent in social media, everyday global dialogues are inevitably transformed into digital texts, which may in turn influence the rationalization of conversations within the lifeworld. The practices entailed in processing global contact experiences also produce material texts: via photos, reports and blogs, global contact experiences are transformed back into monologic types of text and are moved into archives of everyday memory, which may also prevent lively negotiations within the local, everyday lifeworld.

Global society, global community and global communication as a multiple phenomenon

In sum, the time has come to treat global communication as a multiple phenomenon in which different actors may do, or are doing, a variety of things as facilitated by their specific communicative options. Broadly speaking, we can distinguish between three types of actor. Through their communication, generated primarily through observation, the mass media delivers monologic discourses on distant world events that potentially provide information and knowledge for other subsystems. The organized action systems of politics, economy and civil society bring their own observations to bear, but also interactively generate political, economic and social communality, however limited it may be. Finally, we can describe the intrinsic communicative logic of lifeworlds as informally dialogic, despite the potential for strategic, formal, public and text-based communication. How actors make use of specific global communicative options is the subject of this book. But since systems interact in a variety of ways rather than operating separately, the final step in our theoretical presentation requires us to examine the issue of communicative interdependence.

1.4   System dependencies and lifeworld relations

Communication and inter-state relations

So far, we have tried to understand the intrinsic communicative logics of actors and systems in a global framework. However, actors' modes of communication are closely related to certain social concepts such as "global public sphere" and "global community". The integrative systems theorists presented above, among others, recognized early on that, for example, cross-border interaction through letters, the telephone, and so on, creates a density of relationships that is politically relevant

40 Theory of global communication

or, conversely, that a certain intensity of political and economic relations between countries promotes such communication. Communication does not take place for no reason, but is tied into social motivations, whose complexity we have to understand if we wish to analyse global communication – or the lack of it. So far there is no general theory applicable to such macrosocial phenomena. Nonetheless, there are concepts we can harness for the analysis of global communication, although they require supplementation and revision. In what follows, we present three types of approach to interdependence, which thematize different areas and describe complex relationships:

- communication and inter-state relations,
- media and national/international systemic relations,
- relationships between mass media, systems of action and lifeworlds.

Together these theorems do not form a coherent dependency theory of global communication, but they do generate a matrix that sensitizes us to interrelationships between different actors as well as between actors and their environments. Richard Rosecrance describes the interactions between interest structures and communicative relationships in international politics by elaborating three basic relational patterns (1973, p. 136ff.). He uses the term "positive interdependence" when the interest structures of two actors, for example, two states, are fundamentally compatible and a complementary form of relationship exists. In this case, a high level of communication usually contributes to the stability of relations, while a breakdown in or massive disruption to communication may lead to temporary instability and an increase in tensions. In the case of "negative interdependence", on the other hand, that is, incompatible interest structures and "zero-sum" interdependence (one side's profits are the other's losses), a high level of communication generally has no conflict-reducing impact. In these cases, it is necessary either to resolve the conflict, to remain in a long-term state of conflict or to redefine interests. Rosecrance refers to "low interdependence" when international communication partners (states/governments) maintain neither positive nor negative relationships. Communication is the most important relational factor here. If the communication goes smoothly, relations feature a low degree of conflict. If communication is increasingly disrupted, relationships will be beset by growing conflict. Despite the close connection between interaction and national interests, then, interaction is not a panacea. We can expect a conflict-reducing or conflict-intensifying effect of communication only in two-thirds of the model constellations (positive interdependence and, in some cases, a low degree of interdependence). In a third of all cases in the model (negative interdependence), no or only minor effects are achieved through communication.

Media and national/international systemic relations

As a scholar of international relations, from Rosecrance's perspective "communication" consists primarily of direct interaction between political systems. Other theoretical approaches have concentrated on the mass media, in other words on observational forms of exchange between societies, which are in turn significant to a variety of systems and lifeworlds in which mass media functions as a key environmental system for actors, which in turn represent environments for the mass media. In general terms, Kai Hafez works on the assumption that cross-border interdependencies are poorly developed in most mass media – in contrast to politics and the economy – because, as stated above, a transnational media system exists today at most in rudimentary form (2002a, vol. 1, p. 134ff., 2007a). At present, it is primarily national media and media systems that observe other nations (and their media). The mass media system is therefore not only observational and non-dialogic by nature. It is also fragmented nationally, which means that the national environments of the media are generally more significant than the global ones, such that its dependencies are largely shaped by the national context. In principle, there is no "positive" interdependence in the case of the mass media of the kind Rosecrance identifies in the relationship between some states or in the case of multinational entities such as the EU. As a result, there is little pressure on the media to become synchronized with the global public sphere or global society (see p. 40).

The reason for the extensive national decoupling of the mass media lies in the fundamentally different character of the exchange relations involved. In contrast to most material goods in the economy, the media, as a cultural product, is often context-dependent and – in line with Karl W. Deutsch's statement that: "Human relations are … far more nationally bounded than movements of goods" (see p. 16) – is difficult to export. People may drive the same cars around the world, but they use the same media only to a highly limited extent. Cross-border media use is undoubtedly present in certain large linguistic regions (the English-, Spanish- or Arabic-speaking world, and so on), but is otherwise limited to special situations and groups. However, there is a hierarchy in national media: sound and image overcome boundaries more easily than texts, with the import and export of music and films being particularly common in the fictional entertainment sector, albeit with a clear tendency towards a North–South divide (Hafez and Grüne 2016). Media are, therefore, not transnational. Instead, certain foreign products are integrated into national media, contributing to the global exchange that fired the imagination of the first wave of globalization research (which highlighted the demand for Hollywood films in Asia, and so on). However, even in entertainment, it is essentially fictional narratives that can be globalized. When it comes to casting, reality or game shows, only the formats, but not the shows themselves can be imported and exported and they have to be reproduced nationally or regionally, which leads to shifts in the process of production and reception and thus in the synchronization of the media (Grüne 2016). At the level of news journalism, meanwhile, the informational raw material about the world situation is imported and reassembled locally by national media systems.

We need to bear in mind the aforementioned notion of a "dynamic equilibrium", which suggests that media, politics and other social systems feature autonomous programming but are at the same time forced to adapt to their respective

42 Theory of global communication

environment (Kunczik 1984, pp. 205ff., 212ff.; see also Endruweit 2004, p. 67ff.). In the mass media this balancing act does not take place partly across borders, as is the case with other social systems. Instead the interdependencies are to be found almost entirely within the nation state. Based on the current state of research, we can put forward the following guiding principles governing the specific relationships of interdependence characteristic of the mass media (Hafez 2002a, vol. 1, p. 130ff.):

- *Media/politics*: National media policy lays down the political parameters of the media, while national media and national foreign policy usually have a major influence on one another within foreign coverage (indexing hypothesis, CNN effect, and so on, see Chapter 9, Section 9.3). In comparison, the influence of other countries on the national media is usually marginal, which means that the way we view the world is often greatly influenced by national foreign policy, especially at times of extreme crisis.
- *Media/economy*: Media markets are only interlinked globally to a limited degree, especially when it comes to direct investment (see Chapter 2, Section 2.1). The interests of national markets tend to dominate, which means that national demand influences content.
- *Media/society*: In every single media system in the world, the strong dependence on national audiences leads to the constant reproduction of ethnic and religious stereotypes in foreign coverage, though these are potentially changeable under the influence of the (interactive and dependent) political system. Cosmopolitan civil society, at least its organized variant, is for the most part "structurally weak". Cultural and lifeworld environments are diffuse, making generalization difficult (see p. 43ff.).
- *Media/journalism*: At the micro- and meso-level of journalism, media systems mostly consist of nationally socialized journalists. Multicultural editorial teams are more the exception than the rule, which can be explained in light of the highly advanced language skills required. Foreign correspondents can be regarded as a global elite among journalists only to a limited extent, since head editorial offices carry greater weight and cosmopolitan ethics are underdeveloped among journalists, such that journalism generally features strong ties to national cultures (see Chapter 2).

As a result, according to Hafez, mass media feature little global interdependence, less than other organized social systems at least. They may export and import information like other systems to a certain extent. But transnationalization at the production level only takes place to a limited degree, which hinders the global synchronization of discourses (and is even less conducive to dialogic communication, which, as discussed in Section 1.3, is basically a by-product of the mass media system). The observational communicative system of the mass media thus tends to be more local than more interactive systems such as politics and economics, where global dependencies are more advanced, although here too the nation state prevents genuine transnationalization.

As a guiding principle, however, we can state that the global dependence of political and economic systems on one another is generally greater than that of the mass media, which are mostly still embedded in the nation. However, this national orientation of the media in turn makes it highly dependent on national politics, both in terms of regulation through media policy and discursive influence, though we can also discern a secondary dependence of politics on the media (see Chapter 9, Section 9.3).

Relationships between mass media, systems of action and lifeworlds

While plenty of excellent research has been done on the media, this does not apply to the investigation of lifeworlds due to the even more complex and heterogeneous interweaving of interests. Scholars have endeavoured to give up the fixation on mass communication so widespread in the discipline of communication studies through a variety of integrative concepts (Giesecke 2002, p. 18). The aim of approaches as diverse as communicative ecology (Michael Giesecke) and media dependency theory (Sandra Ball-Rokeach and Melvin DeFleur) is to make the individual and the social group more visible than before as actors in social and cultural communication. So far, neither approach has had much to do with global communication, but both can be made productive in this regard. Giesecke, at least, as set out above, has made some initial remarks on intercultural communication. He assumes that Western long-distance communication, as supported by books and mass media, has aroused curiosity but no real interest in other worlds. For Giesecke, the genius of human communication, which he discerns in principle in the interaction between the "fundamentally different" communicative modes of observation and interaction (2002, p. 26), has become unbalanced in close and especially long-distance relationships. "Book culture" has made face-to-face conversations superfluous, resulting in cultural and social imbalances (ibid., p. 35ff.). Yet new opportunities are opening up to rebalance our communicative ecology, not least through modern network technology. The combining of "feedback-intensive and low-interaction forms of communication is becoming a [key] task for the future" in the new knowledge or learning society (ibid., p. 370). Giesecke too draws on the metaphor of "dynamic equilibrium" (ibid., p. 36) when he describes human beings' fundamentally dynamic ability to strike a new balance between forms of communication.

Since Giesecke is chiefly concerned with the equilibrium between forms of communication and less with the relationships between actors themselves, the media dependency theory formulated by Sandra Ball-Rokeach and Melvin DeFleur is also important for the purposes of this book, as it discusses the general relationships between different systems as dependency factors (1976; Ball-Rokeach 1985; Ognyanova and Ball-Rokeach 2015). Much as in Giesecke's work, their starting point is a shift in the modern era from the requirements of interpersonal communication to information control through mass media (Ball-Rokeach 1985, p. 488f.). From this perspective, particularly in democratic societies, the media system cultivates dynamic relationships with other social systems. On the one hand,

44 Theory of global communication

given the fundamentally symbiotic relationship between the mass media and the economy, humans as consumers are broadly dependent on the media (advertising, and so on). On the other hand, however, it is the individual systems' struggle for autonomy that creates a symmetrical "interdependence" and allows the individual to develop trust in the media. As we know chiefly from authoritarian systems where the balance has been upset, this trust may also be lost (ibid., p. 491ff.).

Just as the type of interdependence between the media and other social systems – such as the close relationship between foreign policy and foreign coverage – is important to their position in society, the individual, despite their structural integration, has various ways of shaping their dependence on the media in line with their interpersonal and sociostructural integration (ibid., p. 497ff.). From the perspective of the media dependency approach, intervening variables that can influence the dependence of the individual include changes in the social environment, the activities of interpersonal networks and group memberships. People's dependence on the mass media increases, for example, when it is perceived as the best source of information and no alternative information is available. In principle, the Internet can contribute to a "renegotiation" of dependence structures, though the mass media has often retained its strong position in the Internet age (Ognyanova and Ball-Rokeach 2015, p. 4).

It is difficult to transfer the dependency idea into lifeworld theory since individual actors do not have a uniform systemic functionality. There are times when individuals, in their systemic roles, achieve or seek to achieve organizations' functional objectives through strategic communication. However, everyday communicative action is to a large extent ideally oriented towards understanding and does not pursue any isolable functional goals (Habermas 1995). People's media-related behaviour cannot simply be broken down into strategic relationships with media, in which all that matters is the functional interest in information. The processes of media appropriation are diverse and include habitual positioning vis-à-vis the entertainment on offer or unconscious habitual behaviour. In addition, today's media environments raise the more fundamental question of the media system's coherence, that is, whether individual recipients are actually dependent on a homogeneous system. The audience's media repertoires tend to be increasingly diverse and may thus engender vastly different individual-media relationships, just as sociocultural influences in lifeworlds produce different individual-society relationships. One individual's dependency relationship may have a quite different meaning for another person. This, in other words, is an analytical rather than empirically generalizable relationship.

We can, however, identify tendencies in the general relationship between lifeworlds and systems, as postulated by Habermas in his notion of the "colonization" of lifeworlds by systems (1990). Ultimately, the key question here is what autonomous contribution lifeworlds make. Do the themes and structures of systems determine experiences in the lifeworld? Conversely, how and when does the communicative output of the lifeworld shape systems? In totalitarian systems, authoritarian regimes often govern deep into the private experiential world, because they wish to prevent certain forms of action in that context and seek to prescribe systems of meaning and belief. At first glance, the space for communication in the lifeworld thus appears to be severely restricted. On the other hand, the communicative construction of everyday reality maintains a space of freedom. This is because, theoretically, the collective reworking of pre-existing interpretive schemes is always possible, with the new constructs then challenging systems either subversively (in the sealed-off spaces of subcultures) or publicly (revolutions on the "street"). Without this independence, many processes of change in dictatorships would be inconceivable. This internal communicative contribution is particularly important when individual room for manoeuvre is restricted and the media is forced to act as the state's mouthpiece.

In democratic systems, conversely, we might reverse this argument. Here the individual is released from traditional obligations and relationships and, in the best-case scenario, the media should now perform social systems' feats of critical observation. But in democracies too there are moments when systems close ranks. The above-mentioned "dynamic equilibrium" of system-environment relations then tends to be adapted and harmonized. In democracies too, therefore, moments of patriotic or populist mobilization may result in the marginalization and sanctioning of dissenting views (Grüne 2019a).

Even more important than the special conditions of crisis situations, however, is the conventionalization of communication in the lifeworld. While productive creativity always means self-empowerment in dictatorships, there is often little need for this in democracies. But as Hubert Knoblauch has described, we can also observe the development of communicative conventions and routines in differentiated lifeworlds (1996). In this case, the lifeworld produces "sluggish structures" not suited to exercising an effect on systems. This may explain the slow pace of the shift towards cosmopolitanism in modern societies. Stereotypes and images of the other are surprisingly stable, and the inertia inherent in the reproduction of hackneyed clichés is perpetuated in many people's travels and dialogues.

The relationship between lifeworld and system must therefore be completely re-evaluated against the background of global developments. Social systems have the advantage over lifeworld actors that they have significantly more resources available for the organized observation of the world – regardless of how well or comprehensively they make use of this advantage. Both individuals and small groups can only selectively observe and travel around the world, while foreign policy, for example, can generate a comprehensive picture. The system of scholarship, meanwhile, can produce detailed factual knowledge, whereas individuals mainly accumulate experiential knowledge. In most cases, then, in their private, everyday lives, people are dependent on the knowledge systems of systems to help them navigate globalization.

However, it would be too simple to assume the uniform dominance of systems over lifeworlds. This is because global developments are crucially dependent on lifeworld actors' crossing of spatial boundaries. Such boundary crossing may represent imposed biographical challenges for individuals (such as labour migration), but it

46 Theory of global communication

may also be emancipatory in character, for example, when people have the opportunity to make private trips abroad, or when everyday cultural references are no longer limited to the immediate environment of everyday activity (as in the case of global fan cultures).

Lifeworld actors may also accomplish feats of globalization, especially in the context of their own global experience. Mobile social elites, for example, are in a position to strike a new balance between their own observation of global realities and the observation of observation performed by the mass media. Their specialist knowledge may even be crucial for a society at specific moments of possible global conflict (if they function as country experts, for example). New experiences of contact through brief private moments of global interaction may also unsettle stereotypical public discourses, at least in the private sphere, and may help trigger conflicts over norms as part of a process of cultural transformation. Finally, the digital platforms of Internet-based media environments now allow many people to seek out global contacts and global knowledge, which may impact in turn on the dynamics of global networks if people form cross-border social connections.

Hence, depending on how extensive different local actors' feats of global observation and interaction are, they have a variable influence on horizontal relations of interdependence with lifeworlds beyond national borders as well as on other social systems both within and outside these borders. The global observation carried out by one local actor may thus conflict with another actor's experience of global interaction. This means that differentiating between communicative *modes* will help us characterize *individual* social actors' feats of global understanding. But it also means that the specific communicative *process* of mediation *between* social actors can help us explain often ambivalent global developments.

Conclusion: horizontal and vertical interdependencies in the dominant and accidental mode

What we have seen is that the problem with interdependency theory is its lack of international integration. The potential interdependencies are multiplied in global communication because any number of international influences may be added to national ones (see Figure 1.4).

Ultimately, amid the range of overlapping interdependencies of importance to the analysis of global communication, we can identify two key dimensions.

- *Horizontal/vertical*: *Horizontal* global interdependencies between the same type of system or lifeworld (for example, between two political spheres in the context of diplomacy) have a dynamic reciprocal relationship with *vertical* (local and global) interdependencies between dissimilar systems or lifeworlds (between politics and the media, the media and lifeworlds, and so on). The key question here is whether the influence of local environments diminishes if the global relations between similar systems or similar lifeworlds intensify (see the

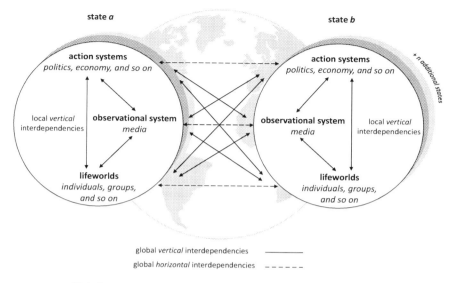

FIGURE 1.4 Global communicative interdependencies

example on win–win situations in foreign policy in contrast to the local character of the mass media on p. 40ff.).

- *Dominant/accidental*: Global long-distance relationships give systems a *dominant* position due to their increased potential for mobility, with the emphasis traditionally being on the dependence of the media on politics and of people on the media. At the same time, however, there are numerous *accidental* mechanisms through which supposedly weaker systems (such as mass media) and lifeworlds (such as groups and communities) can create new local areas of autonomy and may even exercise an inverse social influence on globalization by exploiting new horizontal global ties.

2
MASS MEDIA AND THE GLOBAL PUBLIC SPHERE

One of this book's theoretical premises is that the dominant mode of communication used by mass media can be distinguished from that of other social systems and lifeworlds by a number of traits that are also characteristic of global, cross-border communication. Mass media do not establish an interactive relationship between actors as do politics, the economy or lifeworlds. They are observational systems. Interaction between mass media or between media and recipients is possible, but the primary mode of communication is monologic and discursive. Mass media mostly broadcast in one direction, from producer to consumer. Rather than a "global community", then, this gives rise at most to a "global public sphere".

This means that we have to conceptualize the global communication of the mass media, as an observational system, differently than in the case of action systems, where a distinction must always be made between interactive and observational communicative modes. The greatest challenge for the theory of mass media, meanwhile, is the ambivalence of the concept of discourse. Media discourses are monologic, but media producers are capable of arranging the ideas of different social actors in such a way as to generate an as-if dialogue, in which people do not actively interact across borders but are made aware of others' media agendas and public debates. In a global context, we coined the term "synchronization of the global public sphere" in our theoretical chapter (Chapter 1). Hence, the key question here is not, as is the case with other social systems, what the relationship is between interactive and observational communicative modes, but whether observational communication is practised consistently and a global discourse is facilitated by the media.

The structure of this chapter arises from this basic problem. According to our system-lifeworld-network approach, we must first present the fundamental structure of the system of the mass media, then its feats of discourse and synchronization, before exploring, in a final section, whether or not the achievements and shortcomings of today's global mass communication suggest that it is capable of

DOI: 10.4324/9781003255239-3

producing a synchronized global public sphere. Here, in addition to functionalist and systems-theoretical concepts, we discuss normative democratic and cosmopolitan ideas.

Its theoretical independence is probably the reason why global mass communication is by far the most researched area of global communication. Interpersonal communication and social communication still tend to be marginal topics in the discipline of communication studies, which has for many years chiefly operated as "journalism studies", especially in the Anglo-American tradition (Averbeck-Lietz 2010). In communication studies as well as in other social sciences and humanities disciplines, the idea of media that are supposedly globally available and that inform citizens in real time about the furthest corners of the world has an established place, and this has had a lasting impact on the zeitgeist. The notion of the global power of new technologies, such as satellite television or the Internet, is one of the central myths of the globalization debate, along with the transnationalization of the economy.

However, this notion has generated a certain amount of opposition, so that today global mass communication is probably not just the largest but also the most controversial field of research on global communication. Controversial issues include

- the extent to which mass media have developed transnational organizational structures or have remained chiefly local (and above all national);
- to what extent global or local media ethics and professional standards prevail;
- to what extent mass media are primarily geared towards global or local markets;
- to what extent global or national legal and political parameters play a decisive role;
- to what extent all of this is bound up with global homogenization or synchronization or, alternatively, with the continued local heterogeneity of media discourses (Flew 2007, p. 26f.; Hafez 2007a; McMillin 2007, p. 8ff.; Kübler 2011, p. 28ff.).

Finally, therefore, we have to ask whether the new technological possibilities of digitization have really brought about a new kind of globalization or whether we have merely seen shifts of emphasis that change little about the basic state of global communication. Present-day scholarship features a number of currents (Hafez 2007a, p. 1ff.; Williams 2011, p. 21ff.; Ulrich 2016, p. 45ff.), with "globalization optimists" assuming the progressive convergence of structures and content, while "globalization pessimists" or "globalization realists", envisage a race between local and global structures and discourses in which they effectively cancel each other out. This chapter seeks to tie together and summarize these different research perspectives at every analytical level – structure, discourse and theory of the public sphere. In analysing the contradictions of global mass communication, our goal is to go beyond broad-brush and imprecise notions of "glocalization" (see Chapter 1, Section 1.2) and to bring out fundamental tendencies as clearly as possible. In the context of the globalization debate, German sociologist Ulrich Beck rightly noted

50 Mass media and the global public sphere

that the simplistic notion of "dialectics" has appeared before in history but was ultimately "dismissed by all clear-headed thinkers" (2000, p. 49). We have no desire to revive this misconceived perspective here.

2.1 Systems and system change

A basic model of global mass communication

Mass media form complex systems that are made up of journalists, their professional relations and professional ethics (micro-level), media companies and editorial offices (meso-level), and those environmental relationships of importance to the media system with other subsystems in politics, economy and society (especially audiences) (macro-level). Within the meso-level, there are exchange relations between media, for example, through economic interrelationships, information procurement or an orientation towards journalistic opinion leaders, with news agencies occupying a prominent position. There are relations of interdependence between media organizations and their environmental systems of politics and economy as well as their non-organized systemic environments of audiences. Politics, for example, acts as a social supersystem (Gerhards and Neidhardt 1990, p. 8f.) in that it regulates and controls the media system legally and politically, although politics is also dependent on its representation in the media. The economy plays a dual role, as it is part of the internal media system through ownership, but at the same time it supplies the media system with economic resources, similar to the paying audience, for example, through advertising revenue. The relations of the media system to its environments are dependent, not least, on the character of a given political system. In a liberal system (democracy), these relations can best be described as a dynamic equilibrium between autonomy and adaptation. The media system provides society with independent (critical) observation but is simultaneously exposed to influences from its environment that restrict its autonomy (Kunczik 1984; Marcinkowski 1993; Hafez 2002a, vol. 1, p. 123ff.).

While integrated media systems emerge in this way in the national framework, a global media system does not exist (as yet). Most of the mass media in the world are geared towards national or even smaller local audiences and are linguistically limited. This also applies to global mass communication, whenever it is part of national media systems as "foreign coverage", because here national media edit the world for national audiences. National foreign coverage, in which national editorial offices produce international news with the help of foreign correspondents and the information made available to them by news agencies, is still the dominant form of global journalism and media use (see p. 54f.). In essence, then, the synchronization of the "global public sphere" is carried out by "egocentric", that is, decentralized national media systems. Media systems – and this is closely related to their tendency towards discursive rather than interactive communication – tend to be more egocentric than political or economic systems. As we shall see, other social systems have given up some of their sovereignty in favour of transnational diplomatic spaces, global governance structures and transnational relations of production and ownership.

In those cases in which recipients (at the macro-level) cross borders via technological means such as direct-to-air satellite broadcasting and use the media of other countries, the audience's media spaces have certainly expanded beyond national borders. But regardless of a number of attempts to establish a cross-border media policy, and political PR that is distributed worldwide via news agencies, political regulation is still carried out by nation states, and not by a transnational state, which of course exists only in rudimentary form, within the framework of the European Union, for example. At the meso-level too, the media may maintain exchange relations through import and export, there may be leading international media (such as the *New York Times*) and there may even be joint projects across international boundaries, as in the case of cross-border journalism. But once again, the regulatory environmental systems are always shaped mainly by the national framework. At the theoretical micro-level, journalists may orientate themselves towards universal ethics and conceptions of professionalism, including aesthetic and stylistic standards (see p. 53ff.) – but they remain employees within the legal framework of a particular nation state.

The residual local ties in all forms of global mass communication are present in media that view themselves programmatically as "global media" and whose existence is often regarded as evidence of a transnational media system – though ultimately this is not the case. The television channels CNN, Al-Jazeera English and BBC World News, for example, operate worldwide, but are tied politically to their home systems. This is even clearer in the case of so-called "international broadcasting", that is, media established by states that broadcast in a variety of languages (such as Deutsche Welle, Voice of America, RT and BBC World Service) and that cannot deny their political mandate as part of their home countries' public diplomacy. Even in the twenty-first century, a global media system not tied, in one way or another, to specific nation states is still largely a utopia (Hafez 2007a, p. 13).

In order to understand the basic structure of global mass communication, it is therefore useful to distinguish between three different dimensions (Figure 2.1). Global mass communication is not a self-contained global system, but consists of

- national media *systems* (especially foreign coverage)
- that make use of international communication *flows* (generated by news agencies, foreign correspondents, imports/exports, and so on) and
- that are supplemented by individual transnational media *structures* (global ethics, joint productions, cross-border reception and regulations).

Global communication flows do not constitute a global media system. Local or national systems remain intact but are exposed to global influences and also form transnational network structures.

The key maxim here is that, at all levels, the system of the mass media and journalism is still shaped more by the nation state than by global forces (Hafez

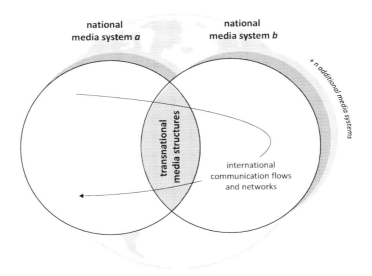

FIGURE 2.1 Dimensions of global mass communication

2002a, vol. 1, p. 134ff.). As a rule, the prevailing features are a journalism imbued by national ethics and socialization (micro-level), national forms of organization and ownership structures (meso-level) and national audiences and environmental influences (macro-level). For the most part, globalization has remained structurally weak in the mass media and generally speaking there is no significant cross-border convergence of media systems.

At the same time, both international communication flows and transnational substructures may well be dynamic. According to our basic theoretical model, namely the system-lifeworld-network approach, whether national systems or globally influenced processes have a greater impact on media discourse cannot be shown without empirical investigation. Furthermore, while it is unlikely that the primacy of national media systems will end before the nation state dissolves worldwide, which is improbable any time soon, we cannot rule out systemic change in the mass media in future.

The first signs of such change emerged in the debate on the "New World Information Order" at the turn of the 1980s. Many commentators assailed the informational pressure exerted by the major Western news agencies, as well as the Western music and film industries, on the rest of the world (Many Voices – One World 1980). There is still a considerable gap between this influence, emanating chiefly from the superpower of the United States, and the "subaltern contra flows" issuing from the countries of Asia, Africa and Latin America (Thussu 2010, pp. 222f., 234). In view of the unequal cultural balance of power, it seems premature to refer to "multi-centred" globalization (Butsch 2019, p. 214ff.). The strong global presence of Western communicative flows does not contradict the absence of a global media system, but points to the possibly increasing impact of international *system environments*, which do not manifest as organized *environmental systems* with formal political and legal regulatory powers (see p. 56f.), but do shape the informational environment of national media systems. In the course of this chapter, we will be discussing the persistent dominance of national systems, but also the international communicative flows and transnational substructures of global mass communication, at all levels – from professional ethics, through media production and reception, to the political and economic environmental factors affecting media systems.

(Trans)national media ethics and professionalism

Professional journalism can be described in terms of the values of journalists, media and journalistic representatives (such as press councils), values that influence the behaviour of the media. These values are in evidence both in formal ethics (ethical codes) and in the informal practices of media professionals. Comparative country studies reveal similarities as well as differences between national and regional journalistic ethics (see, for example, Hafez 2002b, 2003b; Hanitzsch 2006; Löffelholz and Weaver 2008; d'Haenens et al. 2014). In general, with respect to formal ethics we can observe a high degree of congruity in the core areas of objectivity and the search for truth, while the differences are greater when it comes to liberal norms as well as the journalistic emphasis on individuality and community (Christians and Traber 1997). The differences between media systems' media ethics are, however, fluid and dynamic, and professional role models may generate intercultural "contagion" and demonstration effects that we can also observe in journalistic routines, news values and journalistic design aesthetics (Sklair 1995, p. 159f.; Machin and van Leeuwen 2007, p. 8f.). The transnational television broadcaster Al-Jazeera has been called the "Arab CNN" in part because it deploys a mode of presentation similar to that of its Western counterpart.

We should not, however, confuse the harmonization of professional standards with the harmonization of content. Even with identical standards of objectivity, the selection and interpretation of topics in journalism are vastly different at the system level (see Section 2.2.1). Especially at times of war and crisis, conflicting media discourses are not uncommon, and the synchronization of the global public sphere remains underdeveloped. Only the kind of vision put forward by Marshall McLuhan, according to which the medium is itself the message (McLuhan 1964), can ignore differences in content and take the transnational convergence of the profession of journalism as evidence of the globalization of mass communication in the "global village" (see Chapter 1, Section 1.1). How unproductive such an analysis is, however, becomes clear when we consider that international codes of ethics barely exist to date and national values, such as internationalism or cosmopolitanism, are hardly ever mentioned in national codes (Hafez 2008, p. 160f.). The formulation of a global, cosmopolitan and/or postcolonial media ethics remains a task for the future (Ward and Wasserman 2010).

54 Mass media and the global public sphere

(G)local media production

It makes sense to first differentiate between nationally and transnationally oriented mass media. The foreign coverage produced by national media achieves greater reach than transnational media. It is true that national foreign coverage is in crisis worldwide as a result of digitization, declining revenue and a lack of resources that has made itself felt chiefly in the axing of correspondent jobs (Lewis 2010). But this changes nothing about the fundamentally strong position of national foreign coverage. For most recipients, media operating transnationally are more supplement than substitute, and the entire market share of television channels such as CNN, Al-Jazeera English and BBC World, as well as European channels such as Euronews, Eurosports and Fashion TV, to mention just a few examples, is 10 per cent at most (Chalaby 2009, p. 118) but probably even smaller. Transnational media are known the world over and, as the leading media within journalism and the reference media for informational elites, they have a certain opinion-leading influence (see p. 67f.) among recipients (Samuel-Azran 2009). But their market shares are often exceedingly small, which means that many of these media are loss-making and subsidized by their home countries. We will also be examining whether these transnational broadcasters can represent global discourses better than national mass media (Chalaby 2009, p. 228; see Section 2.2.1).

The strong position of national media is, however, put into perspective by global communication flows and new transnational structures. For some time now, national news journalism has been supplemented by various cross-border "collaborative journalism" projects, which became widely known, for example, in the wake of the "Panama Papers" (Alfter 2016, 2019; Heft 2019). Since these projects are essentially exceptions, national journalism continues to dominate and cross-border journalism, like the transnational media, is at best a supplement rather than a real alternative (Grieves 2012, p. 169). In the news business in particular, as a rule it is very difficult to establish transnational media structures, since there is always a need to adapt language, personnel and content to the discursive interests and habits of consumers in the various countries.

At the same time, it is evident – and, again, this qualifies our view of national relations of production – that fictional entertainment has always been imported and exported more than news. The best-known example of this is Hollywood films, but also Latin American telenovelas, which are watched across the world. Compared to the news business, which is characterized by national preferences, the entertainment sector can be described as the core of globalization and the centrepiece of a hybrid cultural development: while national productions are still prominent in this context, they are sometimes less dominant (Hafez 2007a, p. 82ff.; Straubhaar 2014). However, the media-based entertainment industries are still highly local in character (Kawashima and Hye-Kyung 2018). National productions have the greatest reach, especially in the television sector, which is why we should be careful not to overstate the internationalization of the entertainment industry (Flew 2007, p. 127; Hafez 2007a, p. 82ff.; Straubhaar 2007). The major film industries in India

(Bollywood), the Arab world, China and Iran, and animated film productions in East Asian countries, are dominant in their local markets.

However, they have also managed to establish a global "contraflow" in the international export business that at least provides the still dominant American films with a degree of competition (Thussu 2019, p. 191ff.). The notion of Western "cultural imperialism" through globalization is simplistic, since it fails to take account of the simultaneous modernization of cultures centred on a national language and the potential for globalization in the global "South" (Hafez 2007a, p. 94ff.).

The global reception gap: informational masses and elites

In addition to ethics (micro-level) and production (meso-level), reception (macro-level) is a key structural feature of global mass communication. Apart from anything else, the reason why media systems are transnationalizing themselves only haltingly is that national media are still preferred by the vast majority of consumers. The "relative unimportance" (Sparks 2016, p. 61) of transnationally oriented broadcasters is due to the national reception behaviour of a large portion of audiences. No significant change has occurred in these reception structures, despite the growth of direct-to-air satellite broadcasting since the late 1980s and the Internet since the 1990s (Wessler and Brüggemann 2012, p. 98ff.). With all due caution regarding the figures produced by research on global media reach, which are often disseminated by companies themselves and are not always accurate (Zöllner 2004), it seems clear that both the use of transnational media (such as CNN, BBC World, and so on) and the cross-border uptake of other national media services remain a marginal aspect of media use (Hasebrink and Herzog 2009). This finding is by no means trivial, but of the utmost significance. As we shall see, national images of foreign countries often have a negative or at least stereotypical character, such that consumers are increasingly exposed to negative stereotypes as a result of their primarily national media consumption (see Section 2.2.1). The global reception gap is, to a significant extent, responsible for the problems of nationalism and racism, including right-wing populist attacks on globalization.

However, there are also some notable exceptions and countervailing trends to the general rule of national media use, which are associated with special situations (language areas and international broadcasting) and special groups (migrants and global elites). Media are used across borders chiefly in geolinguistically homogeneous language areas if they include several national states, for example, the German-speaking world (Germany, Austria and Switzerland), or the Arabic- and Spanish-speaking regions, each of which comprises more than 20 countries (Sinclair et al. 1996). The development of satellite broadcasting and the Internet has facilitated this "small-scale border crossing", but it is in fact much older and is bound up with a common history and linguistic relationships. Since this kind of media use is not global, but is limited to traditional cultural areas, it is effectively regionalization rather than globalization. On the one hand, national borders are being crossed. On the other hand, the notion of "cultural areas" is being revived by technology, which is an impediment to a cosmopolitan and universal conception of globalization (Hafez 2007a, p. 69ff.).

56 Mass media and the global public sphere

Another special case of media use arises from multilingual international broadcasting, such as BBC World Service (UK), RT (Russia), Voice of America (United States), Deutsche Welle (Germany) and Radio China International (China) (Carvalho 2009). The monolingual middle classes, who do not use foreign language media, may also turn to international broadcasting (Chouikha 1992). The attacks of 11 September 2001 in particular led to an increase in the number of options available in this regard and triggered a new media race between the major and medium-sized powers (Hafez 2007a, p. 118ff.). Despite these developments, cross-border media use is at best a supplementary component of most people's media menu and is not evidence of sweeping globalization.

Such globalization may occur, however, among special groups such as global elites active in the fields of politics, economy and culture, who constantly cross borders, are mobile, and therefore use media outside their countries of origin to a greater extent than other people (ibid., p. 61; Wessler and Brüggemann 2012, p. 98f.). Migrants play a prominent but particular role within the global informational elite. Often, they regularly use media outside their place of residence – from their countries of origin or within a diaspora context (Galal 2014; Robins and Aksoy 2015). It is difficult to determine the exact size of global informational elites, but even if they are small in number, the *qualitative* influence of these "cosmopolitans" on society is likely to be substantial. Migrants in particular can use their multicultural media menus to develop a transcultural subjectivity at the interface between media globalization and postcolonialism, though very little research has been done on this as yet (Merten and Krämer 2016, see also Brennan 2008). This is in fact the source of a common misunderstanding, since these mobile elites tend to regard their own cosmopolitan style of media use as a general trend towards globalization, when in reality it is a phenomenon special to them.

The environmental system of politics: the hegemony of the nation state

Global media policy is a reflection of most people's reception behaviour, which is still strongly influenced by the national context. Where media are rarely used across borders, there is no need for global legal and political regulation of the media. Transnational legal regulations are limited to a few commercial or technology policy fields. The Agreement on Trade-Related Aspects of Intellectual Property Rights or TRIPS, for example, prohibits pirating. The EU television directive harmonizes, among other things, national regulations on advertising, sponsoring and tele-shopping. The International Telecommunication Union (ITU) and the Internet Corporation for Assigned Names and Numbers (ICANN), meanwhile, regulate the technological parameters of satellite broadcasting and the Internet. Ostensibly, a growing number of such actors seems to point to the increasing importance of global media policy. However, a "techno-functional perspective" still dominates here (Berghofer 2017, p. 365), which certainly involves the global regulation of technological issues but otherwise defines media policy essentially as national cultural policy and has virtually no effect on the independence of nation states. Even the European Union, probably the most ambitious confederation of states in the world, leaves the regulation of the media largely to individual countries (Michalis 2016). This leads to some odd outcomes, as a number of European states are classified as "partially free" (Italy, Poland, Hungary, and so on) in the international rankings of media freedom (Freedom House, Reporters Without Borders) because their governments place excessive restrictions on media freedom, with Brussels or Strasbourg doing little to counteract this.

Aside from a few capitalist and technological parameters, global media policy thus remains largely in the hands of the nation state, especially with respect to core policies on media freedom and concentration (Hafez 2007a, p. 142ff.). Ironically, in the "era of globalization", the result has been that freedom of expression and media freedom are under growing threat worldwide from authoritarian regimes and – even within democracies – authoritarian tendencies (Freedom House 2019). Structurally, the synchronization of a cross-border global public sphere is endangered by the hegemony of national media policy (Heft and Pfetsch 2012, p. 158f.). Media freedom, therefore, ultimately remains a privilege of multilingual informational elites who, in the event of threats to domestic media freedom, obtain information from foreign media, though even here the nation state can assert itself through Internet censorship or by disrupting foreign satellite media.

The persistence of the nation state has prompted a rethinking of assumptions in recent times. Previously, numerous scholars criticized the "methodological essentialism" (Kleinsteuber and Rossmann 1994; Couldry and Hepp 2009) typical of comparative research on media systems, with its focus on the nation state. But these critics are now being upbraided for an excessively optimistic view of globalization (Flew et al. 2016, p. 5). Of course, we might argue that state media regulation is only effective to a limited extent. When it comes to the Internet in particular, companies such as Google and Facebook have repeatedly ignored criticism by national governments, which seems to point to the ascendancy of global Internet companies (Iosifidis 2016, p. 23). When things get serious, however, as exemplified by the Erdoğan regime in Turkey, which shut down YouTube and Facebook in that country, the state may well be in position to impose its will. The counter-critique of the "methodological globalism" practised by some communication studies scholars (Waisbord 2014, p. 30) is based on the nation state's ultimate sovereignty over media issues. The fact that the state is struggling with global challenges in the media sector and has made regulatory concessions does not mean that transnational media structures have finally eliminated the national media system and its control of international communicative flows.

The environmental system of the economy: the limits of transnationalization

Global substructures are also found in the field of media economics. American media groups in particular (such as Disney, News Corporation, Netflix and Thomson Reuters), but also French and German "global players" (such as Vivendi,

58 Mass media and the global public sphere

Bertelsmann, and so on) are active exporters of entertainment culture and make direct investments in many media systems around the world. In addition, recent years have seen the (often rapid) growth of companies in the field of telecommunications, the Internet and information and communication technology based in the United States (such as AT&T, Google, Facebook and Amazon) and China (such as Tencent and Baidu). If we add the major powers' already strong position in the world news market thanks to large Western news agencies such as Reuters, AFP and AP, as well as the limited but still visible reach of Western channels like CNN, then it is clear that a number of large powerful states dominate the global media market. In the case of search engines, as non-traditional mass media, more than 60 per cent of all inquiries are made on Google. The latter plus Yahoo, Baidu and Microsoft have an 80 per cent market share (Winseck 2011, p. 36f.). Critical left-wing media scholars have repeatedly quoted these figures to assail what they regard as media imperialism under the guise of globalization policy (Herman and McChesney 1997; Artz and Kamalipour 2003; McPhail 2010).

Against the thesis of global media dominance, revisionist scholars have objected that, despite their influence in certain fields, the large global corporations are far from dominating entire media markets. The transnationalization of media capital is limited and in the nationally imbued media systems of this world it is national (and to some extent regional) media capital that continues to rule the roost (Compaine 2002, Rugman 2002; Flew 2007, 2009, 2011; Hafez 2007a) as even advocates of the Western dominance thesis occasionally concede (Herman and McChesney 1997, p. 9). Rather than a homogeneous global media market, there is now a patchwork of national and regional markets in which transnational substructures and commercial relationships are embedded. Terry Flew refers here to a "statistical illusion" (2007, p. 82), since we would have to compare corporations' impressive international profits with the even larger local profits chalked up in their home countries (mostly in the United States and Europe). Media corporations are thus far less global than companies in other fields, making this sector more of a "laggard" than a pioneer of globalization (Flew 2007, p. 87, 208; see also Hafez 2007a, p. 158ff.).

The second common analytical flaw consists in the fact that a business economics perspective on individual media giants tells us nothing about their market shares in national economies. Yet this is crucial if we want to measure the true influence of "global players", who are in fact outdone by local "provincial princes" of media capital in most countries (Hafez 2007a, p.161ff.; see also Birkinbine et al. 2017, p. 109ff.). There is even much to suggest that, despite increasing foreign direct investment due to rapidly growing local media markets, US corporations are less influential today than at the end of the twentieth century: especially in the press, television and news sectors, "territorialized capital" usually dominates (Christophers 2014, p. 369). Major Indian corporations such as Doordashan have responded to global competition (from Rupert Murdoch's Sky TV, for example) by expanding their regional services. Similar developments have been seen in Hong Kong, Malaysia and Latin America, while countries like China and Indonesia set quotas on international programme imports (McMillin 2007, p. 105ff.). In Arab countries, for political reasons, foreign media groups tend to make silent media investments and do not hold majority stakes, so their influence is limited in terms of both content and politics (Sakr 2001, p. 97). Even the global trade in television formats consists of cooperation between transnational companies and local partners (Grüne 2016). Overall, globalization as technologically possible clearly faces major constraints within local markets.

Against the revisionists, it has been argued with some justification that we need to take into account not only the producers of media content but also media infra-structure capital (Fuchs 2010). In the twenty-first century, the international profits of the Internet, telecommunications and computer hardware giants have in fact grown considerably and their degree of transnationalization – the contribution of international markets to their sales figures – is higher than that of classic media groups (Winseck 2011, p. 6f.). More than one hundred thousand employees work for Dell Inc. worldwide (Gershon 2019, p. 39). The Getty Images picture agency makes around 40 per cent of its sales outside the United States and has customers in more than 50 countries (Machin and van Leeuwen 2007, p. 150ff.). But what we are seeing here is a techno-functional form of capital globalization. Foreign products and services are used whenever they cannot be produced locally or when informa-tional building blocks – such as photos – are required. However, editorial services and programmes, especially in the information sector, are provided *within* most countries. When it comes to politically and culturally complex media products, foreign goods and direct investment tend to plug the gaps in local markets, to supplement and extend rather than replace national products.

Non-traditional mass media: extended hypermediality

Novel services have emerged that can be described as mass media, especially on the Internet. The Internet not only extends the reach of the established media of press, radio and television in a technological sense. It also generates a new basis for media as diverse as search engine news, social media (such as Twitter), blogs, podcasts, and alternative news portals (such as WikiNews). Not every form of digital com-munication can be characterized as "mass media". Much of it is interpersonal or community-oriented (see Chapter 6). However, communicative phenomena that are publicly accessible and appear periodically, so that they resemble journalistic services, can be classified as non-traditional mass media.

To what extent the production and reception structures or the communicative flows of global mass communication change as a result of the Internet is difficult to assess. Once again, there are optimistic and pessimistic views of whether the Internet has really initiated a structural shift in global mass communication. Ethan Zuckerman has demonstrated that even in the age of the Internet, cross-border and above all foreign-language media use has remained a marginal phenomenon. In none of the ten most powerful nations in the world is the average share of for-eign media use online higher than 7 per cent of the population. Often, the usage

60 Mass media and the global public sphere

figures are barely measurable, and things are no different in other parts of the world (2013, p. 52ff., see also Elvestad 2009; Fenyoe 2010; Finnemann et al. 2012). From this point of view, digitization has not fostered transnational structural change (in media use), let alone ushered in a "global media system". From a historical perspective, analogue media revolutions such as the introduction of the telegraph seem to have had a far more powerful effect on global communications than the Internet.

Hans-Jürgen Bucher, however, has pointed out that at times of crisis, global media use increases (2005). Since the Kosovo War, the attacks of 11 September 2001 and the Iraq War of 2003, critical sections of the public have been searching the Internet for information provided by digitized classic and alternative mass media that they cannot get from their national media. The quality of this extended hypermediality is a matter of controversy, as some of the sources are questionable (Lewis 2010, p. 123). But social movements in particular have created media that not only can generate alternative global public spheres, but also can function as "interlocutors" and may link media agendas across borders (Volkmer 2014, p. 141ff., see also Chapter 5). At the same time, given that these processes are temporally limited and restricted to informational elites, they are far from constituting a global "structural transformation of the public sphere" (Bucher 2005, p. 214).

Interdependence gaps and two-speed globalization

In summary, global mass media communication today is still overwhelmingly carried out by national media systems. The worldwide patchwork of egocentric media systems has, it is true, been supplemented by transnational structures of production and reception. This complementarity, however, is governed by the principle of subsidiarity, which means that national systems not only dominate most news production, but also much of the entertainment sector, at most supplementing them with international products. Transnational products – CNN, Al-Jazeera, Hollywood, Bollywood, and so on – are major prestige projects that add an important global component to media consumption, but without eliminating the pre-eminence of local structures.

When it comes to media policy and media law, moreover, the nation state still sets the key parameters, which are supplemented rather than replaced by functional global regulations relating to technology. Media markets are only globally interdependent to a very limited extent. In contrast to the interactive social systems of politics, the economy, and so on, in its primary mode of (world) observation the mass media's cultural production remains highly self-referential in structural terms. The exceptions to this tendency are alternative flows of information and public spheres that point to a "two-speed" globalization. Global mass communication is a minority phenomenon, with informational elites, among both producers and consumers, systematically trying to move beyond the national borders of the media realm and create a stable global public sphere.

2.2 Communicative system connections

According to our system-lifeworld-network approach, a purely structuralist view of global mass communication is insufficient. Media systems communicate across borders, but does this mean that their feats of observation are synchronized in the sense of creating a common global media discourse and a transnational global public sphere? Or are we in fact dealing with separate national media discourses that remain unconnected to one another? Our analysis involves two steps. First we review the state of empirical research on, and above all the content analysis of, global mass communication, before going on to evaluate present-day realities in light of the differing requirements for synchrony found in the theory of the deliberative public sphere and systems theory.

2.2.1 Discourse analysis

Fundamentals: interdiscursivity, convergence and the domestication of media discourses

The media's "worldview" is a discourse that consists – in terms of text linguistics – of macro- and micro-propositions (van Dijk 1988,; Hafez 2002a, vol. 1, p. 45ff.). "Topics", for example, are the macro-propositions of a text. These are closely associated with the theory of agenda-setting within the discipline of communication studies, that is, with the question of what issues the media (and, consequently, its recipients) are thinking *about*. Topics include micro-propositions such as frames and stereotypes, in other words, action-oriented argumentational constructs in a text as well as attributive characterizations (of nations or social groups, for example) (Entman 1993; Thiele 2015). While we may examine topics, framing and stereotypes on the basis of individual texts, the concept of discourse also includes relationships *between* texts (the key term here being intertextuality; see Konerding 2005). Public discourse is not an interactive dialogue in the sense of the shared production of meaning. It remains monologic but has dialogue-like attributes in that we can identify intertextual references to other texts. Intertextual discourses, meanwhile, have an integrative function and create discursive communities (public spheres) through their linguistic comprehensibility.

The question is to what extent the national media systems of this world, which are relatively separate in structural terms, function as transcultural mediators by synchronizing national discourses with one another and creating a global and transcultural "interdiscourse" in which understanding of self and other are fused (Hafez 2002a, vol. 1, p. 163ff.). This would require the producers of foreign coverage to investigate and "translate" the congruence and difference between local discourses. Such a role may entail considerable difficulties, not only because topic choice and interpretations may differ in different discursive communities, but also because contextual knowledge naturally decreases in line with one's distance from international events and has to be imparted by the foreign correspondent (ibid.,

62 Mass media and the global public sphere

vol. 1, p. 65f.). This process is further complicated by the fact that acoustic, visual and textual signs have different logics within global communication. While music and images cross borders relatively easily and are seemingly "self-explanatory", texts have to be translated, processed and contextualized. But even the straightforward character of images is more apparent than real, such that they are often highly manipulative.

Varying standards are imposed on interdiscursive synchronization. From the *convergence* perspective, the task of journalism is not only to reproduce the discourses of other systems comprehensively and precisely, but also to explain them meaningfully in the context of the reporting system's own discourse and thus to connect national discourses and generate global perspectives (Hafez 2002a, vol. 1, p. 24ff.; Stanton 2007). The key attributes are (1) thematic convergence, (2) temporal synchrony and intensity, and (3) convergence of interpretations and speakers (Tobler 2006; Ulrich 2016, p. 114). The distinction between the convergence of interpretations and the convergence of speakers is important in that while interpretations of topics may diverge nationally, non-national discourses must be represented by speakers in such a way as to ensure global responsiveness. The idea of convergent interdiscursivity in the global public sphere takes its lead from the theory of the deliberative public sphere (see Section 2.2.2).

From the *domestication* perspective, foreign coverage is designed for national target groups only. Here the construction of a worldview requires no references beyond the national, virtually self-contained observational system (Renneberg 2011, p. 45ff.). The exponents of this view criticize the convergence perspective as "methodological connectivism" (Werron 2010, p. 143), which they counter with a kind of disjointed media modernity. We flesh out these different theoretical approaches in Section 2.2.2. First, though, we examine the current empirical state of global media discourse, which is also subject to contestation by media scholars.

A fragmented news agenda: the tip of the globalization iceberg

It is a fundamental paradox that in the era of globalization the attention paid to foreign news has diminished rather than grown (Norris 1995; Willnat et al. 2013; Ulrich 2016, p. 118ff.; Russ-Mohl 2017, p. 162f.). The public's interest in foreign affairs is not uniform. It is often greater in smaller countries and intensifies as soon as local actors are involved ("home news abroad") (Hanitzsch et al. 2013). But historical turning points have an impact, with the end of the East-West conflict triggering a decline in interest in the world. Talk shows in large, industrialized countries such as Germany focus overwhelmingly on national issues and very few international ones (Schultz 2006, p. 168ff.). Interest may, however, fluctuate greatly over the short term. In particular, international crises and wars of a threatening character, such as the attacks of 11 September 2001 or the Iraq War of 2003, led to a temporary increase in attention.

In general terms, an interesting logic seems to govern which countries and topics receive attention or are ignored in the various national media systems. This is best explained by a number of key theorems relating to the structure of discourse (Hafez 2002a, vol. 1, p. 51ff., 2007a, p. 39ff.). For the most part, foreign news crosses the reporting threshold only if it comes either from other countries in the same region or from the "global metropolises" (such as the United States, Russia and China), in other words from countries with the status of a major power. Such news often focuses on political affairs, foregrounds elites rather than lifeworlds and privileges negative reports on conflicts, wars and disasters. This logic is not only corroborated by numerous empirical case studies, but is based on news-related factors such as political and economic importance, an orientation towards conflict, and cultural proximity or distance (Williams 2011, p. 146ff.; Cazzamatta 2014, 2018, 2020a, 2020b). The result of these gatekeeping processes is the extremely fragmentary worldviews constructed by the media, in which many countries devoid of acute conflicts or with little power are largely disregarded, while crisis-hit regions and major powers are over-represented and engender a hegemonic global news scene. Negativism is a general tendency of journalism in domestic reporting as well, but in the case of foreign news, country images are particularly severely affected due to time constraints. Developing countries especially rarely make an appearance and, when they do, the coverage is mostly negative (Hafez 2002a, vol. 2, p. 125ff.; Zuckerman 2013, p. 79ff.).

However, since every country has a different regional environment, media systems' "news geographies" are not uniform. Very different topics and countries are discussed below the thin "tip of the iceberg" of world news about crisis-hit regions and "metropolitan" states. The result is a dual global discursive displacement, consisting of an extremely narrow global agenda that is shared across the world and that underscores the North–South divide, and separate national news geographies and agenda setting. Despite the strong convergence of news values and professional media ethics worldwide (see Section 2.1), then, there has been little change in the domestication of global news through mass communication. There is currently no prospect of the kind of expansion and qualitative consolidation of discourses that might consciously compensate for thematic gaps and restructure news values in such a way as to achieve global interdiscursive synchrony. Strong domestication prevails.

Large-scale comparative studies have attested to this for decades (including Sreberny-Mohammadi et al. 1985; Wu 2000, 2003; Pietiläinen 2006; Cohen 2013a; Heimprecht 2017). Local factors are thus decisive in the selection of topics and countries in foreign coverage. Regionalism holds sway in every country, though a little less in developing countries than in industrialized ones, as a metropolitan orientation and global agenda are more pronounced in the former (de Swert et al. 2013; Wilke et al. 2013). Even within regions such as Europe, while the attention paid to individual neighbouring countries is greater (due to regionalism), EU issues and EU actors play a merely secondary role within the nationally fixated public spheres (Machill et al. 2006; Pfetsch et al. 2008). At the level of content, nationally imbued and fragmented media agendas challenge the assumption of the globalization of media discourses, let alone a cosmopolitan "global village" (McLuhan) (Cohen 2013b).

64 Mass media and the global public sphere

A number of studies have shown that online journalism and search engines such as Google News and Yahoo, that is, non-traditional mass media, have barely improved anything in this regard, contrary to the hopes harboured by many. The news geography remains as restricted as ever (Gasher and Gabriele 2004; Wu 2007; Wang 2010). To quote Kevin Williams: "The geography of online content reflects the imbalances of the traditional mainstream media; web technology has not drastically changed what is reported as international news" (2011, p. 161). Even hyperlinks to foreign websites have failed to catch on in online journalism (Chang et al. 2009).

Only a few topics, such as the climate issue, manage to become firmly established in the mass media worldwide and feature similar sub-topics, which is probably due to the nature of environmental themes, which receive a similar degree of attention in different parts of the world (Ivanova 2017). When it comes to political issues such as the United Nations, what we find is that views of international institutions are country-specific or thematic clusters form in particular countries, with armed conflicts tending to dominate in the media of industrialized countries and structural crises such as poverty holding sway in the developing countries' media (Ulrich 2016, p. 301ff.). Certainly, prevailing professional standards and news-related factors, leading global media and news agencies prevent media systems from being completely self-contained or sealing themselves off and facilitate the dynamic opening up and short-term internationalization of discourses, especially at times of crisis. But social and cultural developments often tend to be ignored and are poor predictors of a global media discourse that shows little sign of convergence. Two-thirds of the land mass and population of this planet, in Asia, Africa and Latin America, remain largely invisible in Western media, with just a few, often negative exceptions (Williams 2011, p. 145f.).

Global framing or domesticated discourses?

In order to assess the synchrony of global media discourses from the perspectives of convergence and domestication, we have to examine not just macro-propositions such as the media's thematic agenda but also micro-propositions such as stereotypes and frames. In contrast to thematic repertoires, the key issue here is not *what* is reported, but *how* this is done. The work of Michael Gurevitch, Mark R. Levy and Itzhak Roeh is now regarded as the *locus classicus* of research in this field. As early as 1991, they showed that one and the same topic can be presented very differently in different national media systems, a phenomenon they call the "domestication of the foreign" (1991, p. 206). The idea that we are automatically provided with global perspectives in a world connected by news agencies and global media corporations emerges as untenable in view of the media's character as a national system, with stereotypes and frames still often being nationally imbued.

This is most clearly apparent in national and religious stereotypes. Unlike frames, stereotypes are blanket attributions of character traits, of a cultural mentality that is supposedly typical of a certain group or country. Such ideas have shown an astonishing capacity for survival even in modern media systems, generating a vast number of studies that defy easy summation (see the meta-study by Thiele 2015). Since it is difficult analytically to differentiate between stereotypes (as the sweeping attribution of characteristics to nations and groups) and frames (as the argumentational framing of an action) (Hafez 2002a, vol. 1, p. 47f.), researchers often examine these different micro-propositions of discourse in combination. Many studies show the strong tendency to fall back on prejudices in foreign coverage, when it comes to topics such as Islam, for example (Hafez 2002a, vol. 2, p. 207ff.; Schiffer 2005; Poole and Richardson 2006; Mertens and de Smaele 2016), or national stereotypes (Marten 1989; von Bassewitz 1990; Tzogopoulos 2013). At present, stereotypes are especially in evidence in the field of fiction. Arab stereotypes in Hollywood films, for example, have been extensively researched (Kamalipour 1995; Shaheen 2009). Ethnic and religious stereotypes in fictional and non-fictional media are not just the raw material for worldviews centred on racism and right-wing populist anti-globalism (Hafez 2014a, 2017a). In a globally integrated media system they would probably have no chance of survival, as they would be rejected by those who are discriminated against. Because of the structural lacunae in the interdependence of global mass communication, however, they can persist in what are still highly isolated national discursive communities. While mass media do more than just produce stereotypes, also informing people of facts and realities, the mere existence of stereotypes in mass media is evidence of the strong domestication of global mass communication.

Assessment is more difficult with respect to non-stereotypical frames. However, numerous studies point to domestication effects in the argumentational mediation of international issues as well. Just a few examples follow.

- Media discourses after the attacks of 11 September 2001 were diametrically opposed in Western and Middle Eastern media and showed how strongly national media systems are exposed to local influences (Hafez 2007a, p. 41ff., see also Dimitrova and Strömbäck 2005).
- The Palestinian-Israeli conflict has for decades been framed extremely differently by the two sides (Müller 2017).
- The widespread characterization of wars in Africa as ethnic "tribal wars" rather than wars over power and resources is an exogenous framing (Allen and Seaton 1999; Williams 2011, p. 150ff.).
- While both Western media discourse and its Arab counterpart reject terrorism, the two are notoriously different, with the former tending to ignore the way in which Western policies towards the Middle East have contributed to terrorism, while the latter mostly disregards the Arab world's own political failings (Badr 2017).
- Since actors often appear as "speakers" and thus bearers of frames in the media, it is significant that the speakers' references are clearly national in character, even with respect to apparently global topics such as the United Nations (Ulrich 2016, p. 398f.).

66 Mass media and the global public sphere

- On the subject of Europe too, in spite of increasing awareness of the subject and transnational speaker references (above all among EU personnel and high-ranking European politicians), a number of studies highlight the sometimes glaring differences in content in a European media discourse that is still highly segmented (Sievert 1998; de Vreese et al. 2001; Koopmans and Erbe 2003; Brüggemann et al. 2006; AIM 2007; Hepp et al. 2012).
- Even projects on the Internet rooted in citizen journalism such as OhmyNews International or Groundreport often generate similar processes of domestication as in the professional media (Dencik 2012, p. 171).

In the wake of numerous studies over the past decades, authors such as Akiba A. Cohen (2013b), Kai Hafez (2000b, 2002a, 2007a, 2009, 2011), Richard C. Stanton (2007), Bella Mody (2010), Kristina Riegert (2011) and Miki Tanikawa (2019) have emphasized the continued domestication of media content even in the era of globalization (especially at times of crisis) and tend to cast doubt on transnational convergence. This once revisionist and globalization-sceptical view, which asserts that the promise of convergence inherent in global mass communication has gone unfulfilled, is now regarded as the new "standard" or even the new "orthodoxy" by scholars (Curran et al. 2015, pp. 1, 14). Some more optimistic authors have criticized these ideas by underlining that comparative analyses of media content in different countries do reveal convergence in the framing carried out by mass media, which they explain in light of the unifying effect potentially exercised by global news agencies (Curran et al. 2015; see also Bucher 2005, p. 187f.; Wessler and Brüggemann 2012, p. 91f., Lück et al. 2016; Volkmer 2014, p. 3f.). But even these analyses reject any return to the convergence-based metaphor of the "global village", which seems a wholly inadequate means of characterizing the current state of global news.

Furthermore, the more optimistic studies, which assume greater convergence, ignore the systemic parameters of the news, examining, for example, attitudes to the Greek government-debt crisis in countries facing very similar economic issues or investigating the discourse on the climate crisis as a globally unifying topic. The domestication of framing usually increases strikingly in tandem with nation states' degree of conflictual involvement in a given topic because national systems' internal self-interests almost always make themselves felt to hegemonic effect in the media. In addition, the convergence of frames is not just a matter of whether given arguments are reflected in various national media discourses, but also whether their responsiveness relates to the frames *central* to the conflict – which is not the case with respect to terrorism, despite a certain convergence in discourses on this topic. Copy-and-paste journalism, that is, taking material wholesale from the global agencies, usually gives way quickly to strong influences from national media discourse once a public debate has taken off. Convergence in global mass communication is thus an unstable variable at best. Domestication is still the deep structure of media globalization.

Visual globalization and stereotypes

Synchrony through interdiscursivity potentially exists not only at the level of texts, but also in the visual arena. In the international news system, it is above all images that steer recipients' emotions when it comes to countries and global developments (Chaban et al. 2014). There is also a close text-image relationship: text framing can influence the perception of images and, conversely, image perception can influence the understanding of text. Pictures cross borders more easily than words, yet this simplified access is more apparent than real, because images are just as context-dependent and require just as much explanation as texts (Müller and Geise 2015, p. 24ff.). Because of the lack of an "explicit propositional syntax" (Geise et al. 2013, p. 52), it is difficult to formulate an image analysis based on the principle of "visual framing". Hence, stripped-down methods of the analysis of "visual stereotypes" examine only isolated and frequently recurring elements and symbols, rather than the propositions inherent in images (Petersen and Schwender 2009). In any case, images do in fact require interpretation in the same way as texts, while journalists have to approach them "interdiscursively" within a global framework, "translating" them into national discourses.

Since the image is an integral part of a discourse, it is not surprising that scholars discuss the same basic problem of convergence and domestication in this context. At present, for example, women's magazines are often produced by publishers that operate internationally, and visual discourses are increasingly aligned thematically despite differences in gender roles (Machin and van Leeuwen 2007). Nonetheless, foreign coverage in particular seems to reproduce cultural and political stereotypes in a variety of ways. The EU, for example, is often presented visually as a bureaucratic and crisis-prone organization (Chaban et al. 2014). Visually, Afghanistan is almost exclusively a war-torn country in which women are oppressed – a widespread image across the world that local photojournalists are keen to correct (Mitra 2017). Although fictional media productions have greater freedom of manoeuvre in this respect than the news system even in censored media systems, the notion of transnational hybridity, "glocalization" and convergence in the visual arena requires major qualification, with local production and reception contexts remaining important (McMillin 2007, p. 111ff.).

Transnational media: contraflows without cosmopolitanism

Global news agencies are at least strengthening interdiscursive thematic synchronization, as we have seen, although national media convert content only to a very limited degree. But what role do leading transnational media such as BBC World, CNN, Al-Jazeera English, CCTV or Telesur play here? Studies have shown that they too are essentially the "tip of the iceberg" of established global news and thus generate an interdiscursive thematic contraflow only to a limited extent (Schenk 2009, p. 131; Atad 2016, p. 10). However, we can discern subtle shifts towards a more constructive and less negative media agenda when, for example, the English-language

68 Mass media and the global public sphere

channel Al-Jazeera English no longer presents Africa solely as a continent of poverty and conflict but also as one of economic success and diverse lifeworlds (Seib 2012; Robertson 2015). When it comes to framing, however, the literature largely agrees that global broadcasters tend to reflect the nationally imbued perspective of their home countries. This even applies to much-praised media such as BBC World, a broadcaster that, despite its interdiscursive ("dialogic") aspirations, cannot deny that its choice of themes, hegemonic rhetoric and trust in Western institutions reflect the attitudes and priorities of the UK (Baumann et al. 2011; Dencik 2012, pp. 39f., 56ff., Atad 2016).

However, certain aspects of transnational broadcasters are worthy of note. The thematic congruence in their agendas seems to correspond to the minimum definition of the global public sphere as an agenda shared across the world, even if, as we have stated, the tendency towards the consolidation of power typical of this transnationalization, driven by major powers, is evident in both topics and frames. National interpretations also circulate through international communication flows and although there is no cosmopolitan pluralism within states, we are seeing the emergence of a globally accessible external pluralism when these media are used in parallel (El-Nawawy and Iskandar 2003, p. 54). Finally, we can discern the first evidence of the adaptation of mass media to transnational audiences and markets, particularly in their more positive interpretations of topics. A hybrid field of tension thus arises between the contexts of national production and global reception. Through global media, transnational substructures are formed in national media systems. These arenas, having undergone a limited form of global expansion, are of particular importance to informational elites, who often utilize multiple global media and thus experience a slightly enhanced form of thematic co-orientation. This is certainly not yet an integrated global public sphere in which media synchronize national discourses globally and independently of the nation state as, so to speak, a UN-like "United Media". And it is unclear whether the leading global media's external pluralism, which, as evident in the animosity between CNN and Al-Jazeera in 2001 and 2003, can be highly conflictual, is stabilizing international relations or not.

Incomplete synchronization of global media discourses

Overall, the structural characteristics of the mass media largely seem to determine global media discourse. Fragmented and unreliably networked by egocentric media systems and a number of centrally controlled news flows and transnational media, it is apparent that incipient synchronization is occurring through convergent discourses both thematically and in terms of content, but its most striking attribute is its diverse forms of local domestication. Global news agencies and transnational opinion-leading media foreground key topics with no guarantee of interdiscursive quality. Especially under conditions of international crisis, we are still a long way from an integrated global media system or at least a responsive global public sphere in which national media systems reliably extract global issues and frames from local

Mass media and the global public sphere **69**

discourses on the basis of an emphatically global journalistic ethics. The question we have to answer is how best to evaluate this state of affairs theoretically and what alternatives we might identify.

2.2.2 Public sphere theory

Theoretical perspectives on the "global public sphere"

We may assess the discursive practice of global mass communication, as we have outlined it so far, not just from the vantage point of discourse analysis but also from a media-theoretical perspective. The theory of the deliberative public sphere, which goes back chiefly to Jürgen Habermas (1990, 1992, 1995) but has inspired many other authors as well, makes high demands on the quantity and quality of public discourse. It envisages the public sphere as playing a crucial legitimizing role for democracy (Beierwaltes 2002). The public sphere must also be "ubiquitous", in other words, deal with questions of general relevance, "reciprocal", that is, simulate listener and speaker positions, be as "open" as possible to various topics, and be "discursive" in the sense of taking rational objections into account (Peters 1994, p. 45ff.). It is also imagined as building consensus to solve problems and accomplish social integration, though the agonistic theory of the public sphere disputes this notion on the basis that agreement is often difficult to achieve and integration takes place through discourse *per se* (Mouffe 2005, p. 69ff.). These criteria describe in detail what we have so far referred to as "responsiveness" and "interdiscursivity". In the realm of the global, what this means is cross-border reflection on perspectives from other countries. The key question from the point of view of public sphere theory is thus whether national media systems and a small number of transnational media can adequately represent their system environments – the public spheres of other countries – despite weak system interdependence.

It is interesting to note here that most empiricists of convergence (see Section 2.2.1), regardless of whether they are essentially pessimists or optimists, tend to endorse the same ultimate goals of convergence – as articulated in theories of the public sphere and from a normative perspective – even if they evaluate their present-day realization quite differently. In other words, discourse pessimists too want convergence, but they view domestication as predominant, since both thematization and framing, as well as visual arrangement, have a strong local hue. A functioning global public sphere cannot arise if synchronization is restricted in this way (Sparks 1998, 2000; Couldry 2014).

Nancy Fraser has pointed out that the concept of the public sphere has to be rethought if we wish to apply it to the global realm because, to take just one example, it is not immediately obvious in which language discourse should be conducted and who the relevant actors (states, counter-elites) and publics are (2014, p. 27). A global public sphere can be achieved either by synchronizing national public spheres in media systems that are separated along national lines or by establishing a transnational media system (Ulrich 2016, p. 111ff.). Both models have advantages

70 Mass media and the global public sphere

and disadvantages, since a transnational media system would liberate itself from the filtering of national systems, but national systems may function as national "aids to translation" and help contextualize international problems. Most theorists therefore tend to embrace the pragmatic notion of synchronization by national systems, though so far this seems to have largely failed to ensure interdiscursivity. Furthermore, in a technical sense the development of a "consensus" in the global public sphere is virtually impossible in the national model, so we need to retain transnationalism, at least as the second pillar of the global public sphere.

From the perspective of another theory, namely systems theory, the theory of the deliberative public sphere, regardless of whether it is optimistic or pessimistic, is in any case nothing but an expression of "hyperglobalism" (Werron 2010, see Section 2.2.1). From the point of view of systems theory in the tradition of Niklas Luhmann, what matters is not so much *how* nations connect through media discourses and whether they synchronize with one another, but *that* they connect, because every form of connectivity entails the potential for follow-up societal communication (Luhmann 1970; Axford 2012, pp. 38, 45). Systems theory foregrounds the reduction of environmental complexity; the structuring of topics by the media is more important than any specific participatory and democratic mode we might ascribe to it (Böckelmann 1975). In Luhmann's work, "global society" is therefore defined in a comparatively open way: it emerges out of any kind of cross-border communication and is in no way akin to the construct of global civil society (see Chapter 5). In systems theory, what matters is neither the quality of journalism nor the question of whether information or entertainment is being communicated. Instead the focus is on a postmodern assemblage of dispersed individual opinions. From this point of view, there is nothing wrong with the current state of global media discourse. In this school of thought, fragmentary thematic agendas and frames, verbal and visual stereotypes or even deficient speaker references are all legitimate elements in the postmodern construction of worldviews.

The role of the global public sphere in global society

However, the limits of this perspective become clear when we understand that it can be used to justify war propaganda and racist constructs in the mass media (Hafez 2010b, 2017b). It is true that we must recognize the excessive structural demands made of the theory of the deliberative global public sphere. At the same time, we need to be alert to the structural deficiencies of systems theory. As a rudimentary macro-theory, it does not appear to provide a practicable theory of society. From the perspective of the theory of the deliberative public sphere, the media have an "ambivalent potential" in that their offerings lay the foundations for creating a public sphere, yet the media "hierarchize and restrict" the realm of potential communication (Burkart and Lang 2004, p. 63ff.). In the case of global communication, we can observe the potential effects of global mass communication within and outside of national systems, effects that may trade under the names of "cosmopolitanism" and "global governance".

Foreign coverage has a direct impact on a society's attitudes to issues of cosmopolitanism, multiculturalism and racism. People tend to rely on media knowledge when constructing their ideas about distant people and events and on their own experience when it comes to their local counterparts (Kruck 2008). Problems arise because racism is based on prejudices against the "absent other", that is, it is not a reaction to others in the immediate environment, but to the "chaotic world" constructed in the media, which is then transferred to "others" in local contexts ("foreigners", and so on), with whom there is no contact and of whom there is therefore no direct experience-based knowledge (Hafez 2002a, vol. 2, p. 261ff.; Chouliaraki 2006). However, we should not underestimate the influence of other agents of socialization (family, community and institutions) on people's core values (Hafez 2011, p. 488f.).

As far as the question of international impact is concerned, a large proportion of recipients are considered to be "passive" because they are not much interested in foreign news or react mainly to the opinions of elites that they find in the media (though these in turn anticipate public values and sentiments) (Powlick and Katz 1998). Most studies, however, seek to establish recipients' interest in international politics rather than the world as such (Hafez 2011, p. 490f.), probably because researchers assume that most audiences react more to specific and conflictual events than to developments in the lifeworld (Wanta and Hu 1993). In any case, there is agreement among scholars that without media coverage of the global, there will be no debates about the global. The greater the quantity of reports about a country, the more likely recipients are to assume that this country is significant; the more negative these reports are, the more negative people's image of the country tends to be (Wanta et al. 2004, see also Iyengar and Simon 1993). Most people's media dependence increases in tandem with the audience's distance from world events (see also Chapter 9, Section 9.2).

Alternative theories of the public sphere: dialogic, constructive and cosmopolitan journalism

When it comes to both the impact of foreign journalism within societies and cosmopolitanism, Hans Kleinsteuber (2004) issued an early plea for a "dialogic" approach. His idea of greater inclusion of local and cultural perspectives in journalism is an attempt to stimulate the "dialogue of cultures". This dialogue is intended to give fresh impetus to multicultural society and improve interdiscursivity, which should attach far less importance to negative, elite-focused and politically oriented news or stereotypical entertainment products and instead extend the imaginative space of intercultural relations. In a similar way, Richard C. Stanton has highlighted the need for a new "conversational model" that ought to complement the informational paradigm typical of journalism at present (2007, p. 190ff.). On this view, there should be a shift of emphasis in news reports away from elite action and towards the interests of citizens and civil society.

If we interpret these approaches in light of the Habermasian theory of the public sphere, what both authors are pushing for is a shift from coverage of systems to coverage of lifeworlds. Perspectives that foreground "constructive" or "positive journalism" point in the same direction, aiming to correct the negative bias of foreign news by embracing lifeworld issues (Hafez and Grüne 2015). Such models make it clear that the negative fixation of foreign coverage strengthens populism (Haagerup 2014; Russ-Mohl 2017). Against this background, they call for the redefinition of news values.

Approaches centred on "cosmopolitan journalism" have similar goals but set about achieving them in a different way. Their exponents contend that journalism should not focus less on negative events such as refugee crises, as in "constructive journalism", but instead make a point of discussing them. These events, however, should be interpreted differently than in conventional media coverage. The focus should no longer be on the stereotypical portrayal of refugees as a threatening mob, but on the fate of individuals and, above all, the ways in which the international political sphere and the major powers have contributed to creating such crises. Attention should also be given to the complexities of global political and economic relations (Chouliaraki 2006; Silverstone 2007; Lindell and Karlsson 2016; Schmidt 2017).

This perspective has affinities with both dialogic and constructive journalism: in cosmopolitan journalism too, interdiscursivity is important as a means of improving reflexivity vis-à-vis "self and other" and thus helping inject cosmopolitanism into societies with significant numbers of immigrants. To a great extent, all three alternative currents of public sphere theory merge in Ingrid Volkmer's approach to the "reflexive interdependence" of the global public sphere, a new and expanded framework that fuses interdiscursivity, an orientation towards the lifeworld and cosmopolitanism (2014, p. 163ff.). Referring explicitly to Habermas, but also to Georg Wilhelm Friedrich Hegel, Immanuel Kant and John Rawls, she describes the social changes wrought by globalization as fundamental in the sense that in global reflexive journalism people appear not as "strangers" but as a global "self". This can mitigate the social reproduction of local identities generated in part by isolated media discourses.

Global public sphere and global governance: the case of Europe

Europe and the European Union provide an example of how media coverage affects international politics. The key finding of content analyses is that there is a certain thematic convergence in coverage of Europe in the continent's national media, which is the minimum criterion for a European public sphere. However, the framing is often nationally imbued and shows little sign of interdiscursivity. In the academic literature, media domestication is seen as an impediment to the specific form of global governance within the EU, which is not a federal state but has been a confederation of states with strong transnational competencies since the Maastricht Treaties of 1992 (Splichal 2012, pp. 145ff.). The media and media policy, however, are almost entirely in the hands of the nation states, so the influence of national politics on the media is enormous, strengthening local perspectives and hampering European consensus building. Those responsible for policies emanating from Brussels, meanwhile, face a constant battle to present them in a positive light, because the EU is the only political force that has no structurally secure media influence.

In light of this situation, most authors call not so much for the creation of transnational media as for better interlinking of national media in order to improve media interdiscursivity (Habermas 2001, p. 120; see also Gerhards 1993, 2000; Wessler and Brüggemann 2012, p. 62). The idea of establishing transnational European media, on the other hand, is referred to as a "naive model", because there will "certainly never be" a global news broadcast that reaches a large audience (Wessler and Brüggemann 2012, p. 65; see also Lingenberg 2010, p. 118). It is likely, however, that historically no political formation has arisen that lacked its own media. Just as the modern nation state was accompanied and enabled by national media, global political constructs will probably only be successful if there are *real* transnational media that are no longer linked to nation states in the manner of today's media such as CNN, Al-Jazeera, and so on. The new media would not have to replace national media, as these are ideally adapted within their language areas and are potentially important "translators" in the context of globalization. Especially under crisis conditions, however, they would be less susceptible to "going it alone" on a national basis and could thus more effectively offset European citizens' informational deficits (Morganti and Audenhove 2011). The model of the national arena as found in the work of Habermas and others is thus referred to elsewhere as a "misconception", indicating a simmering scholarly controversy over the establishment of independent European media (Ambrosi 2011, p. 240).

Europe is thus exemplary of the complex developmental problems facing other transnational realms such as Mercosur, NAFTA, the OECD, ASEAN or the United Nations. If the public sphere is important to legitimizing political authority in the modern age, then global governance will probably require the support of a complex interplay of more strongly synchronized national media and transnational mass media established as independent entities. We might also refer to a combination of horizontal and vertical global mass communication. Both Brexit (from 2016 onwards) and the Greek crisis (beginning in 2010) were due not only to various political and economic upheavals, but also to the failure of national media with respect to the EU. Continuing to regard mass media as national cultural goods, as EU treaties do, while simultaneously holding European elections, is an approach whose internal contradictions cannot be resolved solely through appeals to pan-European media ethics. Existing media systems also require major modification. In addition to national arenas as sites of transnationalization, then, it is vitally important to establish a direct media-based connection between European citizens, the Parliament in Strasbourg and the Brussels executive through pan-European media and improved journalistic networks (Ratavaara 2013). As these pan-European media became more popular among consumers, they would grow into a leadership role for national European journalism as national public spheres are Europeanized,

74 Mass media and the global public sphere

something current media, such as Euronews, have not yet managed to achieve (Brüggemann and Schulz-Forberg 2009).

Conclusion: global public sphere, global society and lagging structural change of the mass media

In summary, global mass communication is characterized by transnational communicative flows as well as by an increasing number of transnational media and transnational media structures at all levels (media ethics, production, reception, regulation and economics). However, the national or geocultural character of most media cannot be denied in structural terms, that is, with respect to the organizational structures and primary environmental references of politics, economy and markets. Without wanting to argue in excessively structuralist terms, this global interdependence gap in global mass communication correlates to a high degree with the fragmentary media discourses of a national or otherwise local hue. So far there are no indications that the Internet is spawning a genuine global alternative to particularist journalism to any great extent, apart from niches.

Largely irrelevant from a systems-theoretical point of view, from the perspective of theories of the deliberative public sphere the current situation is a challenge to the notion of the global public sphere because we have yet to see the kind of structural change in the media that might ensure the desired synchronization in perceptions of global society. Global civil society would, therefore, do well to establish its own forms of communication beyond the mass media (see Chapters 5 and 6). The fact that these cannot replace the mass media's core orienting function with respect to either domestic or international politics is highlighted by alternative theories of the public sphere and remains a key problem of globalization.

3

POLITICS

The state's global communication

Political systems are characterized by various forms of sovereignty that shape the nature of their global communication and they must in every respect be considered "hybrid systems". They are the global all-rounders among social systems, with sufficient resources to engage in all communicative processes – information gathering and observation, as well as both discursive-monologic and interactive-dialogic communication. These communicative dimensions go hand in hand with certain social processes. Alongside the state's potential to help form global communities through diplomatic interaction, national foreign policy and propaganda act as a permanent block on the emergence of a synchronized global public sphere. It is no accident that in his definition of political communication Gerhard Vowe made a distinction not only between interpersonal communication and mass communication, but also between strategic and understanding-oriented action (2002, p. 10).

At the end of the day, there is a certain potential for communitization in the state's international communication. If you believe the statistics on war, we are currently living in the most peaceful of times, which is due in part to the densification of global diplomacy as engendered by modern means of communication. However, the global public sphere, which is shaped by the political system, remains highly antagonistic and the propagandistic impulses of the nation state make it anything but easy for media, systems and lifeworlds to prioritize truth with respect to international relations. Systemic difference-inducing pressures undermine the capacity for interactive adaptation in the global community.

DOI: 10.4324/9781003255239-4

3.1 Systems and system change

Actors, target audiences and "third spaces" of global communication

In line with the system-lifeworld-network approach introduced earlier, which not only considers the "relations" between systems but also the substance of the systems themselves, we begin by introducing the actor – the political system. The basic functions of the state include ensuring security and securing resources for the economic system. To do this, it has to develop and manage a certain complexity of organization and actor networks within the system. Externally, the state has to communicate with other political systems as well as with various environments at home and abroad. One-to-one communication between the same or similar actors (diplomacy) thus plays a role here, as does one-to-many communication (public diplomacy/propaganda). In order to be able to do both successfully, a third element must be added: the state has to observe itself, other systems and its environment in order to be able to act meaningfully.

Since the complexity of the requirements in each individual communicative sphere is constantly increasing, the number of actors involved in state communication is also growing, giving rise to a highly heterogeneous constellation of actors and target audiences. The extended systemic field of the nation state now also includes multinational systems (such as the UN or the EU), NGOs, think tanks and even lifeworld actors (such as bloggers), while the environmental field includes multipliers, media, public spheres and entire populations. What ultimately emerges when we consider global political communication is something like the following actor matrix (see Figure 3.1).

Actors in the political system and, depending on the role they have been assigned, other intermediary systems and lifeworlds in society, may be described

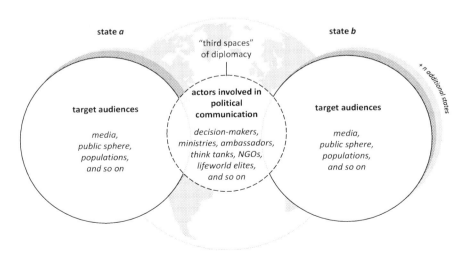

FIGURE 3.1 Actors and target audiences of international political communication

Politics: the state's global communication **77**

as the "insiders" of politics. Environmental systems and system environments at home and abroad, on the other hand, operate as "outsiders". In the diplomatic inner zone of political communication there are no longer actors of just one state, but of several states. Figure 3.1 shows concisely that through interpersonal diplomatic communication states effectively form "third spaces" centred on an (often secret) diplomacy, in which governments are in more intensive dialogue with each other than with their own citizens. It is here that we are most likely to see the emergence of a "global community" through interactive communication – in contrast to the discursive "global public sphere".

Diplomacy: realism versus constructivism

In order to fulfil their basic functions, political systems have always had to communicate with other political systems. The natural forum for this state-state interaction is diplomacy, which can take place bilaterally, multilaterally or through processes of mediation. What is casually referred to as the "state" has, however, changed considerably over the course of time. Diplomatic communication has a long history. Political authority and communication have always been closely linked. Early city states such as Ebla and Mari in present-day Syria were already exchanging envoys by the second millennium BCE and concluded treaties as well (Cohen 1999). Nevertheless, communication in ever-larger empires became more and more difficult as antiquity gave way to the Middle Ages: without modern transmission technologies, messages reached their destinations only after much delay. The medieval state was therefore what is called an "association-of-persons-state" (*Personenverbandsstaat*), which was based on a network of individuals who owed allegiance to a king or emperor (in the feudal system, for example). But decisions were not always made centrally. It was typical of medieval rulers to be constantly on the move to make their presence felt, because a loss of communication usually strengthened the vassals' independence. Centralized administration functioned by means of faster and more efficient communication across large areas: the superiority of the huge medieval Mongol empire, which reached as far as Europe, was due in significant part to its revolutionary fast courier system, while the carrier pigeons used in the Arab empires could travel up to a thousand kilometres a day (Frederick 1993, p. 15ff.). The ability to establish centralized, bureaucratic rule of the kind typical of the modern state clearly went hand in hand with the development of enhanced forms of communication.

Nevertheless, it was to be some time before scholars recognized this. We can divide the analysis of political decision-making broadly into three approaches: traditional, cognitive, and organizational (Mansfield 1990). The traditional analysis provided by the "realist school" focuses solely on the supposed substance of state interests. Since the 1960s at the latest, it has been supplemented by the cognitive interpretation of political decision-makers' perceptions. Christoph Weller has rightly pointed out that the constructivist school of international relations, as this strand is often called, has yet to develop a unified theory and that it is advisable to distinguish between state constructivist and social constructivist approaches, with the former

78 Politics: the state's global communication

foregrounding the state as communicative actor, while the latter emphasizes the state's dependence on social constructions (2003/4, p. 111f.). In accordance with our system-lifeworld-network approach, we try to include both perspectives by asserting that the political system is more than a diffuse actor, namely an organized social system that acts in specific ways, while recognizing the existence of lifeworld influences in the political system (see our remarks on informality on p. 89f.).

It is crucial to state constructivist analysis, however, that over time the realist school has not only been supplemented by psychological and sociological approaches, but that realist scholars have recognized the communicative complexity of the state when it comes to the group dynamics of political decision-makers and communicative flows in state bureaucracies (Mansfield 1990). It seems fair to say that the discipline of communication studies has only begun to interpret foreign policy decisions thanks to its recent embrace of organizational sociology, which has prompted it to consider the (successful and unsuccessful) interactions between people and groups.

Second-track diplomacy and global governance

A complex analysis of the state informed by organizational sociology is necessary because nowadays we have to consider not just state but also non-state actors as a result of changes in modern political systems. The key developments here were, first, the emergence of bureaucratic authority in Max Weber's sense (1922), the enshrining of the rule of law and the development of large-scale institutions and organizations that integrate increasing numbers of actors in the executive and – in democracies – the legislature and judiciary into foreign policy communication. Second, and just as significant, was the transition that took place mostly in the twentieth century (1) from a purely state foreign policy to an expanded social form of foreign policy, and (2) to global governance, which has been established at a rudimentary level.

1. *Second-track diplomacy or multi-track diplomacy*: There are many types of diplomacy, such as conference diplomacy, crisis diplomacy, summit diplomacy and "shuttle" diplomacy (Rofe 2016), each of which is practised by different actors. While summit diplomacy mainly brings together high-ranking decision-makers, conference diplomacy usually involves more than two states. The constellation of actors involved in conference diplomacy thus expands the realm of actors both vertically, through the inclusion of key decision-makers, and horizontally, through multilateralism. A new "diagonal" variant has emerged only in the last few decades: second-track or multi-track diplomacy. In principle, here members of quite different systemic origins interact with one another. In addition to politicians and professional diplomats, think tanks, NGOs, scholars and religious leaders play a role (Werkner and Hidalgo 2014). The reason for this lies in a development that James Rosenau calls the "linkage" policy. He assumes that the division into domestic and foreign policy is too simplistic, as

Politics: the state's global communication **79**

there are numerous connections between the two, which creates a third, linked discursive field. According to Rosenau, the more a foreign policy issue affects the material resources or the intellectual and moral foundations of a society, the lower the probability that this problem will be dealt with by the political class alone (1967, p. 49). From the perspective of our system-lifeworld-network approach, multi-track diplomacy has considerable consequences for communication, since in the new networks the need for strategic communication is significantly reduced, while dialogic communication and processes of interaction become increasingly important. The new actors in this context are free to articulate alternative information and new dialogues can develop. However, it must be recognized that the decision-makers of traditional state diplomacy still hold a superior position of power: it is they who decide whether new forms of international communitization will come into effect or whether the interests of individual nation states will prevail. The willingness of state diplomacy to include multi-track diplomacy is still considered negligible (Diamond and McDonald 1996, p. 158). At the same time, however, the number of NGOs accredited by the UN has increased significantly (Turek 2017, p. 356). But it remains unclear whether this quantitative increase indicates greater political relevance for second-track diplomacy, that is, whether actors involved in multi-track diplomacy are equal "insiders" in the sphere of political communication. Successful NGO lobbying obviously takes place chiefly in areas such as economic, environmental and human rights policy (such as debt relief for developing countries), in other words, when, in addition to the state's core concerns of security and territorial sovereignty, other social subsystems of great domestic political relevance are involved (Saner and Yiu 2008).

2. *Global governance*: Global governance is a way of describing the system of institutions and rules that was created after the Second World War to stabilize international relations. Numerous international organizations, rules and agreements came into being, such as the World Bank, the International Monetary Fund (IMF), the Organization for Security and Cooperation in Europe (OSCE), as well as anti-crime, environmental, anti-discrimination and trade agreements (UN 2012). The goal was to establish basic standards for intergovernmental action and to standardize foreign policy in order to prevent chaotic international conditions (Block 1977; Brand et al. 2000; Held and McGrew 2002). Global governance again expanded the constellation of actors involved in global relations. While traditional diplomacy takes place irregularly and is geared towards crises, global governance creates a kind of "hotline" between nations. Due to the large number of participating states and transnational institutions, global governance (like second-track diplomacy) cannot be investigated solely with reference to interpersonal negotiation communication but requires a complementary theoretical understanding of organizational communication. Nonetheless, negotiation communication remains central to the systemic communicative relationships of global governance since the sovereignty of the nation state is not restricted and transnational state formations

80 Politics: the state's global communication

are rare – the European Union being the exception. International agreements, such as the Kyoto Protocol in the environmental field, must also first be ratified by national politicians before they come into force in a country – and they can be terminated. Hence, global governance, much like multi-track diplomacy, has not yet managed to emancipate itself definitively from national foreign policy. Here too, then, the interplay between the substantive interests of the nation state and its interactive actions in the global community essentially persists. For the discipline of communication studies this means that the inter- and multi-state interactions of diplomacy remain the true site of analysis. The nascent "third spaces" of community building are ephemeral. Multi-state institutions, conferences, summits, and so on are situational extensions of national negotiation communication rather than independent institutions. But perhaps transnational organizational communication really is the future, which would then change not only the constellation of actors involved in foreign policy communication, but also its target audiences.

Target audiences of public diplomacy

So far, every nation state has carried out public relations geared towards its own interests, the international dimension of which is known today as "public diplomacy". In terms of content, it is extremely difficult to distinguish it from classic propaganda or public relations. In any case, the state pursues various forms of public relations abroad, such as foreign cultural policy, international broadcasting and national marketing. "Public diplomacy" borrows from the classic concept of diplomacy but is categorically different. J. Simon Rofe has thus rightly referred to public diplomacy a "distinct concept" (2016, p. 40) – but more on this later. In order to understand systems and system change, all that matters for now is that the modern state no longer communicates only with other states, but increasingly also with entire populations, the media and public spheres. Through public diplomacy, then, the complex constellations of actors in diplomacy are constantly being joined by new "target groups" for the state's messages.

It is of course historically attested that the Romans already carried out systematic propaganda. The reports of the deeds of Augustus (*Res Gestae Divi Augusti*) are perhaps the most famous sources. But with the development of modern politics towards participatory systems and mass democracies, this dimension has become ever more elaborate and important. When the Romans and Egyptians carried out propaganda, their primary aim was to reach their own peoples and perhaps other governments. Modern public diplomacy, meanwhile, not only aspires to spread its messages globally, but also seeks to precisely define opinion-leading disseminators and elites abroad – from journalists through educated elites to social opinion leaders and specific sociological segments (such as young people). Even if the attainability of this objective remains a matter of controversy, the demand for target group specificity is high and growing.

New communicator roles in foreign policy

The link between interactions directed inwards, towards political systems, and discourses directed outwards, towards public spheres, is the state's global information policy (see p. 96ff.). In line with the modes of communication we introduced earlier at the theoretical level, we might put it like this. The state not only engages in dialogues (diplomacy) and produces monologues (public diplomacy), but also observes and gathers information. The latter function is realized in a variety of ways, for example, through the state's own ambassadorial system and the reports it produces, secret services and media monitoring.

The role of political actors is constantly changing due to the technological development of communication. Since it is now extremely easy for governments to communicate directly, the ambassador has largely lost their former role as an intergovernmental negotiator. In the course of this development, many countries have gone so far as to reform the office itself. Today, ambassadors are essentially information gatherers or even propagandists, but play less of a role than they used to in interactive negotiation diplomacy. One expression of this process was the decision by the second Schröder-Fischer government in Germany – after the attacks of 11 September 2001 – to relocate the Directorate General for Communication, Public Diplomacy and the Media ("Department K") from the Federal Press and Information Office to the Federal Foreign Office in 2003; another was the establishment of Germany Centres at key German embassies.

Again, the resulting shifts within the state's constellations of actors change nothing about the negotiation-based communication characteristic of diplomacy because other actors – often special envoys or teams representing heads of government or the ministries of foreign affairs, defence, foreign trade, and so on – take on the ambassador's former role as direct interlocutor. For foreign policy, however, these shifts mean that a form of expertise rooted in communication studies and enhanced by a knowledge of public relations is required to understand the complex informational environments of the political sphere.

Inconsistent shifts towards a "global domestic policy"

Despite the increasing number of actors involved in foreign policy, which performs a growing array of observational tasks internally, integrates civil societies, practises global governance and communicates with entire populations, the nation state has proven to be strong and viable even in the era of globalization. The vision of the complete overcoming of the nation state through a "global domestic policy" has not come to fruition (Bartosch and Gansczyk 2009). The end of the East–West conflict did improve the opportunities for global governance. But the global political crisis following the terrorist attacks of 2001 fostered unilateralism among the superpowers and major powers. Global political communication thus still consists not so much of internal organizational communication as of intergovernmental

82 Politics: the state's global communication

negotiation communication and state PR within the framework of a multipolar world order.

3.2 Communicative system connections

In order to understand the state's global communication, we need to keep several theoretical aspects in mind. Central here is our communicative distinction between observation/discourse and between interaction/dialogue. The key question is thus: where and how does the state interact in diplomacy, propagate a certain discourse in public diplomacy and observe through intelligence across borders? Since state foreign policy and global governance are steered not only by individual diplomats, but also by ministries and institutions, we have to consider the basics of organizational communication in addition to negotiation theory, for example, the relationship between text and speech and the relationships between face-to-face interaction and interpersonally mediatized communication, as well as between formal and informal communication and between internal and external communication. As we shall see, we can discern dialogues chiefly in the interior of systems as well as in diplomatic system-system relations. It is primarily strategic communication that takes place in the external sphere and vis-à-vis system environments (media, business and social lifeworlds). How one assesses political communication in the context of globalization – with a view to the concepts of the global public sphere and global community – ultimately depends on the blend of communicative forms.

3.2.1 Interaction and dialogue

Interests, values and communication

The mass media only interact with one another to a very limited extent across borders, while the world remains a dispersed system environment beyond its own broadcasting borders. In contrast, the state is a system of action that truly interacts with other political systems and environmental systems. Diplomacy thus becomes a counterpoint to the lack of interaction between peoples and media. It is governments that, as representatives of societies, conduct a dialogue on their behalf and thus stabilize international relations. As long as political systems do not merge transnationally, the network relationships *between* systems are crucial to communicative globalization.

It is thus reasonable to state that international relations are based on diplomacy and that diplomacy is synonymous with communication: "In fact, diplomacy is often defined in terms of communication" (Jönsson 2016, p. 79). Paradigmatically, within the framework of our system-lifeworld-network approach, we cannot deny that substantive interests may shape communication just as communication itself influences systems. How the communicative "third space" of diplomacy is configured can be contemplated theoretically but must be investigated empirically in each specific case. As mentioned in our theoretical introduction in Chapter 1, Richard Rosecrance has clarified that the likelihood of success in diplomatic communication is greater when interests are positively interdependent (win–win situations) and lower when they are negatively interdependent. This is not just a matter of material interests or power, but also of values and norms, which do not necessarily dovetail in international diplomacy as they may be linked with separate national interests. It is true that human rights are binding for all states under international law. But their exact content requires constant reinterpretation. From a constructivist perspective, what speaks against Rosecrance's neo-institutionalist point of view is that it is often not so easy for those involved in diplomacy to clearly define their own interests, since a wide range of actors are involved in democracies (Meerts 1999). Hence, what the "interests" of a state are often has to be clarified through communication. This points to a complex interrelationship between power, values and communication that is at the core of diplomacy. In international politics, successful communication can turn seemingly conflicting interests into a new global communality, as we explained in our theoretical introduction (see Chapter 1, Section 1.1).

Diplomatic process stages and metacommunication

If we wish to better understand the relationship between power and communication in diplomacy, it makes sense to consider different process stages or process variants of diplomatic communication, especially the phases before, during and after negotiations, as well as during possible mediation. What is often left out of account is that communication takes place in all aggregate states and should be appraised with the tools of communication studies. The focus on the negotiation itself, which is common within the discipline, leads to a foreshortened view of the communicative process that is so decisive to the relationship between states. Global communality emerges and reflects decisions at all stages and at all levels of diplomacy. Interestingly, global governance basically seeks to abolish these phases and create a kind of permanent negotiating situation through "hotline diplomacy", which would eliminate the hidden meta-levels of communication *before* and *after* negotiations and mediations. But let's look at the processual elements in turn.

Anyone wondering why some states refuse even to enter into negotiations on a contentious issue when they seem to have nothing to lose and might garner sympathy has failed to grasp the character of diplomatic interaction. Dialogue changes those who conduct it, and negotiations thus represent a risk that states only take when they have a reasonable expectation of substantial gains. Participation in negotiations itself sends a meta-message, so it is not without consequence. It entails recognition of the interlocutor, that is, the relational level of communication has already been activated before a single day of negotiations has been completed. Even before the negotiations, however, important decisions have already been made at the level of content, because willingness to negotiate is explicit recognition of the existence of a problem to be solved and implies an outline agenda for talks. There is implicit acceptance that the other side has legitimate interests, because willingness

84 Politics: the state's global communication

to compromise and the overcoming of selfish goals are in the nature of diplomatic dialogue: total intransigence makes it almost impossible to leave the negotiating table without losing face. We are thus on solid ground in asserting that communicative events before negotiations (at the relational as well as content level) are just as significant as communication during negotiations.

When Israel negotiated with the PLO in the course of the Oslo peace process in 1993, this marked the organization's breakthrough as the Palestinians' legitimate representative. The Islamists of Hamas still hesitate to speak to Israel because every diplomatic contact with the country underscores the legitimacy of its existence and there are different camps of maximalists and minimalists among the Islamists. Older and far more famous cases reveal how, in the 1970s, US Secretary of State Henry Kissinger and the subsequent administration under Jimmy Carter made significant decisions before the negotiations between the Israelis and the Arab states had even begun. Through "step-by-step diplomacy", in contrast to the "basket approach" of a comprehensive Middle East peace conference, they decoupled issues such as troop withdrawals and the return of Sinai to Egypt from the question of Palestine. Kissinger makes it more or less clear in his memoirs that he never intended to pursue the establishment of a Palestinian state (1982). Step-by-step diplomacy was therefore more than a process variant. It was a substantive preliminary decision. The space for communicative negotiations was reduced considerably through this steering of the agenda, with the probability of success being increased in some areas but significantly reduced in others. The modern concept of the "roadmap", according to which negotiations are planned in a certain chronological order, is similar to that of step-by-step diplomacy, even if short-term and long-term goals are more clearly defined in roadmaps than in earlier times. Nevertheless, here too there is a risk of getting stuck at every step. Hence, the limiting of the communicative agenda at a given moment and the prioritizing of problems may end up creating political facts.

Agenda-setting and framing in political negotiations

As far as the negotiation phase itself is concerned, the well-known "Harvard Concept of (Principled) Negotiation" has elucidated how the two components of power/interests and communication are related (Fisher et al. 2004). This text distinguishes between "positions" and "interests" and the first principle of successful negotiation is to focus on one's own interests and those of others, not on verbally expressed positions. To take an example: two countries are arguing over a piece of land, with both claiming that it is important to their national security. The official positions are that both want the same bit of land, which amounts to a zero-sum game, that is, one side's gains are the other side's losses. What really matters is the two countries' security interests. The disputed area is strategically important. Security as a core interest can, however, be guaranteed in a different way than implied by the stated position, which envisages total control of the territory, for example, through

Politics: the state's global communication **85**

an agreement on its division and de-militarization. A space is created for a rational dialogue – diplomacy comes into play. Through interaction there is an opportunity to spur a shift from positions to interests in order to reformulate positions in the spirit of compromise and thus turn a zero-sum game into a win–win game that serves both sides. From a communication studies perspective, we might refer to a shift of topic or agenda. The prevailing discourse is deconstructed through direct international dialogue in order to better express the interests of both sides, and through diplomatic dialogue the (propagandistically charged) "global public sphere" becomes a new "global community", albeit one limited to the participating states.

The second principle of the Harvard concept is to flesh out options in order to find creative solutions. The dialogue must therefore proceed in a qualified way. Developing options and scenarios is part of the core business of diplomacy. From the vantage point of communication studies, we might refer here to the diversification of framing. Only when all causal relationships and moral evaluations with respect to the agreed topics are on the table can solutions be found and consensus achieved. It is here that diplomatic dialogue must be informed by public as well as non-public discourses. In the process of political globalization too, "rational dialogue" is only possible if sufficient knowledge and information are available (see our comments on information procurement on p. 93ff.).

Diplomatic mediation: from interaction to dialogue

Diplomatic negotiations sometimes take place with recourse to mediators. Famous examples are Kissinger's "shuttle diplomacy" in the Middle East conflict between Israel, Egypt and Syria and the Camp David Accords between Egypt and Israel of 1979, which were facilitated by Jimmy Carter. In their "contingency approach" Jacob Bercovitch and Allison Houston examine both the "context variables" and "process variables" of mediation: a bifurcation that corresponds to our system-lifeworld-network approach, as both the structures of the actors and the interactions between them are taken into account (1996, p. 14ff.). Context variables relate to the question of which actor constellation increases the likelihood of successful mediation. For example, whether democratic states are involved; there is a fair degree of similarity between the political systems and a reasonable balance of power; the relationship history has not been overly problematic; the conflict is not at its peak; the number of victims is not too high; and the problem is not a matter of vital interest and is thus a potential subject for negotiations (ibid., p. 20ff.). The process variables represent the true communicative substance of diplomatic negotiations, with the three main forms of mediation applying to different aspects of communication (ibid., p. 28ff., see also Bercovitch 1992, p. 17f.):

- *Communication facilitation.* The moderator has little control over the agenda or the content of the negotiation but focuses on maintaining an atmosphere conducive to dialogue between the actors.

86 Politics: the state's global communication

- *Procedural mediation.* The mediator is more active in this case, exercising an influence on the agenda, laying down the type and order of the subjects for discussion and engaging in a sort of topic management.
- *Directive mediation.* Moderators not only control the agenda of the negotiations, but also the framing. They work out proposed solutions, prepare treaty texts and fine-tune their wording. Here, then, topic management is joined by text management.

Article 33 (1) of the UN Charter enshrines the position of mediators, which means nothing other than that the role of communication in international relations is recognized under international law (even if the literature underscores that power-political interests play a major role, and the probability of successful communication should not be assessed naively; Rosecrance 1973). Mediation potentially enables a genuine dialogue that can pierce through the erratic discourses of national public spheres, reorganize them on a rational basis and thus foster global collaborative action.

Signalling as non-verbal global communication

Even if no negotiations are being conducted at a particular point in time, states still communicate with one another. The frequent equation of diplomacy with verbal negotiations is misleading in that there are also non-verbal forms of communication that make a global impact, which are referred to as "signalling" (Jönsson and Aggestam 1999; Jönsson 2016). Signalling is communication between states through action rather than language. The most researched form of signalling is related to violence and war, for example, naval manoeuvres, which may be interpreted as threatening war, or the transport of weapons. Perhaps the most famous example here is the Cuban Missile Crisis of 1962, in which every military manoeuvre was interpreted by the participating states, the United States and the Soviet Union, as evidence of acute aggression and there was a serious risk of a Third World War (Winter 2003). Terrorists, too, are less focused on killing civilians as such and intend their attacks to send political messages (Tuman 2003). But there are also less harmful forms of signalling, such as the exchange of gifts during state visits, silence and inaction, the body language of politicians and diplomats, the selection of diplomatic staff and diplomatic protocol: "There is simply no escape from producing message value" (Jönsson 2016, p. 80). How important shaking hands can be was evident in 2017, when new and controversial US President Donald Trump tried to intimidate other heads of state with a particularly martial handshake, until new French President Emmanuel Macron responded in like manner, which was viewed within the global public sphere as restoring the balance of transatlantic power relations.

Signalling, then, is the continuation of diplomatic negotiations by other means. It is frequently used to avoid negotiations or to increase the costs of unsuccessful negotiations. Often, we can observe nested processes of the type negotiation/breaking off/signalling/renegotiation. We may place signalling within the

Politics: the state's global communication **87**

interactive spectrum of communication, although it appears to entail monologic gestures that can at most be observed. This is because action and reaction are usually related to one another in the manner of a dialogue. The interactive cycle is not completely closed, however, as the messages only appear to be directly transmitted at first glance, but in reality have to be "interpreted". Hence, as the visual transmission of non-verbal political gestures, signalling entails an increased risk for international relations since images are generally more open to interpretation than language (Pious 2001). Diego Gambetta articulates the fundamental problem of the greater openness to interpretation of political signals compared to language:

> Signaling theory tackles a fundamental problem of communication: how can an agent, the receiver, establish whether another agent, the signaler, is telling or otherwise conveying the truth about a state of affairs or event which the signaler might have an interest to misrepresent? And, conversely, how can the signaler persuade the receiver that he is telling the truth, whether he is telling it or not?
>
> *(2009, p. 168)*

It is fortunate that Kennedy and Khrushchev did not mistakenly interpret the other side's actions during the Cuban Missile Crisis as a declaration of war.

Global governance as a diplomatic "hotline"?

Traditional diplomatic communication can create global communality, but it is anarchic, unpredictable and risks war. A "hotline" of diplomatic communication through functioning transnational institutions, as envisaged in the concept of global governance, would not abolish states as such, but would do away with processual phases of negotiation, such as the interplay between negotiation and signalling. Global governance would be more than mere global crisis communication. In addition to occasional references to "negotiation theory" (Benz and Dose 2010, p. 33), representatives of this school call above all for "structures of communication and cooperation designed for the long term" that would be conducive to "dialogue and understanding" in order to facilitate "complex learning" – because "simple learning", as found in traditional diplomacy, amounts to conforming to existing regulatory systems but is incapable of transcending them and harmonizing them on an enduring basis (Messner 2005, pp. 48, 51). Other authors advocate new spaces for "global communication and interaction" in order to enable "collective thought processes" that cannot arise through established multilateralism alone and are conceivable only on a transnational basis (Begemann et al. 1999, p. 11).

Michael Strübel has recognized that these approaches are not yet fully developed conceptually:

> The more [the global governance concept] is used in different contexts, the more it lacks precision and an analytical dimension. We can identify the

88 Politics: the state's global communication

> following as typical features of the 'global governance' construct. As a process, it presupposes a great need for willingness to cooperate and broad participation by various actors. These include states, multinational, supranational and international organizations as well as financial and trade organizations, NGOs and the media. The levels of cooperation vary. They are local, regional, national and global and – like multiple interconnected cobwebs – are linked to one another by threads of interaction. This is intended to guarantee stability and a certain durability.
>
> *(2008, p. 63f.)*

One can imagine that this complex interaction goes far beyond traditional diplomacy, which at most has to forge links between several states but does not pursue multi-track diplomacy at the local, regional and global levels. Yet despite their importance, the communication processes involved in global governance have as yet barely been researched. In structuralist fashion, relevant handbooks highlight either the performative power of economic globalization, which – like Hollywood – also has communicative and cultural effects (Brand et al. 2000, p. 76ff.), or they discuss the regulation of the media by the political sphere – but not the other way around (Perri 6, 2002). So far, then, researchers have largely ignored the mutual influencing of actor structures and communicative networks as in the system-lifeworld-network approach. When it comes to global governance, this mutual influence needs to be thought through with far greater determination if the concept of an interactive global "hotline" of global governance is to get off the ground.

3.2.2 Interaction and organizational communication

Informality at the relational level of global communication

Having delved into theories of negotiation, the next desideratum is to flesh out the analysis of interaction by drawing on organizational theories. Ultimately, the key difference between discourse and dialogue is not our only theoretical yardstick: also relevant are typical theorems of organizational communication such as the distinction between formal and informal, internal and external, spoken and written, and interpersonal and mediatized communication.

The coexistence of formal and informal communication is one of the foundations of organizational sociology. Organizations develop structures, giving rise to hierarchies and ideal-typical decision-making and communication processes. Informal communication occurs when dialogue takes place in an unplanned way through "unofficial channels" (Endruweit 2004, p. 180), which in the first instance seem unrelated to the organization's functional goals. Personal relationships also play a role in diplomatic interaction that can scarcely be overestimated. It is true that international diplomatic exchange is not a matter of internal organizational communication, as the transnationalization of states has so far rarely been realized and what we tend to find are separate national bureaucracies. But the "third space" of

Politics: the state's global communication **89**

international diplomacy is so strictly regulated by protocol, in a bureaucracy-like manner, that informality arises as a near-inevitable response. To return once more to Kissinger, it has become the stuff of legend that he had to endure Israeli prime minister Golda Meir's anti-Arab rants in order to negotiate rationally with her once she had calmed down (see, for example, Brown 1980; Rubin 1983). Jimmy Carter's dealings with the offended Egyptian President Anwar al-Sadat, who was on the point of walking away from Camp David after repeated Israeli affronts, has also gone down in history. Carter threatened to end their friendship, prompting Sadat to stay after all.

Negotiation interaction, like any communication, takes place at the content level as well as the relationship level (Watzlawick et al. 1990, pp. 53ff., 79ff.). Here the term "international relations" takes on a whole new, far more human meaning. There is a certain tragedy in the fact that the success of diplomacy, which often determines whether or not nations go to war, seems to depend to a large extent on the subjective attitudes of individuals. The positive flipside of informality, however, is that it can be astonishingly productive and generate consensus that would not be achieved through formal dialogue alone. The evaluation of informal communication has therefore always been a matter of controversy in the literature (Tacke 2015, p. 13). In diplomacy, the alleged by-product of communication between states – personal networks between individuals – often becomes the true focal point of globalization and can trigger multi-track diplomacy at times of crisis, thus opening up alternative channels of communication. Politicians' personality structures and lifeworlds influence how they perform their professional roles.

Trends in informality: networks of associated states rather than cultural boundaries

One bone of contention, however, is whether informal communication is a matter of cultural or individual influences. Essentialist cultural assumptions such as "The Chinese are generally recognised to have a tough negotiating style" (Zhu and Zhu 2004, p. 207) can often be found in the literature (Requejo and Graham 2008). The problem that arises here is not just of a logical nature, because what is referred to as "cultural" and thus as a typical feature of an organization or even country or state can no longer be declared "informal", since unwritten rules – as a matter of "customary law", so to speak – operate with almost as much formality as written rules (von Groddeck and Wilz 2015, p. 20). Moreover, the fact that the cross-cultural belief in cultural differences is a factor in common and therefore evidence against the belief in essentialist cultural differences is an amusing marginal note on the illogical character of culturalism.

Even more important is the argument put forward by Paul W. Meerts, who contends that the pronounced formality in diplomatic relations implies that any "third space" has its own laws, thus leaving little room for cultural influences exercised by negotiating styles (1999, p. 86). It is not surprising, then, that whenever actors assert that cultural differences are present in diplomacy, they fail to provide

90 Politics: the state's global communication

empirical evidence that personal and informal influences are based on cultural typologies. Until this has been empirically proven, it makes far more sense to assume that in diplomacy, as in any other area, people get on to varying degrees, that is, that informality, as a relational level of communication, is mostly a personal rather than cultural variable – which is why those who analyse diplomacy now regard it as crucial to include biographical information (Carstarphen 2004).

Another key question is what the connection might be between informality and expanding global governance. Global governance outside the framework of the United Nations, which is binding under international law, for example, at the G7, G8 or G20 get-togethers of the major industrialized countries, is "informal" in that it is not binding under international law and is therefore sometimes referred to in the literature as the "informalization of global politics" (Rinke and Schneckener 2013). At the same time, this informality points to a level different than the significance, discussed so far, from a communication studies perspective, because G20 meetings, to mention just one example, are basically traditional, formalized meetings of national leaders and diplomats. They are not personal networks. The concept of informality is thus ambiguous and sometimes means political informality beyond international law, and at other times informality beyond diplomatic protocol. The latter level is crucial to global communication, because only it represents a dimension of communicative action in its own right.

Diplomatic protocol as global symbolic communication

Indeed, because of the attention paid to informality and "cultural" influences in diplomatic communication, there is a tendency to forget that informality must necessarily have a counterpart: formality. As a kind of compensation for the largely absent transnational bureaucracy and due to the highly sensitive nature of international relations, diplomacy is characterized by extremely sophisticated procedures, which are commonly known as "diplomatic protocol". These structures are in fact by no means just a secondary aspect of the content of negotiation communication, but quite often its primary focus. There is no need to be a radical constructivist or relationist to recognize that, especially in the absence of demonstrable results, the form of diplomatic communication – non-verbal signalling (see p. 86f.) – and its symbolic staging are often more important than its content.

In his study of the rituals of the UN General Assembly, Christian Becker has described this fact as the "meaning-creating myth of community" that evokes a "global community", a mythic construction that "holds members together as ideational cement" (2014, p. 281). This is a matter of rituals and symbolic orders that seem to be deeply rooted in human history. A symbolically egalitarian order holds the global community together even if interactive diplomatic relations between states have been disrupted. It is this superordinate symbolic authority that – much like a family – makes it possible for disputes to occur between family members without wars breaking out. But it may also prevent real dialogue through an excess

Politics: the state's global communication **91**

of habitual structures. Symbolic politics alone cannot keep a community alive in the long run. But if, as we have set out theoretically, "community", in contrast to mere sociality, is in fact characterized by a high level of emotionality and identification, then symbols and diplomatic rituals are indispensable elements of the cosmopolitan global community created by diplomatic communication. At the end of the day, both informal and formal communication contribute to the success or failure of diplomatic communication in the sense of a dialogue-based global community.

Cyber-diplomacy: new dynamics, old substance

Formal and informal communication may take place in a direct and mediatized form. "Mediatization" is in fact one of the most controversial topics in present-day research on diplomatic communication. We can make a distinction here between the intellectual schools of "cyber-utopians" and "cyber-realists", with the former assuming major changes in diplomacy in the wake of digitization, while the latter believe few substantial alterations have occurred (Hocking and Melissen 2015, p. 5). These profoundly different assessments stem from the failure to distinguish clearly enough between the basic communicative modes of dialogic interaction and persuasive discursive communication. Too often, the two phenomena are conflated, as evident in the following example. The German Federal Foreign Office recently appointed a commissioner for "cyber foreign policy", while the term "cyber-diplomacy" is also used in the English-speaking world. However, these terms denote something rather different than we might imagine. Cyber-diplomacy is a subdivision of public diplomacy and an outward-facing field of public relations or propaganda (see p. 96ff.) but is not an aspect of negotiation communication. It should really be called "cyber public diplomacy". Digital communication thus supports public diplomacy rather than interactive negotiation diplomacy.

Scholars who study the role of information and communication technology have concluded that there have been no essential changes in diplomacy in the digital age (ibid., p. 13). There was no substantial change in diplomatic negotiations, which largely exclude the public, either in the first analogue media revolution (telegraph, telephone and telex) or in the second digital revolution (emails, video conferences, and so on) (Kurbalija 1999). At decisive political moments, people still often interact face-to-face (Kronenburg 1998, p. 385f.). Diplomacy's approach to the public sphere has not been modified by digital social media. All the developments in media technology have not changed the basic dichotomy of a non-public interactive diplomacy and a monologic public diplomacy. The idea that each and every foreign policy is now being "tweeted" is thus incorrect (Fletcher 2016, p. 171f.). As Christer Jönsson notes: "Yet the basic premises of diplomatic communication – searching for the optimal combination of verbal and nonverbal instruments, of noise and silence, and of clarity and ambiguity – remain" (2016, p. 88). Overall, then, the presence and understanding of basic communicative principles, such as dialogue and discourse, are more important to the role of communication in global

92 Politics: the state's global communication

relations than their aggregate technological state. Content and form need to be clearly distinguished here.

It is not the substance of diplomatic communication that has changed but certain communicative routines, as captured by terms such as "directness" and "speed", which has in turn contributed to certain shifts in actors' positions. As Brian Hocking and Jan Melissen put it: "Experience suggests that technologies rarely create new diplomatic functions but rather influence the ways in which those functions are performed" (2015, p. 29). Telephone calls and video conferences between heads of government, national ministries and diplomats are now the order of the day, whereas historically such face-to-face meetings took place rarely and required a great deal of travel. The final downgrading of the ambassador, whose services as a transmitter of diplomatic messages are now used less and less by governments, thus took place in the wake of digitization (ibid., p. 7). The digitally optimized direct line between state decision-makers has in fact strengthened the hierarchies within diplomacy.

Nevertheless, it should be noted that in organized social systems communicative networking by means of digital media is of secondary importance and does not change the substance of the diplomatic sphere, because (1) it remains the case that, as a dialogic phenomenon, diplomacy features a non-public "backstage", even when it involves interpersonal, mediatized communication, and (2) the analogue revolution was more significant than its digital counterpart as it enabled permanent direct contact between state decision-makers.

Global spaces of interpretation through the text-speech relationship

Of great importance to diplomacy, however, is the text-speech relationship. Text-based interactions – such as protocols, memoranda or treaties between states – are considered particularly valuable. In contrast to spoken dialogue, the written text is believed to be characterized by a strict logic. Like the behavioural protocols and rituals of diplomacy, diplomatic texts are an expression of an important institutionalization of international relations, which stabilizes the system of nation states. In diplomacy, a single negotiating text is often used to put the agreements reached on record, identify problem areas and ensure the clear use of language (Kaufmann 1996, p. 150). Ideally, this text enshrines a consensus satisfactory to all parties, renders it unambiguous and lends it long-term stability, eliminating the need for constant renegotiation. Treaties strengthen the connection between parties and secure their relationships over the long term. A contractual community is established.

But we have to be careful here. The text's role is not necessarily to engender clarity. A certain ambiguity of the text is often part of the business of diplomacy. This is also known as "constructive ambiguity" (Jönsson 2016, p. 82). The text only needs to be clear when it comes to short-term actions. The topics that were essentially excluded from step-by-step diplomacy (see p. 83f.) are often formulated in a vague and unclear manner. Both sides should be able to read the text in the corresponding passages as they wish. Hence, the ambiguity of interaction is just as much a component of written diplomacy as clarity and logical interpretation.

UN Resolution 242 on the Middle East conflict after the 1967 Six-Day War is an example of this. The English version demanded of Israel the "withdrawal of Israeli armed forces from territories occupied in the recent conflict", while the French version referred to the "retrait des forces armées israéliennes des territoires occupés lors du récent conflit". Instead of the originally planned phrasing of "all territories" or "the territories", the English version in particular left Israel with a small loophole that enabled it to continue its occupation of the Palestinian territories, at least in part, while the French version did not. The global governance approach warns that such unresolved problems can lead to instability in the international community over the long term, though the question is whether ambiguity is not an inherent feature of communication, one that would persist in qualitative terms even if there were a quantitative increase in intergovernmental exchanges through the "hotline" of global governance.

Continuities within changing global diplomatic communication

Mediatized interpersonal communication has not changed the essence of (interactive and mostly non-public) face-to-face communication in diplomacy but has led to the temporal consolidation of diplomatic networks, to new routines and shifts in actors' roles. New networks of mediatized interpersonal interaction have made global diplomatic communication more direct and thus seemingly strengthened "global communality". Yet the basic formation of organizational communication within the political realm – formal symbolism, personal dialogic relationships and scope for interpretation of treaty texts – remains fundamentally in place. One of the oldest human institutions, diplomacy, has thus proved astonishingly persistent from a communication studies perspective.

3.2.3   Observation and diffusion

The state's communicative multi-competence

Let us turn now to the discursive forms of communication in international politics. The political sphere not only interacts, it also observes media discourses and other systems and tries to influence them. In communication studies terms, we can characterize this as a feat of interpretive observation. The social system of politics is so prominent because it combines the capacity for interaction and observation to the greatest possible extent and on a global scale (see Chapter 1, Section 1.3). Later we discuss the fact that, in addition, it not only observes discourses, but also tries to influence them strategically. In light of the state's communicative multi-competence, Jürgen Gerhards and Friedhelm Neidhardt are right to describe politics as the supersystem of public sphere theory (1990). The state has considerable power

94 Politics: the state's global communication

and financial resources and therefore, in case of doubt, also the most differentiated structures of global communication.

Ambassadors and secret services as information gatherers

Various forms of analysis and observation of other systems and environments exist whose purpose is to obtain and disseminate information. Ambassadors play multiple roles in this regard, as interaction partners and information gatherers and, as we will see on p. 96ff., as actors involved in external communication as well (Jönsson and Hall 2005, p. 73ff.). The main reason for the introduction of permanent, resident ambassadors was in fact to gather and transmit information, something that is often overlooked in the romanticized image of his or her "Excellency". Governments today spend more on information gathering than on diplomatic interaction. In this context, ambassadors cooperate and compete with secret services as well as the mass media. But they have lost their former informational monopoly as well as their monopoly of representation within negotiation diplomacy (see p. 81), increasingly turning them into practitioners of public diplomacy (see p. 96ff.).

Obtaining information from secret services is a precarious business in that it is often non-transparent. Much like the Internet's so-called "dark web", international politics too has a barely visible flipside known as the "deep state" (Morisse-Schilbach and Peine 2008). Not everything that secret services do violates the international and contract law negotiated at the diplomatic level or infringes relevant national laws. Secret services are in many ways information gatherers that resemble other information systems, such as scholarship. Secret services seek to collect facts, produce analyses and provide assessments, in other words, they are concerned with the basic heuristics of information acquisition, processing and dissemination. But the clandestine aspect of information gathering – espionage – defies the scholarly ethics of communicative action with its insistence on source transparency, duty of public disclosure and willingness to engage in dialogue, and is clearly an example of the state's strategic, monologic action. It is thus effectively impossible to deploy the tools of scholarship to reach conclusions about the secret services' contribution to diplomatic information acquisition.

Media monitoring as the global observation of observation

In addition to the regular reports produced by ambassadors and secret services, foreign policy today is increasingly engaged in so-called "media monitoring". The political sphere thus not only observes the world as such, but also other observers, especially mass media or social media, to cull information of relevance to diplomacy. Media monitoring is expensive and is, therefore, mainly practised at present by the richer industrialized countries. The best-known examples are the BBC Monitoring Service (BBCM) and the US Foreign Broadcast Information Service (FBIS). BBCM translates media from around 150 countries in approximately 70 languages on a daily basis. The goal is not only to use the media as an

Politics: the state's global communication **95**

educational resource, but also to keep an eye on it as a potentially disruptive factor in foreign policy. In principle, this gives rise to new interfaces between media and social systems. While the average citizen has virtually no direct knowledge of foreign language media (see Chapter 2, Section 2.1), their own government often has an informational advantage in this regard.

However, assessments of the importance of media monitoring to foreign policy vary tremendously, which is probably due in part to the fact that media are strictly censored in many countries, which limits their value as a source (Rawnsley 1999, p. 136f.). Nevertheless, there are those who consider the diplomatic procurement of information (by ambassadors) increasingly obsolete due to the development of modern media, which are faster, more comprehensive and more efficient than the information gathering of the diplomatic corps (Jönsson and Hall 2003). This would seem logical, given our above conclusion that ambassadors are increasingly excluded from diplomatic dialogue, such that their value as a source would obviously decrease. However, neither mass media nor social media are likely to represent a true substitute in this regard, as they are not part of the other systems and only have very limited access to diplomacy as "insiders". It is more probable that there is a new appreciation for analysts within the political system who are capable of carrying out media monitoring, while also producing analytical summaries and enriching their monitoring with insider knowledge of diplomacy and access to the secret services. Once again, the development of the modern media seems to be fostering a tendency towards the centralization of communication in decision-making centres, in the form, for example, of IT analysts and IT planning teams in foreign ministries.

However, foreign policy does not necessarily have its own scholarship-based departments or planning staff and is thus partly dependent on the assistance of experts, that is, on policy advice. Political think tanks such as the Carnegie Endowment for International Peace in the United States, the Stiftung Wissenschaft und Politik (SWP) in Germany and the Al-Ahram Center for Political and Strategic Studies (ACPSS) in Cairo, to mention just a few examples, are centres of non-university research that are wholly or partially financed by the political sphere. Again, we might describe such institutions as an interface between the political system and another social system – in this case, that of scholarship. It would certainly not be amiss to refer here to the "interpenetration" of systems, because these bodies' financial dependence in particular sometimes calls their independence into question. Experts from independent universities consulted on an irregular basis are essentially "outsiders" to the political system compared to these "insiders". There is in fact an antinomy between autonomy and communicative access (Gellner 1995; Hafez 2002c).

Knowledge management between rationality and power politics

Ultimately, as Max Weber and Jürgen Habermas have recognized, there are different logics of policy and scholarship, of value-based power action, information

96 Politics: the state's global communication

procurement and knowledge diffusion. As is increasingly evident, the rational aspect of information gathering and observational communication is just one of the guiding principles of politics. Strategic action is just as important. In contrast to scholarship, where the scholarly community is the central gatekeeper, the idea of the interactive global community is only one of several horizons for politics: both the procurement of sources and their processing and dissemination take place according to procedures that are opaque to the public and underscore the self-interest of the nation state. The ambivalences in the process of the state's global political communication, between global community-creation and national egocentrism, are particularly evident in the procurement of information by secret services. It is thus time to take a closer look at the state's strategic global communication.

3.2.4 Discursive (external) communication

The non-transparency of action systems

There is another dimension of foreign policy communication that calls into question the notion of an interactively generated global community. Sociologically, we can best explain this with reference to the distinction between the internal and external communication of organizations. Organized social systems in politics and the economy, which are the main societal action systems, are not only characterized by clear hierarchies, but also feature a strictly guarded border between internal and external communication. The economy keeps its company secrets just as politics classifies the records of its diplomatic interactions, often shielding them from the public for decades.

Such systems also put a great deal of effort into public relations and advertising in order to present themselves in strategically effective ways. At the same time, however, there are systems in which this is at least ideally not the case. Scholarship has to be transparent and, in the case of the mass media too, internal and external freedom of expression ought to go hand in hand. The only exceptions here from an ethical point of view are third parties, that is, mainly anonymous or protected sources. Observational systems thus differ from action systems precisely with regard to the distinction between internal and external communication, though this requires qualification in that the differences become blurred when scholarship or journalism are run on a commercial basis or influenced by politics.

Public diplomacy/propaganda

There are numerous fields of action centred on external communication that are of relevance to foreign policy, such as the marketing of nations, foreign cultural policy, international broadcasting and war propaganda. "Public diplomacy" has established itself as a generic term for this (see, for example, Snow and Taylor 2009). Public diplomacy includes instruments such as national marketing, brochures and websites, state activities on social media, educational soaps, events featuring journalists and cultural professionals, information centres at embassies, state-financed exhibitions of artists, lecture tours by scholars from a given country and cultural bodies operating internationally such as the Chinese Confucius Institute, the Russkiy Mir Institute, the German Goethe Institute, the British Council and the Institut français. The use of the term "public diplomacy" indicates an attempt to shift away from the concept of propaganda, which was discredited by totalitarianism and the Cold War. Ideally, this is intended to signal that states interact with the global community not only through internal diplomacy but also in the field of public communication, that they are willing to engage in dialogue, are prepared to change, and are responding to issues of political legitimacy.

But is this really the case? There is good reason for classifying the term public diplomacy itself as a marketing tool, one intended to camouflage the state's propagandistic interests. If propaganda is viewed not only as the preserve of authoritarian states, but as a form of persuasive one-to-many communication, then it is also practised by democratic countries and, as strategic monologic communication, stands in contrast to the dialogic communication of negotiation diplomacy. Public diplomacy too is a form of global communication by the state, though one that does not foster the synchrony of the global public sphere, let alone the integration of a global community, instead providing a stark contrast with both these theoretical horizons of global communication. It is interesting to note the comment by Vladimir Ivanovich Fokin et al. that there may be a causal connection between the increasing complexity of state interactivity and the simultaneous growth in persuasive communication, a link that illustrates the egocentricity of the nation state in the wake of globalization:

> The explosive expansion of the number of international relations actors at the world community level has triggered globalization processes that have increased the peoples' interdependence. The increased impact of public opinion on foreign policy and on shaping the world order has caused a reciprocal desire of states to exert influence on stereotyping foreign policy in the mass consciousness.
>
> *(2017, p. 46)*

What this suggests is that, in response to its impending loss of control as a result of multi-track diplomacy, global governance, and so on, the modern state is developing persuasive, in other words, propagandistic forms of communication in order to avoid becoming overly dependent on other countries.

"Understanding"-based persuasion

The concept of public diplomacy is controversial in the scholarly literature. In any case, its core objective is to facilitate communication between the state and a dispersed range of target audiences in other countries. The idea here is that if political systems are becoming increasingly participatory or even democratic, then

98 Politics: the state's global communication

the state can no longer communicate only with other state leaderships within the framework of diplomacy but must expand its space of communication. Today, Joseph Nye's concept of "soft power" is often cited as the origin of public diplomacy. The Harvard-based political scientist made the term famous as the antithesis of the "hard power" characteristic of the politics of war and power politics. Soft power is the state's ability to disseminate a positive image through the appeal of its ideas, values and culture and thus to promote its interests abroad (1990). From this point of view, the US music and film industries are just as important to American interests as US military and economic power. Often, they are even more effective because they help bring about a situation in which other states and people cooperate with the US without coercion and at no major cost. Nye has therefore repeatedly made it clear that soft power should not be confused with persuasion or propaganda: "The best propaganda is not propaganda" (2012).

The fact that exponents of public diplomacy like to invoke the concept of soft power while pursuing a persuasive agenda becomes clear if we look at official statements made by the government of the United States in which the objectives of public diplomacy are described as to "inform, engage, and influence" (GAO 2007, p. 1). A 2003 report produced by the US Congress in response to the attacks of 11 September 2001 and the subsequent wars in Afghanistan and Iraq openly refers to external communication as "strategic communication" (GAO 2003, p. 18). The report proposes measures to disseminate American perspectives in the Middle East. There was no noticeable difference here between the Republican administration of George W. Bush and that of Democrat Barack Obama. Under Obama too, the goal was "strategic communication", though supplemented by an emphasis on "connecting with" and "listening to" (Biden 2009, p. 3f.). The concept of dialogue, however, was absent from the Democrats' statements as well. Even those who believed they could discern a shift in emphasis in the Obama administration from persuasion to understanding, concede that: "The term [public diplomacy] was not initially intended to connote propaganda, yet retains an implicit mandate to 'persuade' as much as inform or educate in order to forward the strategic ambitions of the United States" (Hayden 2015, p. 212).

Sandra Busch-Janser and Daniel Florian are thus quite right to propose subdividing the concept of public diplomacy into lobbying, public relations and nation branding (2007). As Jan Melissen argues, public diplomacy is evidence that modern states are viewing persuasive communicative processes as increasingly important. It also indicates a shift away from the realistic school of international relations theory. It is now recognized that the "battle of values and ideas" is every bit as important as classic power politics (2005, p. 4). Public diplomacy does not, however, follow the same communicative rules of dialogic understanding as classic diplomacy, but is instead part of the field of public relations or even classic propaganda. "Understanding" is an essential principle, but it serves chiefly to optimize persuasion. Here communication is fundamentally monologic rather than dialogic.

When Melissen seeks to distinguish a "new public diplomacy" from propaganda (ibid., p. 11) or even describes it as dialogic (2011, p. 10), this contradicts his own call for scholars to think more in terms of marketing (2005, p. 8). He himself certainly recognizes this problem by making it clear that public diplomacy is not an "altruistic affair" (ibid., p. 14). Richard Holbrooke, a senior US diplomat, minced no words in this connection: "Call it public diplomacy, call it public affairs, psychological warfare, if you really want to be blunt, propaganda" (2001). And British diplomat Tom Fletcher writes: "One man's propaganda is another man's spin is another man's public diplomacy strategy" (2016, p. 153). Melissen correctly states that the activities of democratic states cannot be compared with the classic propaganda of totalitarian states such as the Hitler or Stalin dictatorships (2005, p. 17). But this distinction applies at most to the idea of democracy propagated by democratic states, not to the form of persuasive communication, which remains surprisingly stable across political systems. Besides, authoritarian states such as China leave little room for doubt about their attempts to exercise an influence through propaganda (Sohn 2015).

Foreign cultural policy: "dialogue" between "cultures"?

While the scholarly literature as well as experienced diplomats criticize the unclear concept of public diplomacy (Ostrowski 2010, p. 27), those responsible for external communication in particular have repeatedly tried to rehabilitate it as alleged "interaction". Albert Spiegel, then head of the Department of Cultural and Educational Policy at the German Federal Foreign Office, made a distinction between public relations and cultural diplomacy. He designated only PR as public diplomacy, while for him foreign cultural and educational policy was responsible for creating a favourable environment for German foreign policy through the "dialogue of cultures" and "intercultural dialogue" (2002). At the same time, he recognized a close connection between these activities and marketing, public relations and public diplomacy, so this perspective too fails to make a convincing conceptual distinction. This contradiction runs through the entire German literature on the subject.

Foreign cultural and educational policy is based on the entirely valid idea of creating cross-border and cross-cultural epistemic spaces as "third spaces" that – when it comes, for example, to the relationship between the Mediterranean region and the rest of Europe or between the Islamic and Western worlds – can enhance the state's knowledge and thus facilitate competent foreign policy (Ernst 2015, p. 24). We can in fact discern a kinship with classic diplomacy here. However, key differences remain between the entire field of public diplomacy and foreign cultural and educational policy, on the one hand, and diplomacy, on the other. From a communication studies perspective, there are three main problem areas:

- *Claims to representation in the "dialogue of cultures" – who is communicating?* To remain with the example of Germany, after 2001, the German Federal Foreign Office sought to open up channels of communication with the young Arab generation (ibid., p. 108). Yet, in reality, this arbitrary approach turned the real actors and interlocutors involved in global communication between states into

100 Politics: the state's global communication

"target groups". The asymmetry of the actors' constellations – the organized state, on the one hand, entire populations, on the other – is simply too great to facilitate serious dialogic communication. There is no sign of any considered concept of culture here (see also ibid., p. 226).

- *The object of dialogue – what is being communicated?* In contrast to traditional diplomacy, the themes of public diplomacy or foreign cultural and educational policy are one-sidedly determined by the interests of the financing state, which thus dictates the agenda. The external communication of German embassies, for example, is dominated by topics suffused with German interests (Ostrowski 2010, p. 190).
- *Dialogic feedback for decision-makers – who is being communicated with?* While multi-track diplomacy incorporates civil society into traditional diplomatic measures, public diplomacy or foreign cultural and educational policy is largely isolated from civil society. It is doubtful that there is feedback between the measures pursued by foreign cultural and educational policy – Goethe Institute, conferences, and so on – and operational policy that would justify the use of the term "dialogue". Kai Hafez himself designed and carried out the "Media Dialogues with the Arab World" from 1997 to 1999 for the German Foreign Ministry, which are now regarded as pioneering achievements in foreign cultural and educational policy (Ernst 2015, p. 128). There was no sign at the time of any substantive participation by the German diplomatic sphere or of genuine interest in dialogue on the part of German foreign policy. More recent empirical studies do not even include the criterion of feedback itself, as it is evidently irrelevant (Ostrowski 2010).

The organizational expression of the still clear distinction between diplomacy and public diplomacy is the fact that the German Federal Foreign Office has its own department for public diplomacy. This "Department K" for culture and communication (*Kultur und Kommunikation*) is separate from the "Political Department", the "Department for Crisis Prevention", and so on (AA, n.d.). Public diplomacy is not, therefore, a cross-cutting task for the entire diplomatic staff, but the domain of (marketing) specialists. A "dialogue" takes place in public diplomacy only to the extent that these specialized diplomats conduct on-site dialogues with journalists, scholars and other disseminators, which may well have a social impact on the professional lives and lifeworlds of those affected (see Chapters 7 and 8). If necessary, foreign policy may fall back on appropriate networks in order to conduct multi-track diplomacy. As a rule, however, the content of the "dialogues" does not reach foreign policy decision-makers. Within the framework of organized social systems, as we will see later with respect to the economy (see Chapter 4, Section 4.2.4), external communication always tends to instigate instrumentalized pseudo-dialogues in order to win over elites and other target groups through a deft form of public relations. But given the asymmetrical communication and the lack of proper feedback between foreign policy and other "cultures" or populations, there is currently no prospect of policy-changing dialogues.

The measures pursued in this context are located within the discursive-mono-logic spectrum of communication and are examples of strategic but not communi-cative action (see also Fähnrich 2012, on foreign science policy). In any case, close consideration of this issue reveals that any major expansion of dialogic communi-cation – which would be desirable for those keen to see a global community, global governance and the transnationalization of politics – poses a risk to the interests of national political systems. In line with the aforementioned analysis by Fokin et al. (2017), by stepping up its efforts in the field of persuasive public diplomacy, the nation state is seeking to compensate for the increasing interactions, compromises and obligations arising from diplomatic dialogue. From a communication studies perspective, then, the state's actions remain intrinsically ambivalent. The unclear dynamics of the "dialogue of cultures" also make sense here in that "dialogues" can be conducted that function as a marketing tool and bind foreign elites to the state but that represent no real challenge to the centres of political decision-making.

War communication: the return of global disinformation

Nowhere is the ambivalence of the modern state in the process of global com-munication more apparent than in the field of war and crisis communication. This form of communication clearly runs counter to the intensifying dynamism of interactive diplomacy, with its growing number of actors, as well as to global governance. For paradigmatic examples of this development, we need look no further than US war propaganda ("information warfare") relating to the Vietnam War, the Gulf War of 1991, the Kosovo War of 1999 and the Iraq War of 2003. US propaganda techniques have been expanded and differentiated over time, from a classic censorship policy, as exemplified by information pools in the 1991 con-flict, to massive and manipulative linguistic and visual propaganda in the 2003 war, including numerous lies about alleged weapons of mass destruction and mass graves in Iraq, while the invading powers denied their own breaches of inter-national law (killing civilians, using cluster bombs, and so on) (Bennett and Paletz 1994; Goff 1999; Miller 2004, Tumber and Palmer 2004, Kumar 2006). Overall, a tendency towards the return of so-called "black propaganda" can be seen even in Western democracies. In contrast to "white" and "grey" propaganda, this does not (selectively) provide information, but actively disseminates untruths. European states, let alone authoritarian states such as Russia or China, are no better than the United States in this regard.

Thymian Bussemer rightly states that propaganda has become a normalized phe-nomenon. His hopes that the state would increasingly struggle to manage the news as the Internet becomes more important have, however, turned out to be overly optimistic (2005, p. 394). Instead, the evidence shows that war propaganda still has the same mobilizing effects on the majority society as it did before the introduc-tion of the Internet (Hafez 2007a, p. 46ff.). The new complexity of digital, global channels of information has thus done little to alter the primacy of politics at times of (supposedly) acute threats from external enemies (Hafez 2007b). In order to be

102 Politics: the state's global communication

effective, state propaganda has no need to be absolute in the manner of the classic totalitarian propaganda of Hitler or Stalin. At least when a state is deeply involved in a conflict and especially when the latter has reached its peak in terms of state action, it is enough to circulate nationalistic stereotypes of the enemy. This stabilizes the "home front". Only in situations of limited state involvement in international conflicts or low-intensity warfare that extends over long periods of time can states lose control of communication.

There is broad consensus in the present-day scholarship that while democracies are relatively peaceful vis-à-vis other democracies, when it comes to confrontations with authoritarian political systems they are no less belligerent (see, for example, Daase 2004). The state's external communication is, therefore, constantly shaped by images of the enemy (Teusch 2003, p. 216), which partly explains the fragmentary worldviews of the media, which absorb state propaganda (see Chapter 2, Section 2.2.1). Democracies tend to ethically delegitimize all other political systems, rendering them vulnerable to "humanitarian" interventions. We need only think of the huge numbers of victims of American wars after the Second World War in Korea, Vietnam, Afghanistan and Iraq (Hafez 2010a, p. 170ff.). As yet, in any case, the "eternal peace" envisaged by Immanuel Kant scarcely seems in prospect. The peace dividend generated by diplomatic interaction goes hand in hand with the tremendous rhetorical valorization of the nation state and with the undiminished mobilizing power of war communication, which can be highly destructive. The stabilization of the global community through interactive diplomatic communication is endangered almost arbitrarily — and in fact to an increasing degree — by hackneyed images of the enemy and propaganda. Interactively generated communality, as verbally constructed and symbolically conveyed by the political sphere itself, is constantly thwarted by war- and crisis-related propaganda.

State international broadcasting: more than persuasion?

Another area of public diplomacy, state international broadcasting, was considered a victim of globalization until 11 September 2001. Ever more national channels could be received directly via satellite, while operating specifically international channels seemed pointless as they were drowned out by the mass of global offerings. As the number of wars in the Middle East increased, however, the West and other major powers became more interested in modernizing state international broadcasting (such as BBC World, Voice of America, Deutsche Welle, RT, CCTV, Radio China International and Radio France Internationale, see also Chapter 2, Section 2.2.1). International broadcasting — radio and television — is in fact the ideal means of overcoming language barriers in the field of international media. Broadcasting in numerous national languages enables the state to target the monolingual middle classes in other countries with far greater precision. The origins of state international broadcasting are, however, clearly propagandistic in nature. We need only think of the role of Radio Free Europe during the Second World War. While so-called "information warfare" is propaganda directed towards one's own population,

Politics: the state's global communication **103**

international broadcasting is an aspect of "psychological warfare" intended to mobilize foreign populations against hostile governments.

RT ("Russia Today" until 2009), for example, courts the right-wing populist movement in Europe in an attempt to destabilize the political systems of the West. Russian domestic broadcasters, in contrast, refer to the return of fascism in Europe. So while efforts are made to bolster right-wing populism externally, internally it serves to justify new stereotypes of the enemy (Pomerantsev 2015). Likewise, international broadcaster Voice of America and the American Arabic-language television channel Al-Hurra allow no real criticism of American neocolonial policies in the Middle East (Hafez 2007a, p. 118ff.). Such broadcasters systematically disregard the understanding of others that is so crucial to dialogue, while staging sham dialogues that can only be interpreted as artful propaganda strategies.

In recent years, Western European international broadcasting has repeatedly tried to distance itself from the propagandistic approach. It has talked of dialogue and referred to international broadcasting as the ideal platform for the "dialogue of cultures" (Groebel 2000; Kleinsteuber 2002). The director of Deutsche Welle, Erik Bettermann, argued that concentrating on conveying a positive image of Germany was a "long-since obsolete" approach and ill-suited to remaining competitive in the era of globalization. Instead, the aim must be to process information "from regions for regions" and to secure the acceptance of international broadcasting worldwide with an "intelligent mix of German, European and target area-related topics" (2004). The Deutsche Welle law of 2005 thus declares "exchange between cultures and peoples" a key objective (DW 2005). Yet there are question marks over the independence of Deutsche Welle. Certainly, in terms of content, broadcasters such as Deutsche Welle or BBC World Service seem to take pluralism with respect to foreign policy issues more seriously than American, Russian or Chinese broadcasters do. In much the same way as in foreign cultural and educational policy, however, the manner in which Deutsche Welle steers topics evinces strong connections with Germany and Europe, which is surely a long way from an ideal dialogue or sustained critique of the foreign policy of its home country or region (see Chapter 2, Section 2.2.1). The marketing of Germany is still clearly in evidence, and not just in terms of content. This link to German interests can be explained partly in light of the funding of Deutsche Welle by the German state and is corroborated by numerous statements by German politicians, and the broadcaster's senior figures, describing it as a marketing tool (Hagedorn 2016, p. 489ff., see also Michalek 2009, p. 100ff.).

At the end of the day, despite all the attempts at renewal in an era of global competition, even international broadcasting remains largely an instrument of public diplomacy. While US politicians have never left any room for doubt that they consider European broadcasters such as Deutsche Welle part of public diplomacy (GAO 2003/2, p. 2), Deutsche Welle itself is now more realistic about its position and at least concedes that it is located between global information source and public diplomacy (DW 2016). Akin to foreign cultural and educational policy, making state-funded mass media dialogic is an unrealizable aspiration because they

104 Politics: the state's global communication

practise one-to-many communication, with a question mark always hanging over how well the "many" are represented. Even without "black" propaganda, the media agenda is geared towards the self-interest of a given state and society, a stance that marginalizes many global issues and acts as a kind of pre-filter of global dialogue. Even state international broadcasting scarcely seeks to provide feedback for a foreign policy field in which the key decision-makers rarely make themselves available for critique and for *real* public diplomacy.

Public diplomacy 2.0

In the wake of the general shift, evident over the last few decades, away from traditional mass media and towards the Internet, we can discern a tendency towards mediatization in the field of public diplomacy, just as in diplomatic communication. Several authors view the use of social media as a stimulus to greater dialogue in public diplomacy. They suggest that the seemingly inherently interactive character of social media, with people potentially being consumers and producers at the same time, also applies to "public diplomacy 2.0" (Hayden 2015). Yet much the same restrictions on dialogue exist in social media as in other media. When Twitter, Facebook and similar media are actively used by ambassadors and others for external communication, they tend to facilitate the collection and dissemination of information rather than dialogic exchange (Hocking and Melissen 2015, p. 29).

It is unlikely that the technological pull of social media is strong enough to turn public relations into ideal-typical dialogues and thus alter systems. Even in the age of the Internet, the foundations of nation states' power politics have changed little, and social media are by no means interactive *per se* within global communication (see Chapter 6, Section 6.2.1). It is far more probable, as in McLuhan's "the-medium-is-the-message" perspective, that modern media are themselves being used as a marketing tool to simulate and stage an openness to dialogue. This would mean that new public diplomacy (Melissen 2005) is not as new as it seems and is in fact more a case of new wine in the old bottles of international PR.

Conclusion: the state's global communication between integration and isolation

Overall, it is fair to say that over time the political system has increasingly expanded its communication into the global sphere, differentiated it and thus, after the experience of two world wars, fostered at least the idea of a communicative global community. At the same time, states today can hardly be described as peace-promoters and cosmopolitans. While they appear, in the context of diplomacy, to be more willing than ever to interact, through public diplomacy they go behind the backs of their negotiating partners to pursue the national self-interest. Even in the age of global political dialogues, then, the nation state's monologues are far from over. External public communication directed towards the systemic environments of the political system – that is, its target groups and "outsiders" – is persuasive in nature.

Foreign policy has certainly discovered the term "dialogue" as a marketing tool, but public diplomacy remains essentially one-way communication, which is launched strategically by the purveyors of state public relations and whose occasional yield is rarely fed back to the real decision-makers. The political system is more interactive than the mass media, but it is also far more propagandistic, more aggressive and one of the main causes of the mass media's global synchrony problem (see Chapter 2, Section 2.2.1).

In international relations, then, the state's feats of communication oscillate between the basic systemic functions of adaptation and differentiation or autonomy. Diplomacy gives rise to fleeting transnational spaces ("third spaces") in which the internal communication of a number of nation states is dialogically coupled, resulting in integrative adaptation to competing environmental systems. Outside these moments of an interactive global community, other states are treated as dispersed system environments. Communication takes the form of persuasion in order to preserve the identity and interests of the nation state and the difference between systems. The ambiguity of the diplomatic text is no accident, but rather the product of an international politics that is based on separate political systems. Regardless of its capacity to engage in dialogue, the state's striving for autonomy will always prevent international political communication from being geared exclusively towards interaction.

Against this background, it is not without a certain irony that the state, of all things, which itself communicates so ambiguously and which, as the most powerful "supersystem", subverts other systems such as the media for propaganda purposes, is the hero of integrative systems theory in international relations (see Chapter 1, Section 1.1). This is because the political system is in theory an ideal space for cross-border interaction that features a high degree of observational competence and thus far-reaching community-building potential. At the same time, however, it must be recognized that the state is also destructive, undermines synchrony, dilutes discourses and thwarts both global dialogues and enduring relationships. Hence, the state has the ability to integrate, but this is very limited and can only be developed further through changes in actor structures (transnationalization) and communicative relations (global governance). At present, global community formation remains unstable and what we find is a form of hybrid statehood between the nation state and transnationalization, which is also noticeable in a communicative sense in the contrast between global interaction and nationalistic monologue. The communicative global community is constantly forming and melting away.

4

ECONOMY

Global corporate communication

In addition to the media, the economy is viewed as a core area of globalization (Giese et al. 2011). Much like the political system, as an organized social system the economy has a wealth of communicative resources at its disposal. In fact, global corporations appear to be more progressive than the political sphere in that they create genuine transnational forms of organization rather than loose communicative networks between basically separate systems as in diplomacy. Despite this potential shift from global negotiation communication to organizational communication, however, this chapter will show that global economic communication too is beset by numerous problems. The economic system is not only highly differentiated in itself, with ownership and power structures potentially impairing cross-border interaction. In addition, corporate cultures, networks and processes of knowledge diffusion are often far removed from ideal-typical forms of globalization, and there is strong pressure to adjust to local markets in the external communication of marketing and advertising.

All of this has consequences that, following Bassam Tibi, we can convey through the term "semi-modernity" (1995). While the range of material goods in different countries is increasingly converging around the world through global trade and integrated markets of investment and labour, interaction, observation and discursive action often remain locally oriented in the economic system. Economic globalization, then, does not automatically shape our awareness and knowledge of the world. The economy's contribution to the formation of a "global community" or "global society" remains contradictory.

DOI: 10.4324/9781003255239-5

4.1 Systems and system change

Shift of perspective: global institutionalism

As always, our first question is which actors and structures characterize the global economy, before we consider communicative processes themselves. Here a distinction must be made between two sectors: classic trade, as the exchange of goods across political boundaries, and global direct investment by multinational or transnational companies. While global trade has multiple historical roots, today's economic globalization is mainly typified by the expansion of direct investment and the development of global corporate or even multicorporate structures. These new structures cross-cut state sovereignty and are primarily a result of the stagnation of domestic markets, the need for growth in industrialized countries, and population growth and unemployment in developing countries. This impels the rise of global economic forms, though these repeatedly trigger protectionist and neonationalist counter-tendencies (Schuldt 2010, p. 11f.).

In addition to this analysis, which is widespread in the discipline of economics (see, for example, Bhagwati 2004; Friedman 2005), critics have asserted that most companies are not "global" in the sense of being oriented towards entire world markets, but are in fact focused, as "international" entities, on a small number of countries – often neighbouring states or limited realms such as the OECD (Hirst and Thompson 1999; see also Läpple 1999, p. 27). Nevertheless, something fundamentally new is emerging in the field of business due to transnational organizational and cooperative structures, the kind of novelty we have looked for more or less in vain within the political sphere. With the exception of special formations such as the European Union, transnational organizations are extremely weak, both in politics and in the mass media. In contrast, global business enterprises or – and this is an important distinction – global business *ventures* (such as joint ventures, production chains, and so on) do not feature communication *between* autonomous, non-integrated systems, as in the case of both trade and political diplomacy, but instead involve global communication *within* (network) organizations. In global companies, it is no longer a matter of *whether* one has interests and topics in common and is willing to enter into relations of dependence: this question has already been answered in the affirmative. The employees belong together, form a unit and pursue common goals. The result is highly likely to be intense cross-border communication featuring pronounced routines and a high problem-solving capacity, which can be described as the *internal communication of the global organization*.

The return of institutionalism within the debate on globalization is in fact a remarkable development. While institutions such as states, and organizations such as political parties, are increasingly losing their cohesiveness within the national realm and there was long talk of the end of institutionalism in the social sciences, global business enterprises have become the core of a renaissance of institutionalism. By linking formerly national and local systemic entities, transnational organizations, as a number of institutional theorists hope, can use new freedoms to develop a new

108 Economy: global corporate communication

"global culture" (Drori 2008, p. 456ff.). The once apparently structureless global space, characterized equally by irregular forms of diplomatic communication as well as by wars and conflicts, is, they imagine, becoming all but pacified in the domain of global business enterprises. The emergence of a "global community", then, ought to be a matter of course. Here the economy seems to be establishing itself as the lead system of modernity.

Power and communication in global companies

However, the construction principle underpinning global business enterprises, which are often referred to as "global players", is significantly more complicated than institutionalism imagines. Simply labelling global companies as "organizations" fails to do justice to the variety of modern network organizations, though most classifications ultimately boil down to similar typologies and have implications for structure-process or hierarchy-dialogue relations in the economy. The literature usually differentiates either between "ethnocentric", "polycentric" and "geocentric" or between "global", "international", "multinational" or "transnational" companies (Pries 2008a, p. 182ff.; Harrison 2010, p. 211). The idea here is that ethnocentric, global or international companies operate as dependencies of a national parent company, which acts as the unambiguous decision-making centre for its foreign subsidiaries. Polycentric or multinational companies are organized on a decentralized basis; the individual companies enjoy extensive freedoms. But only geocentric or transnational companies correspond to the ideal of cross-border cooperation on an equal footing between interdependent parts of the company, which collectively seek to identify economic solutions. This is significant in that we may assume that an equal dialogue, and thus the genuine integration of global knowledge, dominate in the ideal type of the transnational company. It is true that these companies too feature the typical hierarchies and owner interests found in the capitalist economy, which permit dialogic corporate cultures only on the condition of efficiency and profit maximization (Zerfaß 1996, p. 43). Nonetheless, the dialogic space is distributed evenly across borders and the company's innovative core is no longer to be found in just *one* country.

The transnational company type is still extremely rare. Most global players feature clear centre-periphery structures, in other words, they are ultimately national companies that operate internationally (Pries 2008a, p. 186). However, at the same time a flattening process is taking place in such a way that more and more countries are rising economically and dialogic cooperation can be established even between countries usually considered "culturally distant" (Harrison 2010, pp. 34f., 221f.). Internal economic communication in global companies may therefore be limited spatially and hierarchically by capital structures. But such communication is in principle possible on a transnational and transcultural basis. A strong foundation for dialogic communication tends to emerge when actors from different countries are united under one corporate umbrella, while neither being controlled centrally nor acting in an overly decentralized way, but instead – much as in diplomacy, though

Economy: global corporate communication **109**

on a permanent basis and comparable to the concept of global governance – creating a kind of "third space" for cross-border communication.

In all other fields of the economy, the structures are less conducive to dialogic communication. Trade is dominated by the pure exchange of goods. Cross-border services are rarer (ibid., p. 119), but where they do exist, they too provide opportunities for dialogic communication, albeit in diluted form, since this is external communication with customers or markets, so-called "business-to-customer transactions" (B2C). Here there is no prospect of an equal, sustained dialogue of the kind found within transnational companies due to the strategic communicative goals that predominate (see p. 128ff.). In the field of direct investment, ethnocentric companies establish supply chains, which, however, usually represent a pragmatic if not imposed form of border-crossing, since here the supplier industry is transferred to so-called "low-wage countries", but the company's core productive competence remains in the home country. These are poor conditions for genuine dialogues, since the command centres are located in the country of origin of the manufacturing process and the only topics up for negotiation lie outside the core competences. The cross-border transfer of knowledge is viewed as a risk factor when it comes to production chains (Dhar 2008, p. 301f.). Only slowly is the strictly hierarchical relationship between parent companies and foreign companies giving way to heterarchical relationships, even in the case of supply chains (Schmid et al. 1999, p. 101). In the discipline of economics there are now bitter opponents of classic hierarchical thinking about supply chains, who view it as a "classic control fixation" and a waste of opportunities for economic cooperation. This model, they assert, is being ousted by equitable networks (Johnsen et al. 2008, p. 74f.), though the existence of networks in companies or, if several companies are involved, in joint ventures, is not in itself a guarantee of dialogic interaction, as we will see later on.

Polycentric companies are multinational in construction, that is, they have decentralized decision-making structures or, as is often the case, they experiment with a combination of centralized, decentralized and transnationally networked organizational forms (Conrad and Poole 2012, p. 436). Transnational approaches are thus often found in innovation and research departments, making them interesting examples of cross-border dialogic action. In geocentric or transnational companies, this *modus operandi* is significant to the entire business, which is why they have been identified as "key actors in the globalization process" and in the "information society" (Steffans 2000, p. 9). The scholarship now highlights joint ventures and strategic alliances as organizational forms with a particularly high potential for cooperation (Franke 2010, p. 32).

Essentially, every global type of company has more or less interesting potential for internal and external communication across borders. For a communication studies analysis, the challenge is to determine, in each individual case, how much space for dialogic interaction there really is in the global players. The mere spatial expansion of action or conglomerates' degree of internationalization as determined by capital turnover (Bannenberg 2011, p. 142) tells us nothing about their power structures or

110 Economy: global corporate communication

resource structures, which are in turn important to communicative processes. The widespread general assumption of an increasingly intertwined global economy and thus ever more interwoven forms of international communication (Harrison 2010, p. 44) fails to consider the variable consequences of global enterprises' very different structural patterns for the quality and quantity of internal economic communication. In essence, then, the degree of internationalization is never measured by the marker of global communication, but by sales figures.

Technological gaps and cosmopolitan lifeworld capital

In addition to companies' power structures, from a systems-theoretical point of view, technological, human and sociopolitical structures are important. For global companies, possession and mastery of media technology are an especially crucial structural requirement for global business communication. Many commentators consider technological development a driving force of globalization and just as important as global market trends themselves (ibid., p. 37). Despite a general improvement in the communication infrastructure, there is still a major "digital divide" across the world (see Chapter 5, Section 5.2.2). By 2000, as part of its Millennium Development Goals, the United Nations Conference on Trade and Development (UNCTAD) was already calling for improved access to information and communication technology for developing countries, chiefly in order to bolster the development of the digital economy (UNCTAD 2000; see also CSIS 1998). There are also differences in competence in the companies of the industrialized world, with small firms often being more dynamic here than large corporations. The rapid development of technology in isolated pockets exists in developing countries as well. We need only think of India's "Silicon Valley" in Bangalore.

Labour migration is another structural factor of importance to the global economy in the field of human capital. The different organizational structures of global companies, meanwhile, find reflection in the research on elites. Most "business elites" are characterized by a disjuncture between their international working world and national way of life. While people may work outside their home countries, they rarely marry abroad and even more rarely outside their own ethnocultural group of origin: a cosmopolitan lifestyle and attitude towards life are not an inevitable consequence of working in an international company (Weiß 2017, p. 91ff.; see also Hartmann 2016). Such findings are especially important when it comes to the question of informal communication. They signify further complication of the structural, actor-related conditions of communication, since in addition to the organizational and power structures described above, group and individual structures must be considered as well, and they may even interact. In the company itself, a transnational organizational structure may come to grief due to ethnocentric management attitudes, which affect informal communication in particular. But the benefits of global work communication may also resonate in a positive way with employees' lifeworlds (see Chapters 7 and 8). The risk is that professional role boundaries will keep these worlds apart.

Economy: global corporate communication **111**

A critique of essentialism in the discipline of economics

A final significant structural variable is the sociopolitical competence of a global company or business venture. This competence is part of a company's human capital, but at the same time it is an independent factor because the direct exchange between the economy and its environment – organized environmental systems (media, politics, and so on) and dispersed systemic environments (markets, public opinion, and so on) – plays a role that can only be managed if the internal structures of a company are suited to the task. Thus, here too we not only have to understand the observation of the environment and external communication as communicative processes, but also recognize the importance of structural prerequisites if there is to be efficient communication with political systems and other so-called "stakeholders". Global economic action increases the complexity of informational environments and requires more effective management of global knowledge.

In the economic literature, the theme of "culture" as a structural factor clearly dominates in this regard. "Foreign" cultural environments with different values supposedly compel economic actors to adapt and learn. Most widely read and frequently quoted here is the work of management researcher Geert Hofstede and his colleagues (see, for example, Hofstede et al. 2010; see also Clausen 2006; Bertelsmann Stiftung 2007; Humpf 2008; Keup 2010). Hofstede's dimensions of cultural difference (power distance, individuality/collectivism, masculinity/femininity, avoidance of uncertainty, long-/short-term orientation, domination/compliance) have undoubtedly caught on, for example, in the theory of intercultural organizational communication. As Lisbeth Clausen puts it: "When colleagues speak another language and come from a different cultural background, communicating becomes considerably more difficult" (2006, p. 45). However, there are those who oppose this essentialist view, treating national cultures as structural elements of the economy and placing them on the same level as other structural variables such as power, capital, technology and human capital. Jürgen Bolten, for example, regards it as one of the greatest contradictions in intercultural economic communication that, despite general academic awareness of the "factual complexity of supposedly homogeneous constructs", in economic writings, reference is often still made to "the self-contained variants of the expanded concept of culture" (Bolten 2007, p. 48; see also Cambié and Ooi 2009, p. 69; Pal and Dutta 2008; Conrad and Poole 2012, p. 424). Cynthia Stohl calls this type of research "parochial" and disputes the idea that entire societies can be distinguished by certain values that influence communication (2001). Stohl criticizes the empirical basis of such studies, which often generalize specific phenomena arising from a single company study. Karen Lee Ashcraft and Brenda J. Allen go so far as to describe this research as subliminally racist, because it works with categories such as race and cultural difference (2003).

In any case, the hypertrophied essentialism of much of the discipline of economics is highly contested in the modern field of cultural studies. Actors in other countries are equated with whole "cultures" and cultures are viewed as monolithic rather than as consisting of sub-cultures, social milieus, and so on. In reality,

112 Economy: global corporate communication

however, it is not "culture" that is a structure of global economic action, but at most certain references to culture within a specific workforce. Furthermore, "culture" is constructed communicatively in the first place, especially in transnational companies (see p. 114ff.).

The ethical unpredictability of global capitalism

Just as it is wrong to assume that a "cultural structure" is automatically transferred to the global enterprise, the reverse is also true. In the next few chapters, we will continue to grapple with the fact that while a dialogic corporate culture may form a kind of nucleus of a global community, companies' transnational internal structures do not necessarily transfer to the social environment because the economy, much like politics, features egocentric interests that can create new external borders. At bottom, the economy is not even a uniform system, but consists of nothing but autonomous sub-systems that are only interconnected by the logic of the market and the legal framework of politics. Like politics, which constantly endangers the global community by relapsing into nationalism, the globalization of the economy is often fatally undermined by the tension between the capitalist interests of commercial enterprises and the needs of a global community.

The capitalist privatization of communication does extend the space of global action and thus also that of global communication. But this extension is precarious. Global companies withdraw from countries in an almost haphazard fashion, yet often they adapt to local conditions unconditionally. Frequently, then, their transnational structures are not enduring or, if they are, have no social depth. Cultural essentialism actually provides global companies with a kind of moral room for manoeuvre that enables them to circumvent universal ethics and to counteract at any time vis-à-vis the rest of the world the transnationalization that is required internally, as we will see over the course of this chapter. Here, much as in politics, for structural reasons the cosmopolitan global community becomes a minor feature in a broader capitalist narrative of the world economy. The repeated setbacks to globalization as a result of nationalism, racism and protectionism can be explained in part through the systemic properties of the leading global system of the "economy", which easily crosses borders but acts in an ethically unpredictable way.

4.2 Communicative system connections

Due to modern media technology and the increase in human mobility, when it comes to the basic modes of communication – interaction, observation and discourse – at first glance, spatial distance appears to be ever less important (Cheney et al. 2011, p. 364f.). In earlier decades, the transmission of important documents in an international business context often took weeks. International trading companies functioned largely independently. Today, joint economic action across borders in real time is theoretically possible, but in practice it is limited. Further, improved means of observing and analysing distant realities (including digital technology)

Economy: global corporate communication **113**

intensify the asymmetries that typify the global knowledge society and its global informational elites. External communication still often lacks a cosmopolitan marketing approach. Whether this is ultimately fostering a shift, as Michael Giesecke contends, from observational and monologic to interactive and dialogic global communication (see Chapter 1, Section 1.1) and, we might add, whether the integration of the global community is bolstered by economic communication, are the focus of this section.

4.2.1 Interaction and dialogue

New dialogic action and negotiation in global enterprises

Global (virtual) teams in global business enterprises, which have often been described in the economic literature, seem to be something of a blueprint for the transnational communitization of the world. They give rise to a group dynamic across national borders based on a high level of interaction, a "third space", a "third culture" and a truly international community in miniature. However, precise descriptions of the interaction processes in global companies are in strikingly short supply in the scholarly literature, in sharp contrast to the study of politics, in which diplomatic communication is a subject in its own right. The call from German communication studies scholars in the 1990s for a greater orientation towards dialogue in the business world shows at least a sporadic interest in communicative action in economic life (Bentele et al. 1996). It is worth noting that Bertelsmann, a global company, carried out a study on "corporate cultures in global interaction" (Bertelsmann Stiftung 2007). This was at a time of failed mergers between Bertelsmann and AOL Time Warner and between Daimler and Chrysler. Bertelsmann's self-contemplation, which is based on an extensive empirical survey of global management, is sobering. According to the authors, multiculturalism increases value conflicts in global companies. The guiding values of the German parent company cannot be sufficiently enforced, though communication is not understood here as "interaction" and dialogue, but as strategic communication intended to "transfer basic values to the global company as smoothly as possible", "successfully influence foreign social and cultural forms" and prevent "divergent or ambiguous local interpretations" (ibid., pp. 173, 264, 271). This credo, which borders on cultural imperialism, raises the suspicion that dialogic interaction in an *ethnocentric* global enterprise (see Section 4.1) is of no fundamental significance.

But in order to avoid approaching this topic either too idealistically or too pessimistically, the priority must be to systematically locate interaction within the framework of organizational communication. Drawing on the work of Manfred Rühl (see Chapter 1, Sections 1.2 and 1.3), within an organization we can differentiate between goal-oriented programming (on the part of the owner or boss), conditional programming (routine actions, experiential knowledge) and social renegotiations (1979, 1980). This classification is still in use today, with slight deviations, for the analysis of transnational organizations (see, for example, Klemm

114 Economy: global corporate communication

and Popp 2006, p. 203). While the first level operates monologically (top-down), in the event of disturbances to a routine, social renegotiations are necessary and serve to increase a system's processing complexity. The dilemma thrown up by the clash between the will to hierarchy and the need for interaction, a dilemma inherent in all organized social systems, cannot be straightforwardly resolved even in global companies. Ethnocentric companies can make no headway on this issue, as we have seen. But it is intrinsic to geocentrically or transnationally organized companies that they allocate more space for dialogic interaction.

In principle, we could leave it at that, because the precepts of the Harvard concept of negotiation communication (see Chapter 3, Section 3.2) must be understood as universal rules that were designed not least for the field of business. Leading manuals of international management emphasize the need to keep general interests and concrete policy positions apart and to reach agreements through separate or integrated agendas (single or multiple issue management), and so on (Holtom 2009). Antje Hellmann-Grobe's four-stage model of the process of understanding in dialogues – which basically revolves around the clarification of interests, topics, content and options for action – as well as her reference to the ambivalent role of the media-based public sphere, which can stimulate negotiations but may intervene in a disruptive manner as well, also chime with the accepted standards of successful negotiation (2000, p. 270ff.). Global business communication even provides for methods of moderation (ibid., p. 234ff.). Hence, we might make do with stating that global communality arises in global companies when power relationships allow this to happen and negotiation processes are successful.

But the innovative aspect of Hellmann-Grobe's work is her call for recognition of the growing importance of dialogues within globalization: the international reorientation of the economy appears to necessitate altered worldviews (ibid., p. 75ff.). She refers to processes of "dissolution" triggered by the new social risks arising from the decoupling of economic activity from its consequences. She also highlights changing notions of work in the post-Fordist knowledge society and the disappearance of familiar worldviews as economic hegemony is challenged (ibid., p. 75f.). Hellmann-Grobe considers the dialogic search for new narratives in global companies essential because the search for the commonalities of "cultures" within a new business ethics is engendering an "orientation [towards a global] community" (ibid., pp. 82, 120, 130).

Corporate culture and global storytelling

It soon becomes clear that the "dissolution of the various system logics in favour of an orientation towards society as a whole" (ibid., p. 164) for which Hellmann-Grobe calls – within a global framework, no less – is highly normative. Furthermore, at least implicitly this vision presupposes a socially just rather than neoliberal conception of economics. Despite its allure, this does not seem immediately realistic in the face of selfish economic interests. In any event, the key question that must be answered is to what extent transnational, dialogic corporate narratives can arise

Economy: global corporate communication **115**

in global enterprises even under capitalist conditions, narratives of relevance to the principle of global communality, as set out in our theoretical introduction in Chapter 1. Theoretically speaking, this is only the case if, basing ourselves loosely on the Harvard concept, a win–win situation can be crafted onto the foundation of deeper interest structures. Significantly, the economic literature has discovered the subject of "storytelling" and "narrative", which shows that Hellmann-Grobe's conception is a necessity rather than just idealism. A "corporate culture" is a narrative, if, with Rühl, we understand it as a company's conditional programme, which is influenced by the owners' goal-oriented programming but is not identical with it, instead seeking to harness the experiential values within a company (conditional programming). These experiential values must, however, be created anew when companies expand internationally. The corporate narrative works like an unwritten code, which – ideally – reflects the sum of all the owners' targets and the company's social micro-negotiations and is passed on through socialization within the firm. This phenomenon, also known as "loose coupling", has been shown to exist, for example, in the American police force, when, to some extent contrary to its legal mandate, it acts on the basis of motives such as "centrality of [its] authority and responsibility" or "preservation of police autonomy within the political and legal system" (Manning 1992, p. 127, see also p. 77ff.). The fact that writing often plays less of a role here than informal network communication (see p. 119f.) is also the reason why the corporate culture – often referred to as the "company climate" – should be understood mostly as an interactive rather than a discursive event. The company climate has to be experienced and cannot be read or observed.

To this day, we can identify three main types of community-oriented corporate narratives and stories in the global economic context:

- *Anti-racist narratives*, according to which, stereotypes and prejudices are being broken down through communication in global enterprises (Sooknanan 2011).
- *Diversity narratives*, namely the so-called "managing diversity" concept, according to which – based on the principle of cultural difference criticized above – employees have a range of attitudes, but these should be tolerated and recognized (Barker and Gower 2010).
- *Cosmopolitan narratives* asserting that the goal should be neither merely to ward off negative views nor to moderate differences but rather to facilitate a genuine transcultural and transnational form of integration. According to Silvia Cambié and Yang-May Ooi:

> We are moving beyond the paternalistic international communication methods of the past towards a more integrated vision of employee engagement … Encourage employees from different cultural backgrounds to share their knowledge and experience. Introduce processes able to convert this exchange into an integral component of the company's decision-making.
>
> *(2009, p. 82f.)*

116 Economy: global corporate communication

A global corporate culture may certainly be stronger than one limited to its employees' original environments (Varner 2000, p. 46). There are, however, very few relevant empirical studies and those that are available are based solely on textual analyses, of letters from company management to shareholders, for example. This type of research shows that large corporations are still clearly orienting themselves towards local cultural ideas, so that "corporations cannot be expected to resolve the semantic vacuum (at both the analytical and normative level) masked by the term 'globalization'" (Halff 2009, p. 159). We need only think of Apple, which was initially critical of the (racist) Trump administration, but soon bowed to its protectionist economic policies despite its production focus in East Asia. In such cases, global corporate cultures turn out to be unstable "non-identities" not rooted in any substantive intercultural vision (Bolten 2007, p. 99). Critics have increasingly complained that far too little attention has been paid to the connection between the failure of international business cooperation and corporate culture (Franke 2010, p. 8ff.). Particularly in the case of the cross-border fusion of systems to create "third spaces", an overemphasis on considerations of economic utility tends to go hand in hand with a lack of unifying values and attitudes. From a communication studies point of view, this means a lack of "trust", which can ultimately arise only through experiences of interaction.

Of "chains" and "stars": network structures as communicative channels

If, after considering the level of goal-oriented and conditional programming, we turn again to the level of social negotiations in a company, we find that it is not just the basic rules of dialogic communication that matter here, but also their channels. The fact that the economy is not a uniform system but acts in a decentralized manner and consists of a variety of organizations that are held together only by extremely tenuous frameworks (politics, market) has a massive impact on communication. While diplomacy – at least outside of the more recent multi-track diplomacy – features regulated institutional channels of communication, in a global context the economy communicates through the global networks much discussed in the literature. Companies communicate with constantly changing partner firms and customers, buying and selling – a shimmering wickerwork. Global business communication is therefore not just a matter of power structures and corporate cultures: the issue of communication channels – who is communicating with whom? – is of special importance. In other words, in addition to the attributes of the entity sending the messages (company structure) or the message itself (corporate narrative), the type of communication channels or networks that exist within and between companies is always crucially important as well.

Networks in global companies and ventures can develop their own dynamics and in the best-case scenario generate a new transnational communality. Network theory is thus a useful addition to a theory of communication based on systems theory. In the field of corporate communication, a distinction is made between different types of production network, such as the "star structure", the "chain

Economy: global corporate communication   **117**

structure", the "Y structure", the "circular structure" and the "full structure" (Mast 2013, p. 190ff.). Typically, most networks feature specific central decision-makers, as in the star or chain structure, which correspond to the outsourcing of aspects of production within global "production chains" (Johnsen et al. 2008). Not all parts of the network collective are connected in these networks. Instead, individual members each assume a bridging function – special departments with international contacts – which leads to a communicative situation based on a division of labour. In the Marxist tradition, this may be viewed as an indication of the fundamental "alienation" of labour since network members often lack an overview of all contacts, which means that globalization effects cannot reach every part of the network. At the other end of the spectrum, we find the only fully interactive network, the full structure network, where all parts of the network are interactively connected to one another. This formation too can be found in global economic communication, namely when global work teams are formed (see also virtual teams, discussed on p. 123). Global teams are not "loose couplings" as found in corporate culture, but rather "tight couplings" of direct interaction, which – devoid of power imbalances, no less – can be considered dialogues and thus, so the theory goes, generate communality.

Global teams as reconfigured global communities

Chain networks can also develop communality, but this is usually limited to a small number of people, mostly so-called "fast subjects", that is, expatriate or globally mobile managers who maintain a company's global contacts on its behalf (Plattner 2010). Communality in these types of networks remains tightly limited in terms of personnel and thus fleeting and episodic with respect to companies as a whole. As we know from social psychology, contacts with individual so-called "others" or people with experience of the other are treated as exceptional, with stereotypical ideas about "foreign cultures" remaining intact. Hence, if they are to change images of the other, contact experiences must be of high quantity, quality and sustainability (Pettigrew 1998). Here the global team is best equipped to form a new, transnational group culture. Teams are certainly embedded in firms' power structures and corporate cultures, but a number of authors have also identified them as communities in which a shared identity may be formed through trust (Schmidt et al. 2007, p. 130).

Kenwyn Smith and David Berg have described the processes in intercultural groups as a matter of shifting boundaries, featuring the fusion of old (national) company structures with (transnational) subsystems and the emergence of new external group borders as well as altered identities and communities. Crucially, alongside collective product analysis, these novel communities may create a new awareness of growing global political and social interdependence (1997, pp. 10, 13; see also our remarks on informal communication on p. 119f.). From a communication studies perspective, then, here a *reframing* of cultural perception occurs against the background of the shared basic interests of the working group. In such cases,

118 Economy: global corporate communication

globally operating corporate teams do in fact function as the nucleus of a global communality established through interaction.

Is the network the global message?

But the existence of a network in itself tells us nothing about its communicative quality. It is true that global networks emerge when the traditional national organization no longer provides an adequate framework for economic action (Holton 2008, p. 32). New networks may furnish opportunities for new global dialogues. But networks are not structureless. Manuel Castells, one of the pioneers of global network theory, refers sweepingly in this context to "horizontal corporations" and to a "crisis of the vertical model of the corporation", identifying a general shift in power from corporate headquarters to global networks (2010, vol. 1, 176ff.). However, if we take a closer look at network structures, we find that star networks are likely to predominate in ethnocentric corporate structures, so it is wrong to suggest that the vertical corporation is beset by crisis. Some of today's networks are in fact only spatial extensions of fairly hierarchical corporate power structures. Most global firms, as we have established, are not ideal transnational corporations, which means that the networks through which they communicate are also greatly influenced by strategic communicative objectives and the scope of dialogues is severely limited. Only where chain networks or even full structure networks form is there any prospect of the emergence of new communities. Put simply, all other networks are command networks. There are no grounds here for idealizing global networks with a view to horizontal transnational interactivity, let alone global communality.

Ultimately, Castells probably recognized this himself. After all, he underlined that he meant his analysis of a shift in importance from (vertical) systems to (horizontal) networks to be understood as a "hypothesis" (2010, vol. 1, p. 208). At most, however, we have empirical evidence of the proliferation of global networks, but not of the dominance of full structure networks, greater dialogic quality or an increase in transnational ethics, all of which would be crucial to genuine "horizontal" global companies. Networks are significant components of the meso-history of globalization, that is, of an expanded theory of institutions. The theoretical weakness of network analysis, however, is that in and of itself it tells us virtually nothing about the interactive quality of the exchange of messages. Network theory alone, then, cannot ascertain the quality of dialogue or illuminate the extent of community building.

Strikingly, Castells himself expresses pessimism about the potential for a new (global) ethics to emerge through networks:

> [T]he networking form of organization must have a cultural dimension of its own. Otherwise economic activity would be performed in a social/cultural vacuum ... It is certainly not a new culture, in the traditional sense of a system of values, because the multiplicity of subjects in the network and the diversity of networks reject such a unifying 'network culture'.
>
> *(ibid., vol. 1, p. 214)*

Instead, Castells believes there is a unifying code underlying the diversity of ethics and projects, though for him all this means is that those individuals active in networks across the world develop a similar habitus centred on wellness, fitness and the laptop (ibid., vol. 1, p. 447).

Anyone in search of a global community will be reminded at this point of Bassam Tibi's "semi-modernity" (1995): in material modernity, people live in a similar way all over the world, and they may even be globally networked. However, they are not necessarily embedded in multicultural full structure networks, while their ability to develop a global community and an ethical understanding of the other's political, social and cultural contexts and interpretations is often limited. For Castells, the network *itself* is the message – teams, dialogues and ethics play no role in his analysis. Critics of the network approach have therefore rightly highlighted the almost arbitrary use of the term, which thus loses its analytical acuity (Holton 2008, p. 37). They note a lack of micro-analyses going beyond the identification of "pipeline structures", "fluidity densities" and "storage capacities" and they call for greater attention to be paid to the social processes in networks and the systems connected by them (Becker-Ritterspach 2006, pp. 157, 160).

The dimensions of global economic interaction

To strike a rather less pessimistic note than Castells, however, basing ourselves on the authors cited above such as Wallace V. Schmidt, Roger N. Conaway, Susan S. Easton and William J. Wardrope, and Kenwyn Smith and David Berg, we can state that global, community-building dialogues are conceivable in global companies if facilitated by (1) power asymmetries (goal-oriented programmes); (2) corporate cultures (conditional programmes); (3) network structures; and (4) negotiation processes (social negotiations). To conclude, Figure 4.1 clarifies these different dimensions of economic interaction. Empirical evidence of dialogic interaction must be provided in each case.

4.2.2 Interaction and organizational communication

Informality as a research desideratum

After this initial run through the interactive basics of global corporate communication, we now seek to gain a more precise picture with the help of the criteria of formality, informality, textuality and mediatization, as identified in our theoretical introduction in Chapter 1. As far as formality and informality are concerned, a professional relationship is not necessarily a community in the spirit of global society, because different roles are involved. A person from any country in Europe, Asia, Africa or Latin America may work for a US company and still be anti-American. We can only refer to complete interactive communitization if individuals' private actions and attitudes match the patterns of global interaction within the framework of their networks and contacts. At the moment, it is not possible to

120 Economy: global corporate communication

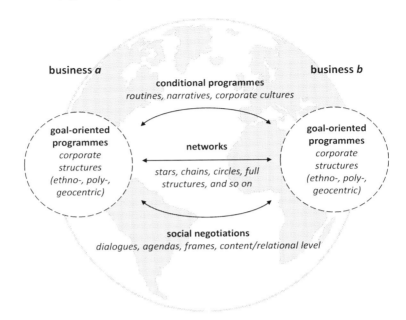

FIGURE 4.1 Dimensions of global economic interaction in transnational companies

precisely quantify the importance of informal communication, though we must assume, with Martin K. Welge, that a large portion of global communication in companies today functions via informal networks (1999, p. 14). However, his concept of informality is considerably broader, including all actions outside official meetings, in other words many of the actions initiated by employees themselves in everyday working life, even when these are not related to private aspects of interaction (ibid., p. 8).

Virtually no research has been carried out as yet on informality in the sense of an influence that professional contacts have on private worldviews. Strictly speaking, the creation (as intimated by Smith and Berg) of a sense of community in global teams that includes social and political aspects would be a matter of informal communication, since this process is not central to economic tasks. The management literature has examined the positive and negative effects of informal communication on formal work processes. But the social and political significance of the informal relational level is seldom reflected upon. What societal and private topics do employees from different countries discuss? How do transnational communities arise and what role do they play in cosmopolitan awareness? Scant research has been done on this, which has to do with the fixation on production in the economic literature, the difficulty involved in defining the subject, but also with methodological problems. Informal communication is difficult to analyse. The observing researcher tends to disturb or destroy the very situation they wish to investigate.

Oral communication and global language skills

If we turn to the text–speech relationship, we find that almost all the process elements of interaction in global companies that we have considered so far – corporate cultures, (informal) networks and chain or team dialogues – are based to a large extent on experiential knowledge, which is itself passed on orally. Although the economy cannot do without the well-known one-text process (see Chapter 3, Section 3.2.2), contracts, unlike in politics, are often not the result of but rather the prerequisite for global networking. Here we can discern the shift from diplomatic external communication to global economic internal communication (in transnational companies). However, neither contracts nor other types of text such as the minutes of meetings document the informal aspects of interaction that are important to community building. In contrast to politics, while global corporate communication is *internal* organizational communication, the interaction does not focus on political and social relationships between countries. Instead, it foregrounds material goods, so that global relationships play no role in business texts. They are at most discussed orally and informally (see p. 119f.). This is the origin of the odd fact that the ostensibly lead system of globalization, the economy, is in some respects based on older modes of communication than other social systems, namely oral modes, an issue that will be coming up again later in connection with observation and the diffusion of knowledge (see p. 124ff.).

However, in the economy, despite the great importance of oral communication, there is no guarantee of a universal lingua franca. While diplomats learn one as part of their profession or can use interpreters, language comprehension is largely unregulated and is usually acquired by employees on a self-taught basis. The main lingua franca in global business relations is English, which may entail a "loss of importance for the mother tongue of everyone outside the English-speaking world" (Walter 2002, p. 31), although transnational regionalization processes continue to ensure that other major languages such as Spanish, Arabic, and so on are hugely significant. As we shall see, the Internet is in any case undergoing a shift away from the exclusive use of English towards a multilingualism made up of large regional languages (see Chapter 6, Section 6.2.1). But as yet little research has been done on the influence of foreign language skills in global companies on production processes and informal aspects of community building.

Mediatization of global economic communication

Things look different when it comes to mediatized interpersonal communication, which has received enormous attention from researchers. Castells has already described the "informational economy" as the basis of the new global network economy. In his definition, the new information and communication technologies transform "signals into commodities by processing knowledge" (2010, vol. 1, p. 188). This shows once again that Castells is no communication studies scholar, as this general definition would also apply to oral interaction in business life, in

122 Economy: global corporate communication

other words, it is not a distinguishing feature of mediatized communication. What distinguishes mediatized from non-mediatized global communication are in fact features such as the following.

- *Textuality*: Much of global long-distance communication is based on written text.
- *Asynchrony*: Unlike face-to-face communication, mediatized interpersonal communication may also be asynchronous (time-delayed) (via written text such as e-mails but also conversations on messenger services such as WhatsApp), which influences the pace and content of the conversation.
- *Intensity of interaction*: Even synchronous processes, such as Skype or Zoom conversations, reduce the intensity of interaction in comparison to direct face-to-face communication, often failing to convey communicative signs of a non-verbal (gestures and facial expressions) and paraverbal nature (vocal pitch, volume, intonation, speaking tempo, speech melody).

Much as in the famous concept of the "virtual community" expounded by Howard Rheingold (2000, see Chapter 6, Section 6.1), global virtual teams may give rise to a "third culture", a further development and synthesis of existing national corporate cultures, especially when internal hierarchies are participatory and permit this (Pan and Leidner 2003; Cheney et al. 2011, p. 381ff.; Zajac 2013, p. 69). But what is the influence of mediatization here?

At the content level, technology-based written communication reduces comprehension problems due to incorrect pronunciation in foreign languages. However, it increases the scope for interpretation of what is said in comparison to face-to-face communication (see p. 123), since interpretations of text cannot be directly reconciled in asynchronous mail exchanges (Grebenstein et al. 2003, p. 136ff.). This is why, in complex situations, synchronous interaction and high mobility of employees for the purpose of direct face-to-face communication are still the order of the day in global companies. In addition, informality in asynchronous mediatized communication (such as e-mails) in global companies is only possible in highly attenuated form, for example, through salutations ("Hi"), the use of informal and formal terms for "you" in certain languages and the use of people's names. Asynchronous communication in the commercial sector cannot do without "human" elements, but it is too limited to generate communality (Zając 2013, p. 169ff.; see also Kruger et al. 2005).

It may be possible to signal forms of habitus, as in Castells's idea of the code typical of the global business elite (captured by phrases such as "nice wellness facilities around here"). But an exchange of differentiated social, political or lifeworld-related messages is unlikely to occur at the informal content level through written long-distance communication, which leaves the level of relations between individuals unresolved. Overall, then, a comprehensive, informality-based notion of a global community is rarely expressed in written form. The text tends to serve the creative

Economy: global corporate communication **123**

stabilization of formal communication. It certainly allows for some work-related informal communication but cannot function as a platform for private, let alone "secret" aspects of informal communication, which are key to the establishment of full-blooded communality.

Face-to-face communication in global virtual teams

In addition to asynchronous e-mails, there are also synchronous forms of communication such as the telephone, Internet telephony, video conferences or mixed forms such as intranet chats, discussion forums and in-house wikis (Cheney et al. 2011, p. 365ff.). The media richness in global companies is tremendous, which in principle enriches interactive relationships. The turn of the twenty-first century can certainly be characterized as heralding a shift from asynchronous to synchronous interaction in companies. After the era of letters, telegrams and telexes, with the advent of instant messaging, video conferences, team chats and mixed forms of these applications, the idea of "the death of distance" has finally established itself (Cairncross 2001; see also Tapscott 1996). It is interesting, however, that with regard to global virtual teams in particular, a rather cautious approach seems to have taken hold. The idea here is that direct face-to-face communication should occur at least occasionally and, if possible, at the beginning of team formation, as only such meetings provide the basis for a human interactive intensity capable of generating a sense of community (Pries 2008a, p. 50; Gronwald 2017, p. 70ff.). The emergence of a new corporate culture and team spirit is often based on informal observations and dialogues, all of which are part of a non-codified experiential knowledge in companies (Kraemer et al. 2008, p. 105). Hans Geser has good reason for assigning mobile communication a subversive role with regard to location-based social systems, since only the "no-techno world of location-based communications" allows "the creation of a discontinuously limited internal context within which system-specific behavioural expectations and rules of interpretation apply" (2005, p. 51).

Ultimately, the question is whether a global "third space" with its own external borders of communality can be created through mediatized communication alone. Today's management literature recommends occasional face-to-face off-line encounters as accompaniments to the widespread digitization of business interactions. Team conflicts in particular are likely to be easier to moderate here than in the digital world. The fact that face-to-face communication also harbours risks (personal antipathies) is usually offset by the richness of team relationships. The interaction between formal and informal communication is important. The loss of informal contexts through asynchronous digital communication or, in the case of synchronous communication, the non- and paraverbal aspects of informal communication, may disrupt the interpersonal relationship level, which may in turn lead to informational reticence at the content level (Amant 2012, p. 82). Virtual global teams can be insidiously limited and excessive virtuality may well be the reason for the failure of global projects.

124 Economy: global corporate communication

"Global cities" rather than "the death of distance"

Since global Internet transmission rates are constantly increasing, especially in the field of corporate communication (Hafez 2014b, p. 648ff.), yet the synchronization of spatial and temporal differences is difficult, while oral communication and informality seem just as important in business communication today as in the past, it is much too early to refer to "the death of distance". Virtual asynchronous and synchronous global communication, which surely make up most of the interaction in global companies in quantitative terms, are more like stuttering than fluid dialogue. They even harbour new risks, as neither complex content-related, let alone informal community-building aspects of communication are automatic concomitants of globalization, which means that opportunities and risks must be weighed up against this background as well (Goodman and Hirsch 2015, p. 6) and there is a need for a new awareness of the "relative benefits of digital and social networks" (Kraemer et al. 2008, p. 94f.). This also explains the new appeal of the concept of "global cities" and a dense regional network of companies. Both have come back into fashion despite all the advances in mediatization and are now considered key nodes of global economic interaction alongside global corporations (Fuchs et al. 1999; Castells 2010, vol. 1, pp. 409ff., 429ff.). In addition to interaction, such regional clusters also facilitate observational communication, to which we now turn.

4.2.3 Observation and diffusion

Economic knowledge gaps

For the global economy, it is not only the interaction in and between cooperating companies that is important, but also the understanding and the learning by observation that are crucial to innovation in firms. Observational communication is part of the spectrum of monologic communication. Since observation and analysis initially remain in the economic system (and in its networks), they are not freely accessible to the public. At most, there is a professional public discourse (such as specialist literature and trade fairs), though here too companies' observational analysis remains concealed from the general public.

However, if the economic system wants to acquire the global knowledge vital to its global action, due to its decentralized organization it must constantly try to expand its feats of observation beyond the boundaries of the company. As we will soon see, however, this does not automatically mean that the company will act more openly than the political system, which systematically hides much of its internal communication from the public. The classification of documents in politics corresponds to the protection of "trade secrets" in business. The economic system is based on knowledge gaps.

Global knowledge diffusion and local adaptation

Observational communication – like interaction – facilitates qualification and knowledge acquisition as a prerequisite for every rational internal interaction in

Economy: global corporate communication **125**

the company. So-called knowledge diffusion for the purpose of innovation is of central importance to the company here because knowledge can never arise solely from inside a system but requires complex environmental processing. Observation is not innovation itself, but targeted imitative action is key to avoiding unpredictable risk investments and to positive corporate development (Nicolai and Halberstadt 2008, p. 271). Contemplation of the global diffusion of knowledge through media quickly became part of the core of communication studies, as in Daniel Lerner's modernization theory (1967), which is geared towards radio and television.

Probably the best-known text in general research on diffusion is *Diffusion of Innovations* by Everett Rogers. Some of its basic categories are still standard today, as follows:

- *Actors of diffusion*: innovators, early adopters, early majority, late majority and laggards (2003, p. 22);
- *Stages of diffusion*: knowledge (becoming aware of an innovation), persuasion (shaping opinion for or against the innovation), decision (act of adoption or rejection), implementation (introducing the innovation) and confirmation (continuing or abandoning implementation) (ibid., p. 169).

Of course, economic enterprises are more complex in that their gatekeeping processes do not depend only on individuals but are negotiated collectively in the organization and its networks, although the overall process features the stages described above. It is interesting to note Rogers's statement that international channels are more important at the knowledge stage than at the later acquisition and implementation stages, when local actors and processes become more important (ibid., p. 207). In a somewhat different way, Castells assumes a global dependency on innovative milieus, chiefly a network of innovation centres (such as Silicon Valley, London, and so on). This makes the concept of local space (especially global cities) even more important in his work than in that of Rogers because it is key to innovation *and* adaptation (2010, vol. 1, p. 419ff.).

Limits to global circulation and global observation

The global diffusion of knowledge may also be thought of as a process of circulation between different innovation centres, though it is always possible for such diffusion to be locally limited (Mayrhofer and Iellatchitch 2005). Unlike innovation or adaptation that remains in the local area, the global circulation of knowledge is in line with the synchronization of global knowledge inherent in our theoretical model. In reality, however, we must assume that local innovation and adaptation constantly generate new variants of knowledge that do not circulate perfectly, giving rise to global imbalances. The limits of the intercultural observation of the world (according to Giesecke 2002; see Chapter 1, Section 1.1) are thus evident not only in the field of interactive community-based communication, but also in the

126 Economy: global corporate communication

always deficient diffusion or circulation of knowledge, not just in the mass media but in the economy as well.

The reasons for these failures of diffusion certainly include competence problems, for example, when it comes to foreign language skills, but also a lack of discursive competencies, that is, an organization's ability to find new, relevant knowledge outside of familiar contexts (Kalkan 2008, p. 393; Nicolai and Halberstadt 2008, p. 279). Particularly competent individuals and institutions in this regard are referred to by scholars as global knowledge brokers or global knowledge gatekeepers. In addition to trade fairs, the most important elements in the global diffusion process are specialist publications utilized by global knowledge brokers (citation ties) (Spencer 2003). "Global cities" and other regional innovation clusters are important because they increase a company's interactional and observational intensity and reduce its dependence on specialized knowledge elites (at universities, for example). However, disastrous routines may arise in local contexts, causing companies to fall behind in the world market, which is why here too globally circulating knowledge is required, which must in turn be procured by special knowledge brokers. In the case of smaller companies, it is scholarship that functions as the main such broker (Kauffeld-Monz and Fritsch 2008). It is by no means certain that global corporations will take on the role of knowledge brokers for small and medium-sized businesses and regional networks, especially since (1) they are not necessarily interested in sharing their knowledge (see p. 126ff.), and (2) their departments of research and analysis themselves may have problems procuring global knowledge (Bertelsmann et al. 2007, p. 182ff.). The structural variable of global expertise and cultural competence, which must be present in a company if it is to function as a knowledge broker, restricts considerably the circle of "innovators" and "early adopters" and impedes the flow of communication. Not every employee in global companies and networks is also a qualified global knowledge broker. A company's global diffusion networks differ from its interaction networks and are often found in separate departments. Global knowledge brokers form global epistemic micro-societies. As a rule of thumb, diffusion and circulation networks, unlike the often still national owners and decision-makers or the partially global interaction networks, have to be truly global in order to be competitive in global markets – but this is not always the case.

Knowledge capitalism rather than a global knowledge society

Yet problems of knowledge diffusion are not just management errors but are also partly due to the logic of the economic system and (national) economic policy. In contrast to the mass media, which rarely features a high degree of market interdependence because its products are chiefly of interest in national markets, the economy is market-interdependent in this sense, though the economic system itself is competitively structured. It thus drives the global diffusion of knowledge more strongly than other systems. However, the new cross-border processes of interaction and observation are interest-based and there is no desire for an

Economy: global corporate communication **127**

ideal-typical "shareware" form of circulation, since knowledge is sought, but is imparted only as commodity and product. Here the economic system is more akin to the organized action system of politics than the organized observational system of the mass media.

Hence, national innovation policy also plays an important role in global knowledge allocation. In contrast to laggards like Japan, successful IT hotspots such as Finland or India are characterized by high levels of government investment in this field (Gómez-Alamillo 2005; Zysman and Newman 2006). In a seeming paradox, however, through *regional* industrial policy *global* innovation is fostering a kind of *re-nationalization* and impeding ideal forms of global circulation. Rogers has already discussed this as a problem of system openness (2003, p. 408).

From a communication studies point of view, observational communication within the economy – in much the same way as in secret services – must be viewed as *non-public internal* corporate communication, despite the trade fairs and specialist public sphere. This communication is open to the environment only in that it obtains information from the environment. But it turns this information into knowledge internally, with at most the networks and subsystems affiliated with the system being involved, not the entire environment. Decision-makers and teams, in their global networks, make decisions about what is communicated to the public and what is not (Nicolai and Halberstadt 2008, p. 276). Hence, the utility of observational communication as generated by global companies is not automatically transferred to "knowledge societies" as a whole – a term applied mainly to social formations in which the production of intellectual goods is growing steadily in comparison with more traditional commodities (Kübler 2005). In capitalism, as in state capitalism, knowledge is based on secret knowledge that is regarded as providing a competitive advantage. Most global legal arrangements such as the WTO agreements or the Agreement on Trade-Related Aspects of Intellectual Property Rights (TRIPS) ensure that companies have copyright on their knowledge and hamper the free circulation of knowledge (Hafez 2007a, p. 142ff.; see also Chapter 2, Section 2.1). In knowledge capitalism, there is a large gap between internal and external communication. It is no coincidence that the concept of public relations originated in the economic system.

The alternative is the radical "shareware" vision of an open knowledge society, which, at least in the corporate sector, seems utopian (Steffans 2000, p. 19; Tapscott 2012; Peters 2014). In knowledge capitalism, the knowledge of global elites in the political and economic spheres is surrounded by an "insulating layer" of strategic interests that restrict diffusion and circulation. Here global elites are inevitably turned into privatizing or even national elites. If these elites have overcome structural hurdles in terms of space, time, power and culture when *collecting* and *evaluating* information, they face structural hurdles when *transmitting* knowledge. Global knowledge diffusion must not be thought of as an ideal-typical form of circulation in the economic system. In the end, the decisive factor is not the structural variable of "culture", which can be given a "cosmopolitan" slant by good management, but the power of capital, which is inherent in the system – unless and until

128 Economy: global corporate communication

Hellmann-Grobe's socially just economy takes off (see Section 4.2.1). The limits of the global diffusion and circulation of knowledge, then, are the limits of the capitalist order.

"Semi-modernity" amid the global flow of knowledge

In summary, global knowledge diffusion is possible in all directions and at all stages, but it is not necessarily completely successful and continues to generate global knowledge elites and local "masses". Knowledge diffusion can, therefore, also create new knowledge gaps. The absorption capacity of those working in the economic system should not be overestimated and global knowledge management requires continuous development (Steffans 2000). In the global knowledge society, entrepreneurial knowledge elites as well as (virtual) teams play an increasingly important role. But local and particularist interests are not decreasing (Eisen 2003, p. 25). The interests of global capital and nationally oriented economic policy not only promote but also inhibit global observational communication within the economy.

These knowledge gaps, which exist not only between industrialized and developing countries, but also between the more global and less global economic elites of each country, are just as much a part of the overall picture of "semi-modernity" as are the constraints on global corporate interaction. Bassam Tibi originally created the term "semi-modernity" to highlight how Islamists have a positive relationship to Western science and modernity while at the same time rejecting Western morality (1995). In much the same way, global capitalism allows goods to circulate – but this does not necessarily involve an increase in intercultural knowledge.

4.2.4 Discursive (external) communication

Direct marketing as global micro-contact

Communication within a company cannot be equated with public communication, so it may have no impact on the global community or global society. But how does a global enterprise communicate with the outside world? We can make a basic distinction between two types of communication in companies: specialist internal communication and specialist-lay communication between firms and their environments, that is, customers, investors, trade unions, NGOs and the media. Specialist-lay communication comes under marketing as a generic term for things like advertising, public relations, branding and market research (Menz and Stahl 2008, p. 135ff.).

Marketing is strategic communication. However limited genuine communicative action may be inside the company, in the marketing context it is meagre indeed and tends to degenerate rapidly into a "façade" (Szyszka 1996; see also Dutta 2012, p. 206), particularly when (viral) direct marketing in the form of advertising via telephone, e-mail or SMS is incorrectly described as a "dialogue" (Lyons 2009, p. 278f.) between a company and its customer. Much the same applies to the direct sales

Economy: global corporate communication **129**

pitch, which in a global context often takes the form of e-commerce:"Traditionally, in EC [e-commerce] there is no human interaction or it has no substantial implication" (Shareef et al. 2009, p. 229; see also Quelch and Jocz 2012, p. 10).

On the other hand, when such global micro-contacts occur somewhat more extensively, for example, through Internet-based business-to-customer (B2C) transactions, they may not be entirely without consequence: the scope for genuine dialogues may be limited, but rudimentary cross-border conversational relationships do at least form between individuals. Much as in the case of firms' network connections, the question arises as to whether the form or the content of this contact is more important. Strategic PR communication may have unintended dialogic side effects, while advertising may play an indirect community-building role (whether the consumers' knowledge and values change through what is in effect observational communication in the context of the daily local consumption of global products is another valid research topic). There are more optimistic as well as more pessimistic assessments of the consequences of consumer capitalism for the formation of a global community. Pessimists regard this economic form as "multiculturalism without migrants", that is, as another variant of "semi-modernity" of the kind we have already encountered in enterprises themselves (Molz 2011, p. 45).

Advertising and PR: dominant culturalism

Despite all these problems, in the first instance this chapter considers marketing less as an interactive event than as part of discursive monologic communication. Our focus is not on the effect on consumers, and so on, which is ultimately an aspect of their lifeworlds, but on the nature of persuasive marketing messages themselves. Marketing is part of the public sphere and thus of the social construction of meaning, which may flow into interpersonal interactions (see Chapter 1, Section 1.1). In this context, we want to address Jürgen Bolten's question as to whether marketing has succeeded in moving away from static cultural concepts and designing campaigns "appropriately" with respect to global and local needs (2007, p. 182). Are global values and knowledge being communicated or is synchrony at least being generated in such a way as to propagate a "glocal" mix of values that reflects the plural character of global society? Here the economy has the potential to formulate cosmopolitan messages that *bypass political systems* and reach people in their lifeworlds. But is the consumer being addressed in such a way that global and local messages are synchronized, or do particularist messages, perhaps even cultural stereotypes, hold sway?

Bolten himself assumes that at present a mixture of global standardization and local differentiation predominates in global firms' marketing (ibid., p. 183). However, this is contradicted by the steady flow of campaigns that tend to emphasize (apparent) national characteristics in order to achieve the highest possible degree of market success and are not afraid to make ethical compromises, as when German manufacturers in Saudi Arabia – a country in which women have fewer rights than anywhere else in the world – advertise using the classic image of the

130 Economy: global corporate communication

housewife (Ramadan 2018). That international companies often shy away from a commitment to globalization has also been evident during Donald Trump's protectionist presidency. Akin to the situation in the political sphere, such developments point to a disjuncture between *partially global* internal and *local, particularist* external communication within the economy.

A glance at today's marketing literature confirms that the focus of marketing discourses in conditions of globalization remains unclear. Much of the literature continues to emphasize the need for international companies to take national sensitivities into account when entering a market (Kiesch 2007; Lützler 2007; Kotabe and Helsen 2008). Global companies are supposed to demonstrate their "commitment to national success" (Freitag and Stokes 2009, p. 217) and become "good local citizens" (Quelch and Jocz 2012, p. 192). By no means should global values be propagated. On the contrary, in some cases the logic of local market adjustment goes so far as to require changes to brand names (Zilg 2013). Cosmopolitan views are considered marginal and outlandish. In a famous polemic, Theodore Levitt accused global firms of giving in to (alleged) national and cultural idiosyncrasies (1983). The global economy, he lamented, does not really take modernity into its own hands, instead knuckling under to an imagined customer whom it does not even know, but who is reconstructed daily through marketing's cultural stereotypes. Much like Levitt, Mahuya Pal accuses the marketing industry and the associated academic discipline of marketing of cultural essentialism, which is blind to new cultural practices and the diversity of the world: "Whereas literature on activism recognizes the complex formation of global activist publics, such theorizations have been inadequate in public relations literature" (2008, p. 171).

"Glocal marketing" without cosmopolitan codes

Mediating concepts such as Bolten's idea of glocalization (see p. 129) are in fact more common (other examples include Lange 2014 and Springer 2007), yet they remain extremely vague when it comes to the essence of what is referred to as a "glocal" compromise. Based loosely on the motto, "as much standardization as possible, as much differentiation as necessary", Monique Schuldt understands this mixed strategy as follows:

> This includes a leitmotif, a specific advertising design and a specific advertising style. All these components must be uniformly enforced by national advertising agencies. However, the concept can be adapted to different national circumstances. In this way, an international image can be constructed and recognition secured worldwide without flouting cultural standards.
>
> *(2010, p. 37)*

This approach thus entails combining a global product idea with local ideas about society. John A. Quelch and Katherine E. Jocz – explicit opponents of Levitt – have discussed a similar strategy with reference to the psychological aura of local

Economy: global corporate communication **131**

places. The most convincing description of this appears in their well-known book *All Business Is Local* (2012). Their core argument is that the customer owns global products, but has no wish to be a global citizen, something global companies have to adapt to. At most, they consider lower transaction costs a reason for standardization. Hence, the vacuum cleaner's global meta-message remains the creation of a hygienic domestic environment. But the local social concept is and remains the mainstream idea of the vacuum-cleaning housewife. In reality, what is referred to as the "glocalization" of marketing very often reproduces local concepts of society.

Empirical studies of global companies' marketing also reveal that they mostly take a communal approach, in order, among other things, to avoid provoking the ire of social activists and to remain virtually inconspicuous (Andres 2004, p. 321). A global symbolic language of advertising (such as hip hop) is systematically overlaid by culture-specific code recombinations (Rathje 2008). Customer research shows that only a minority of consumers with a heightened interest in cultivating their images – most likely cosmopolitan elites, in other words – want global advertising (Jun et al. 2005). Cosmopolitan marketing, if mentioned at all, is referred to as marketing "without nationalistic references" (Brady 2011, p. 11). Explicit mention of cosmopolitan social values, on the other hand, is almost never made and is not even consistently present in the tourist industry (Kefala and Sidiropoulou 2016). Methods of empirical advertising research that take cosmopolitanism into account are being developed only gradually (Cannon et al. 2002).

In sum, the dominant marketing strategies completely avoid global references and values and in fact often advertise on a country-specific basis, through typical local references to personnel, language and visual imagery. Brands either flourish – like the Hollywood film industry – by largely doing without specific cultural symbols and thus achieving global success (Thiermeyer 1994) or they adapt to the local scene. The latter trend seems to be intensifying: the evidence points to the "consistency of the culture-specific" and an "ever more urgent need for distinctive individuality in the symbolic code" (Bendel and Held 2008, p. 7). The label "global" or "cosmopolitan", however, is almost never used to advertise. The international PR industry has grown rapidly as a result of economic globalization but stands out for a form of cultural adaptation that has the potential to reproduce and reinforce stereotypes. Marketing thus tends to strengthen leitmotifs that are remote from globalization, regardless of the worldwide distribution of products.

Conclusion: capitalists are (not) internationalists after all

In summary, the economy's communicative contribution to the "global community", which may be generated to some extent inside the company, remains elitist and at most reaches societies through employees' private lives (see Chapters 6 and 7). The promotion of the global community or global society is not the systemic goal of an economy whose external communication constantly reproduces local stereotypical discourses. Simone Huck's distinction between *global* investment

132 Economy: global corporate communication

relationships, *glocal* internal communication and *local* marketing in globally operating companies provides a good approximation of reality (2007, p. 900f.).

Ultimately, then, capitalists may not be the best internationalists after all. Globalization resembles a "tectonic shift": material interdependencies are increasing, but our ability to communicate lags behind (Hafez 1999, see also the introduction, Chapter 1). In other words, a world is growing together economically, a world that people do not always understand and that can leave them feeling overwhelmed as a result. German senior columnist Heribert Prantl neatly captures the gap between economic and sociocultural globalization:

> A global economy is flourishing, and a mass culture is flourishing along with it. The principle of growth is: everyone is becoming a customer. But it is the universal human rights, that is, the human rights that apply all over the world, that are not flourishing. The world is growing together, but not as an international legal community, not as an intercultural communicative community, but as a consumer community within a global market culture. Many were hoping for a different, more humane spirit.
>
> *(2016)*

5

CIVIL SOCIETY AND GLOBAL MOVEMENT COMMUNICATION

The famous *Manifesto of the Communist Party* by Karl Marx and Friedrich Engels ends with the appeal: "Workers of the world, unite!" (Marx and Engels 1946, p. 36). Even without reference to Marxism, the idea of forging international connections between peoples to pursue joint political action endures to this day. According to modern theorists, a "permanent social contract" (Kaldor 2003, p. 79) should be negotiated within "global civil society", which must act as a counterweight to the power of the state and the global economy.

But this is qualified with regard to actors within global civil society, which is why this chapter is dedicated to "organized social systems". Global civil society is generally understood to include both members of political organizations and associations as well as individuals who join social movements, at least informally, by taking public and collective political action, for example by attending demonstrations or through petitions (ibid., p. 79). The construct of civil society is thus distinguished from the "lifeworld" not only by the political generalizability of private interests, but also by its organizational component (Drake 2010, p. 134f.; Hensby and O'Byrne 2012; Schuppert 2015, p. 226). The lifeworld features political opinions and even communities, but no organized political activism. Civil society, in contrast, is an organized sphere of political activism located between the state and the lifeworld, and it represents a field of research in its own right. There is a border separating civil society from individuals, groups and communities who are not acting in an explicitly political way (see Chapters 6–8).

The fact that – alongside traditional foundations, associations and non-governmental organizations (NGOs) – social movements are now also included in civil society, complicates the transition between lifeworld and civil society (Adebayo and Njoku 2016, p. 64). But it does not change this basic definition as social movements also include civil society organizations and are held together by "social movement organizations" (SMOs). Equating these movements with "communities"

DOI: 10.4324/9781003255239-6

134 Civil society and global movement communication

(Kannengießer 2014, p. 17) thus makes little sense, since this ignores the organized action component. This distinction has largely been preserved in modern research on the Internet, for example, in the delimitation of the "activist" from the state, public, pre-political and journalistic spheres of the web (Dahlgren 2005). A blanket equation of "social media" with "social movements" is thus incorrect because only those parts of social media organized for the purpose of action are considered examples of political activism, while others are usually placed in the public or private lifeworlds.

In any case, from our system-lifeworld-network perspective, there is a shift in global civil society in comparison to the systems of politics and economy in that the technological innovations of digital global communication seem to have a direct influence on civil society's organizational capacity. Civil society has essentially no military or economic power, but it achieves its cohesion through symbolic power. The key questions are where exactly global communication takes place in civil society and to what extent symbolic power also generates real power.

5.1 Systems and system change

International NGOs: grassroots or self-interest?

As the antithesis of the state, civil society must be thought of primarily in political terms and, in addition to NGOs, consists of social movements whose active core is in turn made up of SMOs, which are often referred to in the international context as transnational advocacy networks (TANs). We not only have to differentiate between national NGOs and international INGOs, but also between old and new types of NGO (Schmitz 2001). The older type of INGO, such as Amnesty International, is a member organization. It lobbies governments and the United Nations and makes moderate use of the media. Conversely, a new type, exemplified by Greenpeace, has long got by without a grassroots membership structure and has pursued its political goals primarily through media staging and public pressure. The modernization theory of the 1950s and 1960s did not attach great importance to the meso-level of institutions and was essentially state-oriented (Faist 2008, p. 66). Only in the course of the debates on dependency theory and postcolonialism have NGOs received more attention in research since the 1980s and were even referred to as a new political force in a CIA report (Global Trends 2000).

The enthusiasm for NGOs as grassroots organizations and alternatives to the "corrupt" state was, however, soon dulled. More and more states established so-called "pseudo-NGOs", while NGOs' organizational self-interest became increasingly clear (Dijkzeul 2008, p. 82f.). Günter Endruweit refers to flat hierarchies and a limited division of labour in non-profit organizations that have no material interests. However, he qualifies this by stating that although the members and clients have little self-interest, staff may "have the same interests as the staff of profit-making organizations" (2004, p. 51f.). From the point of view of NGOs and INGOs, then, it is important to be aware of members, donors and supporters as "customers". Even if one "sells" ideal "products" to them, certain "market dependencies" arise.

In addition, there is often a lack of internal democracy. The new type of INGO is highly personalized. Reporters Without Borders was long controlled by its founder Robert Ménard and Wikileaks revolved around Julian Assange. Ludger Pries points out, however, that INGOs in particular act with varying degrees of centralization and that here too, much as with companies, there are different trans- or multinational types of organization (2008b, p. 16; see Chapter 4, Section 4.1). Nevertheless, it is important to scrutinize internal power structures because they may limit the ability to engage in global dialogue and community, as we shall see.

Social movements: the politics of information and mobilization

Not least in response to the limited representational character of INGOs, which have never become mass organizations, the focus of research today is more on social movements. We can identify thematic priorities over the course of history. In the so-called "old social movements", such as the American civil rights movement, or the pacifist and feminist movements, the main focus was on labour rights and welfare issues, but also peace, human rights and women's rights. The "new social movements" emerging since the 1980s added topics such as one-world solidarity, environmental protection and criticism of globalization.

This was the context that spawned the first TANs and globally coordinated campaigns, for example, against landmines, in favour of cheap AIDS/HIV drugs or against the excesses of capitalism, as in the case of the protests against the G7, G8 and G20 groups of industrialized nations. Local protests such as those by the Zapatista movement in Mexico, which attracted worldwide support, were viewed as part of this trend (Kaldor 2003, pp. 80f., 95ff.). TANs are networks of civil society actors who work together internationally mostly on a specific topic, share values and exchange information and services (Keck and Sikkink 1998, p. 2). They consist of a variety of actors, such as INGOs, foundations, churches, trade unions and local initiatives. Protests in earlier decades often had a local (national) character. Since the 1990s and in the wake of the Seattle protests against the WTO in 1999, however, the scholarly literature has identified a greater transnationalization of protests (Rucht 2002a, p. 16f.).

TANs pursue four strategies in confrontation with the state: (1) the politics of information; (2) symbols; (3) accountability; and (4) mobilization (Keck and Sikkink 1998, p. 18ff.). We will be delving mainly into the first two, although these cannot ultimately be separated from TANs' political goals. TANs develop and spread new political ideas and disrupt the routines of politics and economy through ever new international alliances (Jonjic et al. 2016, p. 30). Examples of TANs are Attac, a left-wing alliance that consists of national divisions but also organizes worldwide meetings and campaigns, the Global Campaign for Women's Human Rights, the World Alliance for Citizen Participation and the International Campaign to Ban

136 Civil society and global movement communication

Landmines. The latter is a global coalition of around 1,000 NGOs and initiatives from 100 countries, which prompted 122 governments to sign a treaty against landmines in 1997, earning it the Nobel Peace Prize.

A crisis of global movements?

When it comes to their size, states influential movement researcher Dieter Rucht, transnational movements are often overestimated (2002a, p. 17; see also Heins 2002, pp. 160, 166). Only a few local social movements address themselves to the international level (Rucht 2002b). Since the turn of the millennium, meanwhile, we can discern a marked degree of levelling off. The annual World Social Forum, founded in 2001 in Porto Allegre, is losing members and generating very little media interest (Plöger 2012). The anti-landmine movement failed to achieve some of its main goals, and at the UN World Summit on the Information Society in 2003 and 2005, representatives of civil society failed to get their way on issues such as copyright, Internet governance and communicative rights (Dany 2006; Jonjic et al. 2016, p. 25).

The reasons for this crisis are identified as global terrorism, Islamism and the resurgent reactionary and right-wing populist movements in various parts of the world. The Iraq War of 2003 was both the climax of these developments and a turning point. Although it triggered the largest worldwide demonstrations in human history, they did not stop the war. The financial crisis of 2008 is also seen as a turning point in that the income of NGOs, especially those located within social movements, has subsequently declined (Davies 2013, p. 179). It is nonetheless hard to paint a precise picture of TANs' political power, especially in view of the strong surge of mobilization since 2019 in the shape of the Fridays for Future movement.

Tenuous ideology, fragmentation and global networks

Even TANs are not entirely free of domination. This applies in two respects. Social movements are in principle not homogeneous, because they consist of numerous loosely connected networks, which means freedom from hierarchy, but also fragmentation and a fixation on community-oriented consensus. Probably based in part on experiences of defeat at the hands of the state, "new social movements" are often almost anarchically resistant to grand ideological narratives and integrated political strategies. They thus respond to accusations of an "apolitical" stance by countering that an organization that is overly oriented towards classical ideologies and forms of political organization is "apolitical" ("NGOization"), since in the past this often led to the appropriation of civil society by states (Reitan 2013).

W. Lance Bennett has described modern social movements in an international context as "ideologically thin" and self-contradictory (2003). The polycentric internal structure of social movements marks the transition from "organizational networks", as characteristic of the economy and NGOs, to the "network organization". The "chaotic" anti-capitalist movements in particular, about which activist and author Naomi Klein has written (2017), have achieved few concrete results. Protest tends to become an end in itself, with a focus on achieving "social creativity" instead of concrete political goals (Drake 2010, p. 144f.). The better-organized NGOs have thus struggled to adapt to the "new social movements".

Many in the ranks of the social movements regard INGOs, which are accredited by the United Nations and form part of global governance, as having been co-opted by the political system (Ritzer 2010, p. 166). For INGOs, on the other hand, a governance-protest dilemma arises here. Social movements could in principle strengthen INGOs' legitimacy and influence, but they are often unwilling to do so because they are suspicious of the compromises involved in lobbying and in concrete action within the political system, which in turn diminishes INGOs' legitimacy. This dilemma is also interesting in that it touches on the basic question of how we are to define the key conflicts in the development of modernity. What is the right strategy if one does not wish to be corrupted by states: (anarchic) retreat into small communities, radical protest, political negotiation with the state or a mixture of these tactics? The terms "realism" and "fundamentalism" do not adequately describe these options, which are better understood in terms of the contrast between parliamentary and extra-parliamentary political activism.

In any case, social movements have experimented with different forms of coordination in order to escape this structural dilemma (Andretta et al. 2003, p. 78f.). Internal movement structures are formed through initiative-based, campaigning alliances that now include NGOs (Ruiz 2005, p. 196; Jonjic et al. 2016, p. 11). INGOs have come to form important parts of TANs, which coordinate and mobilize these alliances and attract sympathizers. This gives rise to novel, organization-like "power structures" that we might easily overlook if all we see are protesting masses. The public agenda and timing of protests are often determined by just a small number of actors. Crucially, TANs do not necessarily arise as grassroots movements. The transnational coordinating structure is often established first, with which local groups then affiliate themselves, though this is not always the case (Johnson and McCarthy 2005). INGOs and TANs have, in any case, helped achieve extraordinary successes in the field of ecology and human rights, such as the Ottawa Treaty banning landmines and the Kyoto Protocol. This shows that even "ideologically thin" and fragmented movements can act in the same kind of planned way as organizations. The global network structures of these movements are thus quite meagre overall and certainly do not include every part of civil society, which often operates locally. But they enable global civil society to act in a dynamic, constantly changing and at times highly organized way.

North–South divide and sociospatial ties

The second structural problem can be described as a North–South conflict. Most INGOs were established in the major industrialized nations and many of them in the West, such as Médecins Sans Frontières, the International Red Cross, Amnesty

138 Civil society and global movement communication

International and Greenpeace, but some noteworthy organizations are from the South, like the Buddhist Compassion Relief Tzu Chi Foundation and the Islamic Relief Foundation. Nevertheless, a North–South divide also exists within social movements and TANs. The first striking manifestation of this gap is the sheer number of Western NGOs and actors in transnational constellations. We might refer to a "dual structural weakness" in that social movements are not only weakly organized internally, as we have seen, but also feature a global asymmetry.

The deeper causes of this imbalance lie in the resources and greater freedom enjoyed by the movements of the "North" and in the selfish interests of INGOs and TANs, in other words, the global claim to power or leadership of Western-dominated civil societies. Daniela Tepe refers to a "myth of global civil society" and emphasizes that it is wrong to assume that the same norms and ideas prevail in movements across the world. She argues that nationalism, racism and anti-Semitism can easily appear in left-wing as well as right-wing politics (2012, p. 19f.). What she has in mind here are factors – such as social prejudices or structural power relations between industrialized and developing countries – that may affect civil society activism. Examples include the tendency to critique environmental pollution in countries such as China without assailing the higher per capita ecological impact in industrialized countries, and to disregard the fact that trade unions in the Global "South" are in a more difficult position when it comes to the topic of child labour than their Western counterparts (see also Köpke 2002, p. 64f.; Benedek 2008, p. 174f.; Dany 2013, p. 8f.; Dempsey 2014, p. 459f.).

Rather than imagining a global civil society characterized by an ideal form of communality, it is crucial to grasp that these structural tensions pose a tremendous challenge to TANs' capacity for interactivity. Globalization is not a threat to the "moral ties between the world's sociospatial societal zones" (Heins 2002, p. 162). It is the process through which these ties must be forged in the first place by means of global dialogue on human rights and other issues.

Weak ties and low risk in global civil society

Ultimately, the structure of global civil society is characterized by contradictory features.

- *Postmodern structures*: The evidence points to a general development in social relationships away from so-called "strong" towards "weak" ties (Granovetter 1973). Early social movements, such as the labour movement, with its clear class affiliations and party ties, as well as NGOs, though with a smaller mass base, were often anchored in strong ties. "New social movements", on the other hand, tend to evince weak ties. Lacking even membership structures, they represent loose campaigning groups. This trend towards weak ties has a significant impact on the ability to achieve political goals, enabling flexible alliances even before the emergence of a global state, which would be the pre-requisite for the emergence of an opposition based on strong ties (Petit 2008).

Civil society and global movement communication **139**

Further, scholars tend to associate weak ties not only with postmodern "thin ideologies" but also with low-risk behaviour (McAdam 1986; Gladwell 2012). More traditionally oriented researchers like Rucht thus refer to the "tyranny of structurelessness" and call for more binding organizational structures (2002a, p. 20).

- *Post-postmodern structures*: Still, within this broad shift towards postmodern social relationships in civil society organizations, we can at least make out something of a countervailing trend, namely a will to organization and ideology on the part of INGOs and TANs. Nonetheless, these entities, first, often feature fleeting coalitions and alliances and, second, once again, seem to reproduce the traditional dominance of industrialized countries and former colonial powers.

The literature on global social movements features a certain amount of disagreement about who the actors are whose behaviour is subject to analysis (Stammers and Eschle 2005, p. 52ff.). For us, the development described above means we have to include both the more and less organized aspects equally in the analysis of communication. We must scrutinize the effects of both the more hierarchical character of NGOs and the relatively unstructured nature of social movements, without overlooking the bridging structures typical of TANs.

5.2 Communicative system connections

Social movements often synchronize global value-oriented action in an astonishing way. A communicative approach has become particularly popular in movement research (Richter et al. 2006, p. 17ff.) because, in contrast to the political and economic systems, this growing capacity of global civil society cannot be explained in light of resources such as power and capital but has to do with changes in modern media and communicative relations. On closer inspection, however, the idea that the Internet has made it possible to unite people around the world to the point of achieving interactive communality requires major qualification. Only some parts of global movements interact directly, while other parts are only networked through discourse. Meanwhile, a low-risk protest culture based on weak ties has become established, which explains, for example, the meagre efficacy of the large-scale protests prior to the Iraq War of 2003. This chapter seeks to determine whether social movements are essentially phenomena of an unstable global public sphere rather than examples of stable (interactive) activist community building.

5.2.1 Interaction and dialogue

INGOs and global interaction

As far as questions of internal interaction and dialogue are concerned, INGOs function in a similar way to transnational business enterprises and exhibit comparable multinational or transnational structures (Dijkzeul 2008, p. 84). Problems of

140 Civil society and global movement communication

centralism or decentralism, moreover, lead to interaction processes comparable to those of the economy, that is, to a limited but systematic and enduring species of global interaction in various forms of network, ranging from chain to full structures (in other words, fully-fledged teams) (see Chapter 4, Section 4.2.1). It is reasonable to assume that cross-border interaction through *multinational* structures is mostly limited to superordinate campaigns and axioms (here, of course, knowledge is also diffused through linguistic translation of key studies and other programmatic writings), while *ethnocentric* INGO structures are evident, for example, in the general dominance of NGO head offices in London or Paris (see also Chapter 4, Section 4.1).

Organized internal communication also facilitates interaction with third parties, for example, in the context of multi-track diplomacy or global governance. This is a primordial communicative process, as NGOs force governments to argue and thus limit their power (Chandler 2005, p. 149; Dany 2013, p. 5), but at the very least promote rational communicative action in politics, which can no longer be just classical power politics, but derives its legitimacy from acts of public self-justification. INGOs thus transfer processes of mass democracy into the international framework, even if we questioned how effective global governance really is in Chapter 3 on the political system. INGOs promote the public justification of policies but are located between strong and weak ties. That is, they are organized, but at the same time they are not mass organizations that integrate social classes and are effective enough to prevent wars or save the environment.

Face-to-face communication in social movements

Global social movements represent the genuinely new element of civil society. At the turn of the millennium, there was optimism, especially in communication studies, that transnational networks would grow (Sreberny 2000). However, two leading movement researchers, Donatella della Porta and Sidney Tarrow, quickly concluded that several phenomena were occurring at the same time: transnational interaction was increasing, while the primarily national character of social movements persisted (2005, p. 10). This indicates a separation between global elites and local masses much like the one we will be scrutinizing in the realms of the lifeworld.

Transnational advocacy networks (TANs) hold more or less regular global summits. Direct face-to-face interaction is thus *one* of the different forms of global interaction found in social movements. In particular, falling travel costs have led to more direct activist communication (Keck and Sikkink 1998, p. 16). Typical summit events consist of two components: organized assembly communication, primarily through speeches or artistic interventions, and informal follow-up communication among summit participants (Pianta 2001).

Summit meetings, then, are in principle spaces for creating strong ties, for example, at the annual international meetings of the Attac network (Eskola and Kolb 2002, p. 29). However, we should not overestimate the extent of direct interaction between groups of different national origins. Especially at global meetings, which also function outwardly as protests, local interactions within the participating small groups may dominate, which is bound up with the language and ideological barriers that typify these polycentric movements (Pickerill et al. 2011, pp. 49, 57f.; Rojecki 2011, p. 96). Large meetings in particular, such as the World Summit on the Information Society (WSIS) in Geneva (2003) and Tunis (2005) showed that, at gatherings of up to 20,000 people, interactions certainly took place, but the synthesis of these dialogues often generated extremely vague texts and formulations, so that the rational results of mass interactions appear questionable (Hafez 2007a, p. 147f.; Winter 2010, p. 65ff.). It thus makes more sense to view large-scale summit and protest events as hybrid happenings that fuse internal and external communication, because the outer-directed symbolism often counts for more than interactions within the movement (Adolphsen 2012).

Boomerang effects and domestication

Another aspect is generally referred to in the literature as the "boomerang effect" or "spiral effect" (Keck and Sikkink 1998; Risse and Sikkink 1999). Boomerang effects are phenomena of long-distance communication in which local problems, which cannot be addressed in a given country due to censorship, affect that country via information exchange with social movements and NGOs in other countries. Local censorship is being impeded as global civil society becomes more alert to local grievances. However, it remains unclear whether boomerang effects entail genuine interactions or merely the diffusion of information. As a rule, this phenomenon can probably be located between interaction and co-orientation, as both processes are involved: core groups of activists interact across borders and their texts are then disseminated within local discursive spaces through the media.

Kathryn Sikkink assumes that social movements initially try to solve problems at the local level, as local solutions are more plausible. This is because everyone involved has the same level of knowledge and the nation state is often the key addressee of political protest (2005, p. 164f.; see also della Porta 2005, p. 177). Della Porta and Tarrow have referred to this process as "domestication", while designating the boomerang effect as "externalization" (2005, p. 2). The latter is much more difficult to bring about and transnational coalitions are regarded as unstable and fleeting entities (Tilly and Tarrow 2007, p. 179). Boomerang effects thus receive a great deal of attention in global movement research, but these (partially) interactive processes are by no means omnipresent.

Interaction and global scale shifts

In their essay, "Scale Shift in Transnational Contention" (2005), Sidney Tarrow and Doug McAdam discussed why a complex of themes sometimes leads to interactive networking and sometimes does not. The term "scale shift" refers to the transformation of a national agenda into a global agenda adopted by social movements. Here Tarrow and McAdam differentiate between "relational" international relationships

142 Civil society and global movement communication

in social movements, in other words, those created through interaction, and "non-relational" ones, that is, those created by vehicles such as mass media (ibid., p. 127). They also add a third process of "brokerage", which encompasses both processes and essentially describes exactly what happens in the headquarters of modern TANs: the dissemination of information via the media based on limited interaction (see p. 144f.). These authors conclude that movements that are not connected both interactively and through brokerage spread less quickly (ibid., pp. 128, 130f.). Interaction stimulates the overcoming of national discursive boundaries (attribution of similarity), while brokerage fosters the sustainability of this process through diffusion.

The emergence of a TAN is thus impossible without a critical mass of intensive interactive relationships (della Porta and Tarrow 2005, p. 8). As with diffusion processes in the economy, interactive brokerage is the core of every TAN. These networks often develop their strong ties by chance and through the snowball effect, though this does not mean that TANs are generally based on acquaintance networks (Kiel 2011, p. 82f.). Negotiation processes in TANs are reciprocal adaptation processes intended to produce global frames between existing TANs and newly networked local forces. The most famous example here is probably the Zapatista movement of indigenous people against land-grabbing in Mexico, which quickly learned to articulate its priorities in the language of the struggle against neoliberalism in order to find international alliance partners (Cleaver 1998; Kiel 2011). At the core of transnational brokerage, then, significant negotiation interactions occur. Although they cannot be described as strong ties in the narrow sense of stable organizational ties, they are consistent and goal-oriented.

Networks and North–South elites

If we put these analyses together, it emerges that boomerang and spiral effects as well as transnational scale shifts are probably not always attractive. Further, they only succeed where there are favourable interactions between interactive and non-interactive communication and even an elitist organizational element. The latter is almost reminiscent of the communicative action of diplomacy or the economic system, except that it is "movement elites" that we are talking about here, which are by no means among societies' classic power or capital elites.

Not all local social movements are internationally networked. As Keck and Sikkink remark:

> Our research leads us to believe that these interactions involve much more agency than a pure diffusionist perspective suggests. Even though the implications of our findings are much broader than most political scientists would admit, the findings themselves do not yet support the strong claims about an emerging global civil society. We are much more comfortable with a conception of transnational civil societies as an arena of struggle, a fragmented and contested area …

> *(1998, p. 33f.; for similar statements, see also p. 9)*

The interactive core of transnational movements is primarily formed by an "educated minority" (Kaldor 2003, p. 100). Neera Chandhoke states:

> Yet the idea that all groups across the world who are struggling against the inequalities of globalization, either have access to global civil society or equal voice in this space, is both unrealistic and misleading. For like national civil societies, global civil society is also dominated by a handful of agents ...
>
> *(2012, p. 326)*

In the end, the sphere of the global or transnational tends to be described by these authors as the distant objective of a global civil society, because for most members of social movements, at least with respect to interaction, national borders remain intact.

Another problem, as Ilse Lenz indicates, is that different TANs may exist within the same thematic field without always cooperating closely (2008, p. 109). Hence, interactional deficits are not only to be found in the global/local relationship but also at the global/global level. As a general rule, we can state that TANs are indeed the core interactive structure of global social movements. But due to spatial, linguistic and capacity-related limitations, the interactive density in global social movements is likely to be generally lower than in local social movements (which, by analogy, no doubt applies to the difference between national and local movements as well).

John Keane thus also refers to global civil society as an "unfinished project that consists of sometimes thick, sometimes thinly stretched networks, pyramids and hub-and-spoke clusters of socioeconomic institutions and actors who organize themselves across borders" (2003, p. 8). INGOs and TANs can form full structure or star (also: hub and spoke) networks, where all interactions converge. Chain networks, meanwhile, in which information is transmitted across borders via just a few connected activists through a snowball effect, are often made up of parallel, unconnected chains, certainly just as often – and this Keane forgets – as disintegrated local networks without any global ties at all. Just as politics and the economy do not form unified global communication systems, neither does global civil society.

The NGOs of the Global South in particular are likely to remain un-networked in many cases. According to Andrea Plöger: "The base of social movements – especially in the global South – is usually not involved in this communication" (2012, p. 87). Even in social movements, then, global interactive communality is kindled only in a highly limited and incomplete way. Conflicts between North and South undoubtedly exist in TANs (Kaldor 2003, p. 96f.), but they can only arise and be resolved if there are interactive contacts in the first place and a constructive dialogue can develop as part of the formation of global communality.

For actors in dictatorships, however, international interaction is often dangerous as well. They expose themselves to charges of "treason", which is why NGOs in authoritarian countries are often necessarily characterized by a rather observing,

144 *Civil society and global movement communication*

distanced stance, a refusal to interact and a passive relationship to global discourse. The Ibn Khaldoun Center for Developmental Studies in Cairo, for example, was charged with "treason" in 2001 at the instigation of the then Mubarak government, and its founder, scholar and human rights activist Saad Eddin Ibrahim, was thrown in jail for maintaining what were described as illegal international contacts (Khalil 2001). Similar incidents in dictatorships everywhere have prompted NGOs to adopt a cautious approach to international partners.

Mass media as internal system environment

The fact that interaction and strong ties are limited in global social movements is also related to another phenomenon that clearly distinguishes the "new social movements" as a whole (though not INGOs) from other social systems. In other organizations and organized social systems, the media-based public sphere is a clear "outside", an environment that is reflected upon and processed but does not constitute the organization as an autonomous actor. Social movements, however, are not only connected by the thin layer of interaction involving smaller groups of actors, but also by mass media. As we have seen, economic enterprises also have corporate cultures and even their own media that form a discursive interior space within the firm. But in the case of social movements, the importance of movement-based as well as major media is even greater, because the interactive and contractual basis for cooperation is significantly thinner than in other systems.

For Keck and Sikkink, one of the essential characteristics of social movements is that they can largely be reduced to key symbols, a small number of themes and core demands (1998). Even classic Internet forums such as Indymedia are not sites of global interaction per se, as they consist of national sub-forums and the main focus is on micro-journalism through open posting. Indymedia's motto "Don't hate the media, become the media!" makes its approach clear. Social movements are thus a fascinating mix of the communicative mechanisms found in the political system and mass media, as they contain representational structures that are interactively networked and create agendas, while also forming discursive communities that resemble an open lifeworld rather than a closed social system (see also Chapter 1, Section 1.1).

This strong media dependency creates a problem at a global level. In TANs, movement elites interactively define collective action frames (Benford and Snow 2000) using movement media. These are coordinated in global civil society by INGOs and TANs, which do in fact have to engage in dialogue with one another in order to establish a minimal transnational movement-centred public sphere (Martin Luther King learned about Mahatma Gandhi through the media and formed a strong-tie movement on the basis of this knowledge); present-day Chinese and Western NGOs are discursively networked (Tilly and Tarrow 2007, p. 194f.; Reese 2015). But neither the dialogue of the movement elites nor their transnational media can be understood in the same way by all sympathizers, especially since national movement media exist in parallel, leading discursive lives

Civil society and global movement communication **145**

of their own. Social movements are, therefore, polyvocal or polyphonic and at the global level they essentially share fundamental values and ideas rather than sophisticated programmes and ideologies (Drake 2010, pp. 135, 137). The global Occupy movement, for example, though it coordinates certain key campaigns, is ultimately an association of "millions of people across the world in local (sic!) movements" rather than a transnational movement (Maeckelbergh 2014, p. 354). The lack of global interaction as well as the rather loose cohesion generated by transnational movement media is viewed by many commentators as the genius of grassroots movements' discursive communities, since the high degree of decentralized autonomy facilitates largely independent action within "multinational" structures (ibid., pp. 351, 355).

So far, little attention has been paid to the fact that globally negotiated dialogues and "collective action frames" are likely to remain underdeveloped. Social movements such as Attac or Occupy are absurdly similar to brand formats such as those in the entertainment industry (*Big Brother* or *The Voice*, for example) rather than global diplomacy or the economy, which systematically create "third spaces" of interaction and written agreement that are transmitted through coupled systems. In TANs, conversely, only a shared "product idea" – a so-called "format" – circulates, albeit a non-commercial one (such as "Occupy"). Global movement brokers ensure a certain "standardization" through transnational movement media, but a dialogue, or even just a dense transnational movement-based public sphere between the "format variants", arises only to a limited extent (Grüne 2016, p. 429ff.).

There is another complication. The literature assumes an ideal separation, with movement media (meso media) being responsible for internal communication, while all other mass media have an external effect (on politics and society) (della Porta 2013, p. 29). However, this is highly questionable since the movement's image in the general media may rebound on the movement and influence it. We might describe the general mass media as part of the "inner environment" of social movements (Hafez 2002a, vol. 1, p. 127f.) as they bring in perspectives from outside the system to which social movements react with discourses that shape their social identity. Social movements are thus embedded in "multifaceted media environments" (Mattoni 2013, p. 42). This constitutive importance of mainstream mass media to the interior of movements has hugely significant effects on global civil society. There is a risk that racist frames and stereotypes, which, as we have seen, often characterize the general mass media, will limit a movement's internationalism. Members of TANs, unless they are interactively connected or use transnational movement media, rarely live in the same discursive community, but are exposed to entirely separate media discourses. For example, the anti-Iraq War movement, despite appearing to be transnational, always remained associated with particular media (Murray et al. 2011, p. 60f.). The media discourse in Germany, for example, was very different from that in the UK (Hafez 2004), which may partly explain the national movements' different strengths. Tensions between Northern and Southern movements in TANs are also often causally based on discursive differences in knowledge and experience.

146 Civil society and global movement communication

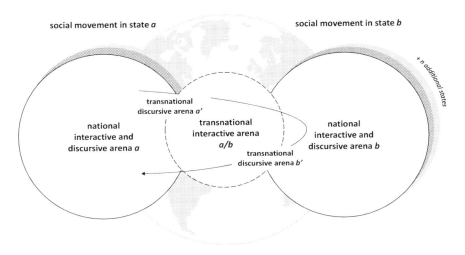

FIGURE 5.1 Discursive and interactive arenas of transnational social movements

A hybrid interaction-media system

The interim conclusion of this chapter on interaction and dialogue can be summarized through a diagram on the "communicative arenas of transnational or multinational social movements" (Figure 5.1).

Arenas *a* and *b* denote local movement spaces, while arenas *a/b*, *a'* and *b'* encompass TANs' global space of action, with *a/b* alone being the interactive space, while *a'* and *b'* are the transnational movement-based public spheres to which TANs give rise and which act as forums for global information exchange (the readings of the same media in these different realms may vary, as indicated here by *a'* and *b'*). Figure 5.1 shows that large portions of global movements are at most synchronized via transnational movement media and their symbols, agendas and frames, but are not networked interactively. Even if there is no aggregate empirical data, both types of phenomena (*ab* and *a'* or *b'*) are presumably underdeveloped in North–South relations, since here communicative processes remain very limited, both interactively and discursively. Global social movements are in many ways more like (special) public spheres than globally interacting organized social systems. Interactive global communality, on the other hand, arises only to a limited extent within the framework of the activities of INGOs and TANs, when they stimulate more concrete political action via direct network communication and brokerage, action that is in turn communicated discursively to the partners of the TANs and to the local parts of their movements (boomerang effects, scale shifts, and so on).

Two points must be noted with respect to the "encounter system" between system and lifeworld:

- Social movements' hybrid interaction–media system gives limited impetus to *people's lifeworlds*, since, in addition to global interactive and discursive experiences, local discursive spaces may continue to exist in which only a very limited number of informational elites ("cosmopolitans") seek to achieve global diffusion and try to advance the circulation of information, while the bulk of people do not interact across borders (see p. 140f.).

- With regard to the *political and economic systems*, TANs' limited interactive communality and limited transnational public sphere may also explain why the weak-tie and low-risk strategies prevalent in "new social movements" achieve only limited success despite a high degree of moral authority, so that the question remains as to whether global civil society is really capable of taking effective action (Bennett 2005, p. 208).

5.2.2 Interaction and organizational communication

The Internet: mediatization as resource

Even if, in contrast to INGOs, we can ascribe organization and organizational communication to social movements only to a limited extent, the question arises as to how things stand when it comes to the other theoretical fields significant to our investigation of global interaction in organized social systems – mediatization, informality and textuality. What has changed, for example, as a result of digital remote communication? Historically, INGOs have had a fractured relationship with the Internet. They have their own resources for external communication and media contacts, so the cacophony of social movements on the web was a source of uncertainty for these organizations at the turn of the millennium. At the beginning of the twenty-first century, W. Lance Bennett observed that the Internet would lay bare the "vulnerability" of the large INGOs, which could no longer control campaigns as they saw fit (2003, p. 145). The so-called "Greenpeace democracy" of the early 1990s assured the INGOs a privileged position in the public sphere (Baringhorst 1998), which is now under threat because their views are being relativized by the multitude of voices on the Internet. Small NGOs, on the other hand, have clearly benefited from the Internet. In developing countries in particular, NGOs with few resources have often emerged, for whose local work the Internet is worth its weight in gold, at least when it comes to obtaining and disseminating information. As far as social movements are concerned, the Internet has not fundamentally changed their logic, but it has increased the pace of information dissemination and the reaction speed within interaction. It has also broadened these movements' reach, which is why the Internet is considered particularly important in transnational relationships (van den Donk et al. 2004, p. 15).

The functions of the web include the following (see also Stein 2011, p. 150ff.; Schade 2018):

- *Protest mobilization*: The Internet facilitates traditional forms of protest, especially when it comes to cases of short-term global mobilization (van den Donk et al. 2004, p. 18) based on familiar mechanisms, such as interaction, brokerage and the discursive global dissemination of information through movement media.

148 Civil society and global movement communication

- *Dissemination of information:* This is not only being strengthened worldwide, but bottom-up dynamics are being fostered. This promotes "thin ideologization" but also grassroots democratic participation and thus reinforces a postmodern turn in global activism (Bennett 2003, p. 146ff.). The various means of information dissemination include (group) emails, list servers, websites and links, Internet portals and special search engines (Winter 2010, p. 51ff.).
- *Increased resources:* The Internet not only makes it easier to collect donations, but also reduces dependency on mass media, which in turn saves resources (van den Donk et al. 2004, p. 11; see also Bennett 2003, p. 144; Castells 2008, p. 870. At issue here are material and immaterial resources such as information and knowledge. Both levels interact.
- *Articulation:* The Internet introduces new forms of political participation, from online petitions to virtual blockades.
- *Identity:* The Internet strengthens the realm of cosmopolitan identity formation through transnational information sharing and the mobilization of large numbers of people – though this is not identical with community formation, since the exchange of information is not necessarily interactive.

The Internet is increasing weak ties involving meagre interaction

Interestingly, the aspect of interaction is missing from most lists of functions in the literature. In addition to optimistic voices (Winter 2010, p. 25), many authors have expressed doubts as to whether the Internet is strengthening global interaction in a sustainable way. Van den Donk et al. already assumed at the start of the millennium that far too little use was being made of movements' interactive potential on the Internet, with a lack even of reciprocal hyperlinking of local movements, which, strictly speaking, is of course an essentially discursive procedure (2004, p. 17). Steve Wright even expressed concern about the increasing shift away from face-to-face interaction (crucial to improving the organization of movements on the basis of activists' personal relationships) towards the proliferation of barely manageable quantities of information on the Internet (2004, p. 89f.). Malcolm Gladwell rightly pointed out that social media reinforce powerfully the weak-tie character of modern social movements, which has in any case been evident since the eras of the labour movement, Luther King and Gandhi, and he sees the danger of more and more informed but increasingly inefficient social movements (2012). Holly Ann Custard complains that there are hardly any studies on the role of intercultural interaction in TANs (2008, p. 7f.).

The available empirical studies confirm these pessimistic impressions. The websites of large US movements and large INGOs are aimed at fundraising and providing information, and they also feature links to other organizations, but direct interaction is severely neglected (Kavada 2005; Stein 2011). The possibility of cross-border conferences on the Internet is hardly used in the anti-war movement across the world, which is why face-to-face meetings have to be used, even in the era of the Internet (Pickerill et al. 2011, p. 46; Yüksel and Yüksel 2011, p. 253). INGOs

Civil society and global movement communication **149**

such as Greenpeace in particular are accused of hardly using social media at all to promote global interaction between large-scale movements (Roose 2012). Even fundamentally optimistic authors like Rainer Winter state that, for example, in the case of the large OneWorld network, interactive possibilities on the Internet are largely ignored, not least because its website has regional divisions featuring different native languages (2010, p. 135f.). All of this chimes with the findings of general research on the quality of online interactions, which repeatedly confirms that in online activism, features of deliberation such as reciprocity of exchange, coherence and decision-oriented communication are underdeveloped and only introduced by a few people, so that instead of dialogues, it is monologues and discourses that predominate (see, for example, Beierle 2004; Jankowski and van Os 2004; Stanley et al. 2004).

In the end, we are left with the fact that the Internet contributes to the rapid global dissemination of information and to short-term political mobilization – but it has not resolved the underlying problems of separate national agendas and frames, which could be converted into a common cosmopolitan programme only through increased strong-tie interaction (Pickerill et al. 2011, p. 42). Conversely, weak-tie mobilizations like the one in Seattle in 1999 would likely have been impossible without the Internet (van Aelst and Walgrave 2004, p. 100). There have always been mass protests historically, but they have rarely been simultaneous across the world. Hence, it takes the Internet to turn local activists into a global civil society capable of effective action (Andretta et al. 2003, p. 72) – however limited this civil society may be. The number of communicative actors who network in TANs has increased enormously worldwide due to the Internet (Dahlgren 2016, p. 11). If we understand global civil society less as an interactive and more as a discursive phenomenon, this positive assessment becomes understandable. Before the Internet, global cohesion in social movements consisted primarily of networks formed by INGOs and was therefore limited to a few people. The digital revolution has at least significantly expanded the transnational space for diffusion and mobilization.

New forms of activism, old (North–South) rifts

There is an objection that might qualify this thesis, namely that genuine "street activism" is turning into virtual activism on the Internet – cyber-mobilization, also contemptuously called "clictivism" or "slacktivism" (Morozov 2009). However, despite indications here and there that civil society was in some cases more strongly mobilized in earlier decades than it is today (Davies 2013, p. 175), there is ultimately no evidence of a decreasing number of real protests in the Internet age – quite the opposite (Andretta et al. 2003, p. 77). At the same time, signing online petitions, and so on, at least articulates political opinions. As we have seen, the Internet may have generated little interaction or organized political resistance – but in no way does it hinder acts of protest as such. The older thesis that preparatory face-to-face contacts are absolutely necessary for street protests has now been largely refuted (Chadwick 2006, p. 139).

150 Civil society and global movement communication

In addition, there is a form of mediatized protest that is original and would not even exist without digital communication: so-called "hacktivism". It is interesting that the language of civil disobedience used by the 1968 generation of protesters can be found today among hacktivists when they refer, for instance, to "digital sit-ins". Such denial-of-service attacks cause servers to be requested so massively by decentralized computers that they collapse. The logic behind this is that a society whose infrastructure is increasingly based on digital networks is exposed to increased risk of cyber-attacks. Of course, these are acts of violence that are only "communicative" to a limited extent. Most of the time, however, the protesters are less concerned with causing destruction than with sending a strong message – digital blockades thus resemble the signalling processes in international politics discussed earlier. The mediatization of protest, then, opens up new fields of communication for political action in the field of weak-tie activism.

The North–South divide is, however, overcome only to a limited extent by the Internet. A fair number of authors take the view that transnational activism, which primarily focuses on the Internet, exacerbates technological, economic and educational differences (keyword: illiteracy) (Custard 2008, p. 5ff.; Jonjic et al. 2016, p. 29). It is true that NGOs and social movements in developing countries are now better represented on the Internet than ever, even if they often act as local NGOs and not as parts of TANs, which is politically awkward under authoritarian conditions. Meanwhile, the digital North–South divide persists, even if it is slowly narrowing (see also Chapter 6, Section 6.2.1). There is therefore no evidence of the fundamental elimination of authoritarian and neocolonial politics in the Internet age (Hafez 2003a) – which perhaps also explains why the Internet has not yet been clearly anchored in the theory of international relations (Rodgers 2003, p. 45).

Global text-conversation cycles?

A social movement can ideally be imagined as a "text-conversation cycle" (Schade 2018, p. 302). Here references to texts from movement media in particular create a social bond of identity. With a view to our previous remarks, we could take the easy route and put forward the following thesis: in social movements, symbols are more important than texts, while topics are more important than frames. Hence, movements' "thin ideology", which arises due to limited global interaction and only a few transnational movement media, generates virtually no core movement texts that might establish a global basis for conversation. If collective action frames have to be negotiated in order to be politically effective, then this process of "self-structuring" (ibid., p. 301) takes place in essentially decentralized fashion in local movement spaces, and only in exceptional cases at the global level through TANs.

Yet in spite of all the ideological and dialogic limitations, through these processes social movements have generated new textual forms that are globally efficacious. The famous online petitions have facilitated innovative forms of campaign. They are often signed by hundreds of thousands of people worldwide, giving a voice to a silent majority. Such petitions are created by a wide range of actors and there are

Civil society and global movement communication **151**

also professional forums for petitions whose political origin is often unclear. INGOs also initiate petitions and use them to counter politicians' argument that their demands are not representative. So these texts are not really about initiating a global conversation in the sense of a genuine dialogue. Rather, the petitions' function is to circulate globally as identical textual templates and thus to help stimulate diffusion and synchronization in such a way as to enable local follow-up discourses and interactions. In the social movement itself, online petitions, at least at a rudimentary level, generate a global discursive community that goes beyond thin symbolism. Externally, they help INGOs and TANs to pursue lobbying (Beato 2014).

But all the ambitious declarations that have played a significant role in movements' recent global history, such as the declaration produced by the 1992 Earth Summit in Rio de Janeiro, came into being in cooperation with the state (the United Nations). So, for now, we can affirm that global civil society is neither interactive across the board, nor does it produce clear, text-based programmes. Sustainability in the sense of ideological consistency and genuine text-conversation-action cycles are more likely to be found in those parts of movements characterized by developed organizational communication – especially the INGOs.

Informality as incivility: who is a member of global civil society?

Although one might think that social movements in particular communicate informally and thus create community, because this is the predominant image of *local* movements, at first glance, the lack of formal organizational communication appears to lead to the exact opposite within the *global* framework. According to Christina Kiel: "During many campaigns, TAN members may never meet or socialize much beyond signing online petitions or loose coordination of strategies, primarily for logistical reasons" (2011, p. 82). Without organization, then, there is no *formal* communication, without which there is no *informal* communication in global civil society. This sounds plausible. But are things that simple?

If global social movements often resemble discursive rather than interactive communities, this acts to reduce the extent of interactive informality. But another effect might be all the stronger. This is generally referred to as "hate speech" or the problem of the "civility" of communication. Ethnic and religious minorities, women, homosexuals and transsexuals, and other social groups suffer massive verbal abuse on the Internet (Hafez 2017b). Andrew Chadwick calls this the "cheap talk" effect, which is, as it were, the flipside of the reduced communication costs that typify electronic networks (2006, p. 121). There are indications that insulting opponents, email bombing, and so on, including through bot programmes, play a role in every kind of social movement communication, because this seems to secure the attention of politicians in particular (ibid.). So even the progressive values that link social movements cannot prevent hateful communication. If we include in civil society – and this is controversial among social scientists – reactionary, identitarian and fundamentalist movements, such as Islamists or right-wing extremists, then digital cheap talk seems to be a ubiquitous problem in global civil society. These

152 Civil society and global movement communication

groups pursue no charitable goals. But they mobilize the partial interests of a society and make extensive use of digital forms of communication.

There can be no doubt that hate speech is a global problem today. Since many actors in this field, unless they are engaged in psychological warfare on behalf of a state or a militant group, use foreign servers for this activity in order to act legally, hateful communication is technically a global, that is, cross-border issue. Because global interactions and public spheres are often restricted in social movements, as we have seen, one might think hate speech is primarily due to cultural deficits at the local level. However, there is increasing evidence of cross-border hate communication. Islamist-jihadist networks were among the pioneers here, as they wish not only to expand their movement networks through social media and recruit supporters, but also seek to threaten and demoralize non-Muslims through the use of propaganda (Torres et al. 2006; de Smedt et al. 2018). Other reactionary TANs, such as the "Baptist-Burqa Network", are, for example, alliances between Christian and Islamic fundamentalists against homosexuality and other liberal rights. They are engaged in a global cultural war across borders and through the Internet (Bob 2012).

Weak-tie globalization through digitization

Overall, the criticism that the Internet has made no contribution to the development of global social movements and has even reinforced processes of global fragmentation (Plöger 2012, p. 87) is overblown. Digital mediatization may foster weak-tie social relationships at the local level and thus contribute to the further destruction of stable political ties and concrete ideologies and solutions. But the dissolution of such social ties began much earlier, at least in Western industrialized countries (Dalton et al. 2000). In the rest of the world, the Internet is often more likely to facilitate the emergence of an opposition, at least in places where no solid opposition structures have previously existed. In any case, the Internet stimulates the circulation of alternative media and informational offerings as well as the specific mobilization required to generate protests via TAN interactions. In many ways, then, the Internet has at least accelerated the emergence of a global weak-tie society, however fragmented it may be due to text-conversation cycles featuring limited interaction. Nevertheless, we cannot ignore the fact that the social movements of this world remain largely separate discursive communities. In the local "bubbles" of the net, the risk of hateful communication is in fact growing, and the tendency is for it to develop into global cheap talk.

5.2.3 Observation and diffusion

Alternative information policy

TANs and INGOs ensure the diffusion and circulation of knowledge and information in global civil society, both in alternative and mainstream media. In line with our remarks so far, transnationalization is based mainly on "mutual symbolic

Civil society and global movement communication **153**

support and information exchange" (Daphi and Deitelhoff 2017, p. 309). Global movements are to a large extent local, weakly relational entities at the interface between the domestication and externalization of problems, entities partially and loosely connected through shared symbols, discourses and political goals. The scale shifts of global agendas as well as the creation of collective action frames are based on social movements' alternative global "information politics" (Keck and Sikkink 1998). Only on the premise of shared topics and concerns is it possible to refer to global movements at all, even if these are not always interactively connected.

Influential authors such as Mary Kaldor and Saskia Sassen even assume the total global presence of information (according to Kaldor: "The local is instantly global, the distant immediately close", 2003, p. 104, see also Sassen 2005). However, this is vastly overstated, since the process of information diffusion, much as in politics and economics, may be situation-dependent, selective and in some cases even distorting, but is in any case dependent on movement brokers.

INGO expertise versus symbolic TAN resources?

The annual reports on the human rights situation by organizations such as Amnesty International, Greenpeace or Reporters Without Borders are important across the globe. As with other organized social systems, INGOs in particular feature an array of communicative modes. They observe the world just as systematically as the media, scholarship and politics, generating knowledge and achieving expert status. Their expertise is often so recognized that as well as politics and the economy reacting to it, it is even used in the academy, although there are certain problems with the transparency of the measurement methods, with INGOs usually suffering a tendency towards partial opacity (Behmer 2003). Nor should one idealize the global flow of information in INGOs. Dennis Dijkzeul's investigation of a Maltese relief agency shows, for example, that the global transfer of knowledge often fails, with knowledge remaining local (2008, p. 97). Nevertheless, INGOs make an important contribution to the recording of human rights and other violations.

The usual perception of grassroots movements, on the other hand, is that, unlike NGOs, they are not a repository of expertise. Social movements thus feature a mix that is difficult to classify and is more reminiscent of everyday communication than formal analysis. Subjectively, the productivity of such movements may well be high for the individual – but the quality of knowledge generation is usually low. The quality of observation typical of TANs, we might think, stands or falls depending on the quality of the INGOs working within them.

Yet a number of scholars are questioning this perception, pointing out that social media in particular seem to have increased the observational skills of social movements' grassroots. Keck and Sikkink describe how pamphlets, eyewitness reports and statistics are spreading globally through TANs even outside of INGOs. Social movements are thus quite consciously seeking to combine emotional and

154 Civil society and global movement communication

personal perspectives with the generally scholarly approach of INGOs. The result is a "dense web of North–South exchange" that represents an effort to break the informational monopoly of the political-economic system (1998, p. 21). The famous boomerang effects are essentially processes of information diffusion. Also significant is Manuel Adolphsen's reference to the role of alternative world summits as "providers of symbolic resources", by which he means not just the dissemination of factual information but also visual stimuli that chime with the "ritualistic" approach of the media and its news factors (2012, p. 58).

Informational quality and circulatory limits

Nevertheless, as we pointed out earlier, even fascinating boomerang effects are not omnipresent phenomena, so the time has come to think more carefully about the quality of information diffusion. There are several levels to consider here. On the one hand, there is a qualitative difference between information and resources that are disseminated via websites, lists and other media of organized TANs, and pure hashtag-lay journalism. Especially with respect to the North–South relationship, in which recipients' knowledge of countries and capacity for meaningful assessment are multiply limited, such journalism is susceptible to falsification and distortion (Cooper and Cottle 2015). The role of TANs as movement organizations and gatekeepers is thus an important one.

On the other hand, TAN-based diffusion and circulation must also be subjected to critical scrutiny.

- *Informational quality*: So far there is no yardstick for rating the global informational density generated by social movements. An increase in information turnover brought about by the Internet does not mean we already live in a global knowledge society, because all too often factual knowledge is subject to ethnocentric limitation, even in social movements (Hafez 2007a, p. 109ff.). Much as in the economy or the mass media, global knowledge is domesticated in social movements, which may lead to fragmentary informational cultures.
- *Theoretical knowledge*: Further, there is a contradiction between the "thin ideologization" of social movements identified above and their aspiration to act as knowledge managers. Daniel Innerarity has pointed out that information is not knowledge as long as there is no theoretical basis for knowledge processing (2013). It is important here not only to differentiate between technological and social networks (Marres 2006), but also to question the idea of movement networks (especially in contrast to network organizations, such as NGOs) as reliable knowledge institutions, not least because of their limited dialogic quality. Even if we regard movements as (informational) public spheres rather than interactive systems, they do not always correspond to Habermas's ideal conception of a rational public sphere, since they may not produce recognized agendas or rational communication (Faltesek 2015).

- *Practical knowledge*: In addition, an informational backlog arises when there are no available routes to turning information into political activity (Chouliaraki 2006). If we leave aside occasional global protests, online petitions, and so on, this last point in particular is likely to be the weakness of a primarily weak ties-based and discursive movement that often engages in perpetual protest without involving itself in politics. The proponents of classic strong-tie movements question the value of postmodern information circulation that is not integrated into concrete political strategies (Le Grignou and Patou 2004, p. 178f.; Wright 2004, p. 84ff.).

New global knowledge elites

INGOs and TANs are new global knowledge elites that meaningfully expand on the often ethnocentric information offered by the mass media, politics and the economy. Alternative political constructs and worldviews circulate in global civil society. Social movements help synchronize the global public sphere, even if their input does not always reach people as it is filtered and domesticated by national media systems. The notion that there is a need for a civil society-based "counterpublic" and the idea of the emergence of new global knowledge elites are both corroborated by the important informational services provided by many INGOs. At the same time, we have to question the primacy of informational over interactive communication and of weak over strong ties, both with a view to the quality of global knowledge and in light of global social movements' capacity for collective action.

5.2.4 Discursive (external) communication

Professionalization of public relations

The quality of global interaction in politics and the economy may be higher than in social movements due to the organizational character of these systems. If at all, social movements are linked more discursively than interactively. But communicative action in politics and the economy is always counteracted by the strategic (propagandistic and PR-related) interests involved in external communication. What role does the relationship between internal and external communication play in INGOs and TANs? Are disruptive vested interests at play here too?

As we have seen, Endruweit distinguishes between organizations' charitable goals and the interests of their elites or staff. This hybridity can lead to strategic problems, the best-known example probably being Greenpeace's manipulation of figures in relation to the Brent Spar scandal of 1995, for which the INGO had to apologize. This affair led many to critically question "Greenpeace democracy", in which a small, non-democratically elected group tried to gain attention and legitimacy by falsifying facts (Baringhorst 1998). This criticism of attention-seeking INGOs with

156 Civil society and global movement communication

scant democratic legitimacy continues to be made (Ritzer 2010, p. 164f.). At the same time, however, we should assume that INGOs' close ties to the interests of civil society prevent excessive hybridity. Internal and external communication should therefore diverge less than in other social systems, as otherwise people would lose their trust in INGOs' expertise.

Despite some setbacks, INGOs have achieved a high degree of stability and they have been particularly successful at improving their position within the framework of the "new social movements" and professionalizing their external communication. In the theory of public relations pursued by INGOs and TANs a distinction is made between latent phases in which topics, frames and symbols are developed by NGOs as well as in alternative movement media, and manifest phases in which communication takes place with the wider public sphere. Researchers have examined the networks that exist between INGOs and mass media as well as the various forms of global event marketing and visual management pursued by social movements (Kolb 2005; Cammearts et al. 2013; della Porta 2013). Forms of civil resistance such as blockades, flash mobs and the like are also part of present-day social movements' PR arsenal (Dempsey 2014, p. 455). Here attention is gained through "exceptional behaviour" (Wolfsfeld 1997, p. 13ff.) in order to compensate for the lack of resources compared to politics and the economy (Schwarz and Fritsch 2014).

By now, however, even TANs can be examined with the help of organizational marketing approaches to organizational communication and here we can ascertain differing degrees of professionalism (Foster et al. 2012). There is broad agreement that despite digital communication there is no evidence that major mass media are any less important to external communication, legitimation or achieving targets (Hutchins and Lester 2011; Rucht 2013). There is no consensus as to whether it is primarily the organized parts of TANs – that is, especially INGOs – that plan public campaigns (Lahusen 2002, p. 41), or whether decentralized, leaderless "permanent campaigns" are being generated at a global level as a result of digitization (Bennett 2003, p. 151ff.).

Cosmopolitan PR?

At least the large-scale campaigns of INGOs and TANs are very similar to advertising campaigns in the economy and politics, though here too the multilevel structure of the global public sphere must be taken into account. Campaigns run by INGOs do not resonate equally in all national media systems (Lahusen 2002, p. 42). This creates a significant problem: while it may not be the interests of INGOs and TANs themselves that generate the strategic ambivalence of communicative action, we can nevertheless expect system environments and environmental systems to exert strong pressure to adapt. As we have seen, even the frames of social movements are not universally oriented from the outset, instead giving rise to strong pressure to negotiate in TANs, for example, with a view to the North–South divide. The cause of these tensions lies partly in the fact that open social movements, unlike

INGOs, are first established in discursive public spheres, that is, in principle, we cannot assume that *exclusively* cosmopolitan narratives will emerge. Islamophobia, anti-Americanism and every type of nationalism must be taken into account at the latest when a global movement communicates with external local environments. Even TANs may find themselves having to make compromises with local interests. To what extent, then, is the PR pursued by TANs and INGOs aimed at achieving global communality?

Keck and Sikkink explain how TANs increase the salience of their topics and frames through information and an emotive, symbolic politics in order to generate "moral leverage" vis-à-vis the political sphere (1998, p. 23). Social values, then, are effectively the "currency" of external movement communication, which of course raises the question of whether the global foundation of values is stable enough to facilitate cosmopolitan public relations. These authors believe that humanitarian issues, especially those relating to children, can be universalized more easily than other topics; in particular, they do not consider individualistic values to be universal (ibid., p. 204ff.). They thus suggest looking for ways to connect new ideas with existing value systems. With reference to transcultural values, they make it clear that what they have in mind is not a local strategy of adaptation to local mainstream values as in large parts of the advertising industry (see Chapter 4, Section 4.2.4). Other texts about social movements, however, lack this goal orientation and thus tend to recommend that INGOs and TANs adapt to local, culturally imbued values (Schwarz and Fritsch 2014, p. 178). The call from Émilie Foster, Raymond Hudon and Stéphanie Yates for social movements to pursue market-oriented rather than product-oriented approaches in order to be successful is perfidious in that market-oriented PR not only involves market research, but also requires "refinement" of the product through local adaptation (2012, p. 318). Is there a danger here that even global civil society, much like politics and the economy, will negate the global communality generated inside it through culturalist external communication?

There are two possible answers to this question, one optimistic and the other pessimistic. The optimistic answer is that, in contrast to the product landscape of capitalism, there is no need to fear a division into global products and local social values in social movements. On this view, for example, within the framework of the intercultural dialogue on human rights, social movements can emphasize the local anchoring of global values without diluting the core message through excessive relativism (Hafez 2000b, p. 13ff.). It is, for example, not hard to demonstrate that "environmental protection" is also an Islamic or Confucian value.

The problem, however, and this is where the more pessimistic reading comes into play, is that PR is not an ideal dialogic space and there may be excessive local contextualization without simultaneous reference to universal values. A number of authors have questioned whether the so-called "anti-globalization movement", for example, is pursuing universal goals (Gopal 2001; Shipman 2002), even if large parts of it tend to call themselves the "global justice movement" to clarify this very point. In any case, what all of this shows is that ideas of global community

158 Civil society and global movement communication

and cosmopolitanism may take a back seat and be sacrificed in social movements in order to achieve other goals – a fair social order, environmental protection, and so on – if this appears opportune. Not every environmental campaign has to emphasize the global meta-value, as in the case of one-world campaigns. One indication of problems in this area is that there are generally no transnational PR strategies even in the case of global events organized by social movements. Instead, local media, governments and the NGOs of larger TANs domesticate these events (Adolphsen 2012, p. 198f.). Hence, if the local adaptation process of PR consists not just in emphasizing local derivations of global values but, as is not uncommon in the economy and politics, in negating the global narrative, then social movements should also be described as hybrids as envisaged in globalization theory, entities that not only generate global communality and synchrony, but also their opposite.

Conclusion: civil society as an expanded global public sphere

In principle, despite all reservations and however much we might qualify the communication practices of social movements, there would appear to be stronger informational foundations for alternative and even cosmopolitan forms of communication in what might be called a "global civil society" than in any other system. This formation creates new interactive global communities, but much of it is in fact home to an alternative global public sphere. This civil society is not a clear manifestation of either a global community or global public sphere, but – much like the action systems of politics and the economy – encompasses both. Globally networked elites and peripheries, organized to varying degrees, shape the image of global social movements. Yet it is non-interactive diffusion processes that dominate via alternative media or even mainstream mass media.

With the exception of INGOs and certain elites associated with transnational advocacy networks (TANs), interaction is less integrated than in other comprehensively organized social systems. Social movements thus tend to practise discursively networked weak-tie politics, while even the strong-tie communication of INGOs does not generate mass organizations. Here too, then, unstable interaction is related to a low-risk policy of limited effectiveness. In the "third space" of diplomatic communication and global governance INGOs are "guests" rather than "hosts". If we regard political diplomacy as an unstable but permanent entity, then the global organizational and interactive character of politics is more pronounced than that of the "new social movements". They, however, often view their weak-tie approach as a strength and as postmodern "culture".

Against this background, we should interpret digital mediatization essentially as an intensified form of the global alternative public sphere generated by INGOs and TANs. There is no clear evidence that interactivity has been fostered by the Internet either. But global civil society is at the same time far from forming a cohesive public sphere because TANs, transnational movement media and a transnational linkage of discourses (boomerang effects, scale shifts, collective action frames, and so on) exist only to a limited degree. Even in "the Internet age", therefore, social movement-based public spheres are still highly local. Because of the limitations of *internal* movement communication in all spheres of interaction and mediated discourse, *external* communication – vis-à-vis the broader public – is also at risk from separatism, even if the global is valued significantly more in some movements than in others.

6

LARGE COMMUNITIES

Global online communication

The "community" part of the "global community" construct comes into play whenever organized social systems in the political or economic spheres, or civil society, exchange, network or even combine to create transnational systems of action beyond the realm of the nation. They then form political, professional, epistemic or scholarly communities (Djelic and Quack 2010, p. 42; see also Linklater 1998; Etzioni 2004). Here the concept of community refers to the values, identities and interactions entailed in the interdependence between nation states, so there is always something strategic going on when systems justify their actions as being in the interests of the global community (Grewal 2007).

In the digital age, however, "community" has become a key scholarly concept from another point of view as well. At issue here is no longer whether organized systems may show tendencies towards communitization, but whether community can take off at the global level without such organizational structures. Since traditional communities are closely tied to face-to-face interaction, the question is whether communities can be expanded into global "online communities" through electronically-based remote communication despite the lack of such structures (Riley and Monge 1998).

So far, no coherent theory of "global community" has been put forward (Djelic and Quack 2010, p. 37), probably because the debate is dominated by political scientists and economists, who focus primarily on social movements. But while large communities often act like social movements, they are in fact completely different phenomena, since they are neither organized in the same way nor pursue short-term political goals, but instead mark the transition from system to lifeworld. Marie-Laure Djelic and Sigrid Quack state: "Communities based on shared convictions, values, or expertise have properties that distinguish them clearly from other modes of social coordination" (ibid., p. 40). To date, little is known about the

DOI: 10.4324/9781003255239-7

Large communities: global online communication **161**

interactive, perceptual, and discursive processes that allow people to become part of a global community or prevent them from doing so.

6.1 Systems and system change

Community and society

Ferdinand Tönnies' classic distinction between society and community was associated with the idea that the "community" is an end in itself for its members, while individuals' and institutions' utilitarian goals come into play in "society" (2010). Since Tönnies's concept of community focuses primarily on relationships among kin, neighbours and friends, from this perspective, small groups (see Chapter 7) or large groups of up to 50 participants are the true sites of community (Stegbauer 2001, p. 83ff.). In principle, then, these groups are interactively networked. National and religious communities, by contrast, may be described as surrogate forms that arose when modernity began to dissolve traditional society. As "communities of fate", they are also referred to as semi-voluntary communities that individuals can only avoid identifying with by emigrating or converting to another faith (In der Smitten 2007, p. 125ff.). Fictions of consensus prevail in the surrogate community. Let's call this the problem of imagination. The imagined community of the nation communicates through public discourses and symbols and no longer primarily through social interaction (Djelic and Quack 2010, p. 9f.). It owes its construction largely to propaganda-based dissemination via mass media as pursued by political actors and institutions. At the very least, however, the definition of the large community must encompass two levels: interactive groups above a certain size and discursive public spheres.

In principle, there is no difference between a large national and global community, as both use media to transcend the locality of interactive groups. It is interesting to note, however, that the aspect of interaction is intensified by the Internet, since online meetings can take place on an ongoing basis, so that people living across the world can form large groups within large communities. However, there may also be counter-tendencies at work within these "online communities", which make their global extent a topic of scholarly controversy to this day. There is no consensus on whether placelessness is possible in large groups without loss of communality. Authors express fundamentally different views on this, ascribing very different degrees of importance to interaction and the real-world existence of a community – that is, so-called "social co-presence" (for an overview, see Jankowski 2002).

Virtual community and the constructivism of placelessness

We can roughly distinguish two currents in the scholarly literature, to which we would add a third, synthetic one. The constructivist school emphasizes the re-forming of community through digital networks (Giddens 1990; Rheingold 2000; Beck, quoted in Stegbauer 2001, p. 53; Barnes 2013). An influential definition formulated

162 Large communities: global online communication

by Howard Rheingold states: "Virtual communities are social aggregations that emerge from the Net when enough people carry on those public discussions long enough and with sufficient human feeling, to form webs of personal relationships in cyberspace" (2000, p. xx). This definition emphasizes sustainable interaction and emotionality. But not all "newsgroups" or digital networks are really communities because the sustainability and intensity of the relationships play a key role (Barnes 2013, pp. 108, 110). Historically, the media revolution brought about by the press, radio and television has fostered individualization, since the community is no longer compulsory. The digital media revolution, meanwhile, is now facilitating social communication (ibid., p. 107). The Internet is thus a correction to modernity that helps offset the anonymity of (capitalist) society by fostering greater communality.

In a certain sense, constructivism points to a return to the original meaning of "community", as this term is derived from the Indo-European stem *mei-* or *moino-*, denoting exchange, and thus refers to communication processes (In der Smitten 2007, p. 113). Tönnies's concept of community was less interactive because though it emphasized the idea of community, this was often transmitted from one generation to the next hierarchically, without being renegotiated through social communication. Ultimately, the imagined communities of early modernity (for example, the nation) chiefly fostered public discourses and turned people into recipients. In the new online communities of the present, meanwhile, there is a great need for interaction since this is the only way to generate the idea of a community in the absence of predetermined social ties between people. This corrective shift from the primordial to the communicative and even to the interactive community is particularly important to globalization research because new agreed communities appear possible beyond people's existing local and national social ties. The principle of location-based communication no longer applies, as modern technologies mean that communities can now form without physical ties (Barnes 2013, p. 106). In this vision, the world is becoming an ideal interactive village.

The relationship between these new large-scale group networks and traditional, semi-voluntary, real and imagined communities remains unclear in the constructivists' writings. Online communities may theoretically exist in isolation from family and neighbours as well as religious and national communities, in other words, they may form a parallel community. But traditional communities may also instigate a process of global re-communitization, that is, a kind of "re-tribalization". This may in fact intensify in an era of globalization if venerable communities capture new spaces of interaction and discourse on the Internet, thus revitalizing themselves (James 2006, p. 293). Here we see the value of Susanne In der Smitten's distinction between "virtual" and "virtualized" communities (2007, p. 128f.).

Structuralist social co-presence and "re-tribalization"

This is the starting point for the constructivists' structuralist opponents (Stegbauer 2001; Bugeja 2005; Curran 2012; Fenton 2012). They emphasize the close connection between digital communities and real-world social conditions, which

Large communities: global online communication **163**

may be described as the problem of social co-presence. The idea here is that *only* "virtualized communities" can be real online communities, while "virtual communities" are not really communities, but merely social networks (probably in the sense of the weak-tie external relations of social entities). From this point of view, there is no community without a place, since this is a key feature of Tönnies's definition of community (Stegbauer 2001, p. 67ff.). As Christian Stegbauer puts it: "Social relationships are usually dependent on co-presence, that is, spatially linked relationships. These relationships can never be completely dissolved *per se* because the point of origin is always a real social place" (ibid., p. 44). Miriam Meckel suggests that at the global level "there must be a close social orientation and connection that also exists 'naturally'" if we are to refer to a global community and she thus considers the concept of society ("global society") more productive when it comes to globalization (2001, p. 43; see also Kneidinger 2013, p. 95ff.). In much the same way, Henrik Enroth and Douglas Brommesson argue that global political culture is not based on interpersonal experiences and that cosmopolitanism is, therefore, unstable because the global dimension lacks the experience of community (2015, p. 69).

If we apply these ideas to digital communication, people can leave virtual networks without social consequences due to the lack of social co-presence, while this is impossible in real-world communities. Stegbauer opposes the "de-structuring fiction" put forward by authors such as Giddens, Beck and Rheingold (2001, p. 38ff.). Ultimately, what this means for globalization research is that we must assume the constant presence (co-presence) of real social ties in online communities. The idea here is that social reality acts like an initial layering that preforms collectives *prior to* digital networking. The real social existence of a community, as emphasized by these authors, is what makes imagined communities (religious community, nation, and so on) possible in the first place. Global online relationships cannot simply be newly forged on the Internet in isolation from offline relationships – in other words, on a cosmopolitan basis. No wonder, then, that Stegbauer not only emphasizes the diversity of cultural symbol systems in a highly essentialist way, but also rejects the myth of the global village: "To embrace the idea that a global village is emerging is to neglect these very cultural identities or consign them to a premodern age" (ibid., p. 45).

As plausible as the connection between virtual and real communality (in the construct of the "virtualized community") is, it is striking that structuralists tend to regard the factor of communication as a dependent variable. There is not much room here for re-communitization through interaction. Transculturality, which is hugely important to constructivists, plays no role from this perspective. What we find instead is the strengthening of traditional community ties since networks can only act within established social relationships. While constructivists see inter- and transcultural communities on the Internet that transcend traditional communities as a possibility, structuralists regard inter- and transcultural interactions merely as a kind of thin and superficial cosmopolitanism. Structuralists see the burgeoning of nationalism and fundamentalism as a far more likely outcome, recalling the problem

164 Large communities: global online communication

of hate speech, which we have yet to discuss. James Curran, for example, contends that the inherent value and belief structures of this world cannot be overcome online through a utopian, virtual, intercultural dialogue. Instead, he asserts, the Internet is inevitably becoming a new combat zone for chauvinistic communities (2012, p. 10).

The reciprocity model of the global online community

In line with our system-lifeworld-network approach, we have to chart a middle course through this dispute. Social structures do play a role, while a technology-centred view of globalization is utopian. Yet under certain circumstances interactive processes can influence global communality more than structuralists believe possible – both in virtual and virtualized communities. It seems reasonable to assume a reciprocity model in which social structures and (digital) interaction influence one another in every situation.

As far as virtual communities are concerned, it must be recognized that even purely mediatized interaction can in principle be just as multimodal as face-to-face communication, especially when communication takes place via visual and sound media, such as Internet telephony or video conferencing. In the chapter on economic communication, we showed that direct communication may have advantages over mediatized communication (see Chapter 4, Section 4.2.2), but ultimately it is the degree of multimodality rather than multimodality itself that is at issue here (Greschke 2013). Hence, just what social co-presence means for interactive communality is yet to be defined with sufficient clarity. The reason we refer to virtual communities as "hyphenated communities" – interest groups, gaming communities, and so on – is not because they are generally less interactive or community-building, but because they do not shape our entire existence, though they do describe part of our identity. They thus have a socially integrative function in that they bring people with different social roots together in a kind of "third space" between the private and the public (Nayar 2010, pp. 44, 59). This does not change a person's socioeconomic circumstances but may change their consciousness under certain circumstances.

In principle, there is no difference at all here between global and traditional local communities, as even the latter do not necessarily have the same formative influence on our lives as in earlier times. We need only think of the large, scattered family whose members have only occasional contact. In light of all these considerations, it is also dangerous to designate modern communities as "thin communities" (Baumann 2000, p. 199ff.) or to assume that global communities are structurally inferior because they tend to be loosely connected (Djelic and Quack 2010, p. 51). From this point of view, football fans can never form real communities, as they take on no reciprocal obligations, getting high on a feeling of supposed communality from which they can escape at any time. Such perspectives underestimate the influence that these forms of communality can exert on everyday life (Brown et al. 2009, p. 6). At the same time, it has to be admitted that the greater the number of

Large communities: global online communication **165**

communities (plural) a person enters, the lower the degree of differentiation (Djelic and Quack 2010, p. 3), so that often the transnational community in particular can no longer be an old-style multiplex community. Instead, it is an addition to an existence that continues to be shaped by local influences.

Even the apparently traditional "virtualized communities" that merely relocate to the Internet essentially create new social facts. Large groups that meet via newsgroups or in chat rooms under national and/or religious auspices – migrant diaspora communities have been subject to a good deal of research here – do not simply strengthen existing communities, but at the same time recreate and change them, as we will see later. The natural, lifeworld-based interlinking of people across borders, people who work, live and marry internationally, as called for by Meckel, has long been a reality rather than pure utopia, and is in fact an expression of the declining significance of monolocalism (Kneidinger 2013, p. 100). Diasporic online communities are home to a blend of virtual and virtualized communality, with old strong ties being joined by new weak ties; new strong ties may even emerge (a mechanism observable within and beyond online extremist communities that recruit followers online before ushering them step by step into small real-world groups).

To refer to the "re-tribalization" of socially co-present ethnic and religious ties in the age of the Internet is thus simplistic. Present-day researchers have good reason for deploying a critical concept of diaspora. The diasporic community not only essentializes the homeland from a distance, but in many ways practises a kind of "strategic essentialism" (Naficy 1993, p. 197), with the apparent focus on the place of origin functioning not so much to spread national and religious beliefs internationally as to adapt them to the new local context. In reality, then, there are no homogeneous diasporas (of Jews, Turks, Muslims, Armenians, and so on), but rather transcultural sub-communities that may arise within the diaspora. A strong influence of global communication – interaction, interpretation, discourses – is just as conceivable here as a communication-resistant insistence on traditional, essentialist views of the community. It is high time for a quite new interpretation of the digital diaspora as, in part, a heterogeneous process of community-building (Karim 2018, p. 12).

Overall, it is fair to say that existing local social structures show strong persistence (reinforced, as we will see, by the fact that the quality of global interaction can vary greatly). Nevertheless, completely new (online) communities are also emerging *beyond and within traditional large communities*, in virtual as well as in virtualized form. Stegbauer's proposal to use the term "network" rather than "online community" (2001, p. 91) fails to adequately capture this social dynamic and Tönnies's concept of community has proven to be outdated in part (In der Smitten 2007, p. 116ff.). Stephen Graham's plea for a multi-perspectival view and a combination of constructivist and structuralist approaches – which he describes as "technological" and "co-evolutionary" perspectives – is absolutely central here (2010, p. 103).

If one wants to understand the communicative processes of online communities, the first step is to keep in mind the variety of forms. As we develop our argument,

166 Large communities: global online communication

the two basic types of virtualized community (such as diasporas) and virtual communities (such as interest groups and gaming communities) and their combinations are particularly important. An adapted layer model, inspired by Stegbauer (2001, p. 281) and In der Smitten (2007, p. 131), but heavily modified, is intended to provide a preliminary overview of types of communality:

1. *Virtualized communities*: Based on semi-voluntary relationships to community as found in local communities, such as family, nationality or religious groups, or based on voluntary local communities, such as online friendship groups.
2. *Virtual communities*: Based on voluntary relationships to community in interest groups and gaming groups of all kinds, whose membership does not depend on social structures but on process variables such as time and duration.
3. *Combined virtualized-virtual communities*: Based on voluntary large-group communication and semi-voluntary community membership, for example, in online diasporas, religious groups and ethnic groupings.

Global social capital: cosmopolitanism or cultural battle between communities?

We have thus highlighted the path dependence of the structures of global online communities, but we have not yet adequately explained it. An action-theoretical perspective is still missing. When it comes to the structures of lifeworlds, we do not refer to organization, system and *function*, but we distinguish between structures and *motives for action* (see, among others, Schütz and Luckmann 2003). The theory of social capital, developed by various authors, which is often used in the analysis of online communities (Barnes 2013, p. 153ff.), is one apt means of capturing motives for action. The focus here is on the social "capital profit" generated by communities. At present, whether online communities have a positive, negative or merely supplementary effect on social capital is as controversial an issue as the formation of the structures of the online community itself (Hofer 2012).

Robert D. Putnam distinguishes between the internal and external capital of communities (which he refers to respectively as bonding and bridging capital). Internal capital is the surplus profit earned by members of a community *in* the community, that is, identity growth, emotional group experience and specific information (2000). This typology, though not identical, is at least similar to Granovetter's division into strong and weak ties (Kneidinger 2010, p. 29). Internal capital may also be generated by purely virtual weak ties, provided that these are sustainable and intense enough to generate a sense of community (see p. 167), because this may produce gains in terms of identity, information and emotion. With respect to the globalization of virtualized communities, it is, for example, ethnically- or religiously-based diaspora networks that facilitate access to the world when travelling and migrating, since members of the community can be found everywhere, regardless of whether these contacts are strong or weak (Quayson and Daswani 2013). In the case of new instances of communitization (virtual communities),

Large communities: global online communication **167**

the principle is similar, though the access requirements are different. It is not the apparent "equality" of origin, but diversity on the basis of universal humanity that promotes transcultural communication, as, for example, in the couchsurfing hospitality network or international gaming communities that may be based on humanistic values (Schumann et al. 2009).

But communities do not generate just one type of internal capital. Diasporic communities are no longer limited to nationalism, contacts with places of origin or specific intentions to return (Mayer 2005, p. 8ff.) and gaming communities are by no means cosmopolitan *per se*, but may, for example, merely focus local fan communities on the same international object (Harrington and Bielby 2007). Both types of community thus generate local and global types of capital. Various communities emerge *within* communities (Djelic and Quack 2010). But we might wonder whether type 3, the "virtualized-virtual community", promises the greatest social capital gains, since it maintains contact with the local co-present community while at the same time forging new contacts. George Rupp has summarized this idea through the concept of an "inclusive global community", arguing that only global communities that do not run counter to the old ones, instead taking them along, as it were, into the global context, are socially relevant (2006, p. 94f.). The best of both worlds? Concepts such as the "rooted cosmopolitanism" proposed by Kwame Anthony Appiah (2006) or the dialogic community of social majorities and minorities envisaged by Kai Hafez (2014a, p. 353ff.) aim in this direction.

However, social capital theory also recognizes the external capital (bridging capital) of communities. External capital and the corresponding networks are important to anchoring the community in society, that is, to achieving benefits not *in* the community but *through* it. However, these weak ties also characterize the cultural struggles between communities, especially since positive internal values may be associated with external boundaries. "The best of both worlds" is difficult to achieve when tensions arise between communities (for example, with respect to national affiliation in cases of dual citizenship). Political-ideological contexts are thus crucial to the sociological understanding of the social capital gains generated by global online communities.

Global community or global society?

Ultimately, the question is whether the digital development of the Internet in particular is contributing to the creation of a space for a growing dialogic global community – beyond global society with its (fragmented) public spheres and (loosely connected) social movements (see also Chapter 1, Section 1.1). Virtual or virtualized communities or their amalgams may in principle generate quite different forms of social capital that either strengthen the agonistic public sphere or the integrated global community. However, questions about community formation cannot be answered with sociological action theory alone. We require an analysis informed by communication studies if we are to understand how and why which individuals choose or maintain which relationships to community and which type of

168 Large communities: global online communication

social capital is preferred: local, cosmopolitan or "rooted" cosmopolitan (see also Walls 1993; Srinivasan 2017, p. 211ff.). Section 6.2 will probe the communication processes on which communities are based and put forward an empirical assessment of the Internet's contribution in this regard.

6.2 Communicative system connections

How exactly do global online communities communicate? The key theoretical modes of communication – interaction, observation and discourse – continue to guide our thinking in this chapter, since (1) interaction through large groups creates the online community in the first place, (2) observation and knowledge diffusion are essential forms of social capital (especially in so-called "wiki communities"), and (3) discourses are significant in communities' internal and external relationships. But it makes no sense to augment the basic modes of communication with organizational theory, as in the previous chapters, since communities are not formal organizations. In the case of online communities, then, it seems more appropriate to use a combination of structuralist analysis of the Internet – how stable and sustainable are networks and communication flows in large groups? – and theories of interpersonal interaction and dialogue. This will enable us to illuminate how emotions are dealt with in global networks and how rational consensus is achieved with regard to the idea of community.

6.2.1 Interaction and dialogue

The cascade model of global online communication

In structuralist Internet research, the intensity of community in large virtual groups such as mailing lists, chat rooms, and so on is chiefly determined in light of the frequency, sustainability and responsiveness of the interaction between members (Stegbauer 2001; Stegbauer and Rausch 2006). This approach is inadequate, however, since no in-depth content analysis is carried out. For example, a dispute on the Internet between different actors may generate interest but will not necessarily lead to a collective consensus. A dialogic space is absolutely essential to negotiating a new communality across borders, especially with respect to global communication, with its often rather low level of cross-border social interpenetration. We thus use the term "relationality" for those aspects of relationships measured in structuralist analysis of the Internet, distinguishing this from "dialogicity" as highlighted both in a negotiation-oriented dialogic approach and in the notion of communicative action (see Chapter 1, Section 1.3). Relationality goes beyond basic "connectivity" in that it no longer only measures *whether* people are connected online, but *how*. This qualitative assessment, however, is most reminiscent of classic network analysis in that we measure frequency, sustainability and responsiveness.

In addition to the triumvirate of elements central to interactional analysis, namely connectivity, relationality and dialogicity, there is another dimension that

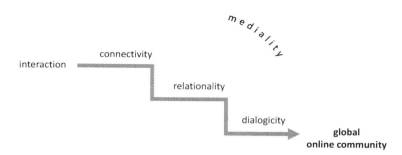

FIGURE 6.1 The cascade model of interaction in the global online community

we are going to call "mediality". In contrast to small groups, large groups and their online communities not only refer to media but produce their own mediality (through newsletters, for instance). Media are not just system environments, then, but part of the system and its imagined communal space.

We can imagine the dimensions of connectivity, relationality and dialogicity as a cascade model, since one level is the prerequisite for reaching the next level and communality and social capital grow as the levels are traversed (see Figure 6.1). Here, as we will see, geocultural (including linguistic) hurdles must be overcome, networks must form a tightly woven fabric and sustainable values must be worked out through dialogue. In this concept, mediality is the space of discursive feedback in which the interactive community and the discursive community interact.

Connectivity: Internet geography and online territories

It makes sense to begin by clarifying the extent to which people are digitally networked across borders, while making no distinction in the first instance between interaction and other forms of communication, such as discourse – as exemplified by the reading of online media – but seeking only to quantify the crossing of borders as such. It turns out that a large part of humanity is still far from being integrated into global communities. It is true that the technical data points to strong growth in international Internet traffic over the last few decades. Both technological transmission (supply) and effective use (traffic) have increased enormously (Hafez 2014b, p. 648ff.). However, data transfers are unevenly distributed and are more extensive between industrialized countries and across the Atlantic, for example, than across the Pacific. In addition, the globalization of the economy promotes the circulation of gigantic amounts of data, but only a – hard to calculate – fraction of this helps establish understanding in diplomacy, economy and society.

Another problem is the ratio of global to local Internet usage. We can refer to real globalization with respect to connectivity only if subregional, regional and national growth rates of Internet-based exchange are lower than international traffic. But this is not the case. The growing Internet traffic in the world arises primarily from an increasing concentration of local communication flows, not from

170 Large communities: global online communication

border crossing (see also Goldenberg and Levy 2009). International hyperlinks are less common than global ones. In the United States, 90 per cent of all hyperlinks remain national in character; in Europe, the figure is no less than 60 to 70 per cent, with about half of the US and European websites studied featuring no international hyperlinks at all (Halavais 2000).

According to Ethan Zuckerman at the Massachusetts Institute of Technology (MIT), averaged out across the industrialized countries virtually no-one uses more than 7 per cent foreign content on the Internet (as measured by the top ten websites used by the individual). By way of comparison, only 3 per cent of US books are translations and only 9.4 per cent of flights are international (2013, pp. 56, 60, 69). Zuckerman concludes that our online travels are amazingly similar to our offline travels and, on average, both point to highly local networks in our lives (see also Warf 2013, pp. 22, 39).

When it comes to the question of whether the rise of Web 2.0, in other words, social media, has fostered the internationalization of the Internet, Zuckerman takes a critical look at data from Facebook from 2010, according to which 15 per cent of "friendship" connections were supposedly international (2013, p. 113ff.). He clarifies that these percentages are mainly generated by travellers and migrants and therefore remain in the same geocultural area. Travellers, then, generate a meagre form of globality that results in misleading statistics. Migrants' digital border crossing is real but takes place within communities featuring social co-presence and the same language, so it can be interpreted as intercultural only to a limited extent. The comparative study produced by Nitish Singh, Kevin Lehnert and Kathleen Bostick on the use of social media, which examined around 4,500 users from the EU, the United States and the BRICS countries, shows that local language use is extremely widespread on MySpace, LinkedIn, Facebook and Twitter, and in many cases local social media are used (2012, p. 698). George Ritzer's assumption that social media are a "truly global phenomenon" (2010, p. 290) is therefore only correct inasmuch as social media are used all over the world. But this occurs predominantly within narrow linguistic or national borders.

Cross-border interactions with other countries or even language areas as prerequisites for global online communities are thus a marginal phenomenon in social media as well. Our online territories resemble geopolitical or geocultural territories. To quote Ethan Zuckerman: "It's not enough to be enthusiastic about the possibility of connection across cultures, by digital or other means. Digital cosmopolitanism, as distinguished from cyberutopianism, requires us to take responsibility for making these potential connections real" (2013, p. 30).

Digital divides and the multilingualization of the Internet

Why is international Internet traffic so meagre? Connectivity is closely related to socioeconomic conditions. Large numbers of people have never made a phone call or used the Internet, which is what is meant by the "digital divide" (Hafez 2014b; Schejter 2017). Internet penetration has been growing in recent decades, but half

Large communities: global online communication 171

the population of Asia and two-thirds of Africa are still excluded from it (Internet World Stats 2018).

Another reason is the increasing multilingualism of the Internet, which has been facilitated by media regulation. The Internet Corporation for Assigned Names and Numbers (ICANN), a worldwide coordinating agency for the Internet, allowed the use of non-Latin language characters for domain names in close consultation with UNESCO. The result was a multitude of linguistic landscapes on the Internet, which fostered local and regional developments online, but also raised major language barriers, subsequently hindering global exchange. The hegemony of English on the net persists but is constantly decreasing. Three-quarters of all Internet users at present are not native English speakers (Internet World Stats 2017). This is reflected at the content level, where English is increasingly losing its function as a link language as other languages spread. Since the 1990s, the proportion of English-language content on the Internet has fallen from more than 80 per cent to around 50 per cent (Web Technology Survey 2018). Exact figures are difficult to determine here because search engines do not adequately capture social media. Zuckerman, in fact, estimates that English makes up less than 40 per cent of the Internet (2013, p. 136f.).

That so much is in fact still communicated in English, though only 25 per cent of Internet users are native English speakers, surely has much to do with the high level of content productivity in Western industrialized societies: around 80 per cent of all domains are registered in Europe and the United States. Asia is significantly less productive in this respect. Japan, for example, has twice as many users as the UK, but less than a third the number of websites (Graham et al. 2015, p. 94f.). Hence, English is still the leading language for online information – but the lifeworld of online communities is dominated by local languages, with German online communities, for example, using English as a foreign language far less naturally and confidently than, for example, their Dutch equivalents due to the Netherlands' historically rooted multilingualism (Dailey-O'Cain 2017).

We might assume in the case of gaming communities that the game itself overcomes language barriers through its universal rules, yet here too the influence of language and region is clearly recognizable. "League of Nations", for example, played by about 100,000 million people around the world in 2016, is dominated by North America and Europe. Only 20 per cent of participants in this game, 80 per cent of which is played in English, come from other continents (Newon 2014, p. 64ff.).

Overall, these – admittedly incomplete – data allow us to conjecture that global connectivity in English or other languages is the exception rather than the rule. Linguistic and cultural boundaries are only overcome by those who not only have the economic wherewithal but also the linguistic competence and the motivation to do so in international link languages or in less international languages. Online communities tend to be nationally oriented or at least geared towards a national language and are not, therefore, globally networked to any great extent. At first sight, this seems to provide backing for those structuralists who believe in the formative

172 Large communities: global online communication

influence of real-world social structures. Beyond professional systems, the Internet seems to have opened up rather small spaces for global communitization. A range of socioeconomic, political-legal and geocultural divides keep people across the world from interactive networking in a global community (see also Jenkins et. al. 2013, p. 286). We have already pointed out that music, sounds and images can often be transported globally more easily than texts because they do not have to be translated (see Chapter 2, Section 2.2.1). However, this form of co-orientation – for example, towards global stars – is not sufficient to produce an interactive community, because it represents at most a *motive* for global interaction, which is prevented, among other things, by the "Babel of languages" on the Internet.

Relationality: asynchrony and community density

We refer to the typical problems of large-community and large-group communication on the Internet as questions of relationality. Large communities can be subdivided into large groups that at most communicate internally or with each other, so that large communities never represent cohesive full network structures, as parts of them are not interactively connected at all (see also Bravo 2013, p. 121). Even within a large-group network, there are numerous aspects relating to the connectedness of individuals that we may summarize under the terms multimodality and asynchrony.

Mediatized interaction may in principle be as multimodal as face-to-face communication if transmission occurs via visual and auditory media (such as Skype or Zoom). While we showed in Chapter 4 on the economy that face-to-face has certain advantages when it comes to informal communication, ultimately, as we have stated, the crucial aspect is the *degree of multimodality* rather than multimodality itself (Greschke 2013). In principle, then, online communication is "media rich", making it a form of communication that also conveys emotions and interpersonal gestures, which may in turn foster community (Tian et al. 2012, p. 234ff.). Social media can certainly have a socially reinforcing effect, and this often outstrips the forces at play in real-world neighbourhoods.

Large groups, however, often generate constraints on ideal interaction and communality, which we summarize here under the term "asynchrony" (Stegbauer 2001, p. 83ff., 155ff.; Stegbauer and Rausch 2006, p. 50ff.; In der Smitten 2007, p. 70ff.). Asynchronous communication is the primary form of interaction in online communities (Mascio 2012, p. 20). In digital networks there are always patterns of hierarchy (opinion leaders, less active people, lurkers, and so on), and the larger a group is, the lower the participation level of individual group members. Topics are not dealt with comprehensively or necessarily in a logical order. Opinions within these groups change when actors do, and many of those who participate in online communication do so with varying frequency, sustainability and reciprocity, which raises the question of whether all participants are really part of a stable "community". Mailing lists increase asynchrony because they are designed to be rolling rather than interactive. In addition to consecutive threads, erratic discourses often spring up in

Large communities: global online communication **173**

chat rooms. Administrators may play a variety of roles, as moderators or technical directors, which affects synchronization.

According to Stegbauer, this means that the problems of relationality that exist in offline assembly communication (just think how hard it is for most individuals to raise their voice and be heard in townhall meetings, and so on) have not been solved in the online world (2001, p. 278ff.). The fact that online communication is a hybrid of active interaction and more passive discourse communication *even within relational networks* does not necessarily mean that online communities do not arise – we just have to acknowledge that these are largely *discursive* communities. A portion of the community consensus is interaction-based, while another part is more discursive, as typical of large imagined and mass media-constructed communities (see p. 164ff.). Hence, a shift towards dialogue in large communities, as perceived by constructivists, does not necessarily occur. Here we already see a difference emerging between "thick" and "thin" communality, which will concern us later, for example, when we address "pop cosmopolitanism" (see p. 175f.).

So far, virtually no structuralist Internet research has been done on global online communities. Still, Stegbauer not only confirms the trend in connectivity mentioned above, namely that even in international Internet forums individuals from the platforms' country of origin are present in far greater numbers than foreigners, but also points out that foreign users often occupy less influential relational positions (2001, p. 277). Furthermore, Hyunji Lee has established that the problems of relationality in large groups also come into play on the Internet: community members are often lurkers and their involvement is irregular and short-term, so there are varying degrees of community engagement (2018). Other network studies measure the frequency and density of interaction, but they are geared primarily towards national rather than global interaction (Drüeke 2013; Kneidinger 2010, 2013). Research on transnational communities remains largely the preserve of the culture-oriented academic disciplines, which focus less on formal structures of relationality than on the content of global interaction, as we shall now see.

Dialogicity 1: global echo chambers

Andreas Hepp has rightly pointed out that transnational diaspora communication is a trend running counter to the otherwise geospatially restricted Internet-based communication experienced by many individuals (2008). Migrants, like other global informational elites, may be viewed as an avant-garde of global communication. At the same time, we have shown that interaction through the primarily asynchronous communication typical of online communities is not necessarily perfectly dialogic, which points to the need for analysis of group communication over longer periods of time (Mascio 2012, p. 23). With its network analyses, structuralist Internet research is not fully capable of capturing dialogicity in online communities. A "narrative network analysis" (Weeks 2012) is also required if we are to answer our initial question as to whether online communities are chiefly defined

174 Large communities: global online communication

by venerable social structures or by new instances of communitization, how people combine different elements with respect to transcultural identities and what sort of social capital is generated in these communities.

In what follows, we present three basic interactive models that can be considered paradigmatic of global online communities:

- the essentialist community of origin (diaspora);
- the limited transcultural community of interest (gaming and fan communities);
- the transcultural community of origin (diaspora).

If we begin with the first type, well-known examples of essentialist global online communities are parts of the Hindu or Muslim diaspora in the United States, which not only collect donations, but also form interactive communities through newsletters and Facebook pages (Mayer 2005, p. 18f.; Mohammad-Arif 2011). The Islamic-jihadist variant of Islamism has been thoroughly researched, from the Taliban and Al-Qaeda to the Islamic State, which are globally active on the Internet (see also Bunt 2003; el-Nawawy and Khamis 2011). Studies on the Latin American diaspora in Germany have also shown that foreign-language media, not least on the Internet, are often associated with a feeling of cultural distinction vis-à-vis the host country and that essentialist cultural views may be perpetuated, especially in the diaspora, through a kind of "cultural exile" (Saucedo Añez 2014, p. 150ff.; see Hafez 2002d). Parallel cultural societies are by no means a universal feature of diasporas, but they do represent a *specific current* within them.

Miyase Christensen, André Jansson and Christian Christensen – drawing heavily on *Spaces of Identity* by David Morley and Kevin Robins – have made it clear that web-based communities delimit "online territories" as they include or exclude members in light of the default settings and "cultural codes" of online interaction (2011, p. 3ff.; see Morley and Robins 1995; see also Sarısakaloğlu 2019). There are also indications that social co-presence, for example, in the form of cultural essentialism, nationalism or fundamentalism, exercises a strong influence here, which appears to confirm the validity of the structuralist approach to research on community. This corroborates Stegbauer's assumption of the persistence of local cultural identities. He contends that local communities are in fact often more heterogeneous than virtual ones, since virtual memberships are based on a set of topics "agreed in advance" (2001, p. 53). In this sense, essentialist global online communities are nothing more than "echo chambers" relocated to global space and featuring little dialogue, since cultural ideas other than essentialist ones barely come into play.

Online territories are, so to speak, the geocultural extension of the Internet's locally and regionally imbued spaces of connectivity. They show that transnationality is not the same as transculturality. Furthermore, the expansion of nationalist and fundamentalist views into global space creates new fields of communicative friction, which we will be considering when we discuss online communities' external communication (see p. 183ff.).

Dialogicity 2: pop cosmopolitanism, gaming and "global metropolis"

A second type of online community is essentially an example of a "virtual community" featuring little local co-presence. This includes global interest groups of all kinds. Fan and gaming communities, for which the term "pop cosmopolitanism" has gained traction, have been well studied. Japanese anime, Korean dramas and Korean pop music (K-pop) have generated global online communities. Henry Jenkins identifies such phenomena as symbols of "semiotic solidarity" (2006, p. 156) in the global community. As an alternative to the often stereotype-ridden film, television and music industries, online communities centred on pop cosmopolitanism are celebrated as a transcultural phenomenon (Shaheen 2009; Lee 2014, p. 198). In contrast to the essentialist diaspora, they seek to escape the parochiality of their cultures of origin (Jenkins et al. 2013, p. 275). Global pop culture may sensitize culturally and transculturalize ideas about culture, but there is no guarantee that stereotypical ideas will not be perpetuated (Jenkins 2006, p. 164). In the case of global gaming communities, it also remains unclear to what extent players transfer transculturality in the "third space" of the game to real-world cultural ideas (Castronova 2007, p. 76f., 176).

Another question is whether this really creates a dialogic communality or – in line with our earlier remarks – an illusory "thin community". Pramod K. Nayar emphasizes the interactive quality of fan sites, which bring people from all over the world together and create a kind of new collective identity (2010, p. 106f.; see also Black 2009). Jenkins too describes the direct interactivity on the fan sites of pop cosmopolitanism as the "beginnings of a global perspective" (2006, p. 166). Nayar concedes, however, that interactivity, especially in the case of computer games, is often limited to the narratives of the gaming world or is influenced by them (2010, p. 36). Jenkins believes there is no guarantee of transcultural understanding because the selectivity of cultural contact is too great (2006, p. 169). "Selectivity" in turn means that – above all due to the problems affecting the relationality of interaction described above – consistent and sustainable dialogues, which are required to produce transculturality, are likely to be the exception rather than the rule.

Taken together, the optimistic and pessimistic perspectives alert us to a range of global online communities in the fields of pop culture and gaming, extending from highly interactive and dialogue-oriented to weakly interactive, discursive, recipient-oriented and essentialistically predetermined. Pop cosmopolitanism has an inherent instability that makes a uniform theoretical description difficult. Even if we recognize that new lifeworld-based global interaction is emerging here, spaces for genuine, concentrated and sustainable dialogues, which, moreover, focus on cultural rather than purely fictional issues, are generally small and as yet under-researched. What Zuckerman calls "unexpected encounters" (2013, pp. 26f., 30), that is, dealing with what is perceived as culturally "other", is likely to be a by-product of their interests for most members of global pop and gaming communities on the Internet – rather than the primary social capital. Online communities do not generate a purely imagined cosmopolitanism as in the case of media

176 Large communities: global online communication

reception (see Chapter 1, Section 1.1 and Chapter 2, Section 2.2.2), as at least the beginnings of interactivity are in evidence here. But they are more reminiscent of life in Robert S. Fortner's "global metropolis" (1993) than in Marshall McLuhan's "global village", as we tend to find fleeting interaction, apparent closeness and a "thin cosmopolitanism" rather than a deep and dialogically cemented cultural knowledge.

Dialogicity 3: digital (trans)cultural salons

Things look entirely different when it comes to post-essentialist online diasporic communities. Jowan Mahmod has produced one of the few narrative network analyses to provide insights into the dialogic processes of online communities. The textual production of the Kurdish diaspora is a first step towards hybridity, as the members of the community themselves are no longer just interpreters and reproducers of traditional writings, but generate their own themes, frames and concepts (2016, p. 180). What is interesting here is a phenomenon that may be described as the distinction between metanarrative and narrative. Some things are obviously less negotiable in the Kurdish diaspora than others, especially the suffering of the Kurdish people, which must not be questioned. However, other traditions relating to gender, religion, politics and sexuality are highly contested (ibid., pp. 181, 183). Central myths of the diaspora thus persist within the online community, constituting the core of community identity, which is, however, constantly being renegotiated in other ways: "[D]iaspora Kurds have, to an increasing extent, adopted a non-essentialist approach to the understanding of their identities" (ibid., p. 197). Other communities also turn out to be diverse, such as the Arab and/or Muslim online communities (Mandaville 2001; Lim 2009). Studies highlighting diversity have also appeared, for example, on the Roma and on Chinese transnational online communities (Kapralski 2014; Ip and Yin 2016).

By now, the notion of the digital diaspora as an essentialist expression of nationalist and fundamentalist social co-presence has been thoroughly revised. Miyase Christensen, André Jansson and Christian Christensen affirm this quite different view of the diaspora despite their references to connected "online territories":

> While there is a temptation to interpret the often observed attachment of dispersed people with a transnational community as a reproduction of the imagined community of the nation beyond boundaries, the diasporic case is significantly different from both the nation and from any primordial bounded community.
>
> *(2011, p. 216; see also p. 268)*

Kevin Robins, one of the authors of *Spaces of Identity*, also concludes, in light of Turkish-language digital media use, that simply applying categories of community such as the "nation" to online communities fails to do justice to the complexities involved (2003; see also Budarick 2014; Mellor 2014, p. 110).

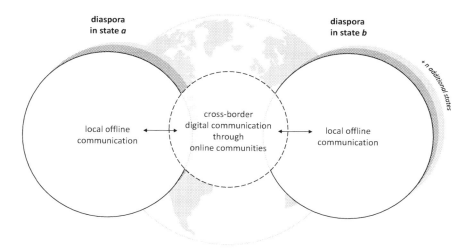

FIGURE 6.2 Diasporic digital networks

Researchers thus need to be aware of the risk of a "methodological nationalism" (De Cesari and Rigney 2014, p. 2) that regards the ethnic and religious basis of an online community exclusively or primarily as the extension into global space of the cultural mainstream in the countries of origin. The opposite is true. The repressive cultural demands characteristic of many of the world's social systems are in fact driving minority attitudes into the new fields of communitization constituted by global networks, which are generating innovative cultural dialogues (Martin 2009).

Another aspect is important. The social co-presence of diaspora communities emits new transcultural impulses not only in digital space, but also through the interaction between online and offline communities. Drawing on the example of the Haitian diaspora in the United States, Michael S. Laguerre has shown that its communication is not only directed towards Haiti, but that the communicative networks always include the migrant's local (US-American) environment (2006; see also Singh 2011, p. 158). Since returnees to Haiti contribute to these networks, transcultural impulses arise at both ends of the diaspora (see Figure 6.2). Mahmod too attests to the experiential aspect of online interaction:

> We saw how dialogues went from essentialist understanding of the Kurdish identity to constructionist views ... Blood and soil, and pride and memories framed much of these answers initially, but as they delved into the questions, participants began to talk about identity as the result of experiences.
>
> *(2016, p. 184)*

Overall, the Internet makes a genuine contribution to the establishment of new transcultural "salons". In some cases, basic assumptions are turned upside down here, such as the idea that voluntary online communities are always more culturally diverse than semi-voluntary communities of origin. The sustainability and density of communication (relationality) as well as the intensity of cultural exchange (dialogicity) may be more pronounced in the diaspora than in often fleeting and unstable voluntary communities that act as echo chambers. Hence, the solid foundation provided by ethnic or religious ties may even strengthen transcultural impulses. Essentialist or transcultural modes of interaction can literally occur in all three basic structural models of online communication: the virtual, the virtualized and the combined form (see also Section 6.1). A purely structuralist view that assumes social co-presence and disregards the role of dialogic interaction on the Internet therefore makes little sense here.

At the same time, it would be a mistake to reject "methodological nationalism" only to lapse into its opposite, methodological cosmopolitanism. First, there are a variety of – essentialist as well as transcultural – online communities. Second, key primordial myths have not gone away and may be revived in the event of crisis. Third, not all differentiated transcultural narratives are automatically part of a cosmopolitan metanarrative (De Cesari and Rigney 2014, p. 6). Fourth, not every differentiation of the virtualized diaspora automatically means increased dialogicity, since differences may lead to the separation of sub-networks, which can find expression in positional shifts in connectivity (the decoupling of networks) or relationality (a sliding into passivity within interaction).

Studies of the Russian diaspora have shown that there may also be crude forms of dispute in online communities (Kuntsman 2010). It would surely be misguided to refer to fully developed dialogues here, given that opinions merely clash antithetically with no prospect of a synthesizing consensus. Still, such studies show that while the fleetingness of digital connectivity and community is likely to be characteristic of the diaspora as well, online communities may be stable enough not to crumble at the slightest sign of pluralism. Such communities then serve as a "third" negotiating space for the modernization of old narratives, which is unlikely to be an entirely harmonious process (Jungbluth 2018, p. 237).

Discursive community through media use

In all large communities, media play a significant role, as they do in social movements. Diasporas are both discursive and interactive communities. The latter often draw on the topics, frames and discourses of the media and process them further (Stegbauer 2001, p. 54ff.; De Cesari and Rigney 2014, p. 15). The exact relationship between online communities and media use is, however, more complicated than in the case of social movements. Here, in the division into local (often large) and transnational (often small) media, we identified a factor that exercises a significant influence on the generally weak cohesion that pertains beyond certain movement elites. When it comes to large communities, however, what matters is the type of community involved. Socially co-present communities, such as diasporas, are likely to feature a dynamic similar to that of social movements, since use is made of both home media and the media of the host countries (Hafez 2002d; Saucedo Añez 2014). While the

Large communities: global online communication **179**

latter reinforce the different experiences of diaspora members, that is, represent centrifugal forces, the media of the home countries play a bridging role, thus enabling a discursive space, renewed daily, to emerge within the diaspora. This space, however, cannot be described as "transnational" any more than other mass media and, as a rule, it features domesticating influences from the home countries (Hafez 2007a, p. 69ff., see also Chapter 2, Section 2.2.1).

Many recipients of a large community's media, moreover, are *not* concurrently members of online communities, in other words, they are not involved in the digital interaction. However, where spaces of media discourse and online interaction overlap, the media agenda is by no means to be equated with the reception agenda or the agenda of the online communities. Qatari television broadcaster Al-Jazeera, for example, long seemed to unite the Arab diaspora, but the discursive and interactive communities that engaged in online follow-up communication were always highly heterogeneous (Mellor 2014, p. 100f.; see also Galal 2014). The role of the mass media thus ranges from the production of essentialist framing with global appeal to the provision of rather weak stimuli to the development of oppositional identities in online communities. Discursive and interactive spaces interact but are not identical.

The function of mass media vis-à-vis "virtual" global communities such as gaming and fan communities is likely to be somewhat different. The further removed the reason for establishing a community is from the agenda of the mass media, the greater the potential is likely to be to create autonomous and alternative spaces of interaction. Gaming communities develop largely unobserved by the mass media. It is true that the consumer product (star, game, and so on), whose origins lie in the economic system, often provides a predetermined framework and steers the interaction. But in virtual online communities the greater distance from the mass media results in greater opportunities to cultivate an interaction that is not influenced by media discourses and thus to simulate alternative social structures of the lifeworld, as social co-presence plays a subordinate role. Here the global community may be severely restricted in connective terms and may be based on a "thin cosmopolitanism". Yet it may provide greater freedom to explore alternative visions of the global.

Interactive global community?

Overall, the findings on the global online community are highly contradictory. There can be no doubt that – much as in social movements – communality is still largely dominated by local structures. Large communities and the large groups active within them are primarily determined by structures of social co-presence. But ideas of a transcultural or even cosmopolitan community exist at the same time and are formed within online communities both in connection with local community structures and independently (virtualized and virtual global communities). This creates a global lifeworld on the Internet, even beyond the private sphere of the small group or individual.

180 Large communities: global online communication

Social networks have to overcome key impediments relating to connectivity, relationality, dialogicity and mediality if they are to create ideally dense, sustainable and dialogic forms of communality. The data on connectivity indicates that the global online community is still a fringe phenomenon in modern societies, as geocultural online territories predominate. Within these formations as well as beyond them, in foreign-language spaces, heterogeneous communities emerge. These partly foster essentialist re-tribalization, but partly stimulate the transcultural and cosmopolitan processes so central to the global community, which then influence local communities.

6.2.2   Observation and diffusion

Global wiki-knowledge community?

Robert D. Putnam and Howard Rheingold, two "stars" of American research on communities, disagree on the role of the Internet. In contrast to Rheingold (see p. 161f.), Putnam is sceptical about the idea of online communities generating social capital because the social context is missing and the interaction is not true to life (2000, p. 170ff.). As he sees it, digital networks instead tend to generate cultural capital through informational gains. In the literature, online communities are generally viewed not only as contemporary variants of interactive community formation, but also as alternative sources of knowledge diffusion. Collective information sites, so-called "wikis", and in particular Wikipedia, are novel forms of knowledge generation that operate according to the open-source principle (Schlieker and Lehmann 2005). Here a large group, which is often also accessible to laypeople, submits to certain rules of internal review and generates epistemic capital through "swarm intelligence", in other words, through a collective effort. This completely new understanding of elites is interesting with respect to the global diffusion of knowledge insofar as it makes emancipation from resources and power structures that are unevenly distributed across the Earth conceivable in principle.

But this distance from the system of professional scholarship raises theoretical issues. Along the continuum of actor-specific communicative modes, we ascribed the qualities of lifeworldly online communities essentially to the sphere of interaction rather than that of observation (see Figure 1.2). In view of the often erratic discourse in online communities, it is quite legitimate to question the existence of a factually correct, logical and consistent online knowledge community. In contrast to the system of professional scholarship, the Internet itself is yet to produce any Nobel Prize-worthy achievements. Which is closest to reality: the emancipatory or the critical view of global knowledge communities on the Internet?

Wikipedia: Eurocentrism of worldview

If we go back to basic diffusion models such as that of Everett Rogers (see Chapter 4, Section 4.2.3), then the ideal informational networking of the world would provide

Large communities: global online communication **181**

for information flows criss-crossing global society in every direction. But in the case of the world's largest encyclopaedia, Wikipedia, which is fashioned by a global online community, the circulation of information is beset by numerous problems that we may characterize as asymmetries of "participation" and "representation". As far as participation is concerned, there is an unequal distribution of editors (in all the roughly 280 language versions), with more than one million edits being made per quarter in the United States, Germany, France and the UK, but just a few thousand in Africa and the Middle East (Graham et al. 2015, p. 95ff.; see also Lieberman and Lin 2009). While the share of emerging and industrialized countries such as South Africa, Argentina, Brazil or Japan is higher, the percentage of edits by authors from Asia, Africa and Latin America is below 25 per cent, despite the fact that they make up the majority of the world's population.

The second problem is the global representation of countries. The number of country mentions and local entries on Wikipedia largely reflects the distribution of wealth among countries and, again, does not correspond with population size (Graham et al. 2015, p. 98ff.). The marked constraints on global online communities inasmuch as they are based on Eurocentric knowledge of the world are clearly evident here (Hafez 2007a, p. 109ff.). The quality of information on the Internet under conditions of extreme spatial distance thus remains limited. Not only is there unequal access to the Internet (see our remarks on p. 170ff. on the digital divide), but this access is related to asymmetries of knowledge production and representation that affect those who are in fact users of the Internet. First, the image of the Global South remains underdeveloped compared to that of the Global North. There is more information about Pokémon and porn stars on Wikipedia than about sub-Saharan Africa (Simonite 2013). Second, the information available about the non-Western world largely reflects an outside perspective. These asymmetries in the flow of information have rightly been described as a process of colonization in the age of the global information society, which would ideally be remedied by decolonization pursued by other authors through the provision of different information (Simonite 2013; Sengupta et al. 2018). The notion of the online community plugging global knowledge gaps is realized only to a meagre extent by Wikipedia.

Separation and quality of knowledge

As a result, in Asia, Africa and Latin America, the versions in languages other than English are far less important than the English pages, which are used by a small, cosmopolitan, educated class (Wikipedia Statistics n.d.). Low rates of participation and usage are not just a matter of magnitude, but also of the quality of the information generated in other languages, which is generally lower, the fewer the number of people involved. Precisely because it is a layperson's format devoid of formal scholarly institutions, Wikipedia requires a "critical mass of users" (Schlieker and Lehmann 2005, p. 258; Stegbauer and Rausch 2006, p. 239). Because this mass is not present in many languages, the generation of knowledge is also at risk. Jaron Lanier's

182 Large communities: global online communication

remark that "swarm intelligence" is better at establishing facts than producing theoretical knowledge (2010) can fairly be applied to Wikipedia. Yet theory is crucial to establishing "knowledge" as the amount of information grows (Innerarity 2013).

For Wikipedia, this means that all non-English language versions can ensure neither factually correct information nor theoretical competence and are thus of only limited use with respect to the global diffusion of information and knowledge. For the English version, on the other hand, the critical mass needed to ensure successful production appears to be in place, but, as we have seen, it is unevenly distributed across the world, again raising questions about the quality of factual knowledge. The general problem of theoretical capacity applies to the English version as well. The quality of global knowledge on Wikipedia is thus limited in many ways.

The separation of knowledge when we compare the different language versions is another significant problem. Wikipedia seeks to standardize its texts to a large extent, and this is often done through borrowing from existing entries, but there may still be considerable differences. A study of more than 20 language versions on Wikipedia showed that 74 per cent of entries are only available in one language (Hecht and Gergle 2010). Even in the same entries we find differences in representation in their various language versions. A well-known example are the famous Mohammed cartoons in Danish newspaper *Jylands Posten*. They are shown in the relevant English entry, but not, for example, in the German one (see also Niesyto 2012). Differences are also evident in other entries. The German version of the entry on "religion", for example, addresses the unscientific nature of religious beliefs, while the Arabic version does not. The main exception here are certain explosive political issues that, especially in the English version, trigger international "editing wars", which may at least be considered a form of global discourse (Graham 2012).

Leaving aside these cases, the global Wikipedia community not only features fundamental quality defects and Eurocentric centres and peripheries, but the centres and peripheries of the diffusion process are also poorly networked. The latter phenomenon, we may note, at least mitigates the problem of cultural colonialism and indicates that cultural stereotypes are constantly being reproduced communicatively (Hafez 2000a) through a culturally separated form of swarm intelligence. This is due to the low level of producer involvement, at least in the non-English versions of Wikipedia. We are still quite far from the ideal-typical circulation of global knowledge in a global online community.

A global knowledge community?

To sum up, we are faced with three basic problems. First, Wikipedia is not a global knowledge community, but rather an informational community, which, second, exhibits ethnocentric informational hegemonies based on producer and thematic structures, which in turn, third, fosters informational autarkies and the disintegration of the global knowledge community into multiple local or regional knowledge communities. The idea of a global grassroots democracy of knowledge, organized

Large communities: global online communication **183**

by the Internet, remains problematic, since the flow of information and the generation of knowledge appear to be impaired in many ways.

Critics working with the idea of "multiple modernities" reject the utopian notion that the circulation of global knowledge in "global society" is generating a universal modernity by pointing out that "global society" is still strongly influenced by subsystems and local actors (Schwinn 2006, p. 18). Wikipedia certainly offers platforms for global knowledge generation, but the interaction within the Wikipedia community is still too shaped by geocultural factors and too sporadic to make a major contribution to a genuine global knowledge society.

6.2.3 Discursive (external) communication

Intercultural dialogue versus online global war

Communities are regarded as having attained an advanced level of development if, having consolidated internally, they communicate externally with other social entities (In der Smitten 2007, p. 115). In the context of global communication, this marks the transition from transcultural to intercultural dialogue. The traditional assumption is that both internal and external communication generate social capital: internal capital (bonding capital) for internal cohesion and external capital (bridging capital) for social anchoring. However, there are also relationships between the types of capital that resemble a zero-sum game. For example, when communities (such as teams) work closely together, they often avoid external contacts that are perceived as disruptive (Schuller 2007). Even where such contacts exist, other communities are often used to support a group's own identity. Rather than conducting an intercultural dialogue with them, it constructs discursive mirror images or even enemy constructs *about* them. Global online communication may generate social capital in a variety of ways, though by no means is there always a balanced relationship between internal and external capital. Communities may also confront one other in cultural struggles.

Junho H. Choi and James A. Danowski's analysis of Usenet shows that different online communities – Asian and Latin American groups, for example – can certainly form "cohesive subgroups", which suggests a dense intercultural interaction (2002). These cross-connections between online communities defy the essentialism of other groups. However, the question remains whether this happens often. Sophie Croisy assumes the dominance of cultural segmentation, while a contrasting intercultural dialogic culture has yet to develop:

> This space of intercultural relationality is to replace the spaces of cultural segmentation in and around which we live today, where cultural groups are clearly hierarchized in public and political discourses regulated by dominant cultural communities and are not given equal access to decision-making processes.

(2015, p. 9)

184 Large communities: global online communication

Similarly, Dominic Busch argues that even on the Internet, which seems predestined for intercultural exchanges, little use is made of such opportunities for cultural exchange (2012, p. 270). As we have seen, the transcultural potential within online communities is sometimes high. But the intercultural exchange between communities is generally meagre. The "web of identity" (Saunders 2011) is spreading faster than communities of intercultural dialogue.

If we can refer to an "exchange" at all, it often takes the form of hateful communication. Barbara Perry and Patrik Olsson differentiate between direct hate speech, in other words attacks on and threats made to other networks, and indirect hate speech, the expression of hatred in communities of the like-minded (2009). We have already noted with respect to social movements that hate speech is also increasingly taking place online at a global level (see Chapter 5, Section 5.2.2). But what the gain is here for an online community, beyond political interests, remains unclear. Conflicts brought in from outside can destabilize a community, but online communities often disintegrate as a result of internal conflicts, while external attacks may strengthen them (Kendall 2013, p. 316ff.). Hence, the aim of such attacks is often likely to be the simulation of a "cyber war" (also known as "cyberbullying"), which does not necessarily have to result in victory for either side, as verbal wars have no clear winners, but are in fact intended to emphasize a community's identity.

Another potential external capital gain from hate communication is that digital culture wars can lead to new alliances between radical communities. On this premise, external capital would consist not in contact with entirely different social forces, but with similar groups outside of one's own. Stormfront.org, for example, a Nazi and racist web community, has found allies across Europe, North America and Australia (Tsunokai and McGrath 2012, p. 43). Global extremist online alliances emerge which, despite all the differences in views, propagate a mythical core of "white" racial affiliation. The main enemies of stormfront.org are Muslims, followed by Jews, "blacks" and "gypsies" but also the EU, liberalism, and so on (Baumgarten 2017). Images of the enemy are not only created here but are also spread outside the community through a kind of psychological warfare (Perry and Olsson 2009, p. 195).

Antinomy between internal and external capital

The external communication of online communities differs significantly from that of organized social systems such as politics, the economy or social movements. While the main problem for the latter lies in strategic communication, which scarcely permits genuine communicative action in the sense of dialogue, the external communication of online communities is both more dialogic but also far more radical than that of organized systems. Leaving aside the fact that political actors may infiltrate and functionalize online communities (Hafez 2017b; Stegemann and Musyal 2020), the differences are probably due to sociological and communicative shifts in the properties of online communities compared to organized systems.

Large communities: global online communication **185**

In many cases, external social capital must be defined completely differently in the global space than in the classic sociology of the community. An online community is not a "normal" social system in that, unlike in organizations, the strong emphasis on an imaginary core may well indicate an identity-based effort to seal the community off from the rest of society. Since the internal capital gain is likely to play a dominant role for most members of an online community, adjustments to the environment are only to be expected in voluntary communities that aim to achieve this form of exchange as an ideal goal (as in the intercultural exchange characteristic of pop cosmopolitanism). All other online communities, especially the essentialist virtualized groups, have no interest in information or contact with respect to weak ties and pursue pure identity politics. They are either transcultural or essentialist in nature (diasporas, for example), exist in "echo chambers" (internally) or even engage in "cyberbullying" (externally). No consideration is given here to "society", "global society" or a "global public sphere". Online communities can be highly anti-modern in this sense.

However, we cannot completely generalize this antinomy between internal and external communication or internal and external capital. Jan Hanrath and Claus Leggewie have rightly pointed out that in authoritarian states the Internet represents a kind of substitute public sphere (2012, p. 165). Hence, intercultural global communication may play a significantly more constructive role for online communities from such countries and for the globally operating online elites of the Global South, making external communication an important resource.

In terms of communication theory, we can identify obstacles to external intercultural communication at every level. Connectivity between online communities is hard to establish, as the constraints on multimodality make initial contact more difficult. Luisa Conti rightly underlines that intercultural dialogue can only develop in a context in which controversies at the content level are rendered safe by a degree of trust at the relational level of communication (2012, p. 308f.). However, this represents a major obstacle, since trust is closely related to the development of multimodal communication, which is limited on the Internet (see p. 168ff.). Networking towards an intercultural community – in other words, relationality and dialogicity – can only be successful once these paracommunicative hurdles have been overcome. In many cases, however, there is no interaction between communities and discourse remains monologic and sometimes hostile.

The intercultural dialogue on the Internet will probably only be strengthened over the long term if organized civil society ceases to be the only source of initiatives that create a framework for trust, and states act more consistently to enforce regulations combating hate speech online. There is a certain logic to ceasing to leave the Internet solely to aggressive online actors, while seeking to harmonize international law against cybercrime and better co-regulate state and society (Perry and Olsson 2009, p. 195ff.; Hafez 2017b, p. 327ff.). The self-regulation of online communities must also be improved. It is interesting to note that racist extremists are also trying to protect themselves. New members of stormfront.org not only have to submit to rules of discussion but must also complete a trial period (Tsunokai and McGrath 2012, p. 43f.). Other online communities protect themselves through moderators (Chua 2009).

Conclusion: social networks as global communities, plural

Global digital communication is not a mass phenomenon. The Internet is far more a localizing than a globalizing medium. The world's political and cultural boundaries are being reproduced on the Internet. However, new virtual communities do emerge. Existing communities also expand virtually into global space and may create new transcultural spaces through interactive processes. The overall picture, however, is complex, with the evidence pointing to a variety of essentialist and hybrid discursive patterns as well as an unstable and sometimes antinomic relationship between online communities' internal and external capital. Beyond interactive communitization, the Internet can only be viewed as a global informational community to a highly limited extent. On closer inspection, we find that the leading knowledge community, Wikipedia, consists of ethnocentric sub-communities. An integrated global community in the singular – "the digital cosmopolitan global community" – is a far distant prospect and the Internet has made it no more tangible than it was before.

7

SMALL GROUPS

Global lifeworldly communication I

If we discuss feats of global communication in the twenty-first century, then we also have to consider the communicative structures and processes of small groups, since global interaction, observation and discursive action are not only communicative phenomena found in systems and large communities, but also take place in people's lifeworlds. Globalization is not configured on an exclusively systemic basis. It is also generated "from below", otherwise it would not be culturally effective (Mau 2007, p. 53; Pries 2008a, p. 46). People act within different social relationships and situations in their everyday life. Here small groups – from friends and families to interest groups – are lifeworld-based social entities that contribute to the socialization of the individual. Our question now is under what conditions processes of communitization ("global community") and socialization ("global society") shift to global space.

We can assume that, consciously or unconsciously, intentionally or unintentionally, people find themselves in cross-border contact situations and experiential contexts in everyday life. These experiences may, first, be the starting point for the formation of new global groups. Second, they may happen in a direct, communal way in an existing group. Third, they may be processed communicatively in an indirect way in the form of individual or collective experiences in existing local groups. These variants of global small-group experiences have varying potential for the communicative construction of a global community and global society.

The third variant is probably the most common because not all groups travel together or maintain international relationships. In general, however, all group formations inevitably have to deal with the global influences emanating from their environments, even if these only consist of fragments of information in the media or talk on the street. Hence, it is reasonable to state that *globality in itself* creates a potentially global realm of action for the small groups of everyday life, even if they act within a largely stationary framework.

DOI: 10.4324/9781003255239-8

188 Small groups: global lifeworld communication

The group thus becomes a nucleus for global motivations for action and interpretive schemes, because values, norms and patterns of action, in other words, cultural codes, are learned and passed on within it. The group's communicative system is theoretically crucial to the cultural safeguarding of society (Keppler 1994; Habermas 1995). The extent to which this cultural safeguarding is based on a cosmopolitan interpretation and integration of the global community, on multicultural or nationalistic value systems, is, therefore, also evident in the lifeworldly niches of everyday communication. Accordingly, we are concerned with the question of how the interactive dialogic and observational discursive communicative patterns of small groups relate to their global knowledge resources, structures of perception and interpretation as well as global motivations for action.

7.1 Lifeworldly structures of global group communication

Neglected research on groups

In view of the relevance of social groups to the processes indicated above, it is astonishing that we are yet to see a theory of "global" or "cross-border" group communication. While the small group is a key factor in social-theoretical and sociological debates (see, for example, Olmsted 1974; Neidhardt 1983a; Schäfers 1994a; Tegethoff 1999), globalization processes are merely marginal phenomena in that context. The same applies to research on small groups in psychology and social psychology (see, for example, Delhees 1994; Arrow et al. 2000; Witte and Davis 2013). However, interethnic contacts and group conflicts have been examined from a behaviourist perspective. There are thus good reasons why the "contact hypothesis" or the theory of social identity, both of which focus on the role of group discrimination, are key points of reference when it comes to issues of intercultural communication (Allport 1954; Tajfel and Turner 1986; Pettigrew 1998).

Overall, the findings of research on the small group are fragmented with regard to our questions and it is difficult to apply them to long-term collective phenomena of globalization, as the focus is often on micro-processes that occur under short-term experimental conditions and are geared towards the individual (see also Girgensohn-Marchand 1994; Schäfers 1994b, p. 30; Neidhardt 2017). Hence, it is a task for the future to apply group research that is more strongly oriented towards communication studies (for example, Harwood and Howard 2005) to long-term change in group communication in the context of global environments. The global communication of groups, then, is probably the most neglected area of research in the present book.

Through a sociological lens, small groups represent the normal setting for social communication (Schäfers 1994b, p. 33). The quotidian integration of the individual into society is achieved through their embedding in groups. But due to individual freedom, leisure time and mobility in modern, differentiated societies, the possibilities of group membership have expanded and, as the debate on individualization underlines, people have been increasingly freed from the roles and structures of "traditional" communities (Beck 1986, p. 205ff.; Kippele 1998; Kron 2000; Junge

Small groups: global lifeworld communication **189**

2002; Kron and Horáček 2009).The shift in the sociological debate away from the primary group towards networks and other collective forms of interaction is thus understandable, even if there is still a lack of integrated empirical assessments of these developments (Tegethoff 2001).

For the purposes of our discussion, we assume the persistence of social groups without overlooking the ongoing changes in their form and function or their empirical heterogeneity (on types of group, see also Tegethoff 2001; Schmidt 2004, p. 21ff.). From a communication studies perspective, it makes sense to retain the group as a category of collective action, since individuals communicate with others in their "small lifeworlds" (Luckmann 1970) and thus variants of collectively shared communicative situations remain an everyday framework for social actions and ascriptions of meaning. Longer-term socialization effects and binding forces may take a wide range of forms today and the narrow definition of primary groups (Cooley 1909) may no longer provide an adequate empirical picture, but communication still takes place in relatively stable and recurring webs of relations and situations, among people who are known to one another – from the family and work groups embedded in our biographies, which we can choose only to a limited extent, through interest and learning groups that we choose strategically, to friendship groups and partnerships that we grow into voluntarily and mostly by chance.These forms of real-world, group-like relationships stand centre-stage here. We consider "target groups" constructed in the media and by the political sphere, statistical groups and erratic group-like assemblages, meanwhile, only as environmental factors (on the definition of the group, see, for example, Neidhardt 1983b; Schäfers 1994a; Bahrdt 1997; Schmidt 2004).

It is important for our discussion to distinguish groups from organized social systems. Groups too develop organizational patterns through the necessary coordination of the actions and values of their members and are internally "organized" social entities. In sociology there are, therefore, systems-theoretical descriptions of the group as a social system (Neidhardt 1983b, p. 14, 2017;Tegethoff 1999, p. 37ff.). Nevertheless, there are no fixed hierarchies or programmes of action that might be equated with those of political and economic systems. Groups arise from different motivations and fulfil different functions. Apart from a we-feeling on which the coherence of groups is based, a feeling ultimately rooted in the closeness and continuity of social relationships, and a crucial permanent and long-term communicative and interactive context that constitutes the group (Schäfers 1994b, p. 21, 2013, p. 108), the forms taken by group-specific structural features vary, and group types thus do so as well. These features include, for example, the informal membership structure (number, access, group members' distribution of roles), the group objective (plus the associated tasks and functions), group identity and the related group norms.

Global action contexts of stationary groups

Before taking a closer look at the communicative processes of small groups, we would like to address groups' lifeworldly structures, which create variable conditions

190 Small groups: global lifeworld communication

for global group communication. Initially, then, we are concerned not with groups' internal structures but with their external structural conditions. The goal here is to illuminate how temporal, spatial and social structures (see also Schütz and Luckmann 2003) influence the potential for, as well as the modalities of, global communication in the everyday lifeworld.

Contributors to the globalization debate have talked a lot about the dissolution of spatial and temporal boundaries (Giddens 2003; Dürrschmidt 2004, p. 47ff.), but from a lifeworld theory perspective a local spatial reference remains central. This is because the communication of individuals and groups, particularly the non-mediatized variant, continues to take place in local environments that can be experienced directly. In certain constellations of migration, diaspora communitization and labour mobility, everyday spatial references may be expanded or multiplied, but we have no findings indicating the total dissolution of primary local references anywhere in the world (see also Castells 2010, vol. 1, p. 453ff.). Nevertheless, the material-physical places in which everyday life goes on provide structures of opportunity for global contacts, as today global references may be integrated into local environments in the form of symbols, goods and people.

Globalization processes and spatial structures have already been linked in the context of the "global city" debates (Sassen 2001, 2002; Eckardt 2004). However, urban sociological research has focused more on organizational patterns and network structures than on groups' contact scenarios or interaction patterns. Interest in the microprocesses of urban life seems generally limited (Dürrschmidt 2000, p. 12). Ethnographically informed studies, meanwhile, provide us with a look at the coexistence of groups in urban areas. Ulf Hannerz describes the coexistence of different transnational groups and their cultural articulation as a characteristic feature of global metropolises (1992, p. 173ff., 1996, p. 127ff.). On this view, the diversity of global metropolises is typified by a mix of transnational economic elites, immigrants from developing countries working in the low-wage service sector, avant-garde cultural workers and tourists. According to Hannerz, only these cities feature the critical mass of people that may lead to the formation of various subcultural groups in the first place (for typologies of city dwellers, see also Clark 1996, p. 106ff.; Abrahamson 2004, p. 23ff.). In addition, metropolises cater to global urban lifestyles, as has also been described for megacities such as Cairo in the Global South, where opportunities for consumption, shopping malls and cafés are becoming symbolic sites in which certain social classes can articulate their cosmopolitan leanings (see, for example, de Koning 2006). As yet, however, the dynamic exchange of knowledge through face-to-face communication, which is in fact a defining characteristic of global cities (Sassen 2004, p. 17), has barely been subject to empirical research.

The geopolitical positioning of urbanity

The global knowledge and contact structures of urban groups may also be shaped by the geopolitical situation of urban areas. Despite the globally apparent similarity

Small groups: global lifeworld communication **191**

of urban modernity, there is reason to doubt the existence of a globally balanced circulation of media and cultural products ("contraflows", see Thussu 2007); the same goes for migration and tourism. With respect to multiple fields of knowledge and cultural production (such as scholarship, art, entertainment and media), postcolonial discourses criticize an orientation towards the symbols, knowledges and consumerist worlds that predominate in Western metropolises. Urbanity is thus no guarantee of integrated global environments of group and individual communication.

By the same token, rural regions are not automatically less global. The very seclusion of rural areas may stimulate global mobility and global interest, while a pre-eminently "local" life may be lived within the "expatriate structures" of global cities. In addition to the multicultural integrative potential that authors such as Hannerz focus on, modern urban structures may foster the countervailing demarcation of milieus and thus the elimination of opportunities for intercultural contact. It is thus an open question whether, for example, the daily routes of tourists, local inhabitants and working labour immigrants intersect in global cities.

A symbol of sociospatial delimitation are "gated communities", which create uniform residential environments for certain groups, mostly elites, shield them from the outside world and can be found across the world. The symbolic and physical separation of urban dwellers is obviously a global phenomenon (see, for example, Jordan 1997; Kieserling 2000; Castells 2010, vol. 1, p. 453; Elsheshtawy 2012; Füller and Glasze 2014, p. 33f.; Leurs and Georgiou 2016), and is an obstacle to integrative communitization at both a sub- and multicultural level. Nor do the global experiences offered by global cities automatically translate into a cosmopolitan orientation on the part of groups (Yeoh and Lin 2018). Attitude research has shown, for example, that while the xenophobic fear of potential threats does decrease in cities, cultural reservations may persist at a high level (Hafez and Schmidt 2015, p. 53f.). Modern and globally networked urbanity, then, has a certain potential but does not necessarily create a global community. To quote Manuel Castells: "Places are not necessarily communities, although they may contribute to community-building" (2010, vol. 1, p. 455).

Mobile horizons of action

Beyond the stationary action space, opportunities for physical mobility open up a mobile horizon of action. But there are significant differences in mobility. There are groups who share a global horizon of experience because their professional life or leisure activities foster mobility, and there are others that remain within stationary local structures and are merely part of the "incoming" global diffusion of knowledge. Even if the lifeworldly reality is physically expanded, for example, through travel, this does not automatically mean that new global groups will emerge. Certain spaces in the "global exterior" may ultimately bring like-minded people together. Studies of young adults' so-called "gap year travel" between education and work have shown, for example, that new, temporary in-groups of backpackers can form

192 Small groups: global lifeworld communication

in hostels. This space brings together kindred spirits in the global exterior while also providing a protective space that may ultimately lead to group-specific isolation from the global environment and thus impede global interactions (Bennett and Johan 2018).

The discipline of tourism studies, too, has investigated the relationship between authentic experience of the world and the staging and "touristification" of spaces (Wöhler 2000, 2005, 2011). As Karlheinz Wöhler puts it: "If the traveller's real-world space was previously identical to the lifeworldly space of the 'travelled', it has been presented and constructed continuously according to tourists' images and desires" (2000, p. 105). On this view, the standardization of tourism and simulated experiences of travel, places and the world, discussed in the social sciences under the heading of "postmodern tourism" (Cohen 1972; Urry 1988, 1990; Munt 1994) prevent authentic dialogues. Even in sustainable tourism projects, despite the benefits for local communities, spaces are created for the staging of traditional cultural symbols and practices. These spaces enable contact between tour groups and the local population only on the basis of staging and marketing and may even promote the re-traditionalization of the local (Ilius et al. 2014).

Preconceived group consensus and assumptions about the world thus influence how it is observed. This is a phenomenon that applies not only to the beaches and villages of the Global South, but also to tourist destinations in the "West". For example, as a reaction to Bollywood films set in the Alps, Indian "film tourists" travel to Switzerland, where they hope their expectations and imaginings will be fulfilled (Frank 2012). Hence, as long as experiences of mobility fail to burst pre-set so-called "environmental bubbles" (Cohen 1972, p. 168), they cannot be equated with the globalization of lived reality.

Digital spatial shifts in group structures

The question is whether, and if so how, digital travel shapes groups' lifeworld. Under the heading of mediatization, scholars have discussed transformations in society as a whole in connection with the increased use and importance of media-based communication (Krotz 2001, 2007; Couldry and Hepp 2013, 2017). In addition to physical spaces, Web 2.0 in particular creates virtual spaces for lifeworldly group communication. It is now possible to be physically present in a local environment while simultaneously interacting in delocalized fashion by means of computer-mediated communication (Zhao 2006).

But if, as in Chapter 6 on large communities, we differentiate between virtualized and virtual groups, new perspectives open up here, because the spatial and social references work differently in small groups and large communities. Social co-presence and interactive density for community building are negligible, at least in "virtual communities", because they are bypassed by overarching value consensuses and ideologies. But they remain constitutive prerequisites for small groups. Furthermore, the characteristics of actors' theoretical anonymity and the potential asynchrony of communication (especially with group members living in

Small groups: global lifeworld communication **193**

different time zones) in digital space are also likely to pose challenges to the emergence of virtual group ties.

Analyses of friendships on social media have shown that the virtual reproduction of local friendship networks is more likely than the creation of new international contacts (Zuckerman 2013, pp. 71f., 110ff.). This is in line with the general trend of Internet communication, which Dominic Busch summarizes with reference to tight constraints of language and culture: "There is potential for intercultural exchange, but it is barely tapped" (2012, p. 270). Hence, online groups do not differ profoundly from offline groups. Here, too, friendships apparently require shared experiences in shared social spaces, though the youth club or playground is difficult to virtualize (see also Reinders 2004; Brandt and Heuser 2016, p. 101).

Individual examples of virtual groups that have been explored empirically are also underpinned by pre-existing commonalities and those forged within the group itself (language, experiential horizon). This includes, for example, the ethnographic case study of a group of émigré Paraguayans, previously unknown to one another, who constructed a shared virtual lifeworld through an online platform, a lifeworld some of them then translated into real-world group meetings (Greschke 2008/2009). There is also evidence of virtual enabling structures in the context of partnerships (Gutekunst 2016). However, these examples are unlikely to represent the normality of everyday global relationships across the world. We are far more likely to find virtualized group communication that sustains socially co-present group relations when the physical boundaries between group members dissolve, as in transnational families.

Tom Postmes and Nancy Baym have looked at virtual contact between different groups and highlighted both the reinforcing of group stereotypes and the positive representation of minority groups through Internet communication, though they conclude rather pessimistically: "[T]he internet by and large has not changed existing intergroup relations but has provided a new forum for the perpetuation and accentuation of familiar forms of racism and sexism" (2005, p. 219). This raises the question of whether it is Internet communication that generates groups' organized, (partially) public, external communication in the first place, communication that does not exist within private and immediate lifeworld structures. What we need, then, is greater knowledge about the patterns of groups' global, virtual, everyday communication.

Temporal structures of global group communication

Another dimension that is related to the communicative processes of the small group is that of time. Short-, medium- or long-term structures not only have a general influence on group formation but are also important to the classification of global contact experiences. For example, a newly formed small group of international students may temporarily be an important lifeworldly point of reference for the group members during a semester abroad but may fade away when they return to their local groups of origin. But we are still waiting for researchers to

194 Small groups: global lifeworld communication

clarify how such episodic, direct, global group experiences relate to processes of social change in the context of globalization.

Conversely, indirectly shared historical experiences have the potential to support cross-border group formation. Through medially stimulated instances of co-orientation, global discursive events may become starting points for cross-border collective narratives and interpretive communities, which we will be returning to when we discuss observational communication. Indirectly, then, a "zeitgeist" that is accessible across borders may also synchronize the actions of small groups at different locations and interactively align them with one another. In youth cultures across the world, we find that despite local specifics, certain trends or narratives become collective global experiences. This applies not only to developments in pop culture, but also to frames that are available across borders and that articulate global motivations for action. Examples include the need to travel as a means of liberation and attaining independence for young people (Desforges 1998) or transnational youth protest cultures that may at least indirectly and loosely refer to one another (Mrozek 2019).

Contact as a symbolic resource of group communication

These observations are related to the social and symbolic structures of group communication. Groups are, therefore, also referred to as subcultural or countercultural manifestations of milieus (Neidhardt 1983b, p. 26), so that "group formation [is interpreted] as a reaction to developments in society as a whole" (ibid., p. 23). The symbolic resources of the small group (special languages, communication patterns, ways of dressing, and so on) may thus generate group consensuses and fictions of consensus that position the group in relation to mainstream interpretations of the world.

It is thus the "group habitus" that explains whether global mobility, global knowledge and global exchange are significant resources for the group. This is in turn related to the internal structures of different types of group. In working groups with an instrumental task orientation and distribution of roles, global action and knowledge may be crucial to their capacity for innovation and thus their competitive advantage. This chimes with the fact that there are numerous discussions of intercultural communication within the field of global corporate communication.

But the global flexibility of a work group is not necessarily linked to a group identity. The group's informal communication and cultural orientation may remain unaffected by the globalization of formal group communication (see Chapter 4, Section 4.2). Conversely, the global working group may be a source of impetus for informal intercultural settings. Apt descriptions of the distinction between formal and informal groups can be found in cross-cultural sociological friendship research. Researchers have, for example, highlighted a specific category of work friends in Indonesia (*teman kerja*), which expresses the continuous exchange that goes on between colleagues, but does not presuppose or necessarily entail an emotional connection between them (Brandt and Heuser 2016, p. 97).

Theoretically, then, the potential and relevance of global contact as groups' internal or external capital ought to differ depending on the type of group (Grüne 2019b). Associations featuring functionally predefined roles, membership and rules of communication (as a goalkeeper in a football club one has certain tasks, choir practice proceeds according to specific rules, and so on) are well placed to facilitate the integration of global others. Such organizations allow for the cultural and social diversity of their members as long as the formal rules and group objectives bridge their differing stocks of knowledge and symbols. At the same time, the greater organization characteristic of hybrid small/large groups relieves members of the need for internal dialogue. A football player with a migration background may be integrated in terms of his functional role as a player while still being marked with difference (as a migrant) in his role as a social actor.

Transformation and persistence of the small group in a globalizing world

So far, we have seen that the lifeworldly structures of small groups provide differing conditions for their integration into globalization processes. At the same time, groups' internal structures are more or less suited to opening up lifeworldly group experiences to global space. In this respect, we can discern a dialectical relationship between groups and globalization: if globalization does not translate into people's lifeworlds, it will not be culturally processed within them. Yet small groups function simultaneously as the lifeworldly "filter" of globalization experiences and may act as an insulating layer even in times of dynamic globalization. In order to discuss the conditions under which group-specific filters foster or impede globalization "from below", we would now like to discuss communicative processes.

7.2 Communicative connections in the lifeworld

The following section explores how small groups' interactive dialogic and observational patterns of discursive communication generate global knowledge and facilitate the cultural transmission of interpretations of global environments. How do people process globalization experiences together? Which communication processes support a global group consciousness or even furnish motives for global action (see also Chapter 1, Section 1.2)? After providing an overview of interactive processes, we discuss forms of observation and mediatization tendencies. We omit the dimension of external discursive communication, which is important in other chapters, since small groups are essentially social "geysers" that do not really communicate with the outside world in a coherent and organized way.

7.2.1 Interaction and dialogue

Transnational connectivity of the lifeworld

The global interaction of small groups is based on cross-border contacts between people who, as we have already seen, continue to maintain real-world, "analogue"

196 Small groups: global lifeworld communication

relationships. But what are their patterns of global interaction? Sociological research on transnationalization tries to capture the cultural geography of global contacts through data on international travel behaviour, exchange programmes and the use of different communicative channels in a given population (Mau and Mewes 2007). Based on this research we will formulate some initial observations on patterns of global connectivity in small groups.

Judging by the available data, for example, just under half (46.5 per cent) of the German population today maintains contact with people abroad, including family members (Mau 2007, p. 103f.). But we cannot be sure whether this indicates changed migration structures, mobility behaviour or a transnational shift within stationary groups in the majority society. It is just as difficult to interpret the rise in binational marriages up to 2005, which still make up only a small proportion of all partnerships in Germany at 6.3 per cent (ibid., p. 117). Contrary to Steffen Mau's interpretation, then, a critical reading is also possible: there is no clear evidence of any opening up of "lifeworldly horizons" (ibid., p. 109) despite opportunities for cross-border contact if more than half of Germans still lack regular contact with people abroad and the cultural geography of existing contacts reflects patterns of political, economic, historical-cultural and geographical proximity (ibid., p. 106).

For example, in 2017, more than half of Germans who did not live in Germany had migrated to European countries (57.3 per cent), and almost 20 per cent to North America (UN DESA and BPB 2017). A picture of cultural closeness also emerges when it comes to the countries of origin of migrants living in Germany. In the shape of Poland, Turkey, Russia, Kazakhstan and other countries, it is largely states considered to be European or part-European that lead the statistics, compared to just under 1 per cent of migrants from Iraq, Morocco, Iran and Afghanistan in 2017. There is no sign here of any truly global opening of potential contact structures encompassing Africa, South America and Asia.

Worldwide too, cross-border lifeworlds are not yet the norm. According to aggregate data from the United Nations, in 2017, only 3.4 per cent of the world's population had lived in a country other than their country of origin. This means that 96.6 per cent of the world's population was *not* in a first-generation, transformative, migration-based situation. Although the absolute number of international migrants has increased significantly, measured against the proportional development of the world population, the migration figures remained relatively stable between 1970 and 2017 (Migration Data Portal 2017).

In addition, the world's largest migration corridors also reflect geographical proximity, for example, between the United States and Mexico, Russia and Ukraine, or Bangladesh and India (UN DESA and BPB 2017). The same applies to temporary stays abroad during education. Here too there is an imbalance in the exchange of students between the "global North and South" (Guruz and Zimpher 2011; on Germany, see Mau 2007, p. 138). Most students worldwide are drawn to the United States, the UK and Australia, followed by Germany, France, Japan, Canada and New Zealand (Verbik and Lasanowski 2007).

Small groups: global lifeworld communication **197**

The social migration of human capital is essentially based on a historically and linguistically established, regional and economic logic. Today's connectivity patterns, then, are obviously geared mainly towards "traditional" group and community structures. Even if we look at the largest country of immigration, the United States, immigration evidently reflects family networks, as Meg Karraker observes: "In fact, two out of every three immigrants admitted into the United States in 2009 were children, spouses, siblings, or grandparents, or family-sponsored individuals being reunited with kin" (2013, p. 59). The data produced by Germany's Federal Statistical Office refers to family reasons with respect to almost half of immigrants to Germany (Statistisches Bundesamt 2019, p. 493ff.).

But in addition to families, which can contribute to enduringly globalized lifeworlds, short-term mobility ought to create global networks as well. Global tourism has in fact seen strong growth since the turn of the millennium (Ilius et al. 2014; World Tourism Organization 2018). In 2017, more than 1.3 billion cross-border tourist arrivals were recorded worldwide (World Tourism Organization 2018). This means that around one in every seven people in the world crosses territorial borders once a year. But these numbers conceal global asymmetries. Most of these arrivals were in Europe (672 million), Asia and the Pacific (323 million) and the United States (211 million). Africa (63 million) and the Middle East (58 million) are significantly less relevant as travel destinations. This means that 63 per cent of all travellers visited the Western world, compared to just under 5 per cent who made their way to Africa. In addition, only 3 per cent of all departing tourists come from Africa and the Middle East, with most from Europe (48 per cent), and 25 per cent from Asia (mainly China). Even if tourism is growing enormously, this does not mean that everyone is travelling equally and globally. Even more significant is the fact that the majority of all tourists travel *intraregionally*. Four out of five travellers thus remain in their own geocultural regions (ibid., p. 14). Regardless of the fact that these data are far from painting a complete picture, they at least raise doubts about whether far-reaching transformations are occurring in cross-border socialization processes when it comes to lifeworldly connectivity. From a comparative perspective, global mobility and the associated globally dynamic social spaces remain the privilege of a few (Gutekunst et al. 2016).

The interaction paradox of global group communication

Connectivity may be an indication of global interaction, but this tells us nothing about the communication processes involved in dealing with these global environments, entered into voluntarily or involuntarily. In addition, we have to consider a theoretical paradox of interaction. Small groups are usually located in a local social space and are in no way oriented towards or dependent on the global expansion of their interactive realm. After all, even migration and travel always create new *local* interactive relationships when new small group contexts arise, or when old ones react to a new global environment.

198 Small groups: global lifeworld communication

However, at a time of increasing migration it may well be advantageous to stationary groups to have global know-how. The ability to come to an inclusive arrangement with globalizing environments may generate positive communitization effects. In theory, adding new group members to small groups can be enriching, as this provides access to alternative observations, experiences and interpretations. If, in addition, it even becomes possible to visit friends, family members or work colleagues in other places, group members can contribute to the extension of the lifeworldly group reality across global social spaces. This would be the lifeworld version of what are colloquially referred to as "expanded horizons".

At the same time, the small group is oriented towards the experiential and interpretive alignment of its members, which requires a dense experiential context (Bohnsack 1994). Small groups create their own systems of meaning, so to speak, which include unspoken consensuses about group identity, action orientations and ultimately the world. These do not necessarily have to be updated constantly through dialogic group discussions. They may also be available as latent fictions of consensus, which has an impact on the extent to which the group is opened up to or sealed off from the outside world.

The internal communicative relations of a group (intragroup communication) are, therefore, closely related to its external communicative relations (intergroup communication). On the one hand, closed groups can generate identificatory stability internally through symbolic updating processes (repetition of narratives of remembrance, special languages, jokes, and so on), but such a set of symbols may serve to delimit the group from the outside world. On the other hand, a consensus of values and action orientations may also help open up the group to dialogues with new or non-group members if the group develops cosmopolitan values. Our analysis thus needs to go beyond a simple in-group/out-group schema.

A theoretical fallacy in intercultural communication research

Studies on intercultural communication, however, often discuss group-specific codes, values and behavioural patterns as core problems of mutual understanding (see, for example, Maletzke 1996, p. 128; Gudykunst et al. 2005; Samovar et al. 2015; Jandt 2016). Small groups are thus equated with large groups, so that everyday forms of expression are soon interpreted as national cultural characteristics and identities, with essentialist explanations dominating. According to the symbolic-interactionist logic of lifeworldly group communication, however, the perceived difference in group action can theoretically be traced back to subcultural variants of collective patterns of communication and action.

The supposed difference between "cultures", then, is essentially a problem of the chosen level of observation. As Kwame Anthony Appiah argues convincingly, family forms and roles in England and among the Asante people of Ghana, for example, may differ greatly, but caring for children seems to be the "thin" universal value shared by groups in both contexts (2006, p. 74ff.). At the same time, like Appiah, rather than potential value dissent, one should emphasize the common response

Small groups: global lifeworld communication **199**

to basic human issues and forms of action. Even if values are not shared, this does not mean they are not understood (ibid.; see also Antweiler 2011, p. 81ff.). Much the same goes for interaction patterns that may cause disruption at first glance. Teenage rebellion, for example, which is unleashed on the parental generation and on society, in no way implies that rules and values are not understood. Instead, young people unsettle the consensus, piling pressure on it with their own interpretations in a "politics of signification" (Hall 1992).

On this premise, intercultural communication would essentially be a consequence of the difference between the communication systems of different groups. While interest groups or family groups can continuously observe tourist groups in the local context and the latter are mainly perceived in their role as tourists, the reverse is only possible temporarily. Theoretically, then, an enduring form of interaction between different groups that reconciles interests or creates mutual understanding can develop here only to a highly limited extent. In addition, local family groups, for example, have different goals than travelling peer groups. If tourist peers encounter familial residents, differences arise once more, which are by no means national or cultural, but are again group-specific. We can say much the same for the oft-discussed global group dynamics in the context of corporate communications. In contrast to the geocultural background of the group members, here too there may simply be different contexts of experience and interpretation that come into contact in artificially assembled teams (see also Chapter 4, Section 4.2.1). It is thus important in what follows to keep in mind the distinction between communication of and between real-world groups with homologous characteristics and the communication between ad-hoc groups that meet in global situations.

In addition, groups with similar experiences may create "intercultures" through global encounters, as described by Gerhard Maletzke (1966, p. 323). Working groups in the professional realm in particular share experiential contexts that bridge other possible differences in experience. The shared orientation towards professional objectives thus helps form small-group alliances that tend to run counter to the much-invoked problems of intercultural communication. Moreover, the premise of the "contact hypothesis" that interpersonal communication is more successful when, for example, based on the same social status and a positive contact atmosphere (Pettigrew 1998) confirm the crucial importance of group-specific characteristics. Since groups' lifeworldly experiential contexts are, therefore, fundamentally multiple and oriented towards different motivations and objects, we can rule out a group's national background as a general criterion for establishing different types of group communication. What we find concealed behind the alleged clash of cultures (Huntington 1997) is in fact a "clash of perceptions" (Hafez 2000b).

Even differing language and symbol systems cannot fully account for cases in which groups' communicative and interpretive systems make interaction impossible. Within the framework of the communicative action in a group encounter, irritant factors are noticed, and remedial action taken. If different language systems are involved, a *lingua franca* or common set of symbols must then be found. It is helpful to keep in mind here that this problem may also arise in cases of shared language

200 Small groups: global lifeworld communication

and national experience, that is, if a group's stock of knowledge and experience as well as special language systems impede understanding. Conversely, as we have just seen, despite linguistic differences the stock of knowledge and experience may be similar enough to help bridge the gap.

Interaction patterns of global group communication: three case analyses

In light of these theoretical considerations, we now turn to differing case analyses of cross-border communication in small groups. Since both interactive and observational communicative modes come into play in small-group communication, we will deal with these one after the other, although they often appear in parallel. We will also be probing the relationship between the group's internal communication (intragroup communication) and external communication in the sense of intergroup communication.

The starting point for the following three case analyses is the small local group that regards its global environment as a potential horizon of experience. This recognition may relate both to global influences on a local environment (globalized symbol systems made available through the circulation of goods, media and people) and to global experiences in distant contexts, for example, when travelling. What matters is that groups grapple with the symbolic and interpretive systems of other people, groups and societies. This, however, results in various forms of interaction and differing relationships to the communicative modes of interaction and observation. First, circular interactive conditions of global group communication may arise that foster a dialogic model of the global community (interactivity 1). Second, group communication may be characterized by reciprocal interaction, as characteristic of a hegemonic model of the global community (interactivity 2). Third, however, this reciprocity may also be oriented more towards global observation and less towards direct interaction, which ultimately amounts to a discursive model of an imagined global community (interactivity 3).

Interactivity 1: circular interaction – the dialogic model of the global community

Let us start by defining the ideal type of global group communication. At the theoretical level, this describes groups that integrate global others within their internal and external communication and, through this global opening, make their communicative and epistemic patterns, as well as their value systems, compatible across borders. These, then, are small groups that participate continuously in a cross-border exchange of experience and knowledge and thus lay the integrative foundations for a global community. We call this interaction circular because here, theoretically, different local experiences of the world interpenetrate.

Small groups of this ideal type not only observe others, but also supplement their observation with interaction, which leads to lifeworldly dialogues and thus to a situation of communicative negotiation in which knowledge and values are reconciled

Small groups: global lifeworld communication **201**

with those of global others. This may include explicit agreements regarding knowledge and views as well as an implicit orientation towards shared situations and the associated accumulation of shared experiences. Thus, over an extended period of time, the original *intragroup* situation may become an *intergroup observational situation* through a process of circular collaboration. The small group then engages in the shared observation and assessment of the world through synthesized and connectable interpretive systems. The symbolic and interpretive patterns of the "multicultural" or "global" group would thus be connected in a circular manner. Theoretically, then, the group knowledge and the internal discourses of such a small group constellation should differ from hegemonic local discourses. The establishment of a sense of togetherness through dialogue and the continuous processing of direct and indirect observation of the world should realize a global community within the microcosm of the small group. But which real-world phenomena illustrate this ideal-typical case of global group communication?

Global education and "intimate tourism"

Groups in global educational contexts provide us with a first example of circular global interactions. The school may become an important "relational locus" for global friendships if it at least temporarily integrates children from different contexts of origin (Köhler 2012). However, the special features of interethnic friendships with respect to socialization have received little attention so far (ibid.; see also Brandt and Heuser 2016). While the empirical evidence is limited, international school classes are of great interest to us at the theoretical level, as here global contact is already institutionalized, and the potential group members can contribute differing experiences that are synthesized – as groups take shape – through shared communicative situations, becoming the basis of the group's internal communicative system.

Communicative action, then, theoretically prompts the new group to coordinate its actions in such a way as to generate a (global) definition of the situation. Since such group interactions are based on the synthesis of systems of knowledge and interpretation, they make adaptation of previously existing patterns an inescapable imperative. Both explicit and implicit action-guiding knowledge change in such a situation of socialization. Whether the group members' value systems undergo adaptation is not decisive here, as long as the global group's action coordination and intergroup dialogue remain effective. Internal communication in this group may thus ultimately lead to a discursive shift if the small group's knowledge system moves from local to more global discursive patterns and content.

However, this does not mean that people in global educational contexts have no contact with family or peer groups in other social spaces or that such contact only arises from isolation in distant places. A study of Korean high-school exchange students in the United States, for example, shows how they maintain their discursive knowledge through intensive use of Korean media, such that they can hold extensive dialogues with their peer group in Korea (Kim 2015). What we find, then, is the

202 Small groups: global lifeworld communication

multiplication of discursive knowledges and overlapping dialogic situations, though there is an urgent need for studies that investigate in more depth the circular connectivity of remote discourses with local group dialogues.

We also find evidence of global group communication in certain generations and milieus. Situations of global small-group communication are inherent, for example, in variants of alternative tourism through the practice of couchsurfing, in which direct and intensive dialogue with global others is the explicit goal of travel-based encounters. Here, random global contacts are integrated into the ritualized everyday actions of local groups, which may create short-term global groups that are referred to as "post-friendships" (Bialski 2012, p. 89ff.; Ullmann 2017, p. 268). However, these encounters, which the authors mentioned explore under the heading of "intimate tourism", are only short-lived. Thus, despite the intensity of encounters in short-term small groups, the long-term effects for the global community may lie in these groups' stimulating effect on individual travellers' schemas of action and thought. We will be scrutinizing the relationship between individual and group in more detail in our chapter on the individual (see Chapter 8, Section 8.2.2).

Family/peer communication and circular global community

In addition to institutionalized forms of education and alternative travel encounters that pre-structure global communication in small groups, longer-term global contexts of experience may be realized in families that maintain cross-border relationships. Although the primary group of the family can thus be a nucleus of the global community, we know little about its global interactions. A number of authors have lamented that there has been insufficient research on internationally mobile and globally oriented families (McLachlan 2007; Diggs and Socha 2013; Karraker 2013, p. 7f.). While some scholars have provided global perspectives on families (Karraker 2013; Beck and Beck-Gernsheim 2014) or country comparisons (Leeder 2004), the focus is often on issues of cultural identity (belonging) and social mobility (labour migration, marriage migration) rather than cross-border family communication and the associated transfer of knowledge and values. Global families are interpreted as "pioneers of interculturalism" (Beck and Beck-Gernsheim 2014, p. 169) and as a microcosmic mirror of global imbalances and communicative problems (ibid.). In neither case is consideration given to dynamic interactive relationships.

Family research has come under fire for its normative and Western biases. This is evident in research on the children of transnationally organized families. Bilingualism and cosmopolitan capital are associated with the "transnational socialization" of "third-culture kids" in cosmopolitan families, but not with children in migrant families (Weidemann 2016, p. 225). Yet Deborah Bryceson and Ulla Vuorela confirm that these families have structural similarities: "[T]he issues of connecting, mixing and networking are very much the same between the mass of international migrants and transnational elites" (2002, p. 8). In this context, Wolf-Dietrich Bukow has highlighted the learning progress of migrant families which, as "test groups" of

Small groups: global lifeworld communication **203**

global change, have an experiential edge over stationary families, albeit with variable consequences (2000, p.14).

The global cultural awareness of cosmopolitan elites may also be more apparent than real, underlining once again the need for a closer analysis of interaction (Cason 2018). This applies generally to supposedly cosmopolitan small groups. The cosmopolitan orientation may be a fiction of consensus generated by the group itself. The "natural" cosmopolitanism of non-elite groups, on the other hand, may exist as everyday practice without a specific value orientation. Koen Leurs and Myria Georgiou have shown in a comparative ethnographic study how young peers in Tottenham felt left behind "globally", yet cultural diversity was a taken-for-granted, everyday experience in their area of North London. The moral-cosmopolitan imagination of middle- and upper-class youth, on the other hand, contradicted their own local practice, which was characterized by exclusive friendship patterns and little openness to cultural variance (2016). Small groups thus have to perform a range of translation services with respect to global communication. This includes the communicative bridging of group members' differing horizons of experience and knowledge, which are prominent in the case of language barriers in multilingual families (Vuorela 2002; Drotbohm 2010, p. 194). Small groups also have to translate the internal system of global values into global external intergroup communication.

The example of the family thus reveals an ambivalent relationship between internal and external communication. Theoretically, families have to reproduce themselves through long-term communicative contexts and routines and require consensus within their knowledge, experiential and communicative systems. They are, therefore, primed for dense global dialogues. However, not every global other can become a permanent part of a family – its access system is exclusive. The expansion of the family to include global others is thus based on chance contacts. Global internal communication and global dialogues in particular presuppose a global membership structure.

If the mobile family only communicates externally with global others and environments, the question is how pronounced the relationship between dialogue and observation is. On the one hand, the withdrawal of understanding into the interior of the family may strengthen family cohesion (internal dialogue, external observation), but this may simultaneously make it difficult to connect with the outside world (McLachlan 2007). Even familial observation of a global environment may unsettle internal communicative and action systems. With respect to global labour mobility, management research emphasizes these adaptive difficulties that arise between local families and the global environment (Caligiuri et al. 1998; McNulty 2015).

However, mobile families do not interact with one another in isolation or exclusively with a global environment. In this context, the scholarly literature has failed to appreciate family members' need to maintain old friendships (Weidemann 2016). This applies to the entire communicative renegotiation of global familial experiences in communication with other local peer groups. Communicative

204 Small groups: global lifeworld communication

channels with "old" friends and family members are mostly viewed negatively by scholars, as homesickness and as an obstacle to integration (ibid., p. 226), rather than part of circular, communicative exchange relationships that might contribute to a synthetic process of global communitization. In sum, then, we are yet to see serious research on the hybrid lifeworldly reality of global families, their patterns of interaction with the "outside world" and the simultaneous renegotiation of global experiences within existing family relationships.

Interactivity 2: reciprocal interaction – the hegemonic model of the global community

Episodic interactions with global others are presumably more common than long-term cross-border communicative relationships. It is from these encounters that we derive the second type of global small-group communication, which is characterized by a hegemonic model of the global community. In the type outlined above, dialogue between group members with different stocks of experience led ideally to internal and external global dialogues, to a discursive shift or at least to overlapping discourses. Now, though, we focus on how small groups observe and reproductively renegotiate global interactions. Here, then, global communication mostly remains linked to the local group's internal communication. Contact scenarios, forms of interactive exchange and dynamic processes of communitization are entirely possible – but they are interpreted within the group's interior. Its knowledge system remains the key stabilizing component in its interpretation of the world.

Examples include groups that travel or migrate together and interact with the outside global world, but do not integrate the global other into the interaction of the original group and thus stabilize structures of knowledge and interpretation. This constitutes a temporary form of "external" integration, but not "internal" integration. From a communication theory perspective, the consequence of such a pattern of action is that the observational mode of global environments remains dominant, whereas the dialogic mode remains unactivated.

The implicit global knowledge of these groups may be changed in light of global experiences of exchange, but the processes of meaning production remain attached to the group's established knowledge systems. People can thus get the hang of other environments and adapt to appropriate routines and forms of articulation, but this does not necessarily mean, for example, that the travel group understands what these articulations mean for others. Despite shared experience in the "outside world", these groups may be surprised by it. Explicit, articulable knowledge thus continues to display familiar patterns of interpretation. Theoretically, then, this impedes synthesis of the group's own observational modes with global alternatives.

Migration and tourism communication

The difference between intergroup interaction with the outside world and intragroup internal communication allows us to explain why international workers (expatriates) find cultural residues in the gated communities described earlier and why – despite the various forms of large community within diasporas (see Chapter 6, Section 6.2.1) – migrant havens are established within small groups. The synthesis of interpretive contexts is also likely to be simulated in the case of mobile young people, package holiday tourists and even travellers with more cultural interests. Global communicative action is a shared value of the group and there is *intergroup* interaction, but there is strong *intragroup* sorting and processing. The reciprocal interaction thus remains within a hegemonic framework, because this interaction is processed within the dominant, pre-established systems of interpretation.

Tourist travel can serve as an illustrative example here, because only a few forms of travel are apt to stimulate circular, participatory interaction between groups of travellers and the stationary. Mass tourism in particular is seen as a hindrance to intercultural dialogue, as the exchange with local environments is reduced and pre-structured on the basis of asymmetrical relationships (Evans 1976; Munt 1994; Herdin and Luger 2001, p. 7; Joseph and Kavoori 2001; Luger 2018, p. 286). It seems doubtful that we can refer here to cultural sustainability of the kind required to create a global community. Accordingly, tourism research focuses on economic and ecological contexts as opposed to cultural issues, as Peter Burns summarizes:

> [W]hile a plethora of social scientists have spent decades dealing with social issues of tourism, there is very little evidence to suggest that cultural sustainability in the form of harmonious relationships between host communities, especially in poorer parts of the world, tourists, and the supplying tourism business sector has gained the same level of importance as the physical environment, or indeed the same level of support as animal protection.
>
> *(2006, p. 13)*

In terms of theories of communication and the lifeworld, we can identify numerous factors that run counter to understanding-oriented action between different groups in tourism situations (see also Garaeva 2012). We can link ideas about the global added value of tourism with the conditions needed to break down prejudice through intergroup communication (Allport 1954; Amir 1969). Studies with a focus on attitude change among travellers have confirmed the slight or non-existent potential for intercultural contact in tourism (for example, Amir and Ben-Ari 1985; Milman et al. 1990; Pizam et al. 1991; Anastasopoulos 1992; Gast-Gampe 1993).

One of the conditions for successful interaction is that groups and their members have a similar status, but this is often not the case in tourism. This status is related to groups' different socioculturally determined capital, and to the different roles that are assumed in a tourist situation. In the form of "disciplined rituals" (Backhaus 2012, p. 183), these roles tend to represent interactive role-plays rather than understanding-oriented action (Urry 1988, p. 38; Wöhler 2000, p. 105). For Christoph Köck, meta-tourism is "an experience-filled process in which tourists observe whether tourism is being staged according to the script" (2005, p. 14). Interaction thus remains at the level of stripped-down or standardized role behaviour, which may also reproduce

206 Small groups: global lifeworld communication

collective clichés. Tourists thus often take on the role of tourists rather than that of ethnographically interested global citizens. Research on travel motives confirms that in many surveys, travellers are less interested in other people's way of life than in individualistic goals such as relaxation or expansion of cultural capital (Stors 2014; Snee 2016).

Tourists and "locals" will rarely define a common cultural goal of their interaction in social situations. Instead, contact often has the character of a mutual business deal and thus tends to reflect a "psycho-economic" relationship (Wilhelm 1993, p. 263). Interaction between guest groups and "locals", then, often involves strategic rather than communicative action. Ideal global communication oriented towards understanding thus shifts from the global to the local group, which observes globally and classifies locally.

The opening up of the world through maintenance of familiar patterns of interpretation is something that we find even in new group structures during travel, provided that the groups involved already feature similar knowledge and communicative structures. When backpackers, for example, retreat to the "third space" of hostels and meet other travellers there, new global groups do form in global space, but across generations they share worlds of experience and meaning and the symbolic capital of travel experience (road status) (Ullmann 2017, p. 275). In the rarest of cases, however, do globetrotters truly become part of a local group in the global environment, as described in the first case analysis (Kayser 2005).

The interactions with their global environments of those who seek to educate and enrich themselves through travel are also contradictory. The interest in global observation is likely to be particularly pronounced in this case. Yet interactive contact occurs in carefully selected travel situations, in which mediators take on the role of cultural translators. In contrast to alternative individual tourism, here one interacts with representatives of other groups, not directly with the groups themselves (Evans 1976). The interpretation of global observation is thus geared towards the interpretation produced by mediators and group-internal dialogues. An emancipatory discursive shift through group communication can only take place through observations and discursive explanations, but not through globalized interpretive horizons generated in dialogue. In terms of communication theory, even travel focused on educating the traveller, which is often praised as the ideal type of intercultural communication (Herdin and Luger 2001, p. 7), is a myth of global communication.

The communication-theoretical peculiarities of such tourist encounters may explain why new stereotypes emerge or old ones are reproduced. This is not only due to persistent attitudes, but also to the lack of potential for a discursive shift. There are no alternative systems of interpretation in the group's interior that might contribute to a hybrid view of the global other. Hence, problems of intercultural communication are not just the result of cultural peculiarities or the human need for distinction but are also due to the fundamental lack of a situation of intercultural communication. Limited and often simulated contact impedes genuine intercultural

Small groups: global lifeworld communication **207**

dialogue, so the dominance of observation may reactivate local group identity (in a potentially stereotypical way) (see, for example, van Rekom and Go 2006).

Intercultural encounters take a different form in the interactive experiences of professional and work groups. Here, contexts of experience that are shared collectively, as in professional knowledge and work systems, precede the intercultural communicative situation. Conferences and work meetings facilitate a "third space" (see p. 199, Maletzke 1966) of relatively homogeneous cross-border professional cultures. Another problem, however, is significant, namely whether the professional dialogue, which can be rapidly established globally, is also translated into informal communicative situations (see also Chapter 4, Section 4.2.2). Here global community arises mainly from the relatively limited range of themes found in the group communication and is laid down systematically in advance. There is a need for more in-depth investigation of the potential transfer of the sense of professional togetherness to contexts of private interaction.

Temporary mobility and the associated global contact, then, can certainly facilitate the global communication of small groups. Theoretically, however, in this case the global community is not constituted in a circular and participatory manner, since experiential contexts in the interior of small mobile groups remain linked to familiar patterns of interpretation. Hence, the constitutive "we" of the small group does not necessarily merge into the "we" of a global community if the group's internal communication is not oriented towards integration.

Interactivity 3: reciprocal discourses – the discursive model of an imagined global community

Continuing to track a diminishing integrative capacity, we turn to the last form of interactive group communication. Here groups do engage with their global environments but do not interact across borders either in their direct observation or in intragroup dialogue. Hence, they are not globally integrative, with their global communication mainly being limited to incoming global discursive offerings via media.

This does not mean these groups have no interest in a global environment or "other cultures" or that they respond to globalization solely with resentment. It is merely the small group's lack of direct interactivity that we are highlighting here. In such cases, recognition of global environments is based on a superficial and locally renegotiated appropriation of global symbolic worlds, which authors taking a similar approach have referred to as "pop cosmopolitanism" or "banal cosmopolitanism" (Beck 2006, p. 40ff.; Jenkins 2006, p. 152ff.; see also Chapter 6, Section 6.2.1).

These groups' knowledge systems, then, may also contain explicit global knowledge if, for example, an interest group achieves expert status vis-à-vis a certain aspect of the global exterior (such as anime fan groups). Such expert groups, however, are more susceptible to essentialist or locally differentialist reproductions of dominant discursive structures, since there is no direct interactive or observational contact with the global other and the group is left with the observation of observation via the media. Here, exchanges about alternative contexts of interpretation, experience

208 Small groups: global lifeworld communication

and action are hampered because group members are not only dependent on the group's interpretive systems, as in the other types of interaction, but are also cut off from the authentically global, which is present only as a pre-interpreted media offering (see Chapter 1, Section 1.1). Certainly, there are modes of hybrid interpretation in media-based observation, as we will see later. Conceptually, however, the reciprocal discursive interpretations are inevitably fragile, because the cosmopolitan consensuses are the imagined constructs of non-interactive lifeworldly groups.

This communicative mode of global exchange helps us understand why there are a variety of local appropriations of globally circulating products or symbols. Furthermore, it provides an explanation for problems of understanding that arise from the difference between group members' personal experiences and collective interpretive contexts, which we will be returning to in Chapter 8 on individuals.

Interactive group communication and participatory global community

In summary, we visualize the shifts in intra- and intergroup interaction in the three types of interactivity we have explored (see Figure 7.1). This clarifies how groups' forms of contact and engagement with global others affect intergroup interaction.

In light of the existing empirical evidence and our theoretical discussion, it is evident that the potential for a global community based on dense group interaction is realized only in the first, rarer type of interactivity. In all other cases, global experience remains theoretically dependent on the discursive structures of world interpretation available to a group that mainly acts locally.

Of course, our typologies are only outlines, and one would have to add many empirical borderline cases. But a more consistent communication-theoretical interpretation of lifeworldly group interaction reveals that the much-discussed problems of intercultural communication are not due only to the adaptability and functions of various groups' communicative and action systems with respect to intergroup communication, but also to differences in small groups' internal interaction. Global integrative capacity may thus vary in line with the dominant communicative modes of observation and interaction in groups' external and internal communication, providing differing degrees of motivation for an opening to the world.

We have seen that although small groups have great interactive potential for dense global relationships in the context of everyday communication, lifeworldly observation remains key to their potential for global integration, because global experiences are subject to negotiation within local groups. In what follows, then, we get to grips with the relationship between discursive knowledge and lifeworldly dialogues.

7.2.2 Observation

Collective observation and medial keyhole

Groups do not communicate *externally* in organized patterns, as do civil society organizations or systems. They communicate *with others* in global environments,

Small groups: global lifeworld communication **209**

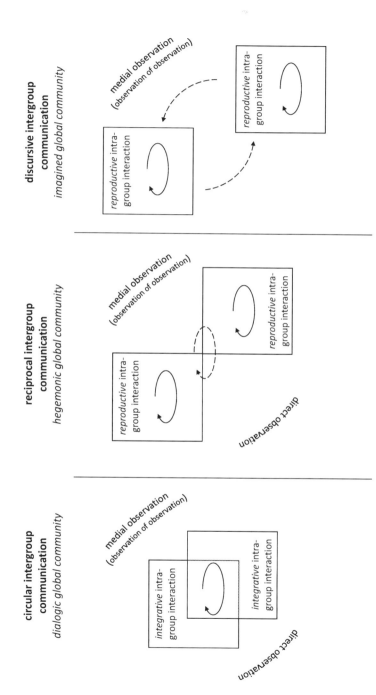

FIGURE 7.1 Variants of global inter- and intragroup communication

210 Small groups: global lifeworld communication

either in an interactive, dialogic manner or through direct and indirect observation. How impressions of globalization are to be interpreted is then decided within the microcosm of the small group. The small group is thus the invisible and non-organized matrix through which globalization is processed.

When it comes to the interpretation of global experiences, the main resource available to the small groups of everyday life is their lifeworldly, experiential knowledge. In contrast to organized systems, they usually lack professionalized tools of research and observation. They have no epistemic or expert archives. In other words, they are devoid of the kind of resources that might be used systematically to observe the world. When interpreting new experiences of the world, then, small groups are dependent on external, media-based interpretive offerings (the observation of observation). This points to the importance of the group filtering mechanisms through which, in non-public dialogues, public discourses are appropriated as group-specific interpretive horizons, and thus come into play again, in circular fashion, with respect to small groups' global interaction.

Small groups in modern societies receive external interpretive offerings through the mass media. However, the structural conditions for groups' observation of the world through the media vary (the key term here being "digital divide") and are shaped by political, economic, social and cultural factors that lead to different forms of world observation. If we also consider the dominance of national media systems (see Chapter 2) and geocultural differences in the use of media (differing media repertoires and forms of media socialization), we have to assume that global media-based observations across the world are extremely heterogeneous, furnishing small groups with quite different stocks of knowledge. International comparison shows that, for recipients, the media's "window on the world" is in fact a "keyhole" that spotlights certain aspects of the world. These images then acquire social relevance through communicative exchange with others, that is, if they are not stored in individual "provinces of reality" (Hepp 1998, p. 76; Schütz and Luckmann 2003, p. 54ff.), but become part of everyday communication and collective interpretations.

That individual use and reception are shaped by exchange with others is underlined both in classic media effects research (the key terms here being multi-step flow of communication and opinion leadership, which we will deal with in more detail in Chapter 8 on the individual) and in media research within the framework of cultural studies. The connection between media experience and the lifeworldly environment is especially important in television research. Under the heading of domestication, scholars have shown how the social rules and role models of the small familial group influence the appropriation of television content in the household (Morley 1986, 2000). Roger Silverstone considers the family's cultural environment to be important, "for it is here that the primary involvement with television is created, and where the primary articulation of meanings is undertaken" (1998, p. 252). The same kind of importance can be ascribed to all small-group situations in everyday life – it is friends, work colleagues and acquaintances from gym class with whom we discuss YouTube clips, news or the latest films and Netflix series. Whether during family conversations around the dinner table

Small groups: global lifeworld communication   **211**

(Keppler 1994), talk in direct response to television or other media within the family environment (see, for example, Hepp 1998; Klaus and O'Connor 2010) or in the clique – media experiences are collectively interpreted, classified and rendered socially compatible. Media offerings take on a cross-group integrative role when they function as an interdiscourse, as described by Andreas Dörner with reference to entertainment products (2010, p. 97), though in our case this role also applies to other content aimed at the most diverse audiences, such as the agendas of foreign coverage.

Media offer, however, meaningful and ambiguous resources that do more than convey manifest messages unilaterally (Fiske 1987, 1989, p. 103ff.; Hall 1992). Even if different social groups are co-oriented towards specific media content, the media repertoires as well as the interpretations differ. According to the paradigms of the active audience, people not only use a variety of media content autonomously (as in the active reception decisions discussed within the uses and gratifications approach), but also produce deviating interpretations, that is, readings (also called active feats of interpretation) that ideal-typically generate hegemonic, negotiated or oppositional positions (Hall 1992, p. 136f.). Individual readings ought ultimately to condense into small-group consensuses in the course of subsequent communication.

What does the existence of different interpretive communities mean for the global communication of the small group? To shed light on this, we take a closer look at (1) the small group reception of local media discourses about the world, (2) the reception of global or hybridized media content, and (3) the reception of global media events.

Local small groups and the media's conception of other countries

Classic foreign coverage provides recipients with explicit knowledge about the world, so there is potential here to generate a cosmopolitan imagination (Robertson 2010). However, the small group shares the reference system of the foreign journalists, who translate distant events for the home audience. As numerous studies on the international image of nations, regions and societies have shown, this translation is mostly politics-focused, selective and not infrequently stereotypical (see Chapter 2, Section 2.2.1). Particularly when small groups have little direct contact with the world and do not observe it themselves, media constructs are their primary source of knowledge. Values and attitudes may promote a critical stance towards the media, but without additional knowledge stocks it is difficult to unsettle these narratives. Negotiated or oppositional readings that not only question conceptions of other countries but introduce anti-stereotypical perspectives, while supplementing or classifying prevailing ideas, require additional knowledge.

Hence, for ideas about other countries to be processed further in small groups, the relevant specialist knowledge must be part of the group's communicative resources. Special discourses or counterdiscourses within the lifeworld that respond to specialist topics in foreign coverage are, however, likely to be the exception. But if such emancipated dynamics exist, theory casts doubt on their public efficacy, since we

212 Small groups: global lifeworld communication

are dealing here with the private appropriation of public constructs and not with the public articulation of opposing points of view by interest-led, organized actors. Determining how everyday interpretations of country constructs impact on social discourse thus remains a theoretical and empirical challenge.

Today, Internet-based social media may give visibility to lifeworldly encounter-based communication and numerous unique interpretive schemes. However, the public dissemination of the "chatty lifeworld" (Knoblauch 1996) does not automatically generate an (alternative) public sphere, let alone a global public sphere and epistemic culture (see also Chapter 6, Section 6.2.2). The problem identified at the start of this chapter of lifeworld actors' lack of observational resources carries over into the virtual public space of lifeworld and here it becomes a problem of transparency. Precisely because lifeworld actors are not formally organized, their expertise inevitably remains nontransparent. If, on the other hand, alternative online publications are used as a source of foreign coverage, we are dealing with a multiplication of statements that must in turn be negotiated and made compatible through lifeworldly group talk. Unfortunately, we still know little about these indirect forms of appropriation of the world.

In addition to the processing of constructs of other countries, research on cosmopolitanism also examines how the local audience can develop feelings of solidarity with global others on the basis of media narratives and whether these feelings have consequences for interactive action (Chouliaraki 2006, 2008). Older reception studies on foreign coverage have shown that satisfying people's interest in engaging or identifying with the problems of others, as opposed to their simple desire to obtain information, is the least significant function of foreign news consumption (Cohen et al. 1996, p. 116).

So far, when it comes to "distant suffering" (Chouliaraki 2006), scholars have investigated the characteristics of reporting but paid little attention to reception. However, existing studies indicate that those productions that establish proximity to lifeworldly realities are more readily stored (Kyriakidou 2014). Media remembering takes on a cosmopolitan character if it relates to a historical event experienced in temporal, geographical and cultural proximity, and if the attention paid to a distant other is supplemented by a shared horizon of action. This was true of Greek groups that remembered the earthquakes in Turkey and Greece of 1999, which were framed as a shared experience and even transcended the discourse of conflict between the two countries (ibid.). But as long as media coverage of political systems, societies and people in other regions of the world remains geared towards national or regional audiences, worldviews will vary. Theoretically, this gives rise to a strong tendency for the media to influence interaction in small groups through self-referential, and sometimes ethnocentric or essentialist ideas.

Self-referentiality and we-identity through media observation

We find a strong dynamic of self-referentiality if we turn to the appropriation of imported or globalized media content. In addition to explicit knowledge transfer

Small groups: global lifeworld communication **213**

through the news, this includes implicit observations of the world through entertainment formats that refer indirectly to their production contexts by taking up discursive and symbolic elements. The intercultural hermeneutic challenge that then arises for local recipients lies in a reflective approach to reception, in which one does not automatically make inferences about social reality in the country of production on the basis of what is staged and fictional. We know that recipients can differentiate between fact and fiction, but the scholarship is yet to sufficiently clarify the extent to which they combine fictional and non-fictional elements in their worldviews.

However, we can confirm the general tendency for perceived or assumed cultural closeness to positively influence how recipients view media offerings. Joseph Straubhaar carried out research on this in Latin America and demonstrated a preference for local productions (2003, 2007). Here group- and milieu-specific cultural proximity, which includes familiarity with genres or historical experiences, ultimately explains media consumption preferences (Straubhaar and La Pastina 2005).

Self-referentiality is also a feature of interpretations that are dependent on culture and society. The famous study by Elihu Katz and Tamar Liebes (1993) on the reception of the television series *Dallas* by couples of differing ethnic backgrounds reconstructs the varying interpretations produced by small groups, which go hand in hand with ethnic differences. Even if ethnic identity is inadequate as an explanation for group-specific differences in reception, it has been shown that different groups produce different interpretations of the same content. In particular, Japanese groups struggled to relate to the series, not necessarily because they were Japanese but above all because they were barely familiar with the genre of the soap opera. Furthermore, in the context of this large-scale project, it was shown that the members of homogeneous groups support each other in their interpretation and thus integrate shared experiences and everyday consensuses in their follow-up communication (ibid., see also Katz and Liebes 1984, 1985).

While studies on the reception of news and entertainment have shown that recipients even from different contexts can have a similarly critical view of the media, the symbolic reference points associated with the in-group and the imagined community (national identity) remain dominant as people engage in interpretation (Kavoori 2011). This tendency has also been demonstrated in the case of media rememberings over longer spans of time (Teer-Tomaselli 2006) and crops up in studies on the connection between media use and diasporic identity construction (Gillespie 1995).

When audiences discuss media content within small groups, theory tells us that they inevitably embed their ideas in common-sense structures and thus contribute to their ongoing self-identification. However, this process of self-identification is not necessarily dependent on whether audiences feel represented in the media. Even if people do not identify with the characters, narratives or style of media texts, their mere engagement with them may still result in the articulation of group identities. The authors of this book have clarified how follow-up discussions of global television formats in both Egyptian and German audience groups prompted critical

214 Small groups: global lifeworld communication

readings that simultaneously led to a recentring on in-group identity (Grüne 2016, p. 341ff; Grüne and Hafez 2018, p. 459ff).

Another key finding is that small groups seem to perceive their own national target audience as fairly heterogeneous based on their critical readings. In contrast, foreign audiences are imagined as more homogeneous entities (Grüne 2016, p. 371ff.). This separate processing of the media creates fictions about other groups and may reinforce stereotypical observations. The circulation of global media products, then, creates a worldwide audience, but one that is fragmented into countless small groups, which in turn act against the background of national and religious large-group influences (see Chapter 6).

One might assume that transnationally available entertainment formats relativize cultural specifics in the text-recipient relationship and lead to the emergence of a culturally hybrid audience. Yet localization simultaneously contributes to the structuring and separating of the audience into national variants. These national target audiences are synchronized to the extent that similar concepts and stylistic patterns ensure similar media experiences across the world. But this does not automatically result in an internally connected audience. The standardization of cultural patterns makes local production and appropriation possible, which certainly networks national and geocultural media landscapes but also maintains their local specifics. The "antinomy between glocalization and globalization" (ibid. p. 429ff.) is likely to lead to the synchronization of the recipient small groups with no integration into a global community as long as they remain local and gain no direct experiences of interaction and primary observation through travel (see pp. 201, 204).

Integration through the culture-connecting interpretation of global media events

Since, as yet, a global public sphere barely exists (see Chapter 2), in just a few cases can small groups' lifeworldly media experiences be oriented towards truly global media discourses. Theoretically, cross-border integrative reception experiences are conceivable in two cases. First, global media events can bring people together. Synchronized world audiences do not, in all likelihood, interact directly with one another, but indirectly these experiences may allow them to interface with cross-border everyday discourses. As global background knowledge, our collective observations of the moon landing, the Olympic Games, football World Cups, and Live Aid and Live Earth concerts, provide starting points for conversations with unknown global others. But while people around the world remember certain global media events (Volkmer 2006; Hug 2017), whether these really help establish community is open to doubt.

On the other hand, interest groups may be linked across borders by exchanging views on global media offerings or producing fan fiction. However, we have already pointed out the limited interactive potential of such entities in the case of large communities (Chapter 6, Section 6.2.1). Although the small local group is likely to be more interactive as part of such a fan community, the interaction here remains

Small groups: global lifeworld communication **215**

strongly limited to the object of the fan culture. The cross-border interactive processing of media discourses that are already globally integrated is, therefore, probably a theoretical utopia.

Conclusion: the small group as norm or disruptive element in global communication?

To conclude, then, little research has been done on the global dimension of small
lifeworldly groups' everyday interactive and observational communicative processes.
As a hub of the processing of globalization, the small group essentially remains a
black box. Our reflections have, therefore, been more conceptual than empirical in
nature. As everyday social sites of understanding-oriented interactions, groups have
much potential to advance the integration of the global community. But this contribution to globality depends on the transfer of small groups' global observations
(the globalization of external communication) to small groups' interactive interior
(the globalization of internal communication).

We have seen that different small groups react to global environments or help
shape environments through global communication. They are thus embedded in
direct and indirect global worlds of experience and form part of a global society
(as travel groups, fan groups, global families or in multicultural, local experiential realms). However, only in a few cases does theory point to a sustained global
density of interaction apt to facilitate the lifeworldly globalization of small groups
by triggering the emergence of new global groups. Global communication is capable of loosening or severing the ties that bind primary groups to their location.
Individuals can find new group forms in cross-border, global networks. To some
extent, however, global communication concurrently fosters a retreat into local primary groups, as evident today in the polarization between nationalistic and cosmopolitan value systems.

Global communication in small groups thus plays a decisive role in society, both
in terms of its interactional and observational contribution. If we start theoretically from the group's key role in socialization, it is group communication that
determines how the knowledge and experience generated by interaction with the
world become collectively anchored stocks of knowledge. The small group may
thus contribute to the "normalization" of everyday globalization, but it may also
disrupt it. One source of potential lies in the small group's feats of interaction –
its dialogic networking and integrative knowledge processing. If these interactive
contributions of the small group prove effective within the global realm, this may
be the key to normalizing the "global community".

8

THE INDIVIDUAL

Global lifeworldly communication II

The last chapter of our attempt at systematization delves into the cross-border communication of the individual. Our focus here, then, is on the smallest social unit of globalization. Opportunities for physical and virtual travel, and the networking of social systems, are opening up global spheres of action for the individual, such that the potential range of individual lifeworlds now extends beyond the local area. At the same time, however, these global options for action are not detached from structural influences such as social, community and individual conditions as well as (social) psychological and sociodemographic factors. Despite the much-postulated international networking, therefore, the conditions for individual global communication are inevitably unequal. In what follows, as in the other chapters, we will first analyse the structural conditions and prerequisites of individual communication in a global framework before going on to map out people's differing modes and types of global communication.

8.1 Lifeworldly structures of individual global communication

Individualization as a meta-tendency of globalization?

The structural detachment of the "modern individual" from traditional community structures and this individual's new and old freedoms and constraints are among the issues that have challenged social scientific debates in recent decades. For us, an intriguing point of departure is the claim that today the more or less "unbound" individual can and must search for a shared meaning and communal identity, often at a distance from traditional communities. In theory, then, environments beyond the individual's contexts of origin may be included in their search for meaning and identity (see also Hitzler 2006, p. 259). This liaison between individualization and globalization ought to be the perfect blend for the development of global

DOI: 10.4324/9781003255239-9

Individual: global lifeworld communication **217**

community and global society in the sense of the foundation of new, cross-border relationships and perceptions. This would make individualization a meta-trend in the context of globalization.

However, individualization also generates toxic side effects, such as the wave of right-wing populist thought that we have mentioned on a number of occasions. But even beyond extreme anti-globalist developments, the social aspects of the large surrogate communities, especially the nation, have not yet completely dissolved (see Chapter 6, Section 6.1). Identity concepts seem to be more variable and dynamic today and there is now evidence of at least weakly developed global identities worldwide. People's transnational experiences too are obviously having a positive effect on the recognition of global interdependencies and global politics and are stimulating a global sense of responsibility (Mau 2006; Pichler 2011). But even the hyphenated identities of modernity are yet to produce a convincing global community. In general, then, the horizon of individual relationships to the world is not entirely cosmopolitan.

New divisions have appeared both within and between societies. Analyses of cosmopolitan attitudes in the European Union indicate, for example, that the elites and the general population are drifting apart (Mau 2006; Teney and Helbling 2014; see also the Introduction). Cosmopolitanism may, therefore, be generating new tendencies towards social disintegration. Does this mean there is an antinomy between individualization and globalization? Florian Pichler has drawn attention to differences in cosmopolitan attitudes in different parts of the world. He distinguishes ethical cosmopolitan attitudes (such as trust in and a tolerant view of various others) from politically oriented cosmopolitan attitudes (such as one's stance on political processes beyond the nation-state) and distinguishes both from a subjective identification with cosmopolitanism (cosmopolitan identity) (2011, p. 24f.). This author found the latter particularly in the less globalized countries of the Global South and, of all things, in so-called "failed states". In addition, political variants of cosmopolitan attitudes were generally less pronounced than ethical ones and primarily to be found in the globalized West, though ethical cosmopolitanism was no more prevalent there than elsewhere. As Pichler states: "[O]ur study has shown that aspects of cosmopolitanism – identity, ethics and politics – do not necessarily go together" (ibid., p. 39).

Cosmopolitans and the paradox of knowledge

The focus of cosmopolitanism research ranges from the cultural study of hybrid identities, through sociological analyses of cosmopolitan capital and forms of practice, to social psychology approaches to the way people deal with the supposedly other (see also Calhoun 2003, p. 540; Werbner 2008a; Delanty 2009, 2018, Meuleman and Savage 2013, p. 231). All make it clear that the development of cosmopolitan values, attitudes and knowledge has a communicative basis. Since individuals are born in local places and can only gradually leave them both physically and imaginatively, it stands to reason that ideas about the potentially global

218 Individual: global lifeworld communication

reach of their own lifeworld, about the potentially global nature of their social environments and contemporaries, and about locating the self historically within a global setting – to bring the structures of the lifeworld into play once again (Schütz and Luckmann 2003) – are imparted communicatively and, to a greater or lesser extent, supplemented by active global experiences.

Individuals' commitment to engaging with other places, people and events beyond their immediate local world is regarded by many authors as a prerequisite for the development of cosmopolitan attitudes (Hannerz 1996; Szerszynski and Urry 2002; see also Skrbis et al. 2014). Reference is often made to the definition put forward by Ulf Hannerz, who has described cosmopolitanism as an individual orientation: "A more genuine cosmopolitanism is first of all an orientation, a willingness to engage with the Other. It entails an intellectual and aesthetic openness toward divergent cultural experiences, a search for contrasts rather than uniformity" (1996, p. 103). Ulrich Beck too views cosmopolitanization as a dimension of self-awareness and individual experience, which are shaped today by "themes of global importance" and thus also change identities (2006, p. 73). At the same time, however, Beck also refers to a "paradoxical relation between knowledge and reality" which, he argues, arises from the discrepancy between increasingly cosmopolitan social structures and processes and a form of experiential knowledge that is stagnating at the local or national level (ibid., p. 87).

Knowledge is the basis for our actions and, at the same time, socially constructed (Knoblauch 2014). Factual and structural knowledge about the world is available through discursive communicative mechanisms and is in this sense dependent on knowledge-producing systems (in other words, media and the systems of scholarship and education). Global experiential knowledge, on the other hand, requires mobility and situations shared with global others. Such conditions, however, do not automatically mean that individuals can truly operate "in other cultures" (Hannerz 1996, p. 103), since global experiences may, for example, be limited to global "third spaces".

Cosmopolitanism as social capital

The social construction of cosmopolitan knowledge is, moreover, embedded in social interpretive struggles. Ultimately, experience of the world may also be used as a strategic resource, as social capital (see Chapter 6, Section 6.1). This is closely bound up with an elitist understanding of cosmopolitanism that attributes cosmopolitan competences primarily to those who have the resources for global mobility and participation. In this reading, mobile business elites are easily identifiable as a global decision-making elite whose members combine certain globally shared characteristics as a result of global educational pathways, professional orientations and lifestyles (Micklethwait and Wooldridge 2000; Levy et al. 2016). Orly Levy, Maury Peiperl and Karsten Jonsen (2016) distinguish these global elites from heterogeneous professional elites, which are united by a high degree of mobility in the work context. But what we can discern here is essentially a "thin cosmopolitanism"

Individual: global lifeworld communication **219**

based on external milieu-based patterns that we can relate to mechanisms of social delimitation. Jonathan Corpus Ong uses the term "instrumental cosmopolitanism" to describe the strategic deployment of individual knowledge of the world (2009, p. 456).

Such cosmopolitanism, which is not necessarily associated with solidary values or a reflective worldview and is generally class-based, has, for example, been demonstrated within elite-oriented schooling in England, in which cosmopolitanism was primarily linked, as a strategic resource, with developing one's career or with individual fulfilment (Maxwell and Aggleton 2016, p. 781). Studies have also appeared on student mobility, which show that students assign a strategic character to studying abroad (Brodersen 2014). The strategic use of holiday experiences, for example, in "culinary tourism", has also been highlighted (Germann Molz 2007). The latter study brings out the way in which leisure travellers stage their experiences as cosmopolitan competence in social media posts, but with no evidence of engagement with the culture and people of the region involved. These few observations make it clear that there is a difference between strategic and understanding-oriented cosmopolitan actions and interpretations.

Elitist concepts of cosmopolitanism have thus been criticized for making it dependent on the resources and action options enjoyed by cosmopolitan elites (see, for example, Werbner 1999; Lamont and Aksartova 2002, p. 1; Ong 2009, p. 457; Høy-Petersen and Woodward 2018). Pnina Werbner asks why those whose mobility is not voluntary or whose access to certain global spaces is restricted are often not considered or recognized as potential cosmopolitans: "It remains unclear … why migrants and diasporics should be distinguished *analytically* from occupational transnationals, the oil engineers or foreign journalists who live in special compounds or the Hilton, wherever they go" (1999, p. 17). Only when cosmopolitanism is not linked to the individual's opportunities and free will can "cosmopolitans from below" be included (Hall and Werbner 2008, p. 346; Werbner 2008b, p. 14f.). This also shifts the focus from global encounters to local realities that are shaped by globalization processes and in which dealing with difference is part of people's everyday life. These forms of cosmopolitanism are also called "vernacular" (Werbner 2008b; Leurs and Georgiou 2016), "banal" (Ong 2009), "ordinary" or "intuitive" (Lamont and Aksartova 2002; Levy et al. 2016). Such broader approaches to cosmopolitanism are also bound up with a conceptual turn to everyday actions and interpretive patterns (Lamont and Aksartova 2002).

From this vantage point, cosmopolitan individuals are likely to be found throughout societies, across class or milieu structures and, ultimately, worldwide. In any case, there is no theoretical reason why, for example, working-class migrants should not develop global identities or empathy (Werbner 1999). Even if migration, such as labour migration, is not motivated by the mere desire to globalize one's horizons and is often an expression of global inequality (Pries 2015, p. 176), migrants still gain global experience. Nor does the positive effect of education on cosmopolitan attitudes (see, for example, Mau 2006, Teney and Helbing 2014) exclude the possibility of everyday cosmopolitan interpretations beyond the educated elite.

220 Individual: global lifeworld communication

These have in fact been traced in qualitative micro-studies. Michèle Lamont and Sada Aksartova (2002), for example, have documented anti-racist argumentational strategies among working-class individuals, and Nina Høy-Petersen and Ian Woodward (2018) have shown how multicultural, everyday experiential knowledge is deployed reflexively in talking about "others". The study by Koen Leurs and Myria Georgiou mentioned earlier also contends that the multicultural environments of underprivileged suburban youths in London induce a normalized approach to different lifestyles and contexts of origin (2016, p. 3730). Conversely, not all elites are automatically global citizens. This is reflected in Europe's right-wing populist parties, which are by no means supported only by the working classes. Nevertheless, the very elites that feel neoracist resentment towards the world are internationally networked. Hence, some elites critical of globalization are themselves to some extent globally operating actors (Bob 2012; see Chapter 5, Section 5.2.2).

Levels of action of cosmopolitanism

In addition, cosmopolitan elites often remain connected to a particular culture and do not constantly advocate universal principles of humanity. Craig Calhoun therefore urges us to consider the relative privileges through which certain action options arise in the first place or that make it easier to translate cosmopolitan attitudes into action (2003, p. 544). For example, business elites or travelling scholars and development aid workers, according to Calhoun, do not have to deal with laborious visa applications or spend time gaining official approval for documents, as do private individuals in certain diaspora communities, who are globally networked in a similar way through their families, but enjoy no privileges arising from their professional status (ibid., p. 543).

Furthermore, individuals' identification with cosmopolitan values does not necessarily converge with their everyday actions. If they derive their cosmopolitan identity from their trips abroad while ignoring the multiculturalism on their doorstep, as Leurs and Georgiou (2016) have documented, there is clearly no inevitable connection between cosmopolitan thinking, feeling and acting. The same ultimately applies to sections of the business elite, such as the "cosmocrats" described by John Micklethwait and Adrian Wooldridge, whose global knowledge is often based on their own globally networked lifeworld but remains cut off from local people and the circumstances in which they operate professionally (2000, p. 241). Earlier avant-garde elites also generated their own cosmopolitan developments in the metropolises of the time but were not connected to local milieus (Werbner 2015, p. 16). The different levels of values and action in the lifeworld may, therefore, have a transnational orientation (physical mobility and cultural immobility) or cosmopolitan orientation (physical *and* cultural mobility) (Werbner 1999).

From a communication studies perspective, two aspects are important. First, two communicative contexts are central to the individual's global communication: global communication in global environments, which arises from the spatio-temporal and social expansion of the individual lifeworld into distant contexts, and

Individual: global lifeworld communication **221**

global communication in local environments, which is generated in immediate settings by an essentially symbolic expansion of the lifeworld that is prompted by the global circulation of people, ideas, goods, and so on. The connection between these lifeworldly internal and external global spaces is important to the development of a global community, as we will see on p. 240. Interaction takes place both between mobile and various immobile local actors within alternating referential systems, and between local actors and various "incoming" global actors. Translated into systems theory, psychological systems constitute environments for one another and thus both mobile and immobile actors, in a variety of interlocking formations, shape the process of globalization. A focus on just one of these types, then, must always be inadequate. Communicative exchanges between mobile and immobile actors are both crucial to the production of meaning within the lifeworld.

Second, individuals differ not only in their mobile or immobile practices, but also in terms of the social roles they assume. We have seen that cosmopolitan elites are often discussed in professional contexts (managers, scholars, and so on). But less attention has been paid to their informal roles (Nowicka 2008, p. 255; Teney and Helbling 2014, p. 269). Yet individuals always occupy a number of roles, whose emergence is determined in part by the communicative situation. In team meetings, the manager of a global team may, for example, pursue global networking and apply knowledge of the world in a strategic and professional manner. But as a private person a manager may act as a friend, parent or partner within a local lifeworldly haven thanks to the Internet connection in her or his hotel room, while making no contacts beyond the hotel lobby. With regard to the business elite in particular, Hannerz recognized early on that in global economic life the experiential space may also carry over to employees' private lives (1996, p. 85f.). The question, then, is, in which areas of the individual biography cosmopolitan practices come into play (for example, only in educational and professional contexts or in private lifeworlds as well) and how they relate to the individual's ethics.

Stereotypes and individual relationships to the world

Concrete analyses of how cosmopolitans are "formed" are rare (Kim 2011, p. 281). But how might we explain the variability of human relationships and attitudes to the world and to global others? While some rescue unknown refugees, this very fact drives others to demand the tightening of asylum laws and to protest against migration. Some take pity on the fate of unknown others in regions afflicted by war and crisis, while others subject them to derogatory jokes over a beer in the pub or even perpetrate violence against supposed "strangers". Between these extreme poles of individual thinking and acting in lifeworlds, there are also those who have no specific attitude towards their global environments or at least do not articulate them.

It is due to the non-organized character of the lifeworld that it follows no uniform internal logic. The lifeworld has no explicit systemic programme but is a site of mutual understanding and cultural validation. The negotiations that this requires between the members of a society generate no uniform consensus of values and

222 Individual: global lifeworld communication

actions, which is why democratic rights and obligations are codified in binding constitutions and why the recognition of legitimate orders must be learned.

The emergence of individual attitudinal and behavioural patterns and their connection with the individual's perception of the world is the focus of social psychology, which has made a lasting impact on communication studies (Littlejohn and Foss 2005, p. 43). In our context, the field of most interest is research on stereotypes and prejudices, which examines the pathologies of perceptual structures – in contrast to cosmopolitanism research, which mainly seeks to determine the vertical attitudes of values and the horizontal attitudes of worldviews and ideologies. In the shape of stereotypes, prejudices, constructions of the other and acts of discrimination, however, it is the categories that prevent the globalization of the everyday world from the perspective of the individual that come into focus. Stereotypes and prejudices impede the crucial openness to other cultural contexts and actors. Discrimination is the opposite of a willingness to engage in exchange. The construct-reality problem (limited or imagined notions of reality), the construct-structure problem (worldview construction in accordance with existing attitudes or ideologies) and the individual-collective problem (the significance of collective stereotypes and images to the individual production of knowledge) ultimately hinder the acquisition of global knowledge (Hafez 2002a, p. 36f.). What is common to all levels of the construction of worldviews and the construction of the global other is that they are the basis of individual patterns of interpretation and action that precede global contact and shape it accordingly. Existing stereotypes may thus prompt people to choose certain travel destinations or avoid contact with particular others.

Here the formation of stereotypes is initially viewed as a general phenomenon rooted in the individual's perception of reality and it is explained in light of the necessity, as derived from theories of cognition, for humans to reduce complexity. Social prejudices are also associated with various individual and social functions – such as the control and orienting of knowledge, the legitimation of existing orders and the preservation of identity (Thiele 2015, p. 60ff.). These functions may serve to safeguard everyday routine actions. But they are a hindrance to extraquotidian contact with global environments, especially when stereotypical perceptual structures and situational perceptions diverge, but certain mechanisms contribute to maintaining the stereotype. This is described by the theory of cognitive dissonance or the theory of case-by-case interpretations, according to which experiences that contradict one's own construct are characterized as exceptions and thus ultimately prove the rule (Lippman 1922; Festinger 1978). In this way, actors avoid constant irritations to their lifeworldly "perspectival security", but constantly reproduce fragmented and generally hostile worldviews. Existing prejudices cannot be broken down in this way.

Conditions for stereotype change

This does not tell us why individual and collective stereotype structures lead to prejudices and discriminatory actions in some people. Certain approaches at the

Individual: global lifeworld communication **223**

individual level direct attention to specific personality structures believed to be conducive to prejudice or highlight experiences of social deprivation, moral-ideological influences and educational shortcomings (Hafez and Schmidt 2015, p. 36ff.; Thiele 2015, p. 90ff.). With regard to these factors, cultural and ideological traditions with a view to the perception of one's in-group play a decisive role in social comparisons within multicultural societies, where segmentation into cultur-ally imagined in-groups and out-groups still constitutes a challenge to social cohe-sion. Here a conflictual perspective comes to the fore. The perceived disadvantage suffered by one's group may go hand in hand with Islamophobic or anti-Semitic attitudes and abasement. Levels of affluence do not necessarily correlate with the rejection of the other, but rather perceived threats to prosperity, in other words so-called relative deprivation, which is ascribed to the group to which individuals feel they belong (Hafez and Schmidt 2015, p. 37). A negative image of the distant out-group and a negative image of the close-by in-group then enter into a toxic mix that may lead to acts of discrimination.

In the context of global communication in the interior of lifeworlds, it is thus important to consider those theoretical approaches that focus on the cultural trans-mission and discursive dependency of stereotypes. Even if attitudes that steer indi-vidual ways of dealing with collectively anchored stereotypes cannot be ignored, selective perceptions of others or essentialist systems of interpretation are based on collective groundwork. With regard to distant, abstract, large communities (such as nations and ethnic groups), such collective stereotypes persist worldwide, so that breaking down fixed stereotype structures and the associated essentialist perceptions is the challenge of today, while the general overcoming of structures of difference is a task for a future utopia.

The theory of social identity emphasizes the importance of the relationship between the interpersonal and intergroup relations of the individual, which influ-ence their conflict behaviour. What is crucial here is the assumption that individ-uals strive for self-respect and a positive identity, which they achieve primarily through processes of social comparison (Tajfel and Turner 1986). The collective and individual perceptions of identity are, therefore, closely related and are in turn dependent on external ascriptions as well as self-attributions. But people tend to evaluate the characteristics of their own reference group more positively than those of an out-group and to act accordingly. Comparisons to the disadvan-tage of the in-group may thus prompt individuals to adopt a variety of strategies, such as searching for a different reference group, confronting the out-group or reinterpreting comparative categories. It is the latter, however, that is most likely in the case of conflict-laden global contacts. Moreover, it seems generally difficult to apply these schemas, which often stem from experiments with ad-hoc groups, to real-world questions of global communication. It is unclear, for example, why – in people's perception – certain characteristic differences between in- and out-groups become markers of distinction and competition. In the context of racism, for example, why does appearance define a distinction between groups rather than profession or living conditions?

224 Individual: global lifeworld communication

Although social psychological attitude measurements have a relatively high predictive value with respect to current trends in public opinion and society, attitudes are not always consistently developed and there is no exact correspondence between attitude and action. For example, racism does not necessarily culminate in discrimination. This is due in significant part to the numerous intervening variables in human behaviour. Here the "contact hypothesis" occupies an important position in the scholarship, the classic formulation of which can be found in the work of Gordon W. Allport and which we already mentioned in the section on small groups (1954, see Chapter 7, Section 7.1). The key point here is that stereotypical ideas are much easier to maintain at a distance than in cases of direct contact with the global other, which may foster individual perception and action. Thomas Pettigrew subsequently made it clear, however, that real change in stereotypes requires common goals, friendships and a lasting relationship (1998).

Why and how individuals become cosmopolitan citizens of the world or xenophobic rejectors of globalization depend on numerous factors. In addition to social psychological studies, informed by theories of cognition and conflict, that try to open up the black box of the human psychological system, we draw on theories of socialization and learning that relate the individual to the intergenerational transmission of collectively anchored images and stereotypes.

Global socialization through family and education

The family, which we introduced in the last chapter as the nucleus of the global community (see Chapter 7, Section 7.2.1), is the immediate lifeworldly realm in which individuals develop their core values. Here symbolic interaction lays the foundation for individual patterns of interpretation and action, which are then available to the individual for subsequent interactions (Mead 1934; Blumer 2010). Growing up in a home with cosmopolitan leanings may, therefore, be a key factor in socialization, prompting individuals to make the world their lifeworld over the course of their lives. The children of mobile parents ("third culture kids" or "global nomads", Weidemann 2016; Cason 2018) thus have a strong basis for the development of global competencies thanks to these framework conditions. Of course, while children's epistemic and experiential worlds are shaped by their parents' worldviews and practices, this does not necessarily make them identical to those of their parents.

In addition, varying ideas of cosmopolitanism may exist within different homes, which recalls our previous remarks. A case analysis by Don Weenink on the cosmopolitanism of parents whose children attend an international school in Denmark prompted the author to distinguish between "dedicated" and "pragmatic" cosmopolitans (2008). For the former, raising their children to be open to other global contexts was crucial. The latter were more strategic in their thinking, focusing on the career opportunities arising from an excellent knowledge of English and experience of internationalization. Here the concept of cosmopolitan capital – which we critiqued earlier – provides stimulus for social advancement and may

Individual: global lifeworld communication **225**

foster the internationalization of the middle class. A pragmatic cosmopolitanism, then, may in fact impede the elite reproduction of cosmopolitan experiences (ibid.).

The individual's global learning is closely linked with their secondary socialization in educational institutions. Schooling, training courses and political education play a part in the development of global knowledge and in inculcating global values. The concepts and practices of "global education" are thus the subject of numerous debates in pedagogical theories of learning, the academic discipline of education and research on education. The entire thematic field of education and "global citizenship" is also a key concern of the United Nations (particularly UNESCO). Without delving further into global pedagogy in worldwide comparison (for further comparative research, see, for example, Hahn and Martin 2008), the point we wish to underline here is that it is vital to reflect epistemologically on the opportunities institutions provide for individuals to acquire global knowledge or knowledge of globalization and on the sort of contact facilitated by exchange programmes or heterogeneous school classes.

Instead of a cosmopolitan outlook, school education often fosters a "banal nationalism" that promotes the individual's affiliation not with global society but with a national community of solidarity, as Anja Weiß has described with reference to Germany (2015, p. 168). England's elite schools too provide a classically English and thus ethnocentric school education, which is paradoxically regarded as guaranteeing advancement into global social strata. Cosmopolitan education is not the focus here (Maxwell and Aggleton 2016). In the latter case study, only a few young people, especially those with origins in other countries, developed a transnational perspective on their future or articulated a global sensibility (ibid., p. 791f.).

If educational content is of a high quality but ethnocentric and prejudiced, education may impede global understanding. Although education generally correlates with openness to the world, as we have already stated, it is, conversely, no sure insulation against the intergenerational transmission of racism. To cite just one example, in Germany, Islamophobia and right-wing nationalist views are present in the middle of society. People can thus be educated and yet ignorant of the world (Hafez and Schmidt 2015, p. 59ff.). The lack of knowledge about the Islamic world is evident in German and European school education (Hafez 2014a, p. 291ff.). In a similarly critical vein, we can question the imparting of knowledge about the societies of the Global South in general, assess whether postcolonial perspectives have made it into school lessons, and scrutinize the sometimes problematic constructs present in school textbooks. Traditions of foreign-language learning, meanwhile, promote limited and region-specific forms of multilingualism, while the potential of migrant multilingualism is barely tapped within the school context. In short, there are major question marks over the globalization of curricula, learning materials and teaching staff (see, for example, Adick 2011;.Oelkers 2011; Treml 2011).

We might include direct global contacts of the kind that may be offered at school or in further education through exchange programmes or the like, yet even these do not automatically lead to participants' global communitization. If the contact does not take place on an equal footing, and distinctions are in fact

226 Individual: global lifeworld communication

emphasized (through differences that the programme fails to compensate for in infrastructure, material resources, and technological and linguistic competencies), it is doubtful that these educational experiences will make individuals cosmopolitan. We also have to consider the regions with which schools, universities and other educational institutions maintain partnerships worldwide. From the perspective of participants, it may well make a difference whether contact is facilitated with people in familiar contexts (for example, in neighbouring countries) or beyond geostrategic relationships between states. The individual's involvement in institutions, then, may either help reproduce their individual relations with the world or open up new horizons.

Individual lifeworlds' ambivalent relations to the world

It is true, however, that the positioning of individuals in relation to the world – through perception, knowledge, values, attitudes, experiences, actions and structural conditions – generates a diverse range of typologies and makes the global development of the individual relatively unpredictable. This has to do with the fact that human beings' expansion into the world and sealing-off from it may relate to the different dimensions of thinking and knowing, feeling and acting. Clearly, individuals do not act and feel in a completely global and cosmopolitan way, making it hard to categorize them as "cosmopolitan" or "local". The individual's specific constitution gives rise to differing requirements for lifeworldly self-optimization through global learning or the cultivation of contact. We take a closer look at the communicative basis of these activities in Section 8.2.

8.2 Communicative connections in the lifeworld

The individual's perception of the world as moulded by their biography is closely related to their communicative actions. On the one hand, individuals learn through their communicative experiences (for example, through direct global experiences). On the other hand, the individual's cognitive, emotional and conative preconditions influence the way they communicate (for example, when they stereotype others in global encounters on the basis of their prejudices). How individuals communicate globally, how they observe their global environments and what they learn discursively about the world cannot be summed up in a simple formula. As we saw above, people may feel empathy for global others while also seeking to isolate themselves in local settings or, conversely, they may travel a great deal but develop no cosmopolitan values or feelings of solidarity for global others. Despite their embedding in social contexts, in their interactive engagement with the world, though not necessarily in its observation, individuals are more autonomous than the small groups discussed earlier. Individuals are not dependent on co-orientation with a group. In contrast to small groups, the individual's relative autonomy is also apparent in the fact that they can communicate with the outside world in their social and professional roles either directly or through media.

Individual: global lifeworld communication **227**

In order to understand the interplay between communicative modes and the crossing of boundaries, in what follows we consider the individual's (1) dialogic quality, (2) feats of observation and information processing, and (3) discursive external communication. The mechanisms of global communication we bring out are primarily conceptual in nature, as the existing research has failed to position individual communication comprehensively within globalization.

8.2.1 Interaction and dialogue

Interpersonal dialogue and global community/society

If we understand the internal communication of the individual as *intra*personal communication, then external communication almost inevitably generates situations of *inter*personal communication. Interpersonal and/or intragroup communication, of a direct nature or via media, is therefore the norm for the communicating individual. In this context the greatest potential for communitization lies in dialogic interaction. Here individuals' epistemic and interpretive systems encounter one another. These are oriented towards each other and towards a shared third, as described in Theodore Newcomb's ABX schema (1953). In addition, through dialogue, the partners to interaction synthesize their symbolic and epistemic worlds, understand each other intersubjectively and construct the world together (see Chapter 1, Section 1.1). According to Jürgen Habermas, the functioning of a global community depends on human beings' cross-border, understanding-oriented action. Only when the local lifeworld is expanded globally can societies stabilize in a similarly global manner, because communicative action has functions that are also relevant to our understanding of global community or global society. Through communicative action, cultural knowledge is reproduced, by means of which the members of a society create a common stock of knowledge to which everyone can relate. Communicative action ensures social integration through individuals' participation in legitimate orders that generate group solidarity. Finally, communicative action is crucial to the socialization through which individuals develop a personal and social identity and gain a capacity for effective action (Habermas 1995, vol. 2, p. 203ff.).

The transfer of these basic theoretical assumptions to global society, however, reveals not only the enormous potential of individual communication for the world, but also its obvious limits. At present, global knowledge is not a matter of course, we are not seeing the emergence of a truly integrated global community and not everyone has developed global competencies. Although Habermas has not written about the ways his theory might be applied at the global level, instead focusing on modern society as moulded by the nation state (Sundermeier 1996, p. 84ff.), the notion of an ideal dialogue is universally valid and transferable to global conditions. In fact, Habermas has defined an ideal type of global communication, because this is tantamount to domination-free exchange that connects and rationally neutralizes the cultural and structural predispositions of those communicating, facilitating their joint development of orientations and situational definitions (Delanty 2009, p. 55).

228 Individual: global lifeworld communication

But the global interaction of individuals poses specific challenges. Familiar linguistic, normative and institutional codes undergo a profound shift when transferred to global processes of negotiation. People speak different languages, have different socialization experiences and to some extent develop different cultural rules and beliefs. There is thus no complete overlap between interpretive and referential systems. The lifeworld with all its content, structures and patterns is challenged when individuals expand into global spaces. Hence, the basic lifeworldly assumptions that lend constancy to the "structure of the world", as well as the "validity of our experience of the world" and the potential to act within it (Schütz 1972, p.153), must first withstand this global expansion.

If the global lifeworld is to function as a source of cultural stabilization for the global community and global society, people need experiential security when dealing with global others as well as the insight that the global environment, which cannot be directly experienced, is structured in much the same way as the everyday local world. However, this is precisely where interactions are preceded by perceptual problems. This is because cultural difference is still chiefly believed to exist *between* societies, although relations of proximity and distance also apply to individuals in different lifeworldly contexts *within* societies. While cultural variations within society are a taken-for-granted component of local lifeworlds, the same sort of cultural disjunctures seems to generate uncertainty when it comes to the outside world.

Dynamics and imponderables of global dialogue

It is evident that an orientation towards the same symbolic and referential systems, above all, language, facilitates interpersonal communication. However, the issue of similarity or difference can hardly be settled *before* an attempt to communicate. While the linguistic symbols used are different, the content conveyed may be identical or at least understandable (otherwise there would be no translations). Although interculturality is not something that can be determined *a priori*, in many situations it is apparent that perceptual and epistemic structures precede dialogue and that people have prejudices about the global other, for example, when an identical situation is interpreted as a "cultural conflict" only if people from other countries or with a "migration background" are involved.

Dialogue, then, is not challenged by interculturality *per se*, but by two representational problems, which we call the individual-collective problem and the interaction-interpretation problem. The first refers to the generalized perception of parties to interaction as representatives of a culture or society or community. In communicative encounters, individuals may focus on another person's imagined cultural imprinting rather than their individual personality and arguments, in such a way that it becomes theoretically impossible to jointly negotiate an understanding of the world, because the individual is always perceived as the "representative" of a larger entity and not as an individual.

The second problem relates to the interpretation of different action routines as representations of differing meanings, although the same function and structure

Individual: global lifeworld communication **229**

may be concealed behind divergent rules and routines (see also Averbeck-Lietz 2011, p. 286). For example, rituals of greeting differ worldwide, but not the basic message inherent in greeting itself. However, if the expression alone is interpreted (for example, bowing as distancing or respectful), the difference (interpretation) inevitably pushes the commonality (function) into the background and confirms assumptions of difference.

Situation-appropriate behaviour, which is central to a rule-oriented understanding of interpersonal communication (Höflich 1988, 1996), is of course not straightforwardly possible if codes have not been learned through a shared process. However, personal dialogue opens up the opportunity for an understanding of people's rule-based behaviour, the elaboration of differences as well as analogies (see also Hafez 2002a, vol. 1, p. 163ff.). In this sense, we can make the reflexive requirement of cosmopolitanism – to recognize the otherness of the familiar – useful to communication theory. The imperative is not to harmonize communicative codes but to understand the universal patterns and analogies behind different codes. Intercultural communication is, therefore, not a means of "repairing" cultural misunderstandings, but rather a precondition for global communality. Through dialogic interaction, differences can be transcended without the understanding of the other requiring assimilation. Not only the understanding of the global other, but also a shared understanding of the world is the bridge to a global community that may be realized through interpersonal encounters.

To this day, however, there are explanatory approaches in the field of intercultural communication that trace the communicative challenges of intercultural encounters back to differences between major cultures. Against this trend, completely new branches of research have emerged, such as the field of critical intercultural communication, which places more emphasis on the social framework within which we find cultural ideas that shape situations, a framework that deconstructs traditional research perspectives (Nakayama and Halualani 2013). To quote Yoshitaka Miike: "When and how can intercultural communication specialists stop talking forever about certain Eurocentric theoretical constructs (e.g., individualism-collectivism, independent-interdependent construals, and high-context and low-context communication) and move beyond these sweeping overgeneralizations that occlude cultural and communicative complexities?" (2013, p. 193f.).

In addition to research on intercultural communication, social psychology too investigates contact scenarios. The contact hypothesis is not concerned with cultural understanding and integration in the narrower sense, but with breaking down prejudices through contact (see pp. 199, 224). Here too, preconceptions about others are an impediment to interaction. An extended version of this hypothesis emphasizes that we can only expect contact to have a positive effect under certain conditions, for example, when interaction partners share a similar status, pursue common goals, speak a common language, when the contact situation is supported by third parties and is not associated with precarious economic realities or other contexts of crisis (Pettigrew 1998). Especially if there is the possibility of sustainable contact that can give rise to friendships, there is an excellent chance of altering

230 Individual: global lifeworld communication

judgements about one another and shifting the boundaries of proximity and distance, of the in- and out-group. The contact hypothesis, however, does not define this contact in a way compatible with the discipline of communication studies, even if, according to Pettigrew, the possibility of self-disclosure points to the need for dense communicative exchange (ibid., p. 78).

Structural variants of global dialogue

Concepts of intercultural and global dialogue are mainly used in politics and education (Leeds-Hurwitz 2015). On the other hand, while conversation analysis and ethnomethodology do investigate everyday conversations, they pay less attention to their specifically global qualities. But everyday dialogues differ structurally from diplomatic dialogues. Institutionally organized dialogues take place in prestructured situations, are mostly solution-oriented and are part and parcel of decision-making scenarios. Concrete goals usually only emerge in the lifeworld when irritations arise. Otherwise, the shared negotiation of everyday meanings takes place implicitly and not through organized communicative formats. Moreover, encounters in the lifeworld are random and open-ended (Cissna and Anderson 1998). The potential for communitization, which individuals develop through sustainable dialogues and that may find expression in "postnational" identities, thus varies as well. Viewed in this way, the more or less culture-bound cosmopolitan identities (Appiah 2006), the hybrid and "both-and" identities, are always partly testimony to the different contact scenarios in lifeworlds.

Research on the effectiveness of interaction in global corporate teams, for example, may blind us to the fact that the dialogues of the lifeworld are not focused on concrete results and are thus uncontrollable. Even in the case of diplomatic dialogue, consensus or agreements are not mandatory, but only desirable. Dialogue partners may continue to have different opinions and views as long as the foundations of mutual acceptance are in place. "Intercultural" communication, then, has not failed if a goal has not been achieved or if the parties to interaction have not "understood" each other, but only if there is no mutual recognition.

Dialogic structural variants are thus closely related to the concepts of tolerance found in recognition theory (Forst 2006), though the latter does not flesh out the communication-theoretical foundations (Hafez 2014a, p. 120). Here "negative tolerance" or "rejection" of the global other must be located at the level of non-interaction. Ultimately, "rejection" would mean the form of dialogue we have just described, one lacking a shared consensus, in other words, a dialogue of a negative character. Only "acceptance" in the sense of positive tolerance and appreciation and the development of a common denominator meet the conditions of an ideal dialogue in the sense of a conversational synthesis and communitization. From this theoretical vantage point as well, then, a community-generating recognition of global others can only be achieved through dialogue. At the same time, for us this raises the question of how we deal with rejecting dialogues, which are the true

Individual: global lifeworld communication **231**

challenge of global interaction. We will discuss this topic later in connection with individual epistemic structures.

Regardless of accepting or rejecting modes of dialogue, we have to consider the sequential nature of interactive encounters (Littlejohn and Foss 2005, p. 161). Dialogues are not isolated components of individual everyday communication (Black 2008). Interpersonal communication is shaped by a whole spectrum of communicative genres. Dialogic sequences may thus be surrounded by moments of debate, gossip or monologic tales of woe. But non-dialogic episodes of encounters are not necessarily counterproductive when it comes to the communitizing quality of the interaction. The shared use of communicative processes in itself already contributes to social reassurance (in everyday family life, for example), not just the content of exchange (Keppler 1994). Monologic narration (storytelling, see also Chapter 4, Section 4.2.1) too may lay the ground for dialogic, power-free mutual understanding by creating a basis for the listener to adopt the other's lifeworldly perspectives and for a shared orientation towards values (Black 2008, p. 99; Antweiler 2011, p. 82f.). Dialogue is thus essentially a communicative snapshot in which those involved in the interaction relate to one another in a particularly conscious way (Cissna and Anderson 1998, p. 67; Black 2008, p. 99).

The communicative quality of global contacts would, therefore, depend in part on the multiplex possibilities of human encounters. Institutional, formalized dialogue situations are easier to organize, but have to achieve a balance between formality and informality in the communicative encounter. Non-organized everyday dialogues, on the other hand, require the temporal and situational conditions vital to fostering the development of multimodal communicative sequences in which shared orientations can be sounded out. This provides a communication-theoretical rationale for the need for different levels of experience within the individual, which we discussed earlier with respect to global contact – as in the development of professional business contacts into private contacts highlighted by Ulf Hannerz (see p. 000).

At the same time, these complex communicative structures explain why online global connectivity is only slowly being realized (see Chapter 6, Section 6.2.1) despite the seemingly limitless possibilities. To quote Nancy Baym: "[T]he range of potential relational partners has been expanded to a broader pool than at any previous point in history" (2010, p. 101). This is no doubt because there already has to be a reason for communication with the global other in virtual space, usually of a strategic nature. There is limited scope here for the chance encounter or a flow of communication encompassing a varied range of genres. The deepening and maintaining of contacts, then, are easily possible, but new intense experiences between people happen only in exceptional cases. It is thus unsurprising that most online relationships do not become intimate and that online contacts arise from offline contacts more often than vice versa (ibid., pp. 124, 132). Hence, opportunities for networking do not simply translate into global lifeworldly relationality, whereas existing lifeworld contacts provide new means of involving others in one's activities and new routes to participation. Once again, as in the case of online communities, the social co-presence of communication is plain to see.

Overlap between observation and dialogue

In direct interpersonal encounters characterized by the dialogic mode of communication the variants of communicative situations, genres and media described so far are accompanied by continuous observation. The perception of non- and paraverbal signs and of the situational context creates a dense text that, like speech acts, requires interpretation. What we often observe routinely in everyday life may have to be reinterpreted in a global context. This also reverses the relationship between verbality and non-verbality, if, for example, looking at things together, pointing and gesturing constitute the only remaining shared symbol system. This is where global individual communication differs from organized social systems, which have separate organizational units for observation, direct interaction and the representation of the world. While in the latter case it is the relationship between the units that matters (for example, between external and internal communication in the economy, see Chapter 4, Section 4.2.4), the key in individual communication is the balance between communicative modes and the effects of shifts between levels for the individual's global communication.

What happens if, for example, linguistic exchange is difficult and is circumvented (for example, when travelling or during migration) and all that is left to the individual is observational experience? Then mobility does not enable one to cross the boundaries of one's lifeworld and structures of perception are transferred to other places. In this way, the potential of interactive exchange in global space remains untapped. Such a radical shift towards an observational stance may in turn become an obstacle in the global encounters that then take place, if one fails to step outside one's own interpretive schemas because the observed situation, in which visible symbols, routines and rules become recognizable, is not decoded at a shared level of meaning.

One example of this is the headscarf, which is often primarily observed as a symbol of religiosity in non-Islamic contexts, although behind it there are personalities who pursue professional careers, have a political opinion and have sex. The interpretation of this piece of cloth tends to define the situation. It continues to determine the agenda even if it gives rise to dialogue. In light of our problems of representation, this would violate the principle of recognition and dialogue from the outset and culminate in a misconceived form of recognition. The "tourist gaze" is another example of learned observational perspectives that tourists adopt without entering into dialogue with local residents (see also Urry 1990; Larsen 2014).

A *dominance* of observation rather than a *balance* between interaction and observation may, however, free the core of communicative statements from grammatical and cultural superimpositions. In any case, not all social meanings can be conveyed verbally. A sense of the taken-for-grantedness of globalized lifeworlds may also be produced through joint action without running the risk of linguistic misunderstandings. If one does the same things in parallel and within the range of mutual observation, there is at least a chance of generating mutual security rather than insecurity through this superimposition of observation on interaction. If the

Individual: global lifeworld communication **233**

person described above wearing a headscarf shares everyday situations with an insecure observer, this may be the first step towards potential rapprochement. The result of observational contacts thus remains unpredictable but is inevitably limited at most to a silent understanding, a (passive) form of recognition that is not necessarily conveyed to the global other.

Influences of digital media

How do opportunities for digital interaction influence the relationship between observation and dialogue for the global individual? We concluded earlier that global interaction on the Internet is generally quite hard to establish as it requires a reason for digital encounters. While people on their travels can, for example, observe the goings-on in a marketplace in a lifeworld that is distant from them, it is difficult to find a counterpart to this lifeworldly situation in digital space. In other words: interaction in the narrower sense can be simulated digitally, but this is scarcely possible when it comes to interaction in the broader sense, which not only entails the exchange of content but also the potential for direct observation in numerous everyday situations. Although research has been carried out on the contextual specifics as well as the social potentials and problems of digitally mediated communication (see, for example, Baym 2002), we still know too little overall about its use in interpersonal cross-border communication. Of course, digital media provide opportunities for the individual to maintain contacts over great distances. But whether they also contribute to the individual's interactive community building is an open question.

We might add that even when people come into contact online, the dominance of individual observation is reinforced, for example, when local knowledge structures act as "digital travel guides" and control observation even while people are travelling, making direct contact unnecessary. In this case, rather than opening a window to the world, technology helps prevent potential global social contacts (Günther and Hopfinger 2009; Garaeva 2012, p. 218; see also Chapter 6, Section 6.1). Overall, for the individual, rather than providing a setting for increased direct interaction beyond the boundaries of their lifeworld, online communication may instead amplify "intercultural observation", from which modern technologies – according to Giesecke (see Chapter 1, Section 1.1) – should actually be leading us away by establishing interactive global communication. We are not yet in a position to assess precisely the role of the digital from the perspective of the individual.

The power and impotence of individual interaction

The specific communicative shifts and superimpositions of global interactive situations generate opportunities and risks for global communitization. Through dialogue, the individual can tap their full potential for creative understanding and explanation in order to enhance global communality. By opening up to the global other, however, the individual runs the risk of disagreement and failure

234 Individual: global lifeworld communication

of recognition. In global dialogue, then, there is no great distance between the individual's power and powerlessness. Sequences of less-demanding hybrid communicative forms may ease the situation, but in turn increase the need for sensitive interpretive work on the part of the individual. But the power of interpretation comes at the cost of impotence in the face of its disconnectedness from global society. Contact as mere connectivity without dialogue does not lead to a "deep globalization" of individual communication in the form of genuine communitization. Hence, a similar mechanism applies here as in the structuralist network analysis discussed earlier (see Chapter 6, Section 6.2.1). Networks alone do not create a global community.

8.2.2 Observation and diffusion

The individual's discursive global knowledge processing

The limits and potentials of global contact result not only from situational and communicative conditions, but also from the epistemic and personality structures available to the individual as resources for interpreting global contacts and observations. The individual faces two challenges here. On the one hand, they cannot know an infinite amount about the world and, on the other hand, they cannot travel constantly in order to gain their own global experience of every part of the Earth. Distant worlds, meanwhile, simply cannot be observed directly in local contexts. How the individual deals with these two shortcomings helps determine how flexible the opening of their lifeworld is.

The individual processing of global knowledge is thus less linear, systematic and uniform than in organized social systems. It also creates ambivalent roles for individuals. While individuals have expert knowledge of that section of the world made up of their own lifeworld over the short or long term, they remain dependent on discursively available knowledge when it comes to other contexts. But the expert knowledge acquired by interpersonal means is often not in keeping with the truncated, selective and often stereotypical discursive knowledge in the public sphere and media (see Chapter 2, Section 2.2.1), which is nonetheless expert knowledge for those without personal experience. Individuals in modern societies thus operate within an everyday field of tension between their own experiences and mediated knowledge, which is exceedingly difficult to process and in fact tends to resemble a form of global ignorance (see also Weiß 2006). Spanish philosopher Daniel Innerarity tells us: "Our ignorance is a consequence of three characteristics found in contemporary societies: the non-immediate nature of our experience of the world, the concentration of information, and the technology that intervenes between us and reality" (2013, p. 3).

Logically enough, then, the debates on a cosmopolitan awareness chiefly emphasize the individual's reflexive competence. Høy-Petersen and Woodward regard ethically based cosmopolitan competence as "reflexive reasoning and the ability to knit together pieces of information drawn from various discourses in order to construct

Individual: global lifeworld communication **235**

the Other as being either 'good' or 'bad', 'worthy' or 'unworthy', regardless of being similar or different" (2018, p. 660). Through this lens, global competence does not consist in predicting differences between cultures (see p. 000), but in the ability to critically combine observation and introspection, knowledge and ignorance.

A critical worldview through media appropriation?

Research on media appropriation has revealed the relative autonomy of individual recipients vis-à-vis media offerings. People are by no means passive media consumers but are in fact creative in their classification and interpretation of media discourses. They sometimes read media texts "oppositionally" and thus ironically (see, for example, Hall 1992, Ang 1985, 2007). However, it is difficult for individuals to produce alternative interpretations if they lack the knowledge that might supplement or correct media constructs. Values and convictions do facilitate a "resistant" attitude, but an alternative vision of the world must remain hazy if one lacks the relevant knowledge.

Media environments today certainly open up new opportunities for individuals to discover the world beyond the traditional mass media. People can access specialist journals, blogs and international media if they wish to seek out global knowledge. Global awareness may thus be inspired by the appropriation of cultural offerings, though as yet we lack sufficient evidence to fully illuminate the connection between media consumption and cosmopolitan awareness (Ong 2009, p. 451) and we have to bear in mind that our remarks here pertain only to those who have regular access to new media and may exclude a huge part of the world's population (reflecting the global digital divide). The field of entertainment communication and pop culture at least suggests that the fictional imagination can spark off an interest in the world. When individuals begin to learn new languages inspired by their favourite series, to translate pop culture (for example, the fansubbing of Korean soaps or Japanese Anime amongst non-Asian fan groups) or to explore the culture of the country of production, we have clear evidence of individual participation in global culture (Jenkins 2006, p. 164; Lee 2018). We may also assume that media offerings influence attitudes towards travel (Skrbis et al. 2014, p. 623).

This means that individuals can greatly enhance their discursive epistemic competence through medial observation and that their attitudes and interests may change. But this does not allow them to escape their discursive dependence on the "information society". The relationship to distant lifeworlds in medial observation must be established and, above all, imagined by recipients. Hence, narratives and forms of representation may impede or facilitate analytical and emotional access to distant realities (Chouliaraki 2006, 2008). Medial accounts of the world may ultimately initiate processes of closure and lead to a rejection of the world of global others. Indifferent and ironic attitudes and "compassion fatigue" are all possible reactions of the receiving individual (ibid.; Höijer 2003; Chouliaraki 2013; Kyriakidou 2014; Scott 2014). But even compassion is no substitute for experience, which remains the reserve of implicit experiential knowledge.

236 Individual: global lifeworld communication

Filters for the processing of global knowledge (or ignorance)

The fact that recipients deal actively with discursive structures of narrative and image does not mean that their readings are detached from the lifeworldly structures and experiences of the individual. Medial knowledge is acquired within the framework of pre-existing patterns of knowledge and identity and the processing of knowledge takes place within group formations (see Chapter 7), in which individual readings are socially embedded and rendered socially compatible. So far, we know little about this process of the social transmission of global expertise (Grüne 2019b) or about the connection between direct and mediatized experience (Robertson 2010, p. 75). Particularly with respect to the globalization of lifeworlds, however, what matters is how the knowledge of the world gained from direct observation can be communicated in interpersonal relationships, since individuals' own experience of the world is limited. How can the knowledge of the individual become the knowledge of the many?

The literature emphasizes the relative autonomy of cosmopolitans in comparison with stationary local groups and communities, problematizing their alienation and experiential difference (Hannerz 1996, p. 110; Rogers 1999). On this view, the opening of the individual to the symbolic systems of an out-group goes hand in hand with a loss of trust and a lack of common-sense experience with the in-group. Individuals' global expertise, then, may benefit them but may also pose risks within their immediate social environment. So does the individual's global integration automatically separate them from their local worlds? If individuals have experiential knowledge shared by neither the media-based public sphere nor relevant reference groups within their local lifeworlds, then media discourse at least will create an imbalance to the detriment of the "knowing" if the "unknowing" base their notion of distant realities on medial knowledge (Kruck 2008). Here, lifeworldly co-orientation is easier to establish with reference to shared medial images than on the basis of exclusive personal experience. This can be illustrated in light of the image of Islam in the German media. Due to the selective focus on conflict inherent in this construct (see Chapter 2, Section 2.2.1), it is probably easier to establish a shared orientation towards the Islamic world with local others by referring to the problems of Islamist terrorism or patriarchal social structures than with reference to environmental movements, new jazz and rock tracks, films or exhibitions in the Islamic world – topics one can learn about "on site" but that are underrepresented in German media discourse.

If, on the other hand, the individual's reference groups share the same alternative experiences, for example, because they have travelled together, the communal nucleus can more easily be teased apart from discursive knowledge. But if the individual's global knowledge stocks and those of their closest interpersonal others diverge, the processing of global knowledge may be obstructed. So do everyday global experts exert any influence within lifeworldly encounter-based communication as opinion leaders? One of the pioneering studies in this field did in fact examine the typological distinction between "local" and "cosmopolitan" opinion

Individual: global lifeworld communication **237**

leaders (Merton 1968). Their biographical experiences (of mobility, for example) and medial orientation were geared more towards either local or national/international contexts. Their experiential structures were associated with different patterns of social bonding and influence. To quote Richard K. Merton: "If the local influentials are quantitativists, the cosmopolitans are qualitativists in this regard" (ibid., p. 451). The structure of connectivity and the structure of relationality were thus different in character in each case. While local opinion leaders mostly served community-oriented spheres of influence (such as local associations) and were able to exert influence with respect to various topics through actional knowledge related to immediate settings (for example, through contacts and networks, implying a polymorphic role), their cosmopolitan counterparts mainly held interest-based positions, providing orientation through essentially exclusive factual knowledge (such as expert opinions on a specific topic, equating to a monomorphic role) (ibid., p. 468).

The reason for communication problems between local and cosmopolitan opinion leaders probably lies not so much in the individual's fear of isolation, as described in spiral-of-silence theory (Noelle-Neumann 1980), as in the multitude's fear of revealing their ignorance. After all, portrayals of personal experience are a typical part of everyday communication and less socially offensive than the expression of political views. The problem of lifeworldly knowledge diffusion is likely to arise from the insecurity of the listening parties to interaction, who classify available interpretations and weigh up their trust in the observational performance of the various systemic (media, scholarship) and lifeworldly (friends, family) actors and sometimes have to admit their own ignorance and impotence. These attributes, however, are important to developing a global consciousness as they help prevent blind faith in erroneous discourses about distant worlds and the perpetuation of ignorance.

While these findings desperately need updating both theoretically and empirically, they point to a problem with which we are familiar from foreign coverage: orientation in distant worlds relies mainly on systemic knowledge structures (especially politics and the media), whereas orientation within immediate settings is based on community-oriented stocks of knowledge (the experiential world of the group – with the other often being assigned to distant worlds within immediate settings and their image thus being open to influence from the media, see Chapter 2, Section 2.2.2). In contexts of communal togetherness, distant settings thus remain a "systemic outside", while the near-at-hand world remains the communal sphere of reference.

From a lifeworld theory perspective, there is no reason why knowledge and contacts gained in far-off settings should not be harnessed in immediate contexts. But this is impeded by the persistence of the individual-collective problem. If cultural premises are included in the observation of others and people seem committed to certain roles, this makes it difficult to resolve perceptual differences. This mechanism exists not only in people's entrenched perceptions, but also appears in systems. If, for example, nation states assess knowledge and abilities with respect

238 Individual: global lifeworld communication

to labour migration and it is language skills that count rather than transnational professional experience, this constitutes a failure to use globally relevant knowledge (Weiß 2018). External perceptions are then dominated by the description "foreign skilled worker" rather than the professional role. Thus, the insights of global opinion leaders and knowledge bearers cannot be achieved solely through the discursive observation of media and lifeworldly environments. This is because the development of role and behavioural expectations occurs relationally, that is, it requires socialization experiences and communication with reference groups (Bahrdt 1997, p. 67ff.).

Today, against the background of stereotypical patterns of perception handed down within lifeworlds, we must assume that people with global knowledge are not automatically opinion leaders. "Dormant experiences" may elude social processing. As Ulf Hannerz states: "Globalization of this kind, diffused within social life, is opaque. Deep personal experiences and their distribution in the world can be in large part a private matter" (1996, p. 89). For globalization-focused research on the lifeworld, then, there is an urgent need to examine the unrecognized cosmopolitans, the "silent experts" (Geise 2017, p. 123), as well as the inactive knowledge processors. The latter too amount to a "black box" in research on opinion leaders, though the field has at least begun to acknowledge as active participants in the impartation of knowledge those subjects who previously seemed passive and were viewed as the recipients of opinion leaders' output (Dressler and Telle 2009, p. 58f.). However, there is still no connection with globalization research or the question of who is selected as global expert and why.

Ignorance as a risk in global society

Both silent observation and intensive dialogue harbour risks when it comes to the global expansion of lifeworldly experience. Often, the fragile knowledge structures involved offer a shaky interpretive basis for classifying new experiences. Contemporary individuals' perception of the world includes an awareness of global risks. Furthermore, the "global risk society" (Beck 2007) is reflected in the communicative microstructures of the lifeworld, where it must be renegotiated. As Daniel Innerarity states: "This is the real social battleground: those who know and those who do not, and the ability to recognize and challenge knowledge and non-knowledge" (2013, p. 41).

From the point of view of the individual, the goal cannot be to counter the uncertainties involved in global contact with ever new knowledge. We thus have to rethink the challenges to the individual's "global competence". Reflexive cosmopolitanism must encompass ways of dealing with the ignorance of both subjects and others. In other words, people have to learn to deal with the fact that "there is always too little knowledge available when assessing complex issues" (Scheunpflug 2001, p. 95; Treml 2001). The recognition of ignorance means that we also have to come up with a way of dealing with this condition. Kai Hafez thus calls for the establishment of a "culture of not knowing" (2014a, p. 301).

Individual: global lifeworld communication **239**

On this view, it is not just global knowledge that is crucial to the individual but also the ability to adequately assess their own ignorance in order to make well-founded intercultural value judgments and engage in a legitimate practice of recognition (see p. 230).

The individual en route to global knowledge optimization

Knowledge acquisition, assessment and diffusion, then, are as demanding a part of everyday communication as dialogue. In principle, the individual has a comparatively meagre capacity for observation with respect to both direct and indirect (discursive) observation (also known as the observation of observation). In addition, it is not always easy for them to acquire and pass on alternative worldviews due to obstacles to social diffusion. Nevertheless, reflexive optimization strategies do exist, something that future research will have to define more precisely.

8.2.3 Discursive (external) communication and global actions

Cosmopolitan action and role adaptation

So far, we have focused on the individual's handling of injections of global knowledge, an approach one might build upon in light of theories of learning. Our final step, however, will be to discuss the individual's potential to help shape global spaces. This means focusing on the conative level of individual communication and thus on the configuration of individual options for action. The individual may develop adjustment mechanisms within a variety of roles and turn cosmopolitan attitudes into visible actions. This is partly bound up with the fact that individuals are capable of strategic external communication. They can convey their globalization experiences in formal and informal, organized and non-organized contexts. They may themselves create a public sphere as well as making an impact as representatives of systems, organizations, professions and civil society groups, an impact that goes beyond individuals' lifeworldly influence.

The individual character of roles that build bridges and translate between different groups, bodies of knowledge and communities of interpretation is of particular importance. We find mediator roles in the field of education (teachers), the media (journalists, foreign correspondents), politics (diplomats), but also at the interfaces of lifeworlds. Here the greengrocer or the individual traveller (such as the globetrotter or couchsurfer) may also take on roles that mediate between people's different worlds of global experience. The proliferation and differentiation of expert roles vis-à-vis the world – from professional cultural translators such as foreign journalists (Hafez 2002a, vol. 1, p. 163ff.) to informal cultural interpreters (such as the famous travellers) – thus go far beyond global elites as conventionally discussed. However, these social positions are dependent on people's normative convictions, communicative reflexivity and pragmatic action orientation. The interplay of interpretive and action patterns remains a deceptive unity.

240 Individual: global lifeworld communication

A person's individual value system may thus be relatively stable, but attitudes can change and worldviews are often not entirely consistent. In addition, individuals activate and articulate different components of knowledge in different contexts. For example, in a qualitative study of ethical cosmopolitanism, Høy-Petersen and Woodward (2018) found that their interview partners not only used either experience-based or knowledge-based schemas to reflect on their cosmopolitan attitudes, but also that they changed their interpretive repertoires and temporarily lapsed into stereotypes. Their openness to cultural diversity was relativized by moments of distance from others (ibid., p. 665). Moreover, professional cosmopolitan roles were not always underpinned by ethical norms (ibid., p. 667). By the same token, ethical attitudes must always be measured against the practice of cosmopolitanism.

Synchronizing "internal" and "external" globalization

There is ethnographic evidence that the "internal globalization" of lifeworlds is not necessarily congruent with individuals' world as actually experienced (Sommer 2015). Their perception of the world may indeed be cosmopolitan, while their specific social world remains limited. A single experience of mobility may spark off the comprehensive globalization of conceptual worlds, while the lifeworld continues to be subject to major limitations (ibid.).

Yet the internal and external globalization of the lifeworld do not depend solely on opportunity structures but also on the individual's feats of mediation. By strategically adapting their actions, people may deprive themselves of global potential. If, for example, the strategic communications of foreign journalists, economic elites and politicians build on stereotypical structures against their better judgement or restrict creative ways of dealing with the world through routines, opportunities for change will be squandered (see Chapter 3, Section 3.2.4, Chapter 4, Section 4.2.4 and Chapter 5, Section 5.2.4). The same applies to unsettling experiences that are not expressed or represented in precipitate efforts to validate the local consensus down the pub or among family and friends. The task for the future will be to emancipate global knowledge vis-à-vis the majority's ignorance, which is shrouded in silence. It is not only the actions of the individual in relation to systems, but also their actions in relation to the actions of the many within lifeworldly encounters that will help determine the extent of global openings and closings.

Conclusion: the global individual between "genius" and "madness"

The global communication of the individual probably harbours the greatest potential and risk for the global community. The human being is both challenged and overwhelmed, a predicament between genius and madness, as it were. On the one hand, in the microcosm of individual lifeworlds, through dialogic long-distance relationships a "global community" in miniature may arise that brings completely new reflective views and horizon-expanding analogies into our lives. This applies

Individual: global lifeworld communication 241

not just to multicultural family contexts, but to all forms of amicable relations with the world, whose dialogic mechanisms of recognition make them vehicles for the emergence of a global community.

On the other hand, this potential is overshadowed by the fragile and overwhelming epistemic structures generated by the various links between local and global lifeworlds, structures that may contribute to persistent interpretive patterns within lifeworlds. The opening of the individual to the outside always risks generating internal boundaries. One's own experiential knowledge can undoubtedly trigger revolutionary changes in one's perspective on the world. However, if these changes remain solitary experiences and if they are in opposition to hegemonic local structures of interpretation, they pose a threat to local cohesion.

If this cohesion is deceptive and is achieved at the cost of marginalized knowledge, there is an even greater need for an injection of individual global experience into the lifeworldly substructure if there is to be any prospect of a reinterpretation of the world and an unsettling of the essentialist consensus. The hard-fought battle over many decades against racism and colonialism lifts the lid on this problem. Enlightenment and education may already have infiltrated the normative value structure of many individuals with respect to these issues. In order to translate this into action, however, that is, if it is to facilitate recognition, individuals must observe in new ways and gain experience of contact and dialogue.

9

INTERDEPENDENCIES OF SYSTEMS AND LIFEWORLDS

In this book, we have mostly dealt separately with the global communication of systems and lifeworld actors. The time has now come to take a closer look at the interactions between social systems and thus to address the reasons for the achievements and shortcomings of global communication as we have identified them, to the extent that they can be understood only in light of the overall social context. Organizations and subjects communicate according to immanent logics. At the same time, however, they are embedded in social environments and encounter the behaviour of other organizations and subjects, with which they have to align themselves. So far, we have taken into account at most interactions between *similar* systems and actors in the contexts of international contact, that is, cases in which politics encounters politics, companies encounter companies and individuals encounter other individuals, and we have shed light on the internal logic of external communication, which involves *dissimilar* systems and actors. But what happens afterwards – when actors truly encounter one another in global and local arenas and have to react to their surroundings? Global communication as an overall system rather than a network of heterogeneous practices is our key focus in this final chapter.

9.1 Foundations of interdependence

The research primacy of local (inter)dependence

In communication research, notions of dependency have so far been mostly national in orientation. For example, in the context of the indexing hypothesis (Bennett 1990, Krüger 2013) or the debate on the so-called "CNN effect" (Robinson 2002), local interactions between politics and the media in the field of foreign policy have been considered. In media dependency theory, as expounded

DOI: 10.4324/9781003255239-10

by Sandra Ball-Rokeach and Melvin DeFleur, local interactions are in fact mostly discussed without reference to global space (1976; see also Chapter 1, Section 1.4). Even well-known theorists in the discipline of communication studies have paid only marginal attention to *global* interdependencies – influences *of* and *on* media, politics, and so on – and have not yet put forward a convincing theoretical model. But how do social systems influence each other globally in terms of interaction, observation and discourse?

Dennis McQuail, whose book *Theories of Mass Communication* enjoys a global reputation as one of the standard texts in communication theory, devotes just a few pages to global interdependence and concludes: "Internationalization of communication would seem to create new kinds of dependency and actually to reduce autonomy" (1994, p. 91). Both parts of this statement are, however, contestable. First, we must ask what McQuail means by "new kinds of dependency". Is every instance of the communicative overcoming of national borders interdependence? True interdependence requires a deeper structural change that connects the communicating systems enduringly, sustainably and above all in a regulatory sense, that is, through the integration of power and capital structures, and that stabilizes "third spaces" of global communication. Have we really reached that point? We also need to reflect on why McQuail jumps to the conclusion that globalization entails a loss of autonomy. A loss for whom or what? For journalists who previously relied chiefly on information from the government of their home country when producing international news (indexing), does globalization bring a loss or gain in autonomy? What McQuail evidently has in mind is a reduction in "national" or "cultural" autonomy, but he overlooks the fact that this form of autonomy is firmly in the hands of local hegemons. He thus fails to see that more globalization always opens up an opportunity for marginalized individual local actors to expand their communicative, political and economic room for manoeuvre.

Evidently, then, as yet, research on interdependence in global communication either (1) has only taken national conditions into account or (2) is based on a highly simplified dynamic of globalization, in which processes of communication are equated with structures and structures are in turn equated with local-global zero-sum games.

Dimensions and levels of interdependence

In reality, however, relations of interdependence are far more complicated and, as set out in Chapter 1, Section 1.4, have to be dealt with in light of several relational dimensions and levels of analysis. The former divide into two types:

- *Local/global interdependencies*: All systems and lifeworlds may in principle be connected to other environmental systems both inside and outside the nation state.
- *Similar/dissimilar interdependencies*: All systems and lifeworlds are linked with similar and dissimilar environmental systems (the political system, for example,

244 Interdependencies of systems and lifeworlds

is linked with other political systems in the form of diplomacy and with national media systems as well as those of other countries).

If we combine these types, we effectively end up with three relational dimensions (see Figure 1.4), which must be examined in the context of globalization:

- *global interdependence between similar systems/lifeworlds* (referred to in what follows as "global horizontal interdependence");
- *global interdependence between dissimilar systems/lifeworlds* (referred to in what follows as "global vertical interdependence");
- *local interdependence between dissimilar systems/lifeworlds* (referred to in what follows as "local vertical interdependence").

A conceivable fourth relational dimension, "local horizontal interdependence", that is, relationships within national systems or lifeworlds – examples include relations between the executive and legislative branches or between different national media – may be omitted here, since this dimension effectively represents basic social scientific theory and is not an object of internationally oriented research.

All relation dimensions also require investigation at two levels of analysis. In accordance with our basic system-lifeworld–network approach (see Chapter 1, Section 1.2), complete interdependence only occurs in cases in which, following the *communicative* coupling of systems/lifeworlds, *structural* integration into corresponding global environments also takes place. Structural connections may take a variety of forms, since systems/lifeworlds may merge with similar systems/lifeworlds or at least enter into close transnational associations (when, for example, local media come together to form a transnational medium). Dissimilar systems/lifeworlds, meanwhile, continue to face each other as separate systems and environments but must be linked in a regulatory sense with respect to finances and/or politics and law if they are to be viewed as interdependent and as characterized by a "dynamic equilibrium" of autonomy and adaptation (see Chapter 1, Section 1.3). In both cases, communicative exchange is not enough and deeper structural ties must be established.

All in all, it seems reasonable to conclude that complete interdependence is that which occurs simultaneously at all levels, something that, as we will seek to show, barely exists at present. Even in cases in which some systems or lifeworldly actors have greater potential for global communication, they usually remain locally dependent in structural terms. This applies in principle to the Middle East specialist who knows the Arab world as an individual but remains a citizen of the United States as well as to the mass media that report on Japan but earn their money in European markets. Even when the communicative coupling of similar systems succeeds, the structural dependence on local environments remains stronger than dependence on global environments. Global communication is thwarted by the influence of local power and capital. In the following analysis, we build on the original approach taken by theorists of integrative systems theory, who examined how the probability of processes structural transnationalization is increased through communicative couplings (see Chapter 1, Section 1.1).

9.2 Global horizontal interdependence

Global communication as a necessary condition

German sociologist Ulrich Beck argues that the transnational dimension runs counter to all the familiar categories of social analysis. While the nation and the international sphere are mutually dependent, Beck contends, the transnational sphere aims to dissolve national structures (2006, p. 61ff., see also Welsch 1995). The problem that arises here, however, is that while the transnational may perhaps be a space, that is, a *system environment*, it is by no means an operational social system, in other words, an *environmental system*. So whether national structures are really dissolving to the benefit of transnational structures, or whether the transnational realm remains a diffuse external space of information and interaction for structures that continue to be locally based, is far from clear. Thus, in Beck's writings, much as in those of McQuail, the analytical levels of the communicative and the structural are unduly mixed. An interpretation rooted in communication theory is no doubt a useful first step in terms of theory building, because it can help explain just what the difference is between spaces and systems and why ideas such as cosmopolitanism and transnationalism, though they cross-cut existing social structures, in many cases make little impact in the face of the nation state and the "tribal" structures of the local sphere.

Global horizontal interdependence between similar systems is necessarily linked to interaction. Without interaction, there will be no exchange relations or relations of global communality. No wonder, then, that it is above all the action systems of politics, the economy and social organizations or movements that interact across borders and thus at least partially integrate, merge or enter into alliances. Lifeworlds often behave more conservatively with respect to globalization, in that they maintain their local social ties. Their range and capacities are often too limited for global communication. Even when it comes to migration, in social discourse "integration" is mostly seen as the immigrants' responsibility, rather than as a matter of global interaction to which everyone might contribute. The local lifeworld fights for its communicative hegemony even when structural couplings occur (interethnic and inter-religious marriages, and so on). The cosmopolitan integration of systems is viewed with suspicion, especially in right-wing populism, and the lifeworldly inhibition on global interaction is the most plausible explanation for the political right's attempt to trigger an anti-globalization counter-revolution (Brexit, Donald Trump, Narendra Modi, Islamism, and so on). Our overall assessment has shown that global interaction occurs to quite differing degrees in different social systems and is at times marked by major shortcomings.

246 Interdependencies of systems and lifeworlds

From a theoretical point of view, we need more global and less local integration in order to create a balance between global and local conditions. Only when we turn diffuse global environments into concrete environmental systems with which we interact, or, to argue in the same vein as Michael Giesecke (see Chapter 1, Section 1.1), depart from the position of cultural observer and enter into a genuine intercultural exchange, can communicative interdependence arise. This is the case if communication, rather than remaining fleeting, becomes sustainable and enduring and moulds relationships. According to Jürgen Habermas, communicative action makes cultural knowledge available, facilitates social integration and enables the individual to develop their personality (1995, vol. 2, p. 182ff.). Rather than a purely discursive possibility, interaction thus has consequences. Communicative actions forge genuine relationships. If interaction does not take place, globalization lacks a social foundation and global communication never gets beyond the superficial sphere of the circulation of goods. However, when Habermas mentions "global society" in this context, he does not do so consistently enough with respect to global communication, so there is a risk of conceptualizing communicative action and community building as limited to the local sphere. His approach thus requires transnational expansion.

Of course, the global realm features well-networked individuals, groups and communities, cosmopolitan "elites", and global informational and interactional elites. Ingrid Volkmer refers here to "reflective interdependence" (see Chapter 2, Section 2.2) and global spaces. In this book we ourselves have often used the term "third spaces", particularly for zones of transnational interaction in diplomacy, the economy, and so on. But "third spaces", to stick with the metaphor, often have few visitors. They are generally quite empty. Furthermore, "spaces" are not systems. They constitute system environments but not environmental systems for the still intact local systems, which have by no means been dissolved by transnational processes, and for lifeworld actors. Third spaces remain ephemeral. They may perhaps be embryonic forms of global interdependence much as the bourgeois salons of nineteenth-century Europe were once the nucleus of the modern democratic public sphere – though ultimately, of course, these salons were not yet national public spheres.

Although communication theory is not the focus of his analysis, Beck does indicate that he understands that the change in social structures through transnationalization that he has in mind is based on interactive premises: "Whereas the epoch of the nation-state produced and institutionalized a monologic imaginary centred on the demarcation and exclusion of others and aliens, the cosmopolitan age is founded on a *dialogical imaginary of the internalized other*" (2006, p. 78f.). But this claim that global dialogue has already reached an advanced level is premature. It fails to take account of horizontal structural interdependence, which is why we can count Beck among the "utopians" of the "first wave" of globalization research (see the Introduction). In sum, global communication is more a *necessary* than a *sufficient* condition for global interdependence. It is a prerequisite that must be in place but it is not enough on its own.

Interdependencies of systems and lifeworlds **247**

Global regulatory coupling as a sufficient condition

Here we are reminded of the contentious debate between structuralists and constructivists with respect to global communities, prompting us to return to our original system-lifeworld-network approach. Both groups considered whether there can be such a thing as stable globalization as long as one of the two levels of analysis – communicative or structural coupling – is dominated by local social structures. A number of organized and non-organized social systems do in fact communicate globally today. But despite all their global activities, their regulatory – political, legal and economic – anchorage often remains local:

- Transnational mass media barely exist. Most media are national in character and produce "foreign coverage".
- The political system creates "third" diplomatic spaces but is generally still a long way from stable global governance as a form of transnational politics.
- In the economy, there are transnational companies that communicate globally both internally and externally. However, the ownership structure of these global players tends to reveal a markedly national configuration (they are often American, Western, Chinese, and so on).
- Social movements develop transnational structures, which, however, are generally weak when measured against local actors. These movements are often global discursive communities (for example, peace or environmental movements) featuring local system structures.
- In the case of large transnational communities as well as other formations in the lifeworld (small groups, and so on), it is difficult to distinguish between communicative and structural interdependence, as these are not formally organized social systems that might be structurally linked. Up to a point, communication is identical with structure.

The global horizontal interdependence between most organized systems, however, remains thoroughly ambivalent, as the analyses in this book have shown. On the one hand, the desire for global communication can be seen in all social systems. On the other hand, actors are still structurally separate and autonomous units of action that do not enter into regulatory linkage. This structural ambivalence then becomes manifest, for example, in a tension between globally integrative internal interaction and nationally autarkic external communication (PR, propaganda) by governments, companies, and so on. Due to the gap between the communicative and structural forms of horizontal global interdependence, then, all that remains is fleeting and unstable "third spaces".

As a result, globalization may go into reverse at any time and can be described as "integration without interdependence". Profound interdependence would give rise to real systemic supranational entities as a result of global communication. As we will now show, however, the main reason for systems' refusal to merge in globally horizontal fashion does not necessarily lie in the systems themselves, but in the

248 Interdependencies of systems and lifeworlds

non-systemic environments in which they are embedded. Horizontal interdependence is thwarted by vertical interdependence.

9.3   Global and local vertical interdependence

Politics, media and the public sphere: globally extended indexing

In our theoretical chapter (Chapter 1) we explained that social systems function as "environments" for other social systems and are connected to them by a complex "dynamic equilibrium" of autonomy and adaptation (see Chapter 1, Sections 1.2 and 1.4). The system-environment complex is largely shaped by the cosmos of vertical interdependencies, since every social system is in contact not only globally with similar systems, but also globally and locally with dissimilar social systems and the number of dissimilar systems is always significantly greater. From the perspective of the media, for example, politics, the economy and lifeworlds are relevant environments. From the point of view of politics, however, it is the media, the economy and lifeworld actors that can be described as such.

Once again it must be remembered that the analytical levels of communication and structure are both important here. A system's own communicative competences exercise an influence on vertical system-environment-relations, because in our system-lifeworld-network-approach autonomy gains arise not just through resources such as power and capital, but also through communicative capacity. At the same time, however, structural aspects play a significant role, such as the ability to redefine social values on the part of the lifeworld, an ability that, as set out in the media dependency theory of Ball-Rokeach and DeFleur, may lead to a loss of confidence in systems, which then increases pressure on the political system to justify itself (see Chapter 1, Section 1.4). Also structurally significant is the ability of a system or of lifeworld actors to form coalitions with other environmental systems in order to emancipate themselves from a third environmental system (for example, the media and the general population may turn against the government or the government and the media may unite against the population, and so on).

These general dynamics of vertical system-environment relations are described in detail by a number of general theories (see especially Ball-Rokeach and DeFleur, and Ognyanova and Ball-Rokeach on media dependence, and Giesecke on media ecology, see Chapter 1, Section 1.4) and specific theories that focus, for example, on relations between media and politics (see especially Bennett on indexing and Wolfsfeld on political conflict; see pp. 249, 251). What these theories seldom address, however, is that when it comes to vertical interdependence we must always also consider the relational dimensions of global and local interdependence. For example, the media are not only influenced by their respective national politics, but also by international politics. There may even be direct political intervention from outside the state in response to media coverage, and so on. Governments, meanwhile, are influenced by public spheres and media beyond the national borders. The real

Interdependencies of systems and lifeworlds **249**

question, however, is *how strongly* global environments affect globally communicating systems and lifeworld actors.

If we first summarize some of the basic findings of classic, locally-oriented research, we find that it concentrates almost exclusively on the relations between politics, media and the public sphere, while disregarding more complex lifeworlds – with the exception of studies informed by the less well-known media dependency or media ecology theories. In communication research, a hypothesis found in so-called indexing theory has gained wide acceptance, namely that the views of national elites on international crises dominate the media (Bennett 1990). This patriotic behaviour of the mass media is not only evident at times of intense and growing national involvement in conflicts (see Chapter 2, Section 2.1 and Chapter 3, Section 3.2.4). It is also evident when no acute crisis is occurring (Krüger 2013), although in such periods the pressure exercised by national environments is lower, allowing more space for the transnational synchronization of differing opinions. This dominant form of local interdependence – the supremacy of national politics over other social subsystems – can be explained both in light of the strength of the political sphere and the relative weakness of the other environmental systems, namely the organized and non-organized public spheres.

Christer Jönsson and Martin Hall describe the hegemony of national politics with respect to foreign affairs chiefly in light of other social systems' dependence on the political sphere as the producer of foreign policy:

> While diplomatic communication has been affected by television in uncontrollable ways, it is also true that statesmen and diplomats may exploit the new media for their purposes in communicating with the world. Diplomats increasingly become engaged in 'media diplomacy'. They are aided by the fact that media susceptibility to 'news management' by the government is perhaps greatest in the realm of foreign affairs. This is an area where journalists often have to rely on official 'primary definers', where references to alleged national security threats can be used to keep the media compliant, and where strong domestic constituencies contesting official sources are relatively rare.
>
> *(2005, p. 95)*

This dominance of politics is reinforced by a weakness of media systems, which Kai Hafez has called the "trickle-down effect". Under great time pressure and lacking the ability to thoroughly investigate crisis news, the media tends to embrace government propaganda and, crucially, to categorize the government of its own country as more trustworthy than others and thus to show it in a more favourable light (2007a, p. 36f.). The view that still prevailed in the 1980s, that large Western news agencies were practising a kind of "cultural imperialism", as also reflected in McQuail's notion, presented above, of reduced autonomy through globalization, may now be regarded as largely out of date. The media technology that has been developed since then, from direct-to-air satellite broadcasting to digital media, has given the local systems even of poorer countries entirely new options for production and

250 Interdependencies of systems and lifeworlds

censorship, making them largely resistant to external influences. International news, too, is currently being processed and "domesticated" in such a way that it jibes with national narratives (see Chapter 2, Section 2.1). In addition, when it comes to the local concentration of media, the use of foreign media has generally remained marginal in most media systems (see Chapter 2, Section 2.1). In view of the polycentric global media situation, then, it no longer makes sense to refer to Western communicative supremacy. Instead, coverage of foreign affairs is clearly dominated by local-national political elites.

In addition to these elements of input (politics) and throughput (media) we must mention an output-related aspect, namely that the national public spheres receiving the news generally have little expertise in foreign affairs, which reinforces the impact of political public relations. Paul Noack's maxim still applies today: "Foreign affairs is the field in which, in relation to its extent and diversity, it is most difficult for public opinion to develop. This means that the pressure emanating from the public sphere tends to remain negligible" (1986, p. 47; see also Powlick and Katz 1998). This is intensified by the so-called "rally-round-the-flag effect", which describes how, at times of crisis, the public is not only passive but may be mobilized by the government to back a war (Mueller 1970). This is a universal and globally demonstrable pattern, which is why governments with domestic political problems often exacerbate foreign policy crises (Kehr 1970). The functioning of elitist indexing and the rally-round-the-flag phenomenon are clear indications of the strength of the local environmental system of the "state" even in the age of global communication.

Nevertheless, according to Uwe Krüger, what we are seeing today is the multilateral extension of local indexing. In his case study of reporting on the annual Munich Security Conference, he shows that German newspapers not only represent German foreign policy interests, but also those of Germany's Western allies (2013, p. 255ff.). Ultimately, however, this apparently increased *global* vertical influence is essentially the geocultural extension of the local and is far from producing an ideal global synchronization of news, since it is the militarily important allies of one's own nation state that are taken into account here. A truly cosmopolitan perspective is absent (see Chapter 2, Section 2.2).

Nonetheless, what is interesting in terms of our analysis is that in such cases local *vertical* interdependencies can clear the way for stronger *global* vertical interdependencies, within whose framework global *horizontal* interdependencies are strengthened. There are other examples of such an extended form of indexing, such as the coverage of the Iraq War of 2003 in the British press, which was less nationalistically charged than during the Falklands War of 1982, a shift that can be explained in part by the greater influence of war opponents Germany and France within the European Union (Hafez 2004). In 2003, it became clear that where political systems are horizontally linked, this may have repercussions for local structures of interdependence by underlining global autonomy and minimizing local pressures to adapt. However, the reverse may also apply. When Brexit took the United Kingdom out of the European Union, the dominant influence of local vertical structures became apparent once again. It was only when the Brexit campaign succeeded in pushing through its nationalist agenda in the media (Gavin 2018), in other words, when it struck a blow against global *communicative interdependence*, that the transnational *structural interdependence* represented by the UK's membership of the EU came to an end.

However, this example shows that it is still too soon to refer to a globally extended form of vertical indexing, because this depends on (1) globally extended horizontal indexing (that is, the elite interests of the national political sphere), and (2) local vertical interdependence (that is, overall global sentiment within a national system). It is thus by no means the case that the global dimension functions as an independent factor. Globality must first be facilitated by national subsystems. Global horizontal interdependence represents an opening and expansion of the politics of autonomy. But local interdependence still holds sway over its global counterpart. In other words, only when the nation state voluntarily accedes to transnationalization does truly global vertical indexing emerge.

Civil society, media and politics: the inversion of dependence

In addition to the dominant mode, there is also an accidental mode of vertical interdependence, which does not represent the standard form but amounts to a so-called "opportunity structure" (Tilly and Tarrow 2007). It is only at this point that the one-sided dependence of the media and society on the political sphere becomes genuine *inter*dependence in the sense of the mutual dependence of politics, media and society. There are various approaches to describe the accidental mode. In the field of communication research, the conflict theory of Gadi Wolfsfeld deserves special mention. His work closely related to systems theory, Wolfsfeld outlines the struggle between government and social challengers for access to the media and the public sphere. Much like Jönsson and Hall, he emphasizes the pre-eminence of the state, which determines international politics. But he also underlines the potential of civil society, for example, its capacity to generate attention through "exceptional behaviour" such as protests, civil disobedience, and so on (1997, p. 20ff.). Another approach focused on increased media power highlights the so-called "CNN effect", in which national media may be able to break through the hegemony of national foreign policy with respect to international conflicts if they gain greater informational power (for example, through the visibility of victims in visual media) and forge alliances with the general population to promote value-based forms of legitimacy and humanitarian policies (Robinson 2002).

However, with the exception of the Internet-based "boomerang effects" of social movements (see Chapter 5, Section 5.2.1), the accidental mode of interdependence has as yet almost always been analysed in a national context. Rather than global influences, the debate on the CNN effect is centred on the pressure exercised by American media on American foreign policy. The question that now arises is whether new global relations between similar systems (global horizontal interdependence) allow these systems to exercise greater influence on their local

252 Interdependencies of systems and lifeworlds

environments (local vertical interdependence), thus creating new types of global vertical interdependence. Is the accidental mode a local or (simultaneously) global phenomenon?

Akin to the globally expanded indexing of the political system, when it comes to global civil society, we have at least qualitative evidence of how local relations of interdependence may be changed through the increased global horizontal communication and global structural linkage of national actors (that is, the emergence of transnational movement networks or TANs). The closer and more stable the transnational coupling of social systems of the same type within civil society, the greater their autonomy in relation to vertical local environments (politics, economy, and so on). A transnational environmental movement such as "Fridays for Future" may challenge any national political and economic system, at least over the short term. This process may be described as the "inversion" of the otherwise usual dependence of society on foreign policy, an inversion that does not occur, as in the work of Ball-Rokeach and DeFleur, due to disruption of a national system (which, moreover, history has shown to be possible at any time) but to the novel communicative and structural embedding in globalization. It thus represents the transcendence of the national system imperative.

Global alliances can change resource relations – especially with respect to information exchange – and create new alliances that compensate for the prevailing local structural weakness that otherwise characterizes civil societies and lifeworlds with regard to international issues. We need to think of accidental inversion as a new ferry of global vertical influence that enables us to avoid the state-controlled bridge over the nation state's border river. While the globally expanded indexing of political communication is essentially a reflection of the nation state's global alliances, global inversion is similar to a revolution in that civil society, which was previously "penned in" by national environmental systems, can unsettle (vertical) power relations with the help of global (horizontal) alliances and replace them with new global vertical power relations.

However, here too the global revolution ultimately fails to occur, since the inversion is not a permanent state of affairs but rather a fleeting event, making it difficult to refer to sustainable global vertical interdependence even in the field of civil society. The Fridays-for-Future effect comes in waves and is unstable, the massive global demonstrations against the Iraq War in 2003 failed to stop the invasion, and perhaps the greatest success of the anti-landmine campaign has been watered down by the Trump administration. Then there is the profound North–South gap in global civil society. While diplomacy is a regular phenomenon and there is a long tradition of more or less intensive political relations between states, global horizontal civil society relationships are far rarer, more sporadic and, as a rule, do not meet the requirements of communicative *and* structural interdependence. In the field of communication, interactive links are the preserve of civil society elites and remain discursive in nature for the majority of people. Even today, global civil society is more of a system environment than an environmental system – it is discourse rather than dialogue that predominates.

The cosmopolitanism of a global civil society, then, is more of an abstract value than the product of real-world experiential knowledge. We can only expect stable expansion of – let alone detachment from – local vertical interdependence in future if there is profound strengthening of horizontal interdependence, if "internationalist" experiences and interactions are fostered on a sustainable basis and if cross-border civil society structures are institutionalized. Nothing less than a major offensive could hope to pose a challenge to the globally expanded state (see Conclusion and Future Prospects).

Another aspect is relevant here, which we might describe as the "technological interdependence" of civil society. A global civil society increasingly focused on the Internet may, at times, exert considerable pressure on the nation state and on local vertical interdependence. But the state provides and controls the technological infrastructure. Due to the international balance of power and the strong position of American corporations, global civil society has so far achieved certain successes against the local state, which are known as "boomerang effects" (see Chapter 5, Section 5.2.1). Yet they occurred chiefly in the early days of the Internet when nation states had yet to adapt adequately to the phenomenon of online political activism. By now the state has passed through a learning curve and even medium powers, but certainly major ones, now exercise technological control with little difficulty. Examples of this are the Chinese firewall, India's frequent shutdown of the Internet in crisis situations, the Turkish ban on Facebook and Iranian or Saudi Arabian Internet censorship. Bruce Kogut of the Massachusetts Institute of Technology (MIT) highlights the limits of global technological interdependence:

> Is the Internet an intrinsically global technology, riding upon the already existing backbone of the global communication network? The simple answer to [this question] is that the Internet has borders. The Internet economy developed differently in each country, reflecting different national systems of law and regulation, business networks, competition, and technological legacies.
>
> *(2003, p. 7)*

This means that despite the global corporate structures of Google, Facebook, and so on, as well as US-dominated ICANN regulations, in principle, each state has the potential to undermine the global horizontal interdependence of the Internet (and thus much of global civil society). The technology of the Internet, a liberating factor for civil society, is a vehicle for cultivating global horizontal and vertical interdependence, while at the same time, absurdly, this technological orientation ultimately underlines local vertical interdependence. Hence, if it is to be successful, the above-mentioned major global offensive to strengthen the global horizontal ties of civil society cannot and should not act within a primarily digital framework but must rely more than ever on direct face-to-face interaction.

Lifeworlds, media and politics: decolonization through globalization?

This book is pervaded by the insight that lifeworldly actors who skilfully facilitate interaction and communitization often find it difficult to deal with globalization. Due to spatial, technological, financial and linguistic hurdles, statistically speaking, our travels, even our digital ones, usually remain captive to a particular geocultural framework, while horizontal global integration is largely absent from most people's lives. Even migration can only be viewed as an anti-cyclical phenomenon to a limited extent. Here, too, communication crosses borders and structural interdependence is generated by family ties, but the social scattering effect in the majority societies is often limited and there is very little impact on the background-based social co-presence of small groups and large communities. Much the same may be said of tourism. This is the only way to explain that even today German tour groups in Namibia are informed, to some extent, of the achievements of German colonialism, but not of the German genocide of the Herero (Scheerer 2011).

However, a section on the *vertical* interdependence of the lifeworld is not the place to simply recapitulate the shortcomings of *horizontal* global interdependence or once again to identify counterexamples of horizon-expanding encounters, which of course also exist. The aim here is to show how the systems of the state and the economy, which are equipped with better resources, repeatedly use the lifeworld as a projection screen for the ambivalence of their horizontal interdependence, their partial anti-globalism and their local systemic egoism or, conversely, how they succumb to the "cultural" braking effect of local lifeworlds. At this point, it is expressly unclear to us whether Jürgen Habermas's notion of the colonization of the lifeworld by systems provides the most plausible conceptual framework or whether it would be better to assume strong reciprocity of local vertical interdependence, with local lifeworlds and states hampering each other when it comes to global integration.

The role of the mass media as moderators in this context is also ambivalent. It can be shown that people's perceptions of globalization fluctuate depending on the coverage of globalization in the media and are therefore influenced by them (Marks et al. 2006). The vertically interdependent national media in particular have a resounding effect when it comes to global long-distance reporting, because most consumers lack alternative sources of information or views anchored in direct experience, that is, there is no independent global horizontal interdependence (see, among others, Chapter 2, Section 2.2.2 and Chapter 7, Section 7.2). At the same time, the media absorb xenophobic cultural undercurrents that still exist throughout much of society. The vertical interdependence between local lifeworlds and national media is significant when it comes to globalization, even if the direction of impact (who "colonizes" whom?) remains unclear. Lifeworlds and cultures are omnipresent, in systems too. They constitute the informal interior of modernity.

If we nevertheless want to consider how the lifeworld might finally free itself of its partial colonization, we will arrive at the astonishing conclusion that this is much easier for the individual than for the lifeworld as a whole. In the context of national "dynamic equilibria" of autonomy and adaptation, the lifeworld's autonomous room for manoeuvre has not increased significantly with the globalization of systems, to the extent that this has occurred at all. It has been augmented at most in the context of politicized civil society and social movements (see p. 251ff.) but not in the everyday world. In the latter, concepts such as "cultural identity", despite their scholarly untenability, display an almost uncanny cohesive force and, today, are even contributing to the "retribalization" of the lifeworld (see Chapter 6, Section 6.1). Still, individual attitudes may change easily. They may be extremely out of date. It is entirely possible to understand the global – unlike McQuail – as an expression of individual autonomy and as a form of resistance to the "colonization" of the lifeworld.

Once the lifeworld, or at least individuals within the lifeworld, are able to expand their horizontal relationships globally, it is theoretically interesting that they can also break through the "ambivalence" surrounding the relationship between horizontal and local-vertical interdependence. An individual can without doubt hold contradictory views – many people who claim not to be racist are Islamophobic (Hafez and Schmidt 2015, p. 27ff.). Nevertheless, the individual has the opportunity to develop basic values, to align their communicative action with them and thus to overcome the schizophrenia characteristic of the relationship between internal and external communication in systems, for the simple reason that the individual, despite all the pressure to adapt, can reflect on the structures of their lifeworld. This special status of the autonomy of the individual generates the potential for the globalization not of the lifeworld as a whole – whose structural inertia appears to make this virtually impossible – but "of the many", that is, the many individuals, who are capable of breaching the blockade of vertical lifeworlds (see, for example, Sezgin 2011). There are many examples today of such movements, which, unlike the historical models of the labour movements, and so on, are not organized but are held together by weak ties. The Arab Spring, the uprisings in Hong Kong, the Occupy movement: all are characterized by a generational conflict (Mustafa 2021) in which young people in particular protest against both political systems and the lifeworldly hierarchies of the established opposition parties, prompting them to enter into international alliances. As we have shown, the energies released here are unlikely to be enough *in themselves* to break through vertical interdependencies and require innovative forms of network organization (see Chapters 5 and 6).

Conclusion: interdependence – diverse but incomplete and reversible

Theoretically, interdependence occurs at different spatial levels of relationship and with respect to a number of dimensions (communicative and structural). Global horizontal communication between similar systems and lifeworld actors may initiate processes of transnationalization, which, however, do not seem to be adequately supported structurally (in terms of power politics, economics and sustainability) in many areas. The main cause of this ambivalence in the horizontal structure of transnationalization is the persistence of local interdependencies. Global horizontal ties may increase the subject's local autonomy, but they may also be impaired by local vertical interdependencies. Global communication has added a factor of creative uncertainty to international interdependencies and generated a diverse array of new social possibilities. In all social systems, however, such communication features interdependence gaps of one kind or another and thus remains incomplete and reversible.

CONCLUSION AND FUTURE PROSPECTS

To seek to summarize a book like this, which is in itself an attempt to condense theoretical themes and bring out empirical trends, is an almost hopeless task. Still, re-emphasizing some of the key features of our analysis provides a basis for a meaningful perspective on the developmental potential of global communication and its role in the future of globalization, whether of the "global community" or "global society".

Overall assessment

If we begin with the mass media as the classic object of international communication research, we can take it as read that so far, despite their fundamental capacity for global synchronization, they have created no more than a fragmentary global public sphere with direct implications for global society. Even if we acknowledge the differences in the performance of the media in this regard and factor in the theory-dependence of the requirements for synchrony, which arise primarily from public sphere theory, in international comparison the worldviews disseminated in the mass media remain highly divergent and asynchronous. The observational, discursive modernity that emerged from the historical revolution of the printing press, the book and the media, then, is capable of conveying consolidated global knowledge only to a limited extent. Even the non-classical mass media of the Internet have not yet managed to remedy this discourse-structural deficit, even if they facilitate new readings in some cases.

When it comes to the organized action systems within the sphere of politics, economy and society (social movements, and so on), non-mediatized global communication processes are just as important to the formation of global communality as mediatized ones. Furthermore, cross-border interaction seems to compensate at least partially for what separates national discourses by creating dialogic "third

DOI: 10.4324/9781003255239-11

258 Conclusion and future prospects

communicative spaces" that maintain the world's capacity to act in a coordinated way. While the mass media are scarcely capable of establishing the public prerequisites for an integrated global society, transnational global communities do at least emerge *in* and *through* action systems. These communities, however, are far from comprehensive, as usually only a limited number of political systems are linked. In addition, politically instituted transnational global professional communities remain exclusive because neither media nor lifeworlds are included in this form of non-public or semi-public communality. The communicative transcendence of national discursive spaces is thus beginning to occur on an enduring basis but remains limited to an elite bubble.

From the perspective of mass media communication alone, with its charged constructs of the enemy and its susceptibility to national propaganda, it is fundamentally incomprehensible why the "international community" ultimately retains its capacity for action and why, despite current wars, we are living in the most peaceful of times, as demonstrated by peace studies (statistically and in other ways). It has certainly been a mistake of the globalization debate to date to concentrate far too much on (discursive) mass communication, while neglecting interactive and interpretive (observational) forms of communication in international and transnational relations. It is vital to leave this theoretical dead end and focus instead on an overall perspective anchored in communicative ecology.

Despite the feats of global communication characteristic of the action systems of politics, economy and society, we must not lose sight of their ambivalences. "Ambivalence" is also the keyword used by sociologist Andreas Reckwitz to characterize modernity as a whole, for example, when it is unable to choose between old and new forms of bourgeois culture or between local essentialist and transcultural perspectives (2019). The anti-global challenges posed by worldwide right-wing populism, neofundamentalism and neofascism are only the extreme forms of the irresolution vis-à-vis global (post)modernity that is deeply embedded in the mainstream of societies. The capacity for global community is difficult to maintain in the long run on the basis of often separate public spheres. In an effort to respond to uneven global and national influences, action systems have become entangled in contradictions. In external communication with their environmental systems – through a rhetoric and politics that insist on nationality and cultural obstinacy – these action systems counteract the "third spaces" that they create within the global sphere in the context of diplomacy, companies and transnational movements. Global communication processes between national systems have increased, but they are inadequately "conveyed" to the local base, to recall a key demand made by Richard Münch with respect to establishing a stable form of globalization (see the Introduction). We might almost refer here to action systems' global communicative schizophrenia.

This behaviour is marked by an almost paradoxical cause-and-effect relationship in the sense that strong horizontal global networking (between similar systems) triggers an at least equally strong vertical communicative counter-reaction (vis-à-vis and on the part of national environmental systems) in order to restore national autonomy. On this premise, modern right-wing populism represents such a backlash against the globalization of systems and a consequence of the self-generated neonationalism of the political, economic and social elites, an ideology from which, apparently, no nation state, regardless of how advanced its global communication may be, is willing to depart.

However, it is important here to understand not only the level of pure communication but also structural interdependence. As a rule, systems are most likely to regress if communicative networking is not followed by systemic integration – in media law, for example – and they are least likely to do so if transnational structures exist, as in commercial law. The instability of the global realm, then, arises not just from discursive insecurity, but always from structural deficits in horizontal and vertical interdependence as well. Global communication may endow national systems with more freedom (as in the Fridays for Future movement), but it may also be repelled by the non-integrated structures of the nation state (such as Western right-wing populism, Middle Eastern or African Islamism and Hindu fundamentalism). What all the examples demonstrating the presence or absence of globalization have in common is that we never see the development of *all levels of globalization* – horizontal and vertical, communicative and structural. Contrary to many earlier predictions, this makes present-day global integration appear fragile and reversible. Globalization and with it the concepts of the global community and global society are characterized by communicative ambivalences and both communicative and structural interdependence gaps. However, these are not the inevitable fate of humankind, but rather a process that can be fashioned, though this can only be done if the resource of "communication" is developed as well.

There is, however, no consensus in the academic debate regarding calls for simultaneous structural *and* communicative global integration. Barrie Axford observes two contrary approaches in the literature: one that highlights the individual and lifeworldly "microstructures" of cross-border interaction, and another that insists on the necessity of a parallel systemic-organizational form of interdependence (2012, p. 47). The latter view is congruent with the system-lifeworld-network approach adopted in the present book, which states that it is only if systems confidently bring their horizontal and vertical communication into national arenas, that is, if the traditional "primacy of domestic politics" (Kehr 1970) is overcome, that lifeworlds as a whole can be incorporated into globalization. This is not so much a normative plea as an insight into the functionality and stability of processes of global transformation.

Under the conditions of long-distance communication, civil societies and lifeworlds are highly dependent on impulses from systems. At the same time, however, they are places in which the traditional dependence on systems may be relativized *by means of* and *as a result* of globalization. Social movements have creatively adopted new digital communication technologies. A global civil society has emerged, focused not so much on direct interaction, which is carried out by just a few intermediaries holding key positions within network organizations, as on the emergence of an alternative media sphere. Even if networks, based on weak

260 Conclusion and future prospects

ties, facilitate only low-threshold risk strategies and their clout does not compare with that of historical formations such as national labour movements, they are at least partially able to penetrate the insulating layers of nationally dependent mass media and self-reproducing large communities and small groups at the local level. Outside the sphere of political activism, digital interactive global communities are also forming, though in the plural and with entirely contrary worldviews that cannot generally be classified as "cosmopolitan". As yet, participation in such global neo-communities has been the preserve of a tiny segment of societies. In addition to language barriers, this is due to the structural prominence of local community-based relationships that persist on the Internet, though often in hybridized form. It is conceivable that the impact of the social co-presence of the local will only diminish when the lead systems of politics and economy finally dissolve the nation state and thus break the cycle of the local reproduction of meaning – a utopia of historic proportions.

The individual, if for a moment we imagine them free of social determination by local groups, communities and systems, is the actor with whom the "global revolution" begins – the champions of global microprocesses are absolutely right. If, however, we wish to get beyond elite cosmopolitanism, the revolution must not end there. It must have a broad social impact. Unfortunately, at present the life-world is also the place where globalization tends to stagnate. The small number of those who can be described as "cosmopolitans", who are globally interacting in an active way, observing and anchored in global discourses, explains the prevalence of national and religious stereotypes, up to and including the fact that much of the world's population is captive to essentialist or racist views. The small group in particular is often more disruptive than typical of globalization. Even if the concept of the "elite" in the traditional form of the power or educational elite cannot endure because communicative elites have long existed in lifeworlds outside organized social systems, globalization as a cultural practice has a very limited capacity to forge consensus, which tends to endow lifeworlds with a braking effect. Even today, lifeworlds may be a source of inspiration for global communality. But if global communication fails to advance at the social base, a huge question mark will hang over the future of a truly global modernity.

Future prospects

We should expect globalization research not only to analyse conditions retrospectively but also to endeavour to provide perspectives on how global communication might develop in future. If we proceed in light of the basic insight that, overall, global communication has so far fostered an essentially heterogeneous discursive global society rather than a densely interacting global community, we will arrive at conclusions similar to those once reached by integrationist systems theory (see Chapter 1, Section 1.1). Thus, a much deeper form of integration must be pursued within international relations through the optimization, within a global framework,

Conclusion and future prospects **261**

of all the basic modes of communication – interaction, observation and discursive communication.

If the global integration of states and populations, and thus *external integration* is accelerated, certain *internal debates on integration* may become superfluous because cosmopolitan horizons shared by national majorities and minorities may emerge that relativize internal ethnic-religious conflicts through greater political, social and cultural recognition. We would therefore like to put forward the credo "more local diversity through increased global integration", against the background of which we wish to highlight the prospects for the development of communication as they relate to the individual social systems and actors discussed in this book.

Starting with the mass media, significant future opportunities can be generated by strengthening two tendencies that would improve the synchrony of the global public sphere: the establishment of transnational media as collaborative multi-national projects and the opening-up of national media to global discourses. These reformist utopias, however, require efforts that would have to originate in national media systems themselves, but which also require the backing of the lead systems of politics and the economy in the context of vertical interdependence.

Within the media, a largely new global journalistic ethics would have to emerge, something that is as yet virtually non-existent. International and cosmopolitan references in national and transnational codes of ethics as well as better networking of national press councils and journalists' unions would be a key desideratum. The existing fixation of professional journalistic ethics, in almost all countries, on basic technical and epistemological skills would have to be overcome, while the training of journalists would have to systematically inculcate a global professional ethics. The development of a "consumer ethics" through measures to monitor the media and media-critical mentoring would be a desirable means of reversing the public's relative passivity towards foreign policy and reinvigorating the paralyzed public debates on international issues in most countries. From an organizational point of view, it would be good to see the mass media investing resources to optimize the global procurement of sources, expand global sites of publication and publishing formats and foster specialist departments – preferably according to the principle of multicultural diversity.

This global "structural transformation of the public sphere" should be supported by political systems, which need to fundamentally revise the division into dip-lomatic internal and (propagandistic) external communication. The goal must be to transfer the dialogic quality of international relations ("global community") as objectively and transparently as possible to "global society". The global public sphere must no longer be a realm saturated with nationalistic sentiment and propaganda. The democratization of international political relations through more effective and sustainable public participation is long overdue. Indeed, the involvement of the people in an interactive global political community and greater transparency would be an excellent way to implement the promised end of secret diplomacy in an age of mass democracy.

262 Conclusion and future prospects

This would have to incorporate improved public access to the internal knowledge of the state's foreign policy departments, their monitoring and information services, including greater access to the global knowledge of the secret services, as well as greater social openness on the part of advisory think tanks, which have so far almost exclusively advised the systemic elites. The true scandal inherent in the repeated publication of internal diplomatic communication by organizations such as Wikileaks is not the release of such information in itself but the high degree of state classification and withholding of information that preceded it. In a more liberal interpretation of information laws (to the extent that they exist at all), such information would have to be made accessible to citizens, enabling them to competently assess international political relations. While politics may require a degree of activity behind the scenes, when it comes to global information, as a matter of principle, nation states' duty of disclosure requires fundamental expansion.

Much the same applies to the economy, the supposed lead system of globalization, which lives up to its communicative responsibilities to a surprisingly meagre extent. There is an urgent need to overcome the culturalism so often present in the business ethics of global corporations as well as in the mainstream of "intercultural" economic research, to develop new global corporate cultures and challenge the separation of internal and external communication within this social subsystem. *Social* models of the global and of cosmopolitanism are grossly underdeveloped in the international advertising industry, while the dominant doctrine of adaptation to assumed local peculiarities (which are ultimately subject to constant cultural change) stands in stark contrast to the universal dissemination of products, which is the core business of the global economy.

If the economic system aspires to be a true lead system of globalization, it must understand and practise globalization as a social concept and not just as a slogan. This would involve companies taking responsibility for the social processes triggered by the globalization of modernity, a development in which they play a major role. The existing gap between growing horizontal and stagnating vertical interdependence can only be closed if transnational dialogic and globally circulating economic communication, as it occurs at least partially within globally operating companies, is also conveyed discursively to the outside world.

This, however, would inevitably bring the economic system up against system-immanent limits to knowledge diffusion. The ambivalence that we observe in other social systems is a polyvalence in the economy. Not only do internal dialogues contrast with external monologues, but the global diffusion of observational communication is impeded by the commoditized character of information. The opening up of interactive and interpretive communication to discursive external communication, which is at least conceivable in the political system, is fundamentally opposed to the capitalist economy. Even global players are far from altruistic institutions determined to promote the circulation of global knowledge. They cross borders only in order to expand transnationally and they establish new borders by buying up global competence, converting it into trade secrets and then regarding them as intellectual property. This should prompt serious consideration of the systemic

Conclusion and future prospects **263**

reform of capitalism or even the establishment of a new kind of economic system capable of turning horizontal into vertical globalization. Those keen to strengthen globalization will have to consider a new global "social economy" approach to transnational corporations. This would require internationally active companies to show far greater responsibility vis-à-vis the societies in which they operate and whose locational advantages they exploit – by actively facilitating the diffusion of knowledge.

However, communicating globally on a more sustainable basis and thus stabilizing globalization as a social process are also a key task for civil societies and lifeworlds, which would ideally overcome the existing division between national interactive and discursive communities. Michael Giesecke has pointed out that a modernity in which it is rare to truly encounter the global other, which is instead "constructed" discursively through the mass media and through the indirect route of the observation of observation, will probably always tend to create, perpetuate and transmit intergenerationally ethnocentric constructs of the other. As grand narratives revolving around the "mentality" and "character" of nations and religions, these remain highly potent even when they function as gross and inaccurate simplifications that nourish the idea of a "clash of civilizations". The lifeworld in particular – but also organized civil society – urgently needs to commit to a radical communicative shift that should consist of at least two components: a much stronger focus on direct cross-border interaction and a complete revision of national traditions of constructing the other in order to help generate genuine global knowledge.

It should be clearly stated at this point that such an endeavour would have to encompass entire education systems in a shift towards a "pedagogy of global inclusion" in order to adapt lifeworldly attitudes to globalization. Despite its educational connotations, we have deliberately chosen the term "pedagogy" because a purely constructivist ideology of networking that proceeds without restructuring the system (education systems, mass tourism, and so on) in a structural and interdependent sense cannot work. It would only force systems, despite their dominance with respect to long-distance communication, ever deeper into an ambivalent and unstable form of globalization.

Global "injections" and islands of cosmopolitan knowledge have been a feature of every society. The real challenge, however, is to bridge the gap between global "elites" and local "majorities". It is utopian to envisage convergence of the symbolic references available in lifeworlds, let alone the total dissolution of social distinctions. However, it will be crucial to achieve new and more balanced concepts of participation as well as mechanisms of cultural connectivity in order to at least mitigate the existing ambivalences of globalization. To this end it is imperative to consider once again all the basic modes of communication. The maxim must be: more direct global dialogue and direct observation of the world, less observation of observation through capture by media discourses, even if – as called for above – media become more transculturally competent. There is an urgent need to bring balance to the communicative ecology of global communication in the lifeworld. The resources

264 Conclusion and future prospects

that might expedite this process include making better use of hidden global knowledge (such as migration-based experiential worlds) and the wide-scale facilitation of direct global contact and interaction through expansion of global exchange programmes, especially in professions that are not specifically global in orientation.

The call for social participation, recognition and active contributions from a wide range of actors again highlights the need to combine vertical and horizontal interdependence, insofar as lifeworlds cannot bring about these changes on their own. Individuals, small groups and local communities are dependent on systems when it comes to global communication because while theoretically they have a tremendous capacity for interaction, their mobility is limited when it comes to observing and achieving contact with the world. At a time of global ecological crisis, it would be wrong to recommend excessive travel. The desired shift in emphasis – in terms of *communicative ecology* – from discursive to interactive exchange and from formal knowledge to experiential knowledge must, therefore, be achieved once again mainly through mediatization. Much as in global corporate teams, the mediatized interpersonal communication of the Internet is definitely no substitute for direct "cultural contact". But it could certainly generate new global communality if it were practised by more people on the basis of genuine principles of dialogicity.

The future of globalization thus depends largely on a comprehensive communicative turnaround in modern societies, one that would require the mass media, systems of action and lifeworldly actors to take on this crucial common task – with each person making their unique contribution, appropriately skilled and in constant exchange with others.

BIBLIOGRAPHY

[AA] (n.d.) Organisationsplan Auswärtiges Amt, www.auswaertiges-amt.de/cae/servlet/contentblob/382698/publicationFile/229074/Organisationsplan-Druckversion.pdf.

Abrahamson, Mark (2004), Global Cities, New York, NY: Oxford University Press.

Adebayo, Kudus Oluwatoyin and Emeka Thaddues Njoku (2016), The Public Sphere and Practice of Democracy in Nigeria: The Context and Contribution of the Nigerian Diaspora, in: Scott Nicholas Romaniuk and Marguerite Marlin (Eds.), Democracy and Civil Society in a Global Era, New York, NY/London: Routledge, p. 60–71.

Adick, Christel (2011), Globalisierungseffekte im Schulsystem, in: Wolfgang Sander (Ed.), Politische Bildung in der Weltgesellschaft: Herausforderungen, Positionen, Kontroversen. Perspektiven politischer Bildung, Bonn: Bundeszentrale für Politische Bildung, p. 146–166.

Adolphsen, Manuel (2012), Communication Strategies of Governments and NGOs. Engineering Global Discourse at High-Level International Summits, Wiesbaden: Springer.

[AIM] (2007) Comparing the Logic of EU Reporting in Mass Media across Europe. Transnational Analysis of EU Media Coverage and Interviews in Editorial Offices in Europe, Adequate Information Management (AIM) Research Consortium (Ed.), Project Co-funded by the European Commission within the Sixth Framework Programme, Bochum/Freiburg: Projekt Verlag.

Albert, Mathias (2009), Globalization and World Society Theory: A Reply, in: International Political Sociology 3/1, p. 126–128.

Albert, Mathias, Lothar Brock, Hilmar Schmidt, Christoph Weller and Klaus Dieter Wolf (1996), Weltgesellschaft: Identifizierung eines „Phantoms", in: Politische Vierteljahresschrift 37/1, p. 5–26.

Alfter, Brigitte (2016), Cross-border Collaborative Journalism: Why Journalists and Scholars Should Talk about an Emerging Method, in: Journal of Applied Journalism and Media Studies 5/2, p. 297–311.

Alfter, Brigitte (2019), Cross-border Collaborative Journalism. A Step-by-Step Guide, Abingdon/New York, NY: Routledge.

Allen, Tim and Jean Seaton (Eds.) (1999), The Media of Conflict. War Reporting and Representations of Ethnic Violence, London/New York, NY: Zed Books.

Allport, Gordon (1954), The Nature of Prejudice, Cambridge, MA: Addison-Wesley.

266 Bibliography

Amant, Kirk St. (2012), Culture, Context, and Cyberspace: Rethinking Identity and Credibility in International Virtual Teams, in: Pauline Hope Cheong, Judith N. Martin and Leah P. Macfadyen (Eds.), New Media and Intercultural Communication. Identity, Community and Politics, New York, NY: Peter Lang, p. 75–89.

Ambrosi, Gerhard Michael (2011), The European Public Sphere and the NUTS. An Approach toward Multilevel Activation of the European Citizenship, in: Luciano Morganti and Léonce Bekemans (Eds.), The European Public Sphere. From Critical Thinking to Responsible Action, Brüssel: Peter Lang, p. 237–254.

Amir, Yehuda (1969), Contact Hypothesis in Ethnic Relations, in: Psychological Bulletin 71/5, p. 319–342.

Amir, Yehuda and Rachel Ben-Ari (1985), International Tourism, Ethnic Contact, and Attitude Change, in: Journal of Social Issues 41/3, p. 105–115.

Anastasopoulos, Petros G. (1992), Tourism and Attitude Change. Greek Tourists Visiting Turkey, in: Annals of Tourism Research 19, p. 629–642.

Andres, Susanne (2004), Internationale Unternehmenskommunikation im Globalisierungsprozess. Eine Studie zum Einfluss der Globalisierung auf die 250 größten in Deutschland ansässigen Unternehmen, Wiesbaden: VS Verlag für Sozialwissenschaften.

Andretta, Massimiliano, Donatella della Porta, Lorenzo Mosca and Herbert Reiter (2003), No Global – New Global. Identität und Strategien der Antiglobalisierungsbewegung, Frankfurt: Campus.

Ang, Ien (1985), Watching *Dallas*, New York, NY: Routledge.

Ang, Ien (2007), Television Fictions around the World. Melodrama and Irony in Global Perspective, in: Critical Studies in Television 2/2, p. 19–30.

Anheier, Helmut, Marlies Glasius and Mary Kaldor (Eds.) (2001), Global Civil Society 2001, Oxford: Oxford University Press.

Antweiler, Christoph (2011), Mensch und Weltkultur. Für einen realistischen Kosmopolitismus im Zeitalter der Globalisierung, Bielefeld: Transcript.

Appadurai, Arjun (1998), Modernity at Large. Cultural Dimensions of Globalization, Minneapolis, MN: University of Minnesota Press (4th ed.).

Appiah, Kwame Anthony (2006), Cosmopolitanism: Ethics in a World of Strangers, New York, NY: Norton.

Arrow, Holly, Joseph Edward E. McGrath and Jennifer L. Berdahl (2000), Small Groups as Complex Systems. Formation, Coordination, Development, and Adaptation, Thousand Oaks, CA: Sage.

Artz, Lee and Yahya R. Kamalipour (2003), The Globalization of Corporate Media Hegemony, New York, NY: State University of New York Press.

Ashcraft, Karen Lee and Brenda J. Allen (2003), The Racial Foundation of Organizational Communication, in: Communication Theory 13/1, p. 5–38.

Atad, Erga (2016), Global Newsworthiness and Reversed Domestication: A New Theoretical Approach in the Age of Transnational Journalism, in: Journalism Practice 11/6, p. 760–776.

Averbeck-Lietz, Stefanie (2010), Kommunikationstheorien in Frankreich: Der epistemologische Diskurs der Sciences de l'information et de la communication (SIC) 1975–2005, Berlin: Avinus.

Averbeck-Lietz, Stefanie (2011), Verständigung und Verhalten in interkulturellen Kommunikationssituationen. Eine kommunikationswissenschaftliche Heuristik, in: Thorsten Quandt and Bertram Scheufele (Eds.), Ebenen der Kommunikation, Wiesbaden: VS Verlag für Sozialwissenschaften, p. 279–301.

Averbeck-Lietz, Stefanie (2015), Soziologie der Kommunikation. Die Mediatisierung der Gesellschaft und die Theoriebildung der Klassiker, Berlin: De Gruyter Oldenbourg.

Bibliography **267**

Axford, Barrie (2012), Mere Connection: Do Communication Flows Compensate for the Lack of a World Society?, in: Georg Peter and Reuß-Markus Krauße (Eds.), Selbstbeobachtung der modernen Gesellschaft und die neuen Grenzen des Sozialen, Wiesbaden: Springer, p. 31–51.

Axford, Barrie (2013), Theories of Globalization, Cambridge/Malden, MA: Polity.

Backhaus, Norman (2012), Die Slum-Tour als touristische Aneignungspraxis: Kulturvermittlung durch eine Exkursion, in: Zeitschrift für Tourismuswissenschaft 4/2, p. 181–195.

Badr, Hanan (2017), Framing von Terrorismus im Nahostkonflikt. Eine Analyse deutscher und ägyptischer Printmedien, Wiesbaden: Springer.

Bahrdt, Hans Paul (1997), Schlüsselbegriffe der Soziologie. Eine Einführung mit Lehrbeispielen, Munich: Beck (7th ed.).

Ball-Rokeach, Sandra (1985), The Origins of Individual Media-System Dependency: A Sociological Framework, in: Communication Research 12/4, p. 485–510.

Ball-Rokeach, Sandra J. and Melvin DeFleur (1976), A Dependency Model of Mass-Media Effects, in: Communication Research 3/1, p. 3–21.

Bannenberg, Ann-Kristin (2011), Die Bedeutung interkultureller Kommunikation in der Wirtschaft. Theoretische und empirische Erforschung von Bedarf und Praxis der interkulturellen Personalentwicklung anhand einiger deutscher Großunternehmen der Automobil- und Zulieferindustrie, Kassel: Kassel University Press.

Baringhorst, Sigrid (1998), Zur Mediatisierung des politischen Protests: Von der Institutionenzur „Greenpeace-Demokratie"?, in: Ulrich Sarcinelli (Ed.), Politikvermittlung und Demokratie in der Mediengesellschaft. Beiträge zur politischen Kommunikationskultur, Bonn: Bundeszentrale für politische Bildung, p. 326–344.

Barker, Randolph T. and Kim Gower (2010), Strategic Application of Storytelling in Organizations. Towards Effective Communication in a Diverse World, in: Journal of Business Communication 47/3, p. 295–312.

Barnes, Susan B. (2013), Social Networks. From Text to Video, New York, NY: Peter Lang.

Bartosch, Ulrich and Klaudius Gansczyk (Eds.) (2009), Weltinnenpolitik für das 21. Jahrhundert. Carl-Friedrich von Weizsäcker verpflichtet, Berlin: LIT-Verlag.

Baumann, Gerd, Marie Gillespie and Annabelle Sreberny (2011), Transcultural Journalism and the Politics of Translation: Interrogating the BBC World Service, in: Journalism. Theory, Practice and Criticism 12/2, p. 135–142.

Baumann, Zygmunt (2000), Liquid Modernity, Cambridge: Polity.

Baumgarten, Nicole (2017), Othering Practice in a Right-Wing Extremist Online Forum, in: Language and Internet 14, www.languageatinternet.org/articles/2017/baumgarten.

Baym, Nancy (2002), Interpersonal Life Online, in: Leah A. Lievrouw and Sonia Livingston (Eds.), Handbook of New Media. Social Shaping and Consequences of ICTs, London: Sage, p. 62–76.

Baym, Nancy (2010), Personal Connections in the Digital Age, Cambridge, Malden, MA: Polity.

Beato, Greg (2014), Civic Engagement: From Petitions to Decisions, in: Stanford Social Innovation Review (Fall), https://ssir.org/articles/entry/from_petitions_to_decisions.

Beck, Ulrich (1986), Risikogesellschaft, Frankfurt: Suhrkamp.

Beck, Ulrich (2000), What Is Globalization?, Cambridge: Polity.

Beck, Ulrich (2006), Cosmopolitan Vision, Cambridge/Malden, MA: Polity.

Beck, Ulrich (2007), Weltrisikogesellschaft. Auf der Suche nach der verlorenen Sicherheit, Frankfurt: Suhrkamp.

Beck, Ulrich and Elisabeth Beck-Gernsheim (2014), Distant Love. Personal Life in the Global Age, Cambridge/Malden, MA: Polity.

268 Bibliography

Becker, Christian (2014), Rituelle Inszenierungen der Staatengemeinschaft. Theorie und empirische Analyse am Beispiel von VN-Generaldebatte und M+5-Gipfel, Wiesbaden: VS Verlag für Sozialwissenschaften.

Becker-Ritterspach, Florian (2006), Wissenstransfer und -integration im Transnationalen Konzern: Eine soziologische Perspektive, in: Ursula Mense-Petermann and Gabriele Wagner (Eds.), Transnationale Konzerne. Ein neuer Organisationstyp?, Wiesbaden: Verlag für Sozialwissenschaften, p. 153–187.

Beer, Francis A. (1981), Peace against War: The Ecology of International Violence, San Francisco, CA: W.H. Freeman.

Begemann, Steve, Carolina Bleser and Maiko Kuchiba (1999), Vereinte Nationen und Sicherheitspolitik, in: Duisburger Arbeitspapiere Ostasienwissenschaften „1999": Ein Gutachten zu den deutschen/europäischen Außen- und Außenwirtschaftsbeziehungen mit Japan, 27, http://duepublico.uni-duisburg-essen.de/servlets/DocumentServlet?id= 36206.

Behmer, Markus (2003), Pressefreiheit in der Dritten Welt – Was heißt "Freiheit"?, in: Michael Haller (Ed.), Das freie Wort und seine Feinde. Zur Pressefreiheit in Zeiten der Globalisierung, Konstanz: UVK, p. 147–160.

Behrens, Henning and Paul Noack (1984), Theorien der internationalen Politik, Munich: DTV.

Beierle, Thomas C. (2004), Digital Deliberation: Engaging the Public through Online Policy Dialogues, in: Peter M. Shane (Ed.), Democracy Online: The Prospects for Political Renewal through the Internet, New York, NY/London: Routledge, p. 155–166.

Beierwaltes, Andreas (2002), Demokratie und Medien: Der Begriff der Öffentlichkeit und seine Bedeutung für die Demokratie in Europa, Baden-Baden: Nomos.

Bendel, Sylvia and Gudrun Held (2008), "Werbung – grenzenlos". Kulturvergleichende Werbeanalysen auf dem theoretischen und methodischen Prüfstand, in: Gudrun Held and Sylvia Bendel (Eds.), Werbung grenzenlos. Multimodale Werbetexte im interkulturellen Vergleich, Frankfurt: Peter Lang, p. 1–11.

Benedek, Wolfgang (2008), The Emerging Global Civil Society: Achievements and Prospects, in: Volker Rittberger and Martin Nettesheim (Eds.), Authority in the Global Political Economy, Basingstoke: Palgrave Macmillan, p. 170–185.

Benford, Robert D. and David A. Snow (2000), Framing Processes and Social Movements: An Overview and Assessment, in: Annual Review of Sociology 26, p. 611–639.

Bennett, Andy and Novie Johan (2018), Young People, Gap Year Travel and the Neo-Tribal Experience, in: Anne Hardy, Andy Bennett and Brady Robards (Eds.), Neo-Tribes. Consumption, Leisure and Tourism, Cham: Palgrave Macmillan, p. 89–103.

Bennett, W. Lance (1990), Toward a Theory of Press-State Relations in the United States, in: Journal of Communication 40/2, p. 103–127.

Bennett, W. Lance (2003), Communicating Global Activism. Strengths and Vulnerabilities in Networked Politics, in: Information, Communication and Society 6/2, p. 143–168.

Bennett, W. Lance (2005), Social Movements beyond Borders: Understanding Two Eras of Transnational Activism, in: Donatella della Porta and Sidney Tarrow (Eds.), Transnational Protest and Global Activism, Lanham, MD: Rowman and Littlefield, p. 203–226.

Bennett, W. Lance and David Paletz (1994), Taken by Storm. The Media, Public Opinion, and U.S. Foreign Policy in the Gulf War, Chicago, IL: Chicago University Press.

Bentele, Günter, Horst Steinmann and Ansgar Zerfaß (1996), Dialogorientierte Unternehmenskommunikation: Ein Handlungsprogramm für die Kommunikationspraxis, in: Günter Bentele, Horst Steinmann and Ansgar Zerfaß (Eds.), Dialogorientierte Unternehmenskommunikation. Grundlagen – Praxiserfahrungen – Perspektiven, Berlin: Vistas, p. 447–463.

Bibliography **269**

Benz, Arthur and Nicolai Dose (2010), Governance – Modebegriff oder nützliches sozialwissenschaftliches Konzept?, in: Arthur Benz (Ed.), Governance – Regieren in komplexen Regelsystemen, Wiesbaden: VS Verlag für Sozialwissenschaften, p. 13–36.

Bercovitch, Jacob (1992), The Structure and Diversity of Mediation in International Relations, in: Jacob Bercovitch and Jeffrey Rubin (Eds.), Mediation in International Relations. Multiple Approaches to Conflict Management, Basingstoke/London: St. Martin's, p. 1–29.

Bercovitch, Jacob and Allison Houston (1996), The Study of International Mediation: Theoretical Issues and Empirical Evidence, in: Jacob Bercovitch (Ed.), Resolving International Conflicts: The Theory and Practice of Mediation, Boulder, CO: Lynne Rienner, p. 11–38.

Berghofer, Simon (2017), Globale Medien- und Kommunikationspolitik. Konzeption und Analyse eines Politikbereichs im Wandel, Baden-Baden: Nomos.

Bertelsmann-Stiftung, Werner Auer-Rizzi, Susanne Blazejewski, Wolfgang Dorow and Gerhard Reber (2007), Unternehmenskulturen in globaler Interaktion. Analysen, Erfahrungen, Lösungsansätze, Wiesbaden: Gabler.

Bettermann, Erik (2004), DW-Intendant Bettermann: „Gesetzentwurf stärkt Unabhängigkeit des deutschen Auslandsrundfunks", 24.3.2004, www.dw.com/de/dw-intendant-bettermann-gesetzentwurf-st%C3%A4rkt-unabh%C3%A4ngigkeit-des-deutschen-auslandsrundfunks/a-1150796.

Bhagwati, Jagdish (2004), In Defense of Globalization, Oxford: Oxford University Press.

Bialski, Paula (2012), Becoming Intimately Mobile, Frankfurt: Peter Lang.

Biden, Joseph R. (2009), National Framework for Strategic Communication, https://fas.org/man/eprint/pubdip.pdf.

Birkinbine, Benjamin J., Rodrigo Gómez and Janet Wasko (Eds.) (2017), Global Media Giants, New York, NY/London: Routledge.

Black, Laura W. (2008), Deliberation, Storytelling, and Dialogic Moments, in: Communication Theory 18/1, p. 93–116.

Black, Rebecca W. (2009), Online Fan Fiction, Global Identities, and Imagination, in: Research in the Teaching of English 43/4, p. 397–425.

Blöbaum, Bernd (1994), Journalismus als soziales System, Opladen: Westdeutscher Verlag.

Block, Fred (1977), The Origins of International Economic Disorder, Berkeley, CA: University of California Press.

Blumer, Herbert (1986), Symbolic Interactionism. Perspective and Method, Berkeley/Los Angeles, CA/London: University of California Press.

Blumer, Herbert (2010), Symbolic Interaction. An Approach to Human Communication, in: Peter Schulz (Ed.), Communication Theory, vol. 1, London: Sage, p. 3–18.

Bob, Clifford (2012), The Global Right Wing and the Clash of World Politics, Cambridge: Cambridge University Press.

Böckelmann, Frank (1975), Theorie der Massenkommunikation, Frankfurt: Suhrkamp.

Bohnsack, Ralf (2014), Rekonstruktive Sozialforschung. Einführung in qualitative Methoden, Opladen: Budrich (9th ed.).

Bolten, Jürgen (2007), Einführung in die interkulturelle Wirtschaftskommunikation, Göttingen: Vandenhoeck und Ruprecht.

Brady, Donald L. (2011), Essentials of International Marketing, Armonk, NY/London: M.E. Sharpe.

Brand, Ulrich, Achim Brunnengräber, Lutz Schrader, Christian Stock and Peter Wahl (2000), Global Governance. Alternative zur neoliberalen Globalisierung?, Münster: Westfälisches Dampfboot.

Brandt, Agnes and Eric Anton Heuser (2016), Kultur und Freundschaft, in: Janosch Schobin, Vincenz Leuschner, Sabine Flick, Erika Alleweldt, Eric Anton Heuser and Agnes Brandt

270 Bibliography

(Eds.), Freundschaft heute. Eine Einführung in die Freundschaftssoziologie, Bielefeld: Transcript, p. 95–106.

Bravo, Vanessa (2013), Studying Diaspora Relations in the Field of Global Public Relations, in: Patricia Moy (Ed.), Communication and Community, New York, NY: Hampton, p. 109–128.

Brennan, Timothy (2008), Postcolonial Studies and Globalization Theory, in: Revathi Krishnaswamy and John C. Hawley (Eds.), The Postcolonial and the Global, Minneapolis, MN/London: University of Minnesota Press, p. 37–53.

Brodersen, Meike (2014), Mobility: Ideological Discourse and Individual Narratives, in: Jürgen Gerhards, Silke Hans and Sören Carlson (Eds.), Globalisierung, Bildung und grenzüberschreitende Mobilität, Wiesbaden: Springer, p. 93–108.

Brown, Adam, Tim Crabbe and Gavin Mellor (2009), Introduction: Football and Community: Practical and Theoretical Considerations, in: Adam Brown, Tim Crabbe and Gavin Mellor (Eds.), Football and Community in the Global Context. Studies in Theory and Practice, London/New York, NY: Routledge, p. 1–10.

Brown, William R. (1980), The Last Crusade. A Negotiator's Middle East Handbook, Chicago, IL: Nelson-Hall.

Brüggemann, Michael and Hagen Schulz-Forberg (2009), Becoming Pan-European? Transnational Media and the European Public Sphere, in: International Communication Gazette 71/8, p. 693–712.

Brüggemann, Michael, Stefanie Sifft, Katharina Kleinen-von Königslöw, Bernhard Peters and Andreas Wimmel (2006), Segmentierte Europäisierung – Trends und Muster der Transnationalisierung von Öffentlichkeiten in Europa, in: Wolfgang R. Langenbucher and Michael Latzer (Eds), Europäische Öffentlichkeit und medialer Wandel. Eine transdisziplinäre Perspektive, Wiesbaden: VS Verlag für Sozialwissenschaften, pp. 214–231.

Bryceson, Deborah and Ulla Vuorela (2002), Transnational Families in the Twenty-First Century, in: Deborah Bryceson and Ulla Vuorela (Eds.), The Transnational Family: New European Frontiers and Global Networks, Oxford: Berg, p. 3–30.

Bucher, Hans-Jürgen (2005), Macht das Internet uns zu Weltbürgern? Globale Online-Diskurse: Strukturwandel der Öffentlichkeit in der Netzwerk-Kommunikation, in: Claudia Fraas and Michael Klemm (Eds.), Mediendiskurse. Bestandsaufnahme und Perspektiven, Frankfurt: Peter Lang, p. 187–218.

Budarick, John (2014), Media and the Limits of Transnational Solidarity, Unanswered Questions in the Relationship between Diaspora, Communication and Community, in: Global Media and Communication 10/2, p. 139–153.

Bugeja, Michael J. (2005), Interpersonal Divide: The Search for Community in a Technological Age, New York, NY: Oxford University Press.

Bukow, Wolf-Dietrich (2000), Die Familie im Spannungsfeld globaler Mobilität, in: Hansjosef Buchkremer, Wolf-Dietrich Bukow and Michaela Emmerich (Eds.), Die Familie im Spannungsfeld globaler Mobilität. Zur Konstruktion ethnischer Minderheiten im Kontext der Familie, Opladen: Lese und Budrich, p. 9–16.

Bunt, Gary R. (2003), Islam in the Digital Age. E-Jihad, Online Fatwas and Cyber Islamic Environments, London/Sterling, VA: Pluto.

Burkart, Roland and Alfred Lang (2004), Die Theorie des kommunikativen Handelns von Jürgen Habermas. Eine kommentierte Textcollage, in: Roland Burkart and Walter Hömberg (Eds.), Kommunikationstheorien. Ein Textbuch zur Einführung, Wien: Braumüller, p. 42–71.

Burns, Peter M. (2006), Social Identities and the Cultural Politics of Tourism, in: Peter M. Burns and Marina Novelli (Eds.), Tourism and Social Identities. Global Frameworks and Local Realities, Amsterdam: Elsevier, p. 13–24.

Bibliography   271

Busch, Dominic (2012), Das Internet als Kulturalisierungsfalle, in: Ursula Reutner (Ed.), Von der digitalen zur interkulturellen Revolution, Baden-Baden: Nomos, p. 267–292.

Busch-Janser, Sandra and Daniel Florian (2007), Die neuen Diplomaten? Public Diplomacy und die Rolle von Kommunikationsagenturen in der Außenpolitik, in: Jens Tenscher and Henrike Viehrig (Eds.), Politische Kommunikation in internationalen Beziehungen, Berlin: LIT, p. 215–233.

Bussemer, Thymian (2005), Propaganda. Konzepte und Theorien. Mit einem Vorwort von Peter Glotz, Wiesbaden: VS Verlag für Sozialwissenschaften.

Butsch, Richard (2019), Screen Culture. A Global History, Cambridge/Medford, MA: Polity.

Cairncross, Frances (2001), The Death of Distance 2.0: How the Communications Revolution Is Changing Our Lives, Boston, MA: Harvard Business School.

Calhoun, Craig (2003), "Belonging" in the Cosmopolitan Imaginary, in: Ethnicities 3/4, p. 531–553.

Caligiuri, Paula M., Mary Anne M. Hyland and Aparna Joshi (1998), Families on Global Assignments. Applying Work/Family Theories Abroad, in: Current Topics in Management 3, p. 313–328.

Cambié, Silvia and Yang-May Ooi (2009), International Communications Strategy. Developments in Cross-Cultural Communications, PR and Social Media, London/Philadelphia, PA: Kogan Page.

Cammaerts, Bart, Alice Mattoni and Patrick McCurdy (2013), Introduction, in: Bart Cammaerts, Alice Mattoni and Patrick McCurdy (Eds.), Mediation and Protest Movements, Bristol/Chicago, IL: Intellect, p. 3–19.

Cannon, Hugh M., Attila Yaprak and Sheila Sasser (2002), Incorporating Cosmopolitan-Related Focus-Group Research into Global Advertising Simulations, in: Developments of Business Simulations and Experiental Learning 29, p. 9–20.

Carstarphen, Nike (2004), Making the 'Other' Human: The Role of Personal Stories to Bridge Deep Differences, in: Hannah Slavik (Ed.), Intercultural Communication and Diplomacy, Malta/Geneva: DiploFoundation, p. 177–196.

Carvalho, Carlos Rubens (2009), International Radio Broadcasting in a Globalizing World: A New Paradigm. A New Information and Communication Order, Saarbrücken: VDM.

Cason, Rachel (2018), Third Culture Kids and Paradoxical Cosmopolitanism, in: Gerard Delanty (Ed.), Routledge International Handbook of Cosmopolitanism Studies, London/New York, NY: Routledge, p. 177–185 (2nd ed.).

Castells, Manuel (2008), The New Public Sphere: Global Civil Society, Communication Networks, and Global Governance, in: The Annals of the American Academy of Political and Social Science 616 (March), p. 78–93.

Castells, Manuel (2010), The Information Age: Economy, Society, and Culture, 3 vols., Malden, MA/Oxford: Wiley-Blackwell (2nd ed.).

Castronova, Edward (2007), Exodus to the Virtual World. How Online Fun Is Changing Reality, New York, NY/Basingstoke: Palgrave Macmillan.

Cazzamatta, Regina (2014), Brasilien-Berichterstattung in der deutschen Presse, Berlin: Frank und Timme.

Cazzamatta, Regina (2018), The Determinants of Latin America's News Coverage in the German Press, in: The Journal of International Communication 24/2, p. 283–304.

Cazzamatta, Regina (2020a), Lateinamerikaberichterstattung der deutschen Presse: Struktur und Entstehungsbedingungen, Wiesbaden: Springer.

Cazzamatta, Regina (2020b), Four Facets of Latin America: A Study of the German Press Coverage from 2000 to 2014, in: Studies in Communications Sciences 20/1, p. 7–23.

272 Bibliography

Chaban, Natalia, Jessica Bain and Serena Kelly (2014), En'vision'ing Europe's Crisis: Intertextuality in News Coverage of the Eurozone Crisis in Chinese, Indian and Russian Press, in: The Journal of International Communication 20/1, p. 1–20.

Chadwick, Andrew (2006), Internet Politics. States, Citizens, and New Communication Technologies, New York, NY/Oxford: Oxford University Press.

Chalaby, Jean K. (2009), Transnational Television in Europe. Reconfiguring Global Communications Networks, London/New York, NY: I.B. Tauris.

Chandhoke, Neera (2012), How Global is Global Civil Society?, in: Frank J. Lechner and John Boli (Eds.), The Globalization Reader, Chichester: Wiley Blackwell, p. 324–331 (5th ed.).

Chandler, David (2005), Constructing Global Civil Society, in: Gideon Baker and David Chandler (Eds.), Global Civil Society: Contested Futures, London: Routledge, p. 149–170.

Chang, Tsan-Kuo, Itai Himmelboim and Dong Dong (2009), Open Global Networks, Closed International Flows, in: International Communication Gazette 71/3, p. 137–159.

Cheney, George, Lars Thøger Christensen, Theodore E. Zorn, Jr. and Shiv Ganesh (2011), Organizational Communication in an Age of Globalization: Issues, Reflections, Practices, Waveland, MS: Long Grove (2nd ed.).

Choi, Junho H. and James A. Danowski (2002), Making a Global Community on the Net: Global Village or Global Metropolis? A Network Analysis of Usenet, in: Journal of Computer-Mediated Communication 7/3, https://onlinelibrary.wiley.com/doi/full/10.1111/j.1083-6101.2002.tb00153.x.

Chouikha, Larbi (1992), Etatisation et pratique journalistique, in: Revue tunisienne de communication 22, p. 37–46.

Chouliaraki, Lilie (2006), The Spectatorship of Suffering, London/Thousand Oaks, CA: Sage.

Chouliaraki, Lilie (2008), The Mediation of Suffering and the Vision of a Cosmopolitan Public, in: Television and New Media 9/5, p. 371–391.

Chouliaraki, Lilie (2013), The Ironic Spectator. Solidarity in the Age of Post-Humanitarianism, Cambridge/Malden, MA: Polity.

Christensen, Miyase, André Jansson and Christian Christensen (2011), Online Territories. Globalization, Mediated Practice and Social Space, New York, NY: Peter Lang.

Christians, Clifford and Michael Traber (1997), Communication Ethics and Universal Values, Thousand Oaks, CA/London: Sage.

Christophers, Brett (2014), Spaces of Media Capital, in: Paul C. Adams, Jim Craine and Jason Dittmer (Eds.), The Ashgate Research Companion to Media Geography, Farnham/Burlington, VT: Ashgate, p. 363–375.

Chua, Cecil Eng Huang (2009), Why Do Virtual Communities Regulate Speech?, in: Communication Monographs 76/2, p. 234–261.

Cissna, Kenneth N. and Rob Anderson (1998), Theorizing about Dialogic Moments: The Buber-Rogers Position and Postmodern Themes, in: Communication Theory 8/1, p. 63–104.

Clark, Cal and Richard L. Merritt (1987), European Community and Intra-European Communications: The Evidence of Mail Flows, in: Claudio Cioffi-Revilla, Richard L. Merritt and Dina A. Zinnes (Eds.), Communication and Interaction in Global Politics, Beverly Hills, CA: Sage, p. 209–236.

Clark, David (1996), Urban World/Global City, London/New York, NY: Routledge.

Clausen, Lisbeth (2006), Intercultural Organizational Communication. Five Corporate Cases in Japan, Copenhagen: Copenhagen Business School.

Cleaver, Harry M. (1998), The Zapatista Effect: The Internet and the Rise of an Alternative Political Fabric, in: Journal of International Affairs 51/2, p. 621–640.

Cohen, Akiba A. (Ed.) (2013a), Foreign News on Television. Where in the World Is the Global Village?, New York, NY: Peter Lang.

Cohen, Akiba A. (2013b), Where in the World Is the Global Village?, in: Akiba A. Cohen (Ed.), Foreign News on Television. Where in the World Is the Global Village?, New York, NY: Peter Lang, p. 319–330.

Cohen, Akiba A., Mark R. Levy, Itzhak Roeh and Michael Gurevitch (1996), Global Newsrooms, Local Audiences. A Study of the Eurovision News Exchange, London: Libbey.

Cohen, Erik (1972), Toward a Sociology of International Tourism, in: Social Research 39/1, p. 164–182.

Cohen, Raymond (1999), Reflections on the New Public Diplomacy: Statecraft 2500 BC to 2000 AD, in: Jan Melissen (Ed.), Innovation in Diplomatic Practice, Basingstoke: Macmillan, p. 1–20.

Compaine, Benjamin (2002), Think Again – Global Media, in: Foreign Policy 133, p. 20–28.

Conrad, Charles and Marshal Scott Poole (2012), Strategic Organizational Communication in a Global Economy, Malden, MA: Wiley Blackwell.

Conti, Luisa (2012). Vom Realen ins Virtuelle und zurück: Wege des interkulturellen Dialogs, in: Ursula Reutner (Ed.), Von der digitalen zur interkulturellen Revolution, Baden-Baden: Nomos, p. 293–316.

Cooley, Charles Horton (1909), Social Organization: A Study of the Larger Mind, New York, NY: C. Scribner's Sons.

Cooper, Glenda and Simon Cottle (2015), Humanitarianism, Communications and Change: Final Reflections, in: Simon Cottle and Glenda Cooper (Eds.), Humanitarianism, Communications and Change, New York, NY: Peter Lang, p. 251–264.

Couldry, Nick (2006), Akteur-Netzwerk-Theorie und Medien: Über Bedingungen und Grenzen von Konnektivitäten und Verbindungen, in: Andreas Hepp, Friedrich Krotz, Shaun Moores and Carsten Winter (Eds.), Konnektivität, Netzwerk und Fluss. Konzepte gegenwärtiger Medien-, Kommunikations- und Kulturtheorie, Wiesbaden: VS Verlag für Sozialwissenschaften, p. 101–117.

Couldry, Nick (2014), What and Where Is the Transnationalized Public Sphere?, in: Nancy Fraser and Kate Nash (Eds.), Transnationalizing the Public Sphere, Cambridge/Malden, MA: Polity, p. 43–59.

Couldry, Nick and Andreas Hepp (2009), What Should Comparative Media Research Be Comparing? Towards a Transcultural Approach to "Media Cultures", in: Daya Thussu (Ed.), Internationalizing Media Studies, London: Routledge, p. 32–47.

Couldry, Nick and Andreas Hepp (2013), Conceptualizing Mediatization: Contexts, Traditions, Arguments, in: Communication Theory 23/3, p. 191–202.

Couldry, Nick and Andreas Hepp (2017), The Mediated Construction of Reality, Cambridge/Malden, MA: Polity.

Croisy, Sophie (2015), Globalization and "Minority" Cultures, in: Sophie Croisy (Eds.), Globalization and "Minority" Cultures. The Role of "Minor" Cultural Groups in Shaping Our Global Future, Leiden/Boston, MA: Brill, p. 1–20.

[CSIS] (1998), Building the Global Information Economy. A Roadmap from the Global Information Infrastructure Commission, Report by Carol Ann Charles, Washington, DC: Center for Strategic and International Studies.

Curran, James (2012), Reinterpreting the Internet, in: James Curran, Natalie Fenton and Des Freedman (Eds.), Misunderstanding the Internet, London/New York, NY: Routledge, p. 3–33.

Curran, James, Frank Esser, Daniel C. Hallin, Kaori Hayashi and Chin-Chuan Lee (2015), International News and Global Integration, in: Journalism Studies 18/2, p. 118–134.

274 Bibliography

Custard, Holly Ann (2008), The Internet and Global Civil Society: Communication and Representation within Transnational Advocacy Networks, in: Global Media Journal (Mediterranean Edition) 3/2, http://globalmedia.emu.edu.tr/images/stories/ALL_A RTICLES/2008/fall2008/issues/Custard_pp_1_11.pdf.

Daase, Christopher (2004), Demokratischer Frieden – Demokratischer Krieg: Drei Gründe für die Unfriedlichkeit von Demokratien, in: Christine Schweitzer, Björn Aust and Peter Schlotter (Eds.), Demokratien im Krieg, Baden-Baden: Nomos, p. 53–71.

Dahlgren, Peter (2005), The Internet, Public Spheres, and Political Communication: Dispersion and Deliberation, in: Political Communication 22/2, p. 147–162.

Dahlgren, Peter (2016), Civic Cosmopolitanism and Political Communication. Media, Activism, and Agency, in: Rita Figueras and Paulo do Espírito Santo (Eds.), Beyond the Internet. Unplugging the Protest Movement Wave, New York, NY/London: Routledge, p. 7–30.

Dailey-O'Cain, Jennifer (2017), Trans-National English in Social Media Communities, London: Palgrave Macmillan.

Dalton, Russel J., Ian McAllister and Martin P. Wattenberg (2000), The Consequences of Partisan Dealignment, in: Russell J. Dalton and Martin P. Wattenberg (Eds.), Parties without Partisans: Political Change in Advanced Industrial Democracies, Oxford: Oxford University Press, p. 37–63.

Dany, Charlotte (2006), The Impact of Participation: How Civil Society Organisations Contribute to the Democratic Quality of the UN World Summit on the Information Society, Bremen: University of Bremen.

Dany, Charlotte (2013), Global Governance and NGO Participation. Shaping the Information Society in the United Nations, London/New York, NY: Routledge.

Daphi, Priska and Nicole Deitelhoff (2017), Protest im Wandel? Jenseits von Transnationalisierung und Entpolitisierung, in: Priska Daphi, Nicole Deitelhoff, Dieter Rucht and Simone Teune (Eds.), Protest in Bewegung? Zum Wandel von Bedingungen, Formen und Effekten politischen Protests, Leviathan Special Edition 45/33, p. 306–322.

Davies, Thomas (2013), NGOs. A New History of Transnational Civil Society, London: Hurst and Company.

De Cesari, Chiara and Ann Rigney (2014), Introduction, in: Chiara De Cesari and Ann Rigney (Eds.), Transnational Memory. Circulation, Articulation, Scales, Berlin/Boston, MA: De Gruyter, p. 1–25.

de Koning, Anouk (2006), Café Latte and Caesar Salad: Cosmopolitan Belonging in Cairo`s Coffee Shops, in: Diane Singerman and Paul Amar (Eds.), Cairo Cosmopolitan. Politics, Culture, and Urban Space in the New Globalized Middle East, Cairo/New York: Cairo University Press, p. 221–232.

Delanty, Gerard (2009), The Cosmopolitan Imagination, Cambridge: Cambridge University Press.

Delanty, Gerard (Ed.) (2018), Routledge International Handbook of Cosmopolitanism Studies, London/New York, NY: Routledge (2nd ed.).

Delhees, Karl H. (1994), Soziale Kommunikation. Psychologische Grundlagen für das Miteinander in der modernen Gesellschaft, Wiesbaden: VS Verlag für Sozialwissenschaften.

della Porta, Donatella (2005), Multiple Belongings, Tolerant Identities and the Construction of "Another Politics": between the European Social Forum and the Local Social Fora, in: Donatella della Porta and Sidney Tarrow (Eds.), Transnational Protest and Global Activism, Lanham, MD: Rowman and Littlefield, p. 175–202.

della Porta, Donatella (2013), Bridging Research on Democracy, Social Movements and Communication, in: Bart Cammaerts, Alice Mattoni and Patrick McCurdy (Eds.), Mediation and Protest Movements, Bristol/Chicago, IL: Intellect, p. 21–37.

Bibliography **275**

della Porta, Donatella and Mario Diani (2006), Social Movements. An Introduction, Oxford: Blackwell (2nd ed.).

della Porta, Donatella and Sidney Tarrow (2005), Transnational Processes and Social Activism: an Introduction, in: Donatella della Porta and Sidney Tarrow (Eds.), Transnational Protest and Global Activism, Lanham, MD: Rowman and Littlefield, p. 1–17.

Dempsey, Sarah E. (2014), NGOs as Communicative Actors within Corporate Social Responsibility Efforts, in: Øyvind Ihlen, Jennifer Bartlett and Steve May (Eds.), The Handbook of Communication and Corporate Social Responsibility, Chichester: Wiley Blackwell, p. 445–466.

Dencik, Lina (2012), Media and Global Civil Society, Houndmills/New York, NY: Palgrave Macmillan.

Desforges, Luke (1998), "Checking out the Planet": Global Representations/Local Identities and Youth Travel, in: Gill Valentine and Tracey Skelton (Eds.), Cool Places. Geographies of Youth Cultures, London/New York, NY: Routledge, p. 175–192.

de Smedt, Tom, Guy de Pauw and Pieter van Ostaeyen (2018), Automatic Detection of Online Jihadist Hate Speech, CLiPS Technical Report 7, Computational Linguistics and Psycholinguistics Technical Report Series, CTRS-007, University of Antwerp, www.uantwerpen.be/en/research-groups/clips/projects-and-publica/clips-technical-repo/.

de Swert, Knut, António Belo, Rasha Kamhawi, Ven-hwei Lo, Constanza Mujica and William Porath (2013), Topics in Foreign and Domestic Television News, in: Akiba A. Cohen (Ed.), Foreign News on Television. Where in the World Is the Global Village?, New York, NY: Peter Lang, p. 41–62.

Deutsch, Karl W. (1964a), Communication Theory and Political Integration, in: Philip E. Jacob and James V. Toscano (Eds.), The Integration of Political Communities, Philadelphia, PA/New York, NY: J. B. Lippincott, p. 46–74.

Deutsch, Karl W. (1964b), Transaction Flows as Indicators of Political Cohesion, in: Philip E. Jacob and James V. Toscano (Eds.), The Integration of Political Communities, Philadelphia, PA/New York, NY: J. B. Lippincott, p. 75–97.

Deutsch, Karl. W. (1970), Political Community at the International Level. Problems of Definition and Measurement, Hamden, CT: Archon Books.

de Vreese, Claes H., Jochen Peter and Holli A. Semetko (2001), Framing Politics at the Launch of the Euro: A Cross-National Comparative Study of Frames in the News, in: Political Communication 18/2, p. 107–122.

d'Haenens, Leen, Michaël Opgenhaffen and Maarten Corten (Eds.) (2014), Cross-continental Views on Journalistic Skills, Abingdon/New York, NY: Routledge.

Dhar, Subhankar (2008), Global IT Outsourcing. Current Trends, Risks, and Cultural Issues, in: Mahesh S. Raisinghani (Ed.), Handbook of Research on Global Information Technology Management in the Digital Economy, Hershey, PA/New York: Information Science Reference, p. 281–311.

Diamond, Jared (2013), Vermächtnis. Was wir von traditionellen Gesellschaften lernen können, Frankfurt: Fischer Taschenbuch Verlag.

Diamond, Louise and John McDonald (1996), Multi-Track Diplomacy. A Systems Approach to Peace, West Hartford, CT: Kumarian.

Diggs, Rhunette C. and Thomas Socha (2013), Communication, Families, and Exploring the Boundaries of Cultural Diversity, in: Anita L. Vangelisti (Ed.), The Routledge Handbook of Family Communication, New York, NY: Routledge, p. 249–266 (2nd ed.).

Dijkzeul, Dennis (2008), Transnational Humanitarian NGOs? A Progress Report, in: Ludger Pries (Ed.), Rethinking Transnationalism. The Meso-Link of Organizations, Abingdon/New York, NY: Routledge, p. 80–103.

276 Bibliography

Dimitrova, Daniela V. and Jesper Strömbäck (2005), Foreign Policy and the Framing of the 2003 Iraq War in Elite Swedish and US Newspapers, in: Media, War and Conflict 1/2, p. 203–220.

Djelic, Marie-Laure and Sigrid Quack (2010), Transnational Communities. Shaping Global Economic Governance, Cambridge: Cambridge University Press.

Dörner, Andreas (2010), Politainment. Politik in der medialen Erlebnisgesellschaft, Frankfurt: Suhrkamp.

Drake, Michael S. (2010), Political Sociology for a Globalizing World, Cambridge: Polity.

Dressler, Matthias and Gina Telle (2009), Meinungsführer in der interdisziplinären Forschung. Bestandsaufnahme und kritische Würdigung, Wiesbaden: Springer.

Drori, Gill S. (2008), Institutionalism and Globalization Studies, in: Roystin Greenwood, Christine Oliver, Roy Suddaby and Kerstin Sahlin (Eds.), The SAGE Handbook of Organizational Institutionalism, Los Angeles, CA: Sage, p. 449–472.

Drotbohm, Heike (2010), Begrenzte Verbindlichkeiten. Zur Bedeutung von Reziprozität und Kontribution in transnationalen Familien, in: Erdmute Alber, Bettina Beer, Julia Pauli and Michael Schnegg (Eds.), Verwandtschaft heute. Positionen, Ergebnisse und Perspektiven, Berlin: Reimer, p. 175–201.

Drüeke, Ricarda (2013), Politische Kommunikationsräume im Internet. Zum Verhältnis von Raum und Öffentlichkeit, Bielefeld: Transcript.

Dürrschmidt, Jörg (2000), Everyday Lives in the Global City: The Delinking of Locale and Milieu, New York, NY: Routledge.

Dürrschmidt, Jörg (2004), Globalisierung, Bielefeld: Transcript (2nd ed.).

Dutta, Mohan Jyoti (2012), Critical Interrogations of Global Public Relations. Power, Culture, and Agency, in: Krishnamurthy Sriramesh and Dejan Vercic (Eds.), Culture and Public Relations, New York, NY: Routledge, p. 202–217.

[DW] (2005), Gesetz über die Rundfunkanstalt des Bundesrechts „Deutsche Welle" (Deutsche-Welle-Gesetz - DWG), www.gesetze-im-internet.de/dwg/BJNR309410997. html.

[DW] (2016), Between Public Diplomacy and Global Information – the Future of International Broadcasting, www.dw.com/en/between-public-diplomacy-and-global-information-the-future-of-international-broadcasting/a-19277319.

Eckardt, Frank (2004), Soziologie der Stadt, Bielefeld: Transcript.

Eisen, Roland (2003), Globalization and the New Economy: Some General Thoughts, in: Journal of European Economy 2/1, p. 21–42.

El-Nawawy, Mohammed and Adel Iskandar (2003), Al-Jazeera. The Story of the Network that is Rattling Governments and Redefining Modern Journalism, Cambridge, MA: Westview.

El-Nawawy, Mohammed and Sahar Khamis (2011), Islam Dot Com: Contemporary Islam Discourses in Cyberspace, New York, NY: Palgrave Macmillan.

Elsheshtawy, Yasser (2012), Urban (Im)Mobility. Public Encounters in Dubai, in: Tim Edensor and Mark Jayne (Eds.), Urban Theory beyond the West. A World of Cities, London: Routledge, p. 219–236.

Elvestad, Eiri (2009), Introverted Locals or World Citizens? A Quantitative Study of Interest in Local and Foreign News in Traditional Media and on the Internet, in: Nordicom Review 30/2, p. 105–123.

Endruweit, Günter (2004), Organisationssoziologie, Stuttgart: Lucius and Lucius/UTB (2nd, revised ed.).

Enroth, Henrik and Douglas Brommesson (2015), Introduction: Transnational and Transdisciplinary Exchanges, in: Henrik Enroth and Douglas Brommesson (Eds.),

Global Community? Transnational and Transdisciplinary Exchanges, London/New York, NY: Rowman and Littlefield, p. 1–77.

Entman, Robert M. (1993), Framing: Toward Clarification of a Fractured Paradigm, in: Journal of Communication 43/4, p. 51–58.

Ernst, Marcel (2015), Der deutsche „Dialog mit der islamischen Welt". Diskurse deutscher Auswärtiger Kultur- und Bildungspolitik im Maghreb, Bielefeld: Transcript.

Eskola, Kaisa and Felix Kolb (2002), Attac: Erfolgsgeschichte einer transnationalen Bewegungsorganisation, in: Forschungsjournal Soziale Bewegungen 15/1, p. 27–33.

Etzioni, Amitai (2004), From Empire to Community. A New Approach to International Relations, New York, NY: Palgrave Macmillan.

Evans, Nancy H. (1976), Tourism and Cross Cultural Communication, in: Annals of Tourism Research 3/4, p. 189–198.

Fähnrich, Birte (2012), Science Diplomacy. Strategische Kommunikation in der Auswärtigen Wissenschaftspolitik, Wiesbaden: Springer.

Faist, Thomas (2008), Transstate Spaces and Development: Some Critical Remarks, in: Ludger Pries (Ed.), Rethinking Transnationalism. The Meso-Link of Organizations, Abingdon/New York, NY: Routledge, p. 62–79.

Faltesek, Daniel (2015), #Time, in: Nathan Rambukkana (Ed.), HashtagPublics. The Power and Politics of Discursive Networks, New York, NY: Peter Lang, p. 77–86.

Fenton, Natalie (2012), The Internet and Social Networking, in: James Curran, Natalie Fenton and Des Freedman (Eds.), Misunderstanding the Internet, London/New York, NY: Routledge, p. 123–148.

Fenyoe, Alice (2010), The World Online. How UK Citizens Use the Internet to Find out about the Wider World, London: International Broadcasting Trust.

Festinger, Leon (1978), Theorie der kognitiven Dissonanz, Ed. by Martin Irle and Volker Möntmann, Bern: Huber.

Finnemann, Niels Ole, Per Jauert, Jakob Linaa Jensen, Karen Klitgaards Povlsen and Anne Scott Sørensen (2012), The Media Menus of Danish Internet Users 2009, Copenhagen: Danish National Research Council, https://findresearcher.sdu.dk:8443/ws/files/146590 573/The_Media_Menus_of_Danish_Internet_Users.pdf.

Fisher, Roger, William Ury and Bruce Patton (2004), Das Harvard-Konzept. Der Klassiker der Verhandlungsdiplomatie, Frankfurt: Campus (22nd revised ed.).

Fiske, John (1987), Television Culture, London/New York, NY: Routledge.

Fiske, John (1989), Understanding Popular Culture, Boston, MA: Unwin Hyman.

Fletcher, Tom (2016), Naked Diplomacy. Power and Statecraft in the Digital Age, London: William Collins.

Flew, Terry (2007), Understanding Global Media, Basingstoke/New York, NY: Palgrave Macmillan.

Flew, Terry (2009), Beyond Globalization: Rethinking the Scalar and Relational in Global Media Studies, in: Global Media Journal (Australian Edition) 3/1, www.hca. westernsydney.edu.au/gmjau/archive/v3_2009_1/3vi1_terry_flew.html.

Flew, Terry (2011), Media and Creative Industries: Conglomeration and Globalization as Accumulation Strategies in an Age of Digital Media, in: Dwayne Winseck and Dal Yong Jin (Eds.), The Political Economies of Media and the Transformation of Global Media Industries, New York, NY: Bloomsbury, p. 84–100.

Flew, Terry, Petros Iosifidis and Jeanette Steemers (2016), Global Media and National Policies: The Return of the State, in: Terry Flew, Petros Iosifidis and Jeanette Steemers (Eds.), Global Media and National Policies. The Return of the State, Basingstoke/New York, NY, p. 1–15.

278 Bibliography

Flusser, Vilém (2000), Kommunikologie, Ed. by Stefan Bollmann and Edith Flusser, Frankfurt: Fischer Taschenbuch Verlag.

Fokin, Vladimir Ivanovich, Sergey Sergeevich Shirin, Julia Vadimovna Nikolaeva, Natalia Mikhailovna Bogolubova, Elena Eduardovna Elts and Vladimir Nikolaevich Baryshnikov (2017), Interaction of Cultures and Diplomacy of States, in: Kasetsart Journal of Social Sciences 38/1, p. 45–49.

Forst, Rainer (2006), Toleranz und Anerkennung, in: Christian Augustin, Johannes Wienand and Christiane Winkler (Eds.), Religiöser Pluralismus und Toleranz in Europa, Wiesbaden: VS Verlag für Sozialwissenschaften, p. 78–83.

Forster, Klaus (2006), Journalismus im Spannungsfeld zwischen Freiheit und Verantwortung. Das Konzept des „Public Journalism" und seine empirische Relevanz, Cologne: Herbert von Halem.

Fortner, Robert S. (1993), International Communication. History, Conflict, and Control in the Global Metropolis, Belmont, CA: Wadsworth.

Foster, Émilie, Raymond Hudon and Stéphanie Yates (2012), Advocacy Coalitions Strategies: Tensions about Legitimacy in Environmental Causes, in: Jennifer Lees-Marshment (Ed.), Routledge Handbook of Political Marketing, London/New York, NY: Routledge, p. 316–328.

Frank, Sybille (2012), When "the Rest" Enters "the West": Indischer Tourismus in die Zentralschweiz, in: Zeitschrift für Tourismuswissenschaft 4/2, p. 221–229.

Franke, Ronald (2010), Kooperationskompetenz im Global Business, Berlin: Logos.

Fraser, Nancy (2014), Transnationalizing the Public Sphere: On the Legitimacy and Efficacy of Public Opinion in a Post-Westphalian World, in: Nancy Fraser and Kate Nash (Eds.), Transnationalizing the Public Sphere, Cambridge/Malden, MA: Polity, p. 1–42.

Frederick, Howard H. (1993), Global Communication and International Relations, Belmont, CA: Wadsworth.

[Freedom House] (2019), Democracy in Retreat. Freedom in the World 2019, Freedom House, https://freedomhouse.org/report/freedom-world/freedom-world-2019/democracy-in-retreat.

Frei, Daniel (1985), Die Entstehung eines globalen Systems unabhängiger Staaten, in: Karl Kaiser and Hans-Peter Schwarz (Eds.), Weltpolitik. Strukturen – Akteure – Perspektiven, Bonn: Bundeszentrale für politische Bildung, p. 19–30.

Freitag, Alan R. and Ashli Quesinberry Stokes (2009), Global Public Relations. Spanning Borders, Spanning Cultures, London/New York, NY: Routledge.

Friedman, Thomas L. (2005), The World Is Flat. The Globalized World in the Twenty-First Century, London: Penguin.

Fuchs, Christian (2010), Global Media and Global Capitalism, in: Nnamdi Ekeanyanwu and Chinedu Okeke (Eds.), Indigenous Societies and Cultural Globalization in the 21st Century. Is the Global Village Truly Real?, Saarbrücken: VDM, p. 556–594.

Fuchs, Gerhard, Gerhard Krauss and Hans-Georg Wolf (Eds.) (1999), Die Bindungen der Globalisierung. Interorganisationsbeziehungen im regionalen und globalen Wirtschaftsraum, Marburg: Metropolis.

Füller, Henning and Georg Glasze (2014), Gated Communities und andere Formen abgegrenzten Wohnens, in: Aus Politik und Zeitgeschichte 63/4–5, p. 33–38.

Galal, Ehab (Ed.) (2014), Arab TV-Audiences. Negotiating Religion and Identity, Frankfurt: Peter Lang.

Galtung, Johan (1973), Imperialismus und strukturelle Gewalt. Analysen über abhängige Reproduktion, Frankfurt: Suhrkamp.

Gambetta, Diego (2009), Signaling, in: Peter Hedström and Peter Bearman (Eds.), The Oxford Handbook of Analytical Sociology, Oxford: Oxford University Press, p. 168–194.

Bibliography **279**

[GAO] (2003), U.S. Public Diplomacy: State Department Expands Efforts but Faces Significant Challenges, Washington, DC: Government Accountability Office.

[GAO] (2003/2), U.S. International Broadcasting: New Strategic Approach Focuses on Reaching Large Audiences but Lacks Measurable Program Objectives, Washington, DC: Government Accountability Office.

[GAO] (2007), U.S. Public Diplomacy: Actions Needed to Improve Strategic Use and Coordination of Research, Washington, DC: Government Accountability Office.

Garaeva, Gulnaz (2012), „Interkul*tour*alität?" oder: Kritische Überlegungen zu interkulturellen Aspekten des Tourismus, in: Zeitschrift für Tourismuswissenschaft 4/2, p. 209–220.

García Canclini, Néstor (2005), Hybrid Cultures. Strategies for Entering and Leaving Modernity, Minneapolis, MN: University of Minnesota Press.

Gasher, Mike and Sandra Gabriele (2004), Increasing Circulation? A Comparative News Flow Study of the Montreal Gazette's Hard Copy and On-line Editions, in: Journalism Studies 5/3, p. 311–323.

Gast-Gampe, Martina (1993), Einstellungsänderung, in: Heinz Hahn and Hans Jürgen Kagelmann (Eds.), Tourismuspsychologie und Tourismussoziologie. Ein Handbuch zur Tourismuswissenschaft, Munich: Quintessenz, p. 132–135.

Gavin, Neil T. (2018), Media Definitely Do Matter: Brexit, Immigration, Climate Change and Beyondc The British Journal of Politics and International Relations 20/4, p. 827–845.

Geise, Stephanie (2017), Meinungsführer und der Flow of Communication, Baden-Baden: Nomos.

Geise, Stephanie, Katharina Lobinger and Cornelia Brantner (2013), Fractured Paradigm? Theorien, Konzepte und Methoden der visuellen Framingforschung. Ergebnisse einer systematischen Literaturschau, in: Stephanie Geise and Katharina Lobinger (Eds.), Visual Framing. Perspektiven und Herausforderungen der Visuellen Kommunikationsforschung, Cologne: Herbert von Halem, p. 42–76.

Geiselberger, Heinrich (2017), Die große Regression. Die internationale Debatte über die geistige Situation der Zeit, Berlin: Suhrkamp.

Gellner, Winand (1995), Ideenagenturen für Politik und Öffentlichkeit. Think Tanks in den USA und in Deutschland, Wiesbaden: Springer.

Georgiou, Myria and Rafal Zaborowski (2017), Media Coverage of the "Refugee Crisis": A Cross-European Perspective, Council of Europe Report DG1/03, https://edoc.coe.int/en/refugees/7367-media-coverage-of-the-refugee-crisis-a-cross-european-perspective.html#.

Gerhards, Jürgen (1993), Westeuropäische Integration und die Schwierigkeiten der Entstehung einer europäischen Öffentlichkeit, in: Zeitschrift für Soziologie 22/2, p. 96–110.

Gerhards, Jürgen (2000), Europäisierung von Ökonomie und Politik und die Trägheit der Entstehung einer europäischen Öffentlichkeit, in: Maurizio Bach (Ed.), Die Europäisierung nationaler Gesellschaften, Wiesbaden: Westdeutscher Verlag, p. 277–305.

Gerhards, Jürgen and Friedhelm Neidhardt (1990), Strukturen und Funktionen moderner Öffentlichkeit. Fragestellungen und Ansätze, Berlin: Wissenschaftszentrum Berlin für Sozialforschung.

Germann Molz, Jennie (2007), Eating Difference. The Cosmopolitan Mobilities of Culinary Tourism, in: Space and Culture 10/1, p. 77–93.

Gershon, Richard A. (2019), Transnational Media and the Economics of Global Competition, in: Yahya R. Kamalipour (Ed.), Global Communication. A Multicultural Perspective, Lanham, MD: Rowman and Littlefield, p. 37–54.

Gerstenberger, Debora and Joel Glasman (Eds.) (2016) Techniken der Globalisierung. Globalgeschichte Meets Akteur-Netzwerk-Theorie, Bielefeld: Transcript.

280 Bibliography

Geser, Hans (2005), Soziologische Aspekte mobiler Kommunikation: Über den Niedergang orts- und raumbezogener Sozialstrukturen, in: Joachim R. Höflich and Julian Gebhardt (Eds.), Mobile Kommunikation. Perspektiven und Forschungsfelder, Frankfurt: Peter Lang, p. 43–59.

Giddens, Anthony (1990), The Consequences of Modernity, Cambridge: Polity.

Giddens, Anthony (2003), The Globalizing of Modernity, in: David Held and Anthony McGrew (Eds.), The Global Transformations Reader. An Introduction to the Globalization Debate, Cambridge: Polity, p. 60–66 (2nd ed.).

Giese, Ernst, Ivo Mossig and Heike Schröder (2011), Globalisierung der Wirtschaft. Eine wirtschaftsgeographische Einführung, Paderborn: Ferdinand Schöningh.

Giesecke, Michael (2002), Von den Mythen der Buchkultur zu den Visionen der Informationsgesellschaft. Trendforschungen zur kulturellen Medienökologie, Frankfurt: Suhrkamp.

Gillespie, Marie (1995), Television, Ethnicity, and Cultural Change, London/New York, NY: Routledge.

Girgensohn-Marchand, Bettina (1994), Ergebnisse der empirischen Kleingruppenforschung, in: Bernhard Schäfers (Ed.), Einführung in die Gruppensoziologie. Geschichte, Theorien, Analysen, Heidelberg/Wiesbaden: Quelle und Meyer, p. 54–79 (2nd ed.).

Gladwell, Malcolm (2012), Social Media Fail to Incite True Activism, in: Dedria Bryfonski (Ed.), The Global Impact of Social Media, Detroit, MI: Greenhaven, p. 95–105.

[GlobalTrends] (2000), GlobalTrends 2015: A Dialogue about the Future with Nongovernment Experts, www.cia.gov/library/readingroom/docs/DOC_0000516933.pdf.

Goff, Peter (Ed.) (1999), The Kosovo News and Propaganda War, Wien: International Press Institute.

Goldenberg, Jacob and Moshe Levy (2009), Distance Is Not Dead. Social Interaction and Geographical Distance in the Internet, in: Computers and Society 2, www.researchgate. net/publication/45857334_Distance_Is_Not_Dead_Social_Interaction_and_ Geographical_Distance_in_the_Internet_Era.

Gómez-Alamillo, Francisco (2005), Technologiediffusion und globale Wissensvernetzung, in: Arnold Picot and Hans-Peter Quadt (Eds.), Telekommunikation und die globale wirtschaftliche Entwicklung. Einfluss der weltweiten Verbreitung neuer Technologien, Berlin: Springer, p. 51–58.

Goodman, Michael B. and Peter B. Hirsch (2015), Corporate Communication. Critical Business Asset for Strategic Global Change, New York, NY: Peter Lang.

Gopal, Shankar (2001), American Anti-Globalisation Movement: Re-Examining Seattle Protests, in: Economic and Political Weekly 36/34, p. 3226–3232.

Graham, Mark (2012), Die Welt in der Wikipedia als Politik der Exklusion, in: Dossier Wikipedia/Bundeszentrale für politische Bildung, www.bpb.de/gesellschaft/digitales/ wikipedia/145816/die-welt-in-der-wikipedia-als-politik-der-exklusion?p=all.

Graham, Mark, Stefano De Sabbata and Matthew A. Zook (2015), Towards a Study of Information Geographies: (Im)mutable Augmentations and a Mapping of the Geographies of Information, in: Geo: Geography and Environment 2, p. 88–105.

Graham, Stephen (2010), The End of Geography or the Explosion of Place? Conceptualizing Space, Place and Information Technology, in: Pramod K. Nayar (Ed.), The New Media and Cybercultures Anthology, Malden, MA/Oxford: Wiley Blackwell, p. 90–108.

Granovetter, Mark S. (1973), The Strength of Weak Ties, in: American Journal of Sociology 78/6, p. 1360–1380.

Grebenstein, Kay, Christian-Andreas Schumann, Claudia Tittmann, Gonpo Tsering, Jana Weber and Jörg Wolle (2003), Globale IT-Infrastruktur für die interkulturelle Kommuni-kation, in: Susanne Bleich, Wenjian Jia and Franz Schneider (Eds.), Kommunikation in der globalen Wirtschaft, Frankfurt: Peter Lang, p. 135–153.

Greschke, Heike Monika (2008), Does it Matter Where You Are? Transnational Migration, Internet Usage and the Emergence of Global Togetherness, in: Remus Gabriel Anghel, Eva Gerharz and Gilberto Rescher (Eds.), The Making of World Society. Perspectives from Transnational Research, Bielefeld: Transcript, p. 275–289.

Greschke, Heike Monika (2009), Daheim in www.Cibervalle.de. Zusammenleben im medialen Alltag der Migration, Berlin: de Gruyter.

Greschke, Heike M. (2013), Wie ist globales Zusammenleben möglich? Die Transnationalisierung der unmittelbaren sozialen Beziehungen und ihre methodologische Reflexion, in: Hans-Georg Soeffner (Ed.), Transnationale Vergesellschaftungen. Verhandlungen des 35. Kongresses der Deutschen Gesellschaft für Soziologie in Frankfurt am Main 2010, vol. 2, Wiesbaden: Springer, p. 371–383.

Grewal, Inderpal (2007), Understanding "Global Community" in Cultural Studies, in: Communication and Critical/Cultural Studies 4/3, p. 332–335.

Grieves, Kevin (2012), Journalism across Boundaries. The Promises and Challenges of Transnational and Transborder Journalism, Basingstoke/New York, NY: Palgrave Macmillan.

Groebel, Jo (2000), Die Rolle des Auslandsrundfunks. Eine vergleichende Analyse der Erfahrungen und Trends in fünf Ländern, Bonn: Friedrich-Ebert-Stiftung.

Gronwald, Klaus-Dieter (2017), Global Communication and Collaboration. Global Project Management, Global Sourcing, Cross-Cultural Competencies, Berlin/Heidelberg: Springer.

Grüne, Anne (2016), Formatierte Weltkultur? Zur Theorie und Praxis globalen Unterhaltungsfernsehens, Bielefeld: Transcript.

Grüne, Anne (2019a), Dys/Functions of Popular Culture in Democratic Transformation: Comparative Perspectives on Germany and Indonesia, in: Anne Grüne, Kai Hafez, Subekti Priyadharma and Sabrina Schmidt (Eds.), Media and Transformation in Germany and Indonesia: Asymmetrical Comparisons and Perspectives, Berlin: Frank und Timme, p. 287–311.

Grüne, Anne (2019b), Gruppenkommunikation und Globalisierung: eine unzeitgemäße Betrachtung, in: Christine Linke and Isabel Schlote (Eds.), Soziales Medienhandeln. Integrative Perspektiven auf den Wandel mediatisierter interpersonaler Kommunikation, Wiesbaden: Springer, p. 185–195.

Grüne, Anne and Kai Hafez (2018), Fördert arabische Populärkultur die Individualisierung? Fernsehnutzung bei jungen Ägyptern, in: Florian Zemmin, Johannes Stephan and Monica Corrado (Eds.), Moderne im Islam. Islam in der Moderne, Leiden: Brill, p. 451–471.

Gudykunst, William B., Carmen M. Lee, Tsukasa Nishida and Naoto Ogawa (2005), Theorizing about Intercultural Communication, in: William B. Gudykunst (Ed.), Theorizing about Intercultural Communication, Thousand Oaks, CA: Sage, p. 3–27.

Günther, Armin and Hans Hopfinger (2009), Neue Medien – neues Reisen? Wirtschafts- und kulturwissenschaftliche Perspektiven der eTourismus Forschung, in: Zeitschrift für Tourismuswissenschaft 1/2, p. 121–150.

Gurevitch, Michael, Mark R. Levy and Itzhak Roeh (1991), The Global Newsroom. Convergences and Diversities in the Globalization of Television News, in: Peter Dahlgren and Colin Sparks (Eds.), Communication and Citizenship. Journalism and the Public Sphere, London/New York, NY: Routledge, p. 195–216.

Guruz, Kemal and Nancy Zimpher (2011), Higher Education and International Student Mobility in the Global Knowledge Economy, Albany, NY: State University of New York Press.

Gutekunst, Miriam (2016), The World Has No Limits, So Why Should You? Migration through Marriage in Times of Increasing Digitalization and Securization of Borders,

282 Bibliography

in: Andreas Hackl, Irene Götz, Julia Sophia Schwarz, Miriam Gutekunst and Sabina Leoncini (Eds.), Bounded Mobilities. Ethnographic Perspectives on Social Hierarchies and Global Inequalities, Bielefeld: Transcript, p. 209–221.

Haagerup, Ulrik (2014), Constructive News. Why Negativity Destroys the Media and Democracy – and How to Improve Journalism of Tomorrow, Hanoi: InnoVatio.

Habermas, Jürgen (1971), Theorie der Gesellschaft oder Sozialtechnologie? Eine Auseinandersetzung mit Niklas Luhmann, in: Jürgen Habermas and Niklas Luhmann, Theorie der Gesellschaft oder Sozialtechnologie: Was leistet die Systemforschung?, Frankfurt: Suhrkamp, p. 142–290.

Habermas, Jürgen (1990), Strukturwandel der Öffentlichkeit, Frankfurt: Suhrkamp (Orig. 1962).

Habermas, Jürgen (1992), Faktizität und Geltung, Frankfurt: Suhrkamp.

Habermas, Jürgen (1995), Theorie des kommunikativen Handelns, 2 vols., Frankfurt: Suhrkamp (4th, revised ed.).

Habermas, Jürgen (2001), Warum braucht Europa eine Verfassung?, in: Die Zeit, June 28.

Hafez, Kai (1999), International News Coverage and the Problems of Media Globalization. In Search of a „New Global-Local Nexus", in: Innovation. The European Journal of Social Sciences 12/1, p. 47–62.

Hafez, Kai (2000a), Medien - Kommunikation - Kultur: Irrwege und Perspektiven der Globalisierungsdebatte, in: Rainer Tetzlaff (Ed.), Weltkulturen unter Globalisierungsdruck. Erfahrungen und Antworten aus den Kontinenten, Bonn: Stiftung Entwicklung und Frieden, p. 93–117.

Hafez, Kai (2000b), Islam and the West: The Clash of Politicized Perceptions, in: Kai Hafez (Ed.), The Islamic World and the West. An Introduction to Political Cultures and International Relations, translated from the German by Mary Ann Kenny, Leiden: Brill, p. 3–18.

Hafez, Kai (2002a), Die politische Dimension der Auslandsberichterstattung. vol. 1: Theoretische Grundlagen; vol. 2: Das Nahost- und Islambild in der deutschen überregionalen Presse, Baden-Baden: Nomos.

Hafez, Kai (2002b), Journalism Ethics Revisited: A Comparison of Ethics Codes in Europe, North Africa, the Middle East and Muslim Asia, in: Political Communication 19/2, p. 225–250.

Hafez, Kai (2002c), Internationale Kommunikations- und Medienforschung in Deutschland: Ein neues Feld der Politikberatung, in: Kai Hafez (Ed.), Die Zukunft der internationalen Kommunikationswissenschaft in Deutschland,, Hamburg: Deutsches Übersee-Institut, p. 135–154.

Hafez, Kai (2002d), Türkische Mediennutzung in Deutschland: Hemmnis oder Chance der gesellschaftlichen Integration. Eine qualitative Studie im Auftrag des Presse- und Informationsamtes der Bundesregierung, Hamburg/Berlin: Presse- und Informationsamt der Bundesregierung.

Hafez, Kai (2003a), Globalisierung und Demokratisierung in Entwicklungsländern: Die Informationsrevolution hat die „dritte Welle der Demokratisierung" verpasst, in: Joachim Betz and Stefan Brüne (Eds.), Globalisierung und Entwicklungsländer, Opladen: Leske und Budrich, p. 39–52.

Hafez, Kai (Ed.) (2003b), Media Ethics in the Dialogue of Cultures. Journalistic Self-Regulation in Europe, the Arab World, and Muslim Asia, Hamburg: Deutsches Orient-Institut.

Hafez, Kai (2004), The Iraq War 2003 in Western Media and Public Opinion. A Case Study of the Effects of Military (Non-)Involvement on Conflict Perception, in: Global Media

Journal 3/5, www.globalmediajournal.com/open-access/the-iraq-war-in-western-media-and-public-opinion-a-case-study-of-the-effects-of-military-non-involvement-on-conflict-perception.pdf.

Hafez, Kai (2007a), The Myth of Media Globalization, translated by Alex Skinner, Cambridge: Polity.

Hafez, Kai (2007b), Die Überlegenheit des Realismus: "Bilderkriege", "Iconic Turn" und die Ohnmacht der Medien, in: Lydia Haustein, Bernd M. Scherer and Martin Hager (Eds.), Feindbilder: Ideologien und visuelle Strategien der Kulturen, Göttingen: Wallstein, p. 126–134.

Hafez, Kai (2008), The Unknown Desire for "Objectivity": Journalism Ethics in Arab (and Western) Journalism, in: Kai Hafez (Ed.), Arab Media – Power and Weakness, London/New York, NY: Continuum, p. 147–164.

Hafez, Kai (2009), Let's Improve "Global Journalism"!, in: Journalism. Theory, Practice and Criticism 10/3, p. 329–331.

Hafez, Kai (2010a), Radicalism and Political Reform in the Islamic and Western Worlds, translated by Alex Skinner, Cambridge: Cambridge University Press.

Hafez, Kai (2010b), Theorielücken als Glaubwürdigkeitsfallen: Öffentlichkeit und Medien aus demokratie- und systemtheoretischer Sicht, in: Carsten Reinemann and Rudolf Stöber (Eds.), Wer die Vergangenheit kennt, hat eine Zukunft. Festschrift für Jürgen Wilke, Cologne: Herbert von Halem, p. 62–78.

Hafez, Kai (2011), Global Journalism for Global Governance? Theoretical Visions, Practical Constraints, in: Journalism. Theory, Practice and Criticism 12/4, p. 483–496.

Hafez, Kai (2014a), Islam in ‚Liberal‘ Europe. Freedom, Equality, and Intolerance, translated by Alex Skinner, Lanham, MD: Rowman and Littlefield.

Hafez, Kai (2014b), How Global Is the Internet? Reflections on Economic, Cultural, and Political Dimensions of the Networked "Global Village", in: Robert S. Fortner and P. Mark Fackler (Eds.), The Handbook of Media and Mass Communication Theory, Vol. II, Malden, MA/Oxford: Wiley Blackwell, p. 645–663.

Hafez, Kai (2016), Compassion Fatigue der Medien? Warum der deutsche „Flüchtlingssommer" so rasch wieder verging, in: Global Media Journal (German Edition) 6/1, www.db-thueringen.de/servlets/MCRFileNodeServlet/dbt_derivate_00035505/GMJ11_Hafez.pdf.

Hafez, Kai (2017a), A Complicated Relationship: Right-Wing Populism, Media Representation and Journalism Theory, in: Global Media Journal (German Edition) 7/2, www.db-thueringen.de/servlets/MCRFileNodeServlet/dbt_derivate_00039851/GMJ14_Hafez_final.pdf.

Hafez, Kai (2017b), Hass im Internet. Zivilitätsverluste in der digitalen Kommunikation, in: Communicatio Socialis 50/3, p. 318–333.

Hafez, Kai and Anne Grüne (2015), Chaotische Fernwelt – getrennte Lebenswelten: Auslandsberichterstattung zwischen negativem und positivem Journalismus, in: Deutscher Fachjournalistenverband (Ed.), Positiver Journalismus, Konstanz/Munich: UVK, p. 99–112.

Hafez, Kai and Anne Grüne (2016), Westernization, in: John Stone, Rutledge M. Dennis, Polly Rizova, Anthony D. Smith and Xiaoshuo Hou (Eds.), The Blackwell Encyclopedia of Race, Ethnicity and Nationalism, vol. V, Chichester: Wiley Blackwell, p. 2205–2209.

Hafez, Kai and Sabrina Schmidt (2015), Die Wahrnehmung des Islams in Deutschland, Gütersloh: Verlag Bertelsmann Stiftung.

Hagedorn, Anke (2016), Die Deutsche Welle und die Politik. Deutscher Auslandsrundfunk 1953–2013, Konstanz/Munich: UVK.

284 Bibliography

Hahn, Carole L. and Theresa Alviar Martin (2008), International Political Socialization Research, in: Linda F. Levstik and Cynthia A. Tyson (Eds.), The Handbook of Research in Social Studies Education, New York, NY/London: Routledge, pp. 81–108.

Halavais, Alexander (2000), National Borders on the World Wide Web, in: New Media and Society 2/1, p. 7–28.

Halff, Gregor (2009), Globalisierung und Wirtschaftssprache: Skizze eines Forschungsfeldes und der Kommunikationspraxis, in: Christoph Moss (Ed.), Die Sprache der Wirtschaft, Wiesbaden: Springer, p. 147–160.

Hall, Stuart (1980), Cultural Studies: Two Paradigms, in: Media, Culture and Society 57/2, p. 57–72.

Hall, Stuart (1992a), The Global, the Local and the Return of Ethnicity, in: Stuart Hall (Ed.), Understanding Modern Societies. An Introduction, Cambridge: Polity/The Open University, p. 304–313.

Hall, Stuart (1992b), Encoding/Decoding, in: Stuart Hall, Dorothy Hobson, Andrew Lowe and Paul Willis (Eds.), Culture, Media, Language. Working Papers in Cultural Studies, 1972–79, London/New York, NY: Routledge in Association with the Centre for Contemporary Cultural Studies, University of Birmingham, p. 128–138.

Hall, Stuart and Pnina Werbner (2008), Cosmopolitanism, Globalisation and Diaspora. Stuart Hall in Conversation with Pnina Werbner, in: Pnina Werbner (Ed.), Anthropology and the New Cosmopolitanism. Rooted, Feminist and Vernacular Perspectives, New York, NY: Berg, p. 345–357.

Hanitzsch, Thomas (2006), Mapping Journalism Culture: A Theoretical Taxonomy and Case Studies from Indonesia, in: Asian Journal of Communication 16/2, p. 169–186.

Hanitzsch, Thomas, Abby Goodrum, Thorsten Quandt and Thilo von Pape (2013), Interest in Foreign News, in: Akiba A. Cohen (Ed.), Foreign News on Television. Where in the World Is the Global Village?, New York, NY: Peter Lang, p. 171–190.

Hannerz, Ulf (1992), Cultural Complexity. Studies in the Social Organization of Meaning, New York, NY: Columbia University Press.

Hannerz, Ulf (1996), Transnational Connections. Culture, People, Places, London/New York, NY: Routledge.

Hanrath, Jan and Claus Leggewie (2012), Revolution 2.0? Die Bedeutung digitaler Medien für politische Mobilisierung und Protest, in: Tobias Debiel, Jochen Hippler, Michèle Roth and Cornelia Ulbert (Eds.), Globale Trends. Frieden, Entwicklung, Umwelt, Bonn: Bundeszentrale für politische Bildung, p. 157–172.

Hansen, Klaus Peter (2011), Kultur und Kulturwissenschaft. Eine Einführung, Tübingen: Francke (4th ed.).

Harrington, C. Lee and Denise D. Bielby (2007), Global Fandom/Global Fan Studies, in: Jonathan Gray, Cornel Sandvoss and C. Lee Harrington (Eds.), Fandom: Identities and Communities in a Mediated World, New York, NY/London: New York University Press, p. 179–197.

Harrison, Andrew (2010), Business Environment in a Global Context, Oxford/New York, NY: Oxford University Press.

Hartmann, Michael (2016), Die globale Wirtschaftselite: Eine Legende, Frankfurt: Campus.

Harwood, Jake and Howard Giles (Eds.) (2005), Intergroup Communication. Multiple Perspectives, New York, NY: Peter Lang.

Hasebrink, Uwe and Anja Herzog (2009), Mediennutzung im internationalen Vergleich, in: Christiane Matzen and Anja Herzog (Eds.), Internationales Handbuch Medien, Baden-Baden: Nomos, p. 131–155.

Hauriou, Maurice (1965), Die Theorie der Institution und zwei andere Aufsätze von Maurice Hauriou, Berlin: Duncker und Humblot (Orig. 1925).

Häußling, Roger (2005), Netzwerke und Organisationen – konträre oder komplementäre gesellschaftliche Mechanismen, in: Wieland Jäger and Uwe Schimank (Eds.), Organisationsgesellschaft. Facetten und Perspektiven, Wiesbaden: VS Verlag für Sozialwissenschaften, p. 265–286.

Hay, Colin and David Marsh (2000), Demystifying Globalization, Basingstoke: Palgrave Macmillan.

Hayden, Craig (2015), US Public Diplomacy: A Model for Public Diplomacy Strategy in East Asia?, in: Jan Melissen and Yul Sohn (Eds.), Understanding Public Diplomacy in East Asia. Middle Powers in a Troubled Region, Basingstoke/New York, NY: Palgrave Macmillan, p. 211–238.

Hecht, Brent and Darren Gergle (2010), The Tower of Babel Meets Web 2.0: User-Generated Content and its Applications in a Multilingual Context, in: Proceedings of the SIGCHI Conference on Human Factors in Computing Systems, April 10.–15., p. 291–300, http://brenthecht.com/papers/bhecht_chi2010_towerofbabel.pdf.

Heft, Annett (2019), The Panama Papers Investigation and the Scope and Boundaries of its Networked Publics: Cross-border Journalistic Collaboration Driving Transnationally Networked Public Spheres, in: Journal of Applied Journalism and Media Studies 8/2, p. 191–209.

Heft, Annett and Barbara Pfetsch (2012), Conditions for the Emergence of a European Public Sphere. Political Actors and Mass Media under Scrutiny, in: Luciano Morganti and Léonce Bekemans (Eds.), The European Public Sphere. From Critical Thinking to Responsible Action, Brüssel: Peter Lang, p. 147–164.

Heimprecht, Christine (2017), Determinanten der Auslandsberichterstattung: eine Mehrebenenanalyse des internationalen Nachrichtenflusses. Wiesbaden: Springer.

Heins, Volker (2002), Weltbürger und Lokalpatrioten. Eine Einführung in das Thema Nichtregierungsorganisationen, Opladen: Leske und Budrich.

Held, David and Anthony McGrew (Eds.) (2000), The Global Transformations Reader. An Introduction to the Globalization Debate, Cambridge: Polity.

Held, David and Anthony McGrew (Eds.) (2002), Governing Globalization. Power, Authority and Global Governance, Cambridge: Polity.

Hellmann-Grobe, Antje (2000), Dialogprozesse: Gestaltungsansätze für Dialoge im globalisierten Umfeld, Bamberg: Difo-Druck.

Hensby, Alexander and Darren J. O'Byrne (2012), Global Civil Society and the Cosmopolitan Ideal, in: Gerard Delanty (Ed.), The Routledge Handbook of Cosmopolitanism Studies, London/New York, NY: Routledge, p. 387–399.

Hepp, Andreas (1998), Fernsehaneignung und Alltagsgespräche. Fernsehnutzung aus der Perspektive der Cultural Studies, Wiesbaden: VS Verlag für Sozialwissenschaften.

Hepp, Andreas (2008), Globalisierung der Medien und transkulturelle Kommunikation, in: Aus Politik und Zeitgeschichte 39, p. 9–16.

Hepp, Andreas, Michael Brüggemann, Katharina Kleinen-von Königslöw, Swantje Lingenberg and Johanna Möller (2012), Politische Diskurskulturen in Europa. Die Mehrfachsegmentierung europäischer Öffentlichkeit, Wiesbaden: Springer.

Herdin, Thomas and Kurt Luger (2001), Der eroberte Horizont. Tourismus und interkulturelle Kommunikation, in: Aus Politik und Zeitgeschichte B 47, p. 6–17.

Herman, Edward S. and Robert W. McChesney (1997), The Global Media. The New Missionaries of Corporate Capitalism, London/New York, NY: Continuum.

Hirst, Paul and Grahame Thompson (1999), Globalization in Question. The International Economy and the Possibilities of Governance, Cambridge: Polity (2nd ed.).

Hitzler, Ronald (2006), Individualisierte Wissensvorräte. Existenzbastler zwischen posttraditionaler Vergemeinschaftung und postmoderner Sozialpositionierung,

286 Bibliography

in: Dirk Tänzler, Hubert Knoblauch and Hans-Georg Soeffner (Eds.), Zur Kritik der Wissensgesellschaft, Konstanz: UVK, p. 257–276.

Hocking, Brian and Jan Melissen (2015), Diplomacy in the Digital Age, Den Haag: the Netherlands Institute of International Relations Clingendael.

Hofer, Matthias (2012), Zur Wirkung der Nutzung von Online-Medien auf das Sozialkapital, in: Leonard Reinecke and Sabine Trepte (Eds.), Unterhaltung in neuen Medien, Cologne: Herbert von Halem, p. 289–307.

Höflich, Joachim R. (1988), Kommunikationsregeln und interpersonale Kommunikation, in: Communications 14/2, p. 61–84.

Höflich, Joachim R. (1996), Technisch vermittelte interpersonale Kommunikation. Grundlagen, organisatorische Medienverwendung, Konstitution "elektronischer Gemeinschaften", Opladen: Westdeutscher Verlag

Hofstede, Geert, Gert Jan Hofstede and Michael Minkov (2010), Cultures and Organizations: Software of the Mind, New York, NY: McGraw-Hill (3rd, revised and extended ed.).

Höijer, Birgitta (2003), The Discourse of Global Compassion and the Media, in: Nordicom Review 24/2, p. 19–29.

Holbrooke, Richard (2001), Get the Message out, Washington Post, October 28.

Holtom, Brooks C. (2009), International Negotiation, in: David J. Newlands and Mark J. Hooper (Eds.), The Global Business Handbook. The Eight Dimensions of International Management, Farnham/Burlington, VT: Gower, p. 69–86.

Holton, Robert J. (2008), Global Networks, Basingstoke/New York, NY: Palgrave Macmillan.

Høy-Petersen, Nina and Ian Woodward (2018), Working with Difference: Cognitive Schemas, Ethical Cosmopolitanism and Negotiating Cultural Diversity, in: International Sociology 33/6, p. 655–673.

Huck, Simone (2007), Internationale Unternehmenskommunikation, in: Manfred Piwinger and Ansgar Zerfaß (Eds.), Handbuch Unternehmenskommunikation, Wiesbaden: Gabler, p. 891–904.

Hug, Theo (2017), Medien – Generationen – Wissen. Überlegungen zur medienpädagogischen Forschung – dargestellt am Beispiel der Frage nach dem Weltwissen globaler Mediengenerationen, in: MedienPädagogik: Zeitschrift für Theorie und Praxis der Medienbildung 3, p. 13–26.

Humpf, Heike (2008), „First Choice" kommunizieren – Erfahrungen aus einem globalen Veränderungsprozess, in: Egbert Deekeling and Dirk Barghop (Eds.), Kommunikation im Corporate Change: Maßstäbe für eine neue Managementpraxis, Wiesbaden: Gabler, p. 141–157.

Huntington, Samuel P. (1997), The Clash of Civilizations and the Remaking of World Order, New York, NY: Simon & Schuster.

Hutchins, Brett and Libby Lester (2011), Politics, Power and Online Protest in an Age of Environmental Conflict, in: Simon Cottle and Libby Lester (Eds.), Transnational Protests and the Media, New York, NY: Peter Lang, p. 159–171.

Igarashi, Hiroki and Hiro Saito (2014), Cosmopolitanism as Cultural Capital: Exploring the Intersection of Globalization, Education and Stratification, in: Cultural Sociology 8/3, p. 222–239.

Ilius, Jennifer, Felicia Akinjemi and Jürgen Schweikart (2014), Community-Based Tourism als Instrument der Armutsbekämpfung am Beispiel von Fallstudien in Ruanda, in: Zeitschrift für Tourismuswissenschaft 6/2, p. 255–272.

In der Smitten, Susanne (2007), Online-Vergemeinschaftung. Potentiale politischen Handelns im Internet, Munich: Reinhard Fischer.

Innerarity, Daniel (2013), The Democracy of Knowledge, translated by Sandra Kingery, New York, NY: Bloomsbury.

Bibliography **287**

[Internet World Stats] (2017), www.internetworldstats.com/stats7.htm.

[Internet World Stats] (2018), www.internetworldstats.com/stats.htm.

[IOM UN Migration] (2018), Global Migration Indicators 2018, International Organization of Migration (Vereinte Nationen), Berlin: Global Migration Data Analysis Centre (GMDAC).

Iosifidis, Petros (2016), Globalisation and the Re-emergence of the Regulatory State, in: Terry Flew, Petros Iosifidis and Jeanette Steemers (Eds.) Global Media and National Policies. The Return of the State, Basingstoke/New York, NY, p. 16–31.

Ip, Manying and Hang Yin (2016), Cyber China and Evolving Transnational Identities. The Case of New Zealand, in: Wanning Sun and John Sinclair (Eds.), Media and Communication in the Chinese Diaspora. Rethinking Nationalism, London/New York, NY: Routledge, p. 165–184.

Ivanova, Ana (2017), Transnationalisierung von Öffentlichkeiten. Eine länderübergreifende Langzeitanalyse der Klimaberichterstattung in Leitmedien, Wiesbaden: Springer.

Iyengar, Shanto and Adam Simon (1993), News Coverage of the Gulf Crisis and Public Opinion. A Study of Agenda-Setting, Priming and Framing, in: Communication Research 20/3, p. 365–383.

James, Paul (2006), Globalism, Nationalism, Tribalism. Bringing Theory Back In, London: Sage.

Jandt, Fred Edmund (2016), An Introduction to Intercultural Communication. Identities in a Global Community, Thousand Oaks, CA: Sage (8th ed.).

Jankowski, Nicholas W. (2002), Creating Community with Media: History, Theories and Scientific Investigations, in: Leah A. Lievrouw and Sonia Livingstone (Eds.), Handbook of New Media. Social Shaping and Consequences of ICTs, London: Sage, p. 34–49.

Jankowski, Nicholas W. and Renée van Os (2004), Internet-Based Political Discourse: A Case Study of Electronic Democracy in Hoogeveen, in: Peter M. Shane (Ed.), Democracy Online: The Prospects for Political Renewal through the Internet, New York, NY/London: Routledge, p. 181–193.

Jenkins, Henry (2006), Fans, Bloggers, and Gamers. Exploring Participatory Culture, New York, NY/London: New York University Press.

Jenkins, Henry, Sam Ford and Joshua Green (2013), Spreadable Media. Creating Value and Meaning in a Networked Culture, New York, NY/London: New York University Press.

Johnsen, Thomas E., Richard C. Lamming and Christine M. Harland (2008), Inter-Organizational Relationships, Chains, and Networks. A Supply Perspective, in: Steve Cropper, Mark Ebers, Chris Huxham and Peter Smith Ring (Eds.), The Oxford Handbook of Inter-Organizational Relations, Oxford/New York, NY: Oxford University Press, p. 61–89.

Johnson, Erik and John D. McCarthy (2005), The Sequencing of Transnational and National Social Movement Mobilization: The Organizational Mobilization of the Global and U.S. Environmental Movements, in: Donatella della Porta and Sidney Tarrow (Eds.), Transnational Protest and Global Activism, Lanham, MD: Rowman and Littlefield, p. 71–93.

Jonjic, Andrea, Papy Manzanza Kazeka, Daniel Metten and Flora Tietgen (2016), Die Transationale Zivilgesellschaft – Hoffnungsträger in der Global Governance?, Würzburg: University of Würzburg.

Jönsson, Christer (2016), Diplomacy, Communication and Signaling, in: The SAGE Handbook of Diplomacy, Los Angeles, CA: Sage, p. 79–91.

Jönsson, Christer and Karin Aggestam (1999), Trends in Diplomatic Signalling, in: Jan Melissen (Ed.), Innovation in Diplomatic Practice, New York, NY: Macmillan, p. 151–170.

Jönsson, Christer and Martin Hall (2003), Communication: An Essential Aspect of Diplomacy, in: International Studies Perspectives 4/2, p. 195–210.

288 Bibliography

Jönsson, Christer and Martin Hall (2005), The Essence of Diplomacy, Basingstoke/New York, NY: Palgrave Macmillan.

Jordan, Rolf (1997), Migrationssysteme in Global Cities. Arbeitsmigration und Globalisierung in Singapur, Hamburg: LIT.

Joseph, Christina A. and Anandam P. Kavoori (2001), Mediated Resistance: Tourism and the Host Community, in: Annals of Tourism Research 28/4, p. 998–1009.

Jun, Sunkyu, Haksik Lee and James W. Gentry (2005), Effects of Global Cultural Positioning Advertisements, in: Asia Pacific Advances in Consumer Research 6, p. 364–368.

Jungbluth, Eva (2018), Narrating Diaspora across Media, Trier: Wissenschaftlicher Verlag Trier.

Junge, Matthias (2002), Individualisierung, Frankfurt/New York, NY: Campus.

Kaldor, Mary (2003), Global Civil Society. An Answer to War, Cambridge: Polity.

Kalkan, Veli Denizhan (2008), An Overall View of Knowledge Management Challenges for Global Business, in: Business Process Management Journal 14/3, p. 390–400.

Kamalipour, Yahya (Ed.) (1995), The U.S. Media and the Middle East. Image and Perception, Westport, CT/London: Praeger.

Kannengießer, Sigrid (2014), Translokale Ermächtigungskommunikation. Medien, Globalisierung, Frauenorganisationen, Wiesbaden: Springer.

Kapralski, Slawomir (2014), Memory, Identity, and Roma Transnational Nationalism, in: Chiara De Cesari and Ann Rigney (Eds.), Transnational Memory. Circulation, Articulation, Scales, Berlin/Boston, MA: De Gruyter, p. 195–217.

Karim, Karim H. (2018), Migration, Diaspora and Communication, in: Karim H. Karim and Ahmed Al-Rawi (Eds.), Diaspora and Media in Europe, Cham: Palgrave Macmillan, p. 1–23.

Karraker, Meg Wilkes (Ed.) (2013), Global Families, Los Angeles, CA: Sage (2nd ed.).

Kauffeld-Monz, Martina and Michael Fritsch (2008), Who Are the Brokers of Knowledge in Regional Systems of Innovation? A Multi-Actor Network Analysis, Jena Economic Papers Nr. 89, Jena: Max-Planck-Institut für Ökonomik and University of Jena, www.econstor.eu/bitstream/10419/31745/1/590822195.PDF.

Kaufmann, Johan (1996), Conference Diplomacy. An Introductory Analysis, Basingstoke/London: Macmillan (3rd revised ed.).

Kavada, Anastasia (2005), Civil Society Organizations and the Internet: The Case of Amnesty International, Oxfam and the World Development Movement, in: Wilma de Jong, Martin Shaw and Neil Stammers (Eds.), Global Activism, Global Media, London/Ann Arbor, MI: Pluto, p. 208–222.

Kavoori, Anandam P. (2011), Trends in Global Media Reception, in: Daya Kishan Thussu (Ed.), Electronic Empires. Global Media and Local Resistance, London: Arnold, p. 193–207.

Kawashima, Nabuko and Lee Hye-Kyung (Eds.) (2018), Asian Cultural Flows: Cultural Policies, Creative Industries, and Media Consumers, Singapore: Springer.

Kayser, Simone (2005), Die Welt der Globetrotter. Selbsterfahrung durch Fremderfahrung, in: Karlheinz Wöhler (Ed.), Erlebniswelten. Herstellung und Nutzung touristischer Welten, Münster: LIT, p. 97–106.

Keane, John (2003), Global Civil Society, Cambridge: Cambridge University Press

Keck, Margaret E. and Kathryn Sikkink (1998), Activists beyond Borders. Advocacy Networks in International Politics, Ithaca, NY/London: Cornell University Press.

Kefala, Stavroula and Maria Sidiropoulou (2016), Shaping the Glo/cal in Greek-English Tourism Advertising. A Critical Cosmopolitan Perspective, in: Languages in Contrast 16/2, p. 191–212.

Kehr, Eckart (1970), Der Primat der Innenpolitik. Gesammelte Aufsätze zur preußisch-deutschen Sozialgeschichte im 19. und 20. Jahrhundert, Ed. and introduced by Hans-Ulrich Wehler, Frankfurt: Ullstein.

Kendall, Lori (2013), Community and the Internet, in: Mia Consalvo and Charles Ess (Eds.), The Handbook of Internet Studies, Malden, MA/Oxford: Wiley Blackwell, p. 309–325.

Keppler, Angela (1994), Tischgespräche. Über Formen kommunikativer Vergemeinschaftung am Beispiel der Konversation in Familien, Frankfurt: Suhrkamp.

Keup, Marion (2010), Internationale Kompetenz. Erfolgreich kommunizieren und handeln im Global Business, Wiesbaden: Gabler.

Khalil, Ashraf (2001), Stunning Sentence by Egyptian Court Jails Rights Leader, in: SFGate, May 22.

Kiel, Christina (2011), How Transnational Advocacy Networks Mobilize: Applying the Literature on Interest Groups to International Action, in: Josef Korbel Journal of Advanced International Studies 3, p. 77–101.

Kiesch, Patrick (2007), Der Einfluss der Landeskultur auf die internationale Werbung. Grundlagen, Wirkungen, Strategien, Saarbrücken: VDM.

Kieserling, Manfred (Ed.) (2000), Singapur. Metropole im Wandel, Frankfurt: Suhrkamp.

Kim, Tae-Sik (2015), Living in a Transnational Room: Transnational Online Communication by Unaccompanied Korean Adolescents in the United States, in: International Journal of Child, Youth and Family Studies 6/4.1, p. 689–708.

Kim, Youna (2011), Female Cosmopolitanism? Media Talk and Identity of Transnational Asian Women, in: Communication Theory 21/3, p. 279–298.

Kippele, Flavia (1998), Was heißt Individualisierung? Die Antworten soziologischer Klassiker, Wiesbaden: VS Verlag für Sozialwissenschaften.

Kissinger, Henry A. (1982), Years of Upheaval, New York, NY: Simon & Schuster.

Klaus, Elisabeth and Barbara O'Connor (2010), Aushandlungsprozesse im Alltag: Jugendliche Fans von Castingshows, in: Jutta Röser (Ed.), Alltag in den Medien – Medien im Alltag, Wiesbaden: VS Verlag für Sozialwissenschaften, p. 48–72.

Klein, Naomi (2017), No Is Not Enough. Resisting Trump's Shock Politics and Winning the World We Need, Chicago, IL: Haymarket.

Kleinsteuber, Hans J. (2002), Auslandsrundfunk in der Kommunikationspolitik. Zwischen globaler Kommunikation und Dialog der Kulturen, in: Andreas Hepp and Martin Löffelholz (Eds.), Grundlagentexte zur transkulturellen Kommunikation, Konstanz: UVK/UTB, p. 345–372.

Kleinsteuber, Hans J. (2004), Bausteine für einen dialogischen Journalismus. Zur Umsetzung des Prinzips „Dialog der Kulturen", in: Jörgen Klussmann (Ed.), Interkulturelle Kompetenz und Medienpraxis. Ein Handbuch, Frankfurt: Brandes und Apsel, p. 41–68.

Kleinsteuber, Hans and Torsten Rossmann (Eds.) (1994), Europa als Kommunikationsraum. Akteure, Strukturen und Konfliktpotentiale, Opladen: Leske und Budrich.

Klemm, Matthias and Michael Popp (2006), Die Lokalität transnationaler Unternehmen, in: Ursula Mense-Petermann and Gabriele Wagner (Eds.), Transnationale Konzerne. Ein neuer Organisationstyp?, Wiesbaden: VS Verlag für Sozialwissenschaften, p. 189–221.

Kneer, Georg and Armin Nassehi (1997), Niklas Luhmanns Theorie sozialer Systeme. Eine Einführung, Paderborn: Fink/UTB (3rd ed.).

Kneidinger, Bernadette (2010), Facebook und Co. Eine soziologische Analyse von Interaktionsformen in Online Social Networks, Wiesbaden: VS Verlag für Sozialwissenschaften.

Kneidinger, Bernadette (2013), Geopolitische Identitätskonstruktionen in der Netzwerkgesellschaft. Mediale Vermittlung und Wirkung regionaler, nationaler und transnationaler Identitätskonzepte, Wiesbaden: Springer.

Knoblauch, Hubert (1996), Einleitung: Kommunikative Lebenswelten und die Ethnographie einer "geschwätzigen Gesellschaft", in: Hubert Knoblauch (Ed.), Kommunikative Lebenswelten. Zur Ethnographie einer geschwätzigen Gesellschaft, Konstanz: UVK, p. 7–27.

290 Bibliography

Knoblauch, Hubert (2014), Wissenssoziologie, Konstanz/Stuttgart: UVK/UTB (3rd, revised ed.).

Köck, Christoph (2005), Die Konstruktion der Erlebnisgesellschaft. Eine kurze Revision, in: Karlheinz Wöhler (Ed.), Erlebniswelten. Herstellung und Nutzung touristischer Welten, Münster: LIT, p. 3–16.

Köhler, Sina-Mareen (2012), Freunde, Feinde oder Klassenteam? Empirische Rekonstruktionen von Peerbeziehungen an globalen Schulen, Wiesbaden: Springer.

Kolb, Felix (2005), The Impact of Transnational Protest on Social Movement Organisations: Mass Media and the Making of ATTAC Germany, in: Donatella della Porta and Sidney Tarrow (Eds.), Transnational Protest and Global Activism, Lanham, MD: Rowman and Littlefield, p. 95–120.

Konerding, Klaus-Peter (2005), Diskurse, Themen und soziale Topik, in: Claudia Fraas and Michael Klemm (Eds.), Mediendiskurse. Bestandsaufnahme und Perspektiven, Frankfurt: Peter Lang, p. 9–38.

Koopmans, Ruud and Jessica Erbe (2003), Towards a European Public Sphere? Vertical and Horizontal Dimensions of Europeanised Political Communication, Berlin: WZB.

Köpke, Ronald (2002), Zur Kompatibilität von Nord-Kampagnen und Süd-Netzwerken, in: Forschungsjournal Neue Soziale Bewegungen 15/1, p. 62–68.

Kotabe, Masaaki and Kristiaan Helsen (2008), Global Marketing Management, Hoboken, NJ: John Wiley (4th ed.).

Kraemer, Kenneth L., Jason Dedrick, William Foster and Zhang Cheng (2008), Information and Communication Technologies and Inter-Corporate Production Networks: Global Information Technology and Local Guanxi in the Taiwanese Personal Computer Industry, in: Juan J. Palacios (Ed.), Multinational Corporations and the Emerging Network Economy in Asia and the Pacific, London: Routledge, p. 89–113.

Kraidy, Marwan M. (2005), Hybridity, or the Cultural Logic of Globalization, Philadelphia, PA: Temple University Press.

Kron, Thomas (2000), Individualisierung und soziologische Theorie, Wiesbaden: VS Verlag für Sozialwissenschaften.

Kron, Thomas and Martin Horácek (2009), Individualisierung, Bielefeld: Transcript

Kronenburg, Stephan (1998), Diplomatische Kommunikation im Rahmen des Zwei-plus-Vier-Prozesses, in: Siegfried Quandt and Wolfgang Gast (Eds.), Deutschland im Dialog der Kulturen. Medien – Images – Verständigung, Konstanz: UVK, p. 381–392.

Krotz, Friedrich (2001), Die Mediatisierung kommunikativen Handelns. Der Wandel von Alltag und sozialen Beziehungen, Kultur und Gesellschaft durch die Medien, Wiesbaden: Westdeutscher Verlag.

Krotz, Friedrich (2007), Mediatisierung. Fallstudien zum Wandel von Kommunikation, Wiesbaden: VS Verlag für Sozialwissenschaften.

Kruck, Peter (2008), Das Nah-/Fernbild-Phänomen im Spiegel. Medienwirkungstheoretische und soziodemographische Implikationen, Saarbrücken: VDM.

Kruger, Justin, Nicholas Epley, Jason Parker and Zhi-Wen Ng (2005), Egocentrism Over E-Mail: Can We Communicate as Well as We Think?, in: Journal of Personality and Social Psychology 89/6, p. 925–936.

Krüger, Uwe (2013), Meinungsmacht. Der Einfluss von Eliten auf Leitmedien und Alpha-Journalisten: eine kritische Netzwerkanalyse, Cologne: Herbert von Halem.

Kübler, Hans-Dieter (2005), Mythos Wissensgesellschaft: Gesellschaftlicher Wandel zwischen Information, Medien und Wissen. Eine Einführung, Wiesbaden: VS Verlag für Sozialwissenschaften.

Kübler, Hans-Dieter (2011), Interkulturelle Medienkommunikation. Eine Einführung, Wiesbaden: VS Verlag für Sozialwissenschaften.

Kumar, Deepa (2006), Media, War, and Propaganda: Strategies of Information Management During the 2003 Iraq War, in: Communication and Critical/Cultural Studies 3/1, p. 48–69.

Kunczik, Michael (1984), Kommunikation und Gesellschaft. Theorien zur Massenkommunikation, Cologne/Wien: Böhlau.

Kunczik, Michael and Astrid Zipfel (2001), Publizistik. Ein Studienhandbuch, Cologne: Böhlau/UTB.

Kuntsman, Adi (2010), Web of Hate in Diasporic Cyberspaces: The Gaza War in the Russian-Language Blogosphere, in: Media, War and Conflict 3/3, p. 299–313.

Kurbalija, Jovan (1999), Diplomacy in the Age of Information Technology, in: Jan Melissen (Ed.), Innovation in Diplomatic Practice, New York, NY: Macmillan, p. 171–191.

Kyriakidou, Maria (2014), Distant Suffering in Audience Memory: The Moral Hierarchy of Remembering, in: International Journal of Communication 8, p. 1474–1494.

Laguerre, Michael S. (2006), Diaspora, Politics, and Globalization, New York, NY/ Basingstoke: Palgrave Macmillan.

Lahusen, Christian (2002), Transnationale Kampagnen sozialer Bewegungen. Grundzüge einer Typologie, in: Forschungsjournal Neue Soziale Bewegungen 15/1, p. 40–46.

Lamont, Michèle and Sada Aksartova (2002), Ordinary Cosmopolitanisms: Strategies for Bridging Racial Boundaries among Working-Class Men, in: Theory, Culture and Society 19/4, p. 1–25.

Lange, Manfred (2014), Die Praxis des internationalen Marketing. Ein Blick hinter die Kulissen der Globalisierung, Munich: FGM.

Lanier, Jaron (2010), You Are Not a Gadget. A Manifesto, New York, NY: Random House.

Läpple, Dieter (1999), Die Ökonomie einer Metropolregion im Spannungsfeld von Globalisierung und Regionalisierung: Das Beispiel Hamburg, in: Gerhard Fuchs, Gerhard Krauss and Hans-Georg Wolf (Eds.), Die Bindungen der Globalisierung. Interorganisationsbeziehungen im regionalen und globalen Wirtschaftsraum, Marburg: Metropolis, p. 11–47.

Larsen, Jonas (2014), The Tourist Gaze 1.0, 2.0, and 3.0., in: Alan A. Lew (Ed.), The Wiley Blackwell Companion to Tourism, Malden, MA: Wiley, p. 304–313.

Latour, Bruno (2014), Eine neue Soziologie für eine neue Gesellschaft, Frankfurt: Suhrkamp (3rd ed.).

Lee, Hye-Kyung (2014), Transnational Cultural Fandom, in: Linda Duits, Koos Zwaan and Stijn Reijnders (Eds.), The Ashgate Research Companion to Fan Cultures, Farnham/ Burlington, VT: Ashgate, p. 195–207.

Lee, Hyunji (2018), A "Real" Fantasy: Hybridity, Korean Drama, and Pop Cosmopolitans, in: Media, Culture and Society 40/3, p. 365–380.

Leeder, Elaine (2004), The Family in Global Perspective, Thousand Oaks, CA: Sage

Leeds-Hurwitz, Wendy (2015), Intercultural Dialogue, in: Karen Tracy, Todd Sandel and Cornelia Ilie (Eds.), The International Encyclopedia of Language and Social Interaction, New York, NY: Wiley Blackwell, p. 860–868.

le Grignou, Brigitte and Charles Patou (2004), ATTAC(k)ing Expertise: Does the Internet Really Democratize Knowledge?, in: Wim van den Donk, Brian D. Loader, Paul G. Nixon and Dieter Rucht (Eds.), Cyberprotest. New Media, Citizens and Social Movements, London/New York, NY: Routledge, p. 164–179.

Lenz, Ilse (2008), Transnational Social Movement Networks and Transnational Public Spaces: Glocalizing Gender Justice, in: Ludger Pries (Ed.), Rethinking Transnationalism. The Meso-Link of Organizations, Abingdon/New York, NY: Routledge, p. 104–125.

Lerner, Daniel (1967), The Passing of Traditional Society. Modernizing the Middle East, New York, NY: Free Press (4th ed.).

292 Bibliography

Leurs, Koen and Myria Georgiou (2016), Digital Makings of the Cosmopolitan City? Young People's Urban Imaginaries of London, in: International Journal of Communication 10, p. 3689–3709.

Levitt, Theodore (1983), The Globalization of Markets, in: Harvard Business Review 61/3, p. 92–102.

Levy, Orly, Maury A. Peiperl and Karsten Jonsen (2016), Cosmopolitanism in a Globalized World: An Interdisciplinary Perspective, in: Advances in Global Leadership 9, p. 281–323.

Lewis, Dannika (2010), Foreign Correspondents in a Modern World. The Past, Present and Possible Future of Global Journalism, in: The Elon Journal of Undergraduate Research in Communications 1/1, p. 119–127.

Lieberman, Michael D. and Jimmy Lin (2009), You Are Where You Edit: Locating Wikipedia Contributors through Edit Histories, in: Proceedings of the 3rd International AAAI Conference on Weblogs and Social Media, p. 106–113, https://aaai.org/ocs/index.php/ICWSM/09/paper/view/204/420.

Liebes, Tamar and Elihu Katz (1984), Once upon a Time in Dallas, in: Intermedia 12/3, p. 28–32.

Liebes, Tamar and Elihu Katz (1985), Mutual Aid in the Decoding of *Dallas*: Preliminary Notes from a Cross-Cultural Study, in: Phillip Drummond and Richard Paterson (Eds.), Television in Transition, London: British Film Institute, p. 187–198.

Liebes, Tamar and Elihu Katz (1993), The Export of Meaning. Cross-Cultural Readings of *Dallas*, Cambridge: Polity (2nd ed.).

Lim, Merlyna (2009), Muslim Voices in the Bloggosphere. Mosaics of Local-Global Discourses, in: Gerard Goggin and Mark McLelland (Eds.), Internationalizing Internet Studies. Beyond Anglophone Paradigms, New York, NY/London: Routledge, p. 178–195.

Lindell, Johan and Michael Karlsson (2016), Cosmopolitan Journalists? Global Journalism in the Work and Visions of Journalists, in: Journalism Studies 17/7, p. 860–870.

Lingenberg, Swantje (2010), Europäische Publikumsöffentlichkeiten. Ein pragmatischer Ansatz, Wiesbaden: VS Verlag für Sozialwissenschaften.

Linklater, Andrew (1998), The Transformation of Political Community. Ethical Foundations of the Post-Westphalian Era, Cambridge: Polity.

Lippman, Walter (1922), Public Opinion, London: Allen and Unwin.

Littlejohn, Stephen W. and Karen A. Foss (2005), Theories of Human Communication, Southbank/Belmont, CA: Thomson Wadsworth (8th ed.).

Löffelholz, Martin and David Weaver (2008), Global Journalism Research. Theories, Methods, Findings, Future, Malden, MA/Oxford: Blackwell.

Lück, Julia, Hartmut Wessler, Antal Wozniak and Diógenes Lycarião (2016), Networks of Coproduction: How Journalists and Environmental NGOs Create Common Interpretations of the UN Climate Change Conferences, in: International Journal of Press/Politics 21/1, p. 25–47.

Luckmann, Benita (1970), The Small Life-Worlds of Modern Man, in: Social Research 37/4, p. 580–596.

Luger, Kurt (2018), Freizeit – Kommunikation – Tourismus. Annäherung an eine Spektrumswissenschaft, in: Thomas Herdin, Franz Rest and Kurt Luger (Eds.), MedienKulturTourismus. Transkulturelle Befunde über Weltbild und Lebenswelt, Baden-Baden: Nomos, p. 281–293.

Luhmann, Niklas (1970), Öffentliche Meinung, in: Politische Vierteljahresschrift, Special Issue Nr. 2, p. 2–28.

Lützler, Thorsten (2007), Internationalisierung in Global Communications – eine Einführung, in: Claudia Langen, Holger Sievert and Daniela Bell (Eds.), Strategisch kommunizieren und führen. Profil und Qualifizierung für eine transparente und internationale Unternehmenskommunikation, Gütersloh: Bertelsmann Stiftung, p. 127–136 (2nd, extended ed.).

Lyons, Tim (2009), Direct Marketing – A Global Perspective, in: Mark J. Hooper and David Newlands (Eds.), The Global Business Handbook. The Eight Dimensions of International Management, Farnham/Burlington, VT: Gower, p. 277–287.

Machill, Marcel, Markus Beiler and Corinna Fischer (2006), Europa-Themen in Europas Medien – die Debatte um eine europäische Öffentlichkeit. Eine Metaanalyse medieninhaltsanalytischer Studien, in: Wolfgang R. Langenbucher and Michael Latzer (Eds.) Europäische Öffentlichkeit und medialer Wandel. Eine transdisziplinäre Perspektive, Wiesbaden: VS Verlag für Sozialwissenschaften, p. 132–155.

Machin, David and Theo van Leeuwen (2007), Global Media Discourse. A Critical Introduction, London/New York, NY: Routledge.

Maeckelbergh, Marianne (2014), Social Movements and Global Governance, in: Martin Parker, George Cheney, Valérie Fournier and Chris Land (Eds.), The Routledge Companion to Alternative Organization, London: Routledge, p. 345–358.

Mahmod, Jovan (2016), Kurdish Diaspora Online – From Imagined Community to Managing Communities, New York, NY: Palgrave Macmillan.

Maletzke, Gerhard (1966), Interkulturelle Kommunikation und Publizistikwissenschaft, in: Publizistik 11/3, p. 318–331.

Maletzke, Gerhard (1996), Interkulturelle Kommunikation. Zur Interaktion zwischen Menschen verschiedener Kulturen, Wiesbaden: VS Verlag für Sozialwissenschaften.

Mandaville, Peter (2001), Transnational Muslim Politics. Reimagining the Umma, New York, NY: Routledge.

Manning, Peter K. (1992), Organizational Communication, New York, NY: Aldine De Gruyter.

Mansfield, Michael W. (1990), Political Communication in Decision-Making Groups, in: David L. Swanson and Dan Nimmo (Eds.), New Directions in Political Communication. A Resource Book, Newbury Park, CA: Sage, p. 255–304.

[Many Voices – One World] (1980), Many Voices – One World. Communication and Society Today and Tomorrow, London: UNESCO.

Marcinkowski, Frank (1993), Publizistik als autopoietisches System. Politik und Massenmedien: eine systemtheoretische Analyse, Opladen: Westdeutscher Verlag.

Marks, Leonie A., Nicholas Kalaitzandonakes and Srinivasa Konduru (2006), Images of Globalisation in the Mass Media, in: The World Economy 29/5, p. 615–636.

Marres, Noortje (2006), Net-Work is Format Work: Issue Networks and the Sites of Civil Society Politics, in: Jodi Dean, Jon W. Anderson and Geert Lovink (Eds.), Reformatting Politics. Information Technology and Global Civil Society, New York, NY/London: Routledge, p. 3–17.

Martell, Luke (2007), The Third Wave of Globalisation Theory, in: International Studies Review 9/2, p. 173–196.

Marten, Eckhard (1989), Das Deutschlandbild in der amerikanischen Auslandsberichterstattung. Ein kommunikationswissenschaftlicher Beitrag zur Nationenbildforschung, Wiesbaden: DVU.

Martin, Fran (2009), That Global Feeling. Sexual Subjectivities and Imagined Geographies in Chinese-Language Lesbian Cyberspaces, in: Gerard Goggin and Mark McLelland (Eds.), Internationalizing Internet Studies. Beyond Anglophone Paradigms, New York, NY/London: Routledge, p. 285–301.

294 Bibliography

Marx, Karl and Friedrich Engels (1946), Manifest der Kommunistischen Partei, Berlin:Verlag Neuer Weg (Orig. 1848).

Mascio, Antonella (2012), Asynchronous Text-Based Community: Proposals for the Analysis, in: Honglei Li (Ed.),Virtual Community Participation and Motivation: Cross-Disciplinary Theories, Hershey, PA: Information Science Reference, p. 18–36.

Mast, Claudia (2013), Unternehmenskommunikation. Ein Leitfaden, Konstanz: UVK/Lucius/UTB.

Mattoni, Alice (2013), Repertoires of Communication in Social Movements Processes, in: Bart Cammaerts, Alice Mattoni and Patrick McCurdy (Eds.), Mediation and Protest Movements, Bristol/Chicago, IL: Intellect, p. 39–56.

Mau, Steffen (2006), Nationalstaatliche Entgrenzung und kosmopolitische Politisierung, Discussion Papers 2006–012, Berlin: Wissenschaftszentrum Berlin für Sozialforschung GmbH, https://nbn-resolving.org/urn:nbn:de:0168-ssoar-196584.

Mau, Steffen (2007), Transnationale Vergesellschaftung, Die Entgrenzung sozialer Lebenswelten, Frankfurt: Campus.

Mau, Steffen and Jan Mewes (2007),Transnationale soziale Beziehungen. Eine Kartographie der deutschen Bevölkerung, in: Soziale Welt 58/2, p. 203–222.

Maxwell, Claire and Peter Aggleton (2016), Creating Cosmopolitan Subjects: The Role of Families and Private Schools in England, in: Sociology 50/4, p. 780–795.

Mayer, Ruth (2005), Diaspora. Eine kritische Begriffsbestimmung, Bielefeld: Transcript.

Mayrhofer,Wolfgang and Alexander Iellatchitch (Eds.) (2005), Globalisierung und Diffusion, Frankfurt/London: IKO.

McAdam, Doug (1986), Recruitment to High-Risk Activism: the Case of a Freedom Summer, in: American Journal of Sociology 92/1, p. 64–90.

McLachlan, Debra A. (2007), Global Nomads in an International School, in: Journal of Research in International Education 6/2, p. 233–249.

McLuhan, Marshall (1962), The Gutenberg Galaxy. The Making of the Typographic Man, Toronto: University of Toronto Press.

McLuhan, Marshall (1964), Understanding Media. The Extensions of Man, New York, NY: McGraw-Hill.

McMillin, Divya C. (2007), International Media Studies, Malden, MA/Oxford: Blackwell.

McNulty, Yvonne (2015), Till Stress Do Us Part: The Causes and Consequences of Expatriate Divorce, in: Journal of Global Mobility 3/2, p. 106–136.

McPhail, Thomas L. (2010), Global Communication. Theories, Stakeholders, and Trends, Chichester:Wiley Blackwell (3rd ed.).

McQuail, Denis (1994), Mass Communication Theory. An Introduction, London: Sage (3rd ed.).

Mead, Georg H. (1934), Mind, Self and Society. From the Standpoint of a Social Behaviorist, Chicago: University of Chicago Press.

Meckel, Miriam (2001), Die globale Agenda. Kommunikation und Globalisierung, Wiesbaden:Westdeutscher Verlag.

Meerts, Paul W. (1999),The Changing Nature of Diplomatic Negotiation, in: Jan Melissen (Ed.), Innovation in Diplomatic Practice, New York, NY: Macmillan, p. 79–93.

Melissen, Jan (2005), The New Public Diplomacy. Soft Power in International Relations, Basingstoke/New York, NY: Palgrave Macmillan.

Melissen, Jan (2011), Beyond the New Public Diplomacy, Den Haag: Netherlands Institute of International Relations Clingendael.

Mellor, Noha (2014), Religious Media as a Cultural Discourse: The Views of the Arab Diaspora in London, in: Ehab Galal (Ed.), Arab TV-Audiences: Negotiating Religion and Identity, Frankfurt/New York, NY: PL Academic Research, p. 95–113.

Menz, Florian and Heinz K. Stahl (2008), Handbuch Stakeholderkommunikation. Grundlagen, Sprache, Praxisbeispiele, Berlin: Erich Schmidt.

Merritt, Davis "Buzz" (1998), Public Journalism and Public Life. Why Telling the News Is Not Enough, Mahwah, NJ/London: Lawrence Erlbaum.

Merten, Kai and Lucia Krämer (2016), Post-Colonial Studies Meets Media Studies. A Critical Encounter, Bielefeld: Transcript.

Mertens, Stefan and Hedwig de Smaele (Eds.) (2016), Representations of Islam in the News. A Cross-Cultural Analysis, Lanham, MD: Lexington Books.

Merton, Richard K. (1968), Social Theory and Social Structure, New York, NY: Free Press (2nd, extended ed.).

Messner, Dirk (2005), Global Governance: Globalisierung im 21. Jahrhundert gestalten, in: Maria Behrens (Ed.), Globalisierung als politische Herausforderung, Wiesbaden: VS Verlag für Sozialwissenschaften, p. 27–54.

Meuleman, Roza and Mike Savage, (2013), A Field Analysis of Cosmopolitan Taste: Lessons from the Netherlands, in: Cultural Sociology 7/2, p. 230–256.

Michalek, Christian (2009), Die Deutsche Welle im Rahmen von Public Diplomacy. Journalistisches Selbstverständnis und politischer Auftrag des deutschen Auslandsrundfunks, Munich: AVM.

Michalis, Maria (2016), Global Communications and National Policies: The View from the EU, in: Terry Flew, Petros Iosifidis and Jeanette Steemers (Eds.), Global Media and National Policies. The Return of the State, Basingstoke/New York, NY: Palgrave Macmillan, p. 122–138.

Micklethwait, John and Adrian Wooldridge (2000), A Future Perfect. The Challenge and Promise of Globalization, New York, NY: Random House.

[Migration Data Portal] (2017), International Migration Stocks, https://migrationdataportal. org/themes/international-migrant-stocks.

Miike, Yoshitaka (2013), Culture as Text and Culture as Theory. Asiacentricity and its Raison d'être in Intercultural Communication Research, in: Thomas K. Nakayama and Rona Tamiko Halualani (Eds.), The Handbook of Critical Intercultural Communication, Chichester/Malden, MA: Wiley Blackwell, p. 190–215.

Miller, David (Ed.) (2004), Tell Me Lies. Propaganda and Media Distortion in the Attack on Iraq, London/Sterling: Pluto.

Milman, Ady, Arie Reichel and Abraham Pizam (1990), The Impact of Tourism on Ethnic Attitudes: The Israeli-Egyptian Case, in: Journal of Travel Research 16, p. 45–49.

Mitra, Saumava (2017), Local-Global Tensions: Professional Experience, Role Perception and Image Production of Afghan Photojournalists Working for a Global Audience, Dissertation in the Dpt. of Media Studies, The University of Western Ontario, Electronic Thesis and Dissertation Repository, 4949, https://ir.lib.uwo.ca/etd/4949.

Mody, Bella (2010), The Geopolitics of Representation in Foreign News, Lanham, MD: Lexington.

Mohammad-Arif, Aminah (2011), Religion, Diaspora and Globalization, in: Deana Heath and Chandana Mathur (Eds.), Communalism and Globalization in South Asia and its Diaspora, London/New York, NY: Routledge, p. 165–178.

Molz, Jennie Germann (2011), Cosmopolitanism and Consumption, in: Maria Rovisco and Magdalena Nowicka (Eds.), The Ashgate Research Companion to Cosmopolitanism, Farnham/Burlington, VT: Ashgate, p. 33–52.

Morganti, Luciano and Leo van Audenhove (2011), Communication and Information Strategies and Policies for the European Public Sphere. Between Rhetoric and Facts, in: Luciano Morganti and Léonce Bekemans (Eds.), The European Public Sphere. From Critical Thinking to Responsible Action, Brüssel: Peter Lang, p. 121–128.

296 Bibliography

Morisse-Schilbach, Melanie and Anke Peine (2008), Demokratische Außenpolitik und Geheimdienste, Berlin: Dr. Köster.

Morley, David (1986), Family Television. Cultural Power and Domestic Leisure, London/New York, NY: Routledge.

Morley, David (2000), Home Territories. Media, Mobility and Identity, London/New York, NY: Routledge.

Morley, David and Kevin Robins (1995), Global Media. Electronic Landscapes and Cultural Boundaries, London: Routledge.

Morozov, Evgeny (2009), The Brave New World of Slacktivism, in: Foreign Policy 19/5, https://foreignpolicy.com/2009/05/19/the-brave-new-world-of-slacktivism/.

Mouffe, Chantal (2005), On the Political, London/New York, NY: Routledge.

Mrozek, Bodo (2019), Jugend – Pop – Kultur. Eine transnationale Geschichte, Frankfurt: Suhrkamp.

Mueller, John (1970), Presidential Popularity from Truman to Johnson, in: American Political Science Review 64/1, p. 18–34.

Müller, Jan-Werner (2019a), Furcht und Freiheit. Für einen anderen Liberalismus, Berlin: Suhrkamp.

Müller, Jan-Werner (2019b), „Spaltung ist das Geschäftsmodell der Rechten", Gespräch mit dem Autor, Der Spiegel, November 15

Müller, Margret (2017), The World According to Israeli Newspapers. Representations of International Involvement in the Israeli-Palestinian Conflict, Berlin: Frank und Timme.

Müller, Marion G. and Stephanie Geise (2015), Grundlagen der Visuellen Kommunikation, (2nd ed.). Konstanz/Munich: UVK/Lucius/UTB.

Münch, Richard (1998), Globale Dynamik, lokale Lebenswelten. Der schwierige Weg in die Weltgesellschaft, Frankfurt: Suhrkamp.

Munt, Ian (1994), The "Other" Postmodern Tourism: Culture, Travel and the New Middle Classes, in: Theory, Culture and Society 11/3, p. 101–123.

Murray, Craig, Piers Robinson, Peter Goddard and Katy Parry (2011), "Not in our Name": British Press, the Anti-War Movement and the Iraq Crisis 2002–2009, in: Simon Cottle and Libby Lester (Eds.), Transnational Protests and the Media, New York, NY: Peter Lang, p. 59–73.

Mustafa, Imad (2021), Revolution und defekte Transformation in Ägypten. Säkulare Parteien und soziale Bewegungen im „Arabischen Frühling", Bielefeld: Transcript.

Naficy, Hamid (1993), The Making of an Exile Culture. Iranian Television in Los Angeles, Minneapolis, MN/London: University of Minnesota Press.

Nakayama, Thomas K. and Rona Tamiko Halualani (Eds.) (2013), The Handbook of Critical Intercultural Communication, Chichester/Malden, MA: Wiley Blackwell.

Nassehi, Armin (2019), Muster: Theorie der digitalen Gesellschaft, Munich: Beck.

Nayar, Pramod K. (2010), An Introduction to New Media and Cybercultures, Chichester: Wiley Blackwell.

Nederveen Pieterse, Jan (1994), Globalisation as Hybridisation, in: International Sociology 9/2, p. 161–184.

Nederveen Pieterse, Jan (1998), Der Melange-Effekt, in: Ulrich Beck (Ed.), Perspektiven der Weltgesellschaft, Frankfurt: Suhrkamp, p. 87–124.

Neidhardt, Friedhelm (Ed.) (1983a), Gruppensoziologie. Perspektiven und Materialien, Kölner Zeitschrift für Soziologie und Sozialpsychologie, Special Issue Nr. 25, Opladen: Westdeutscher Verlag.

Neidhardt, Friedhelm (1983b), Themen und Thesen zur Gruppensoziologie, in: Friedhelm Neidhardt (Ed.), Gruppensoziologie. Perspektiven und Materialien, Kölner Zeitschrift für Soziologie und Sozialpsychologie, Opladen: Westdeutscher Verlag, p. 12–34.

Neidhardt, Friedhelm (2017), Das innere System sozialer Gruppen, in: Kölner Zeitschrift für Soziologie und Sozialpsychologie 69/1 Supplement, p. 433–454.

Newcomb, Theodore M. (1953), An Approach to the Study of Communicative Acts, in: Psychological Review 60/6, p. 393–404.

Newon, Lisa Ann (2014), Discourses of Connectedness: Globalization, Digital Media, and the Language Community, Dissertation im Fachbereich Anthropology, University of California at Los Angeles, CA, UCLA Electronic Theses and Dissertations, https://escho larship.org/uc/item/9395364s.

Nexon, Daniel (1999), Relations before States: Substance, Process and the Study of World Politics, in: European Journal of International Relations 5/3, p. 291–332.

Nicolai, Alexander and Jantje Halberstadt (2008), Die internationale Diffusion von Geschäftsideen: eine Forschungsagenda, in: Sascha Kraus and Katherine Gundolf (Eds.), Stand und Perspektiven der deutschsprachigen Entrepreneurs- und KMU-Forschung, Stuttgart: Ibidem, p. 269–285.

Niesyto, Johanna (2012), Konsens in zwei Sprachversionen. Wissenskulturen in der en- und de-Wikipedia, in: Dossier Wikipedia/Bundeszentrale für politische Bildung, www.bpb. de/gesellschaft/digitales/wikipedia/145818/konsens-in-zwei-sprachversionen?p=all.

Noack, Paul (1986), Außenpolitik und öffentliche Meinung, in: Wichard Woyke (Ed.), Handwörterbuch Internationale Politik, Leverkusen: Leske und Budrich, p. 42–48.

Noelle-Neumann, Elisabeth (1980), Die Schweigespirale. Öffentliche Meinung – unsere soziale Haut, Munich, Zürich: R. Riper und Co.

Norris, Pippa (1995), The Restless Searchlight: Network News Framing of the Cold War World. Cambridge: Cambridge University Press.

Nowicka, Magdalena (2008), "Do You Really Talk about Emotions on the Phone?": Content of Distance Communication as a Structuring Moment of the Modern World Society, in: Remus Gabriel Anghel, Eva Gerharz and Gilberto Rescher (Eds.), The Making of World Society. Perspectives from Transnational Research, Bielefeld: Transcript, p. 253–274.

Nye, Joseph (1990), Bound to Lead. The Changing Nature of American Power, New York, NY: Basic Books.

Nye, Joseph (2012), China's Soft Power Deficit to Catch up, its Politics Must Unleash the Many Talents of its Civil Society, in: The Wall Street Journal, May 8.

Oelkers, Jürgen (2011), Globalisierung als Herausforderung für den Unterricht: Kompetenzentwicklung und Heterogenität, in: Wolfgang Sander (Ed.), Politische Bildung in der Weltgesellschaft: Herausforderungen, Positionen, Kontroversen. Perspektiven politischer Bildung, Bonn: Bundeszentrale für Politische Bildung, p. 167–189.

Ognyanova, Katherine and Sandra J. Ball-Rokeach (2015), Political Efficacy on the Internet: A Media System Dependency Approach, in: Laura Robinson, Shelia R. Cotton, Jeremy Schulz, Timothy M. Hale and Apryl Williams (Eds.), Communication and Information Technologies Annual: Politics, Participation and Production, Bingley: Emerald Group Publishing, p. 3–27.

Olmsted, Michael S. (1974), Die Kleingruppe. Soziologische und sozialpsychologische Aspekte, Freiburg: Lambertus-Verlag (2nd ed.).

Ong, Jonathan Corpus (2009), The Cosmopolitan Continuum: Locating Cosmopolitanism in Media and Cultural Studies, in: Media, Culture and Society 31/3, p. 449–466.

Ostrowski, Daniel (2010), Die Public Diplomacy der deutschen Auslandsvertretungen weltweit. Theorie und Praxis der deutschen Auslandsöffentlichkeit, Wiesbaden: VS Verlag für Sozialwissenschaften.

Pal, Mahuya and Mohan J. Dutta (2008), Public Relations in a Global Context: The Relevance of Critical Modernism as a Theoretical Lens, in: Journal of Public Relations Research 20/2, p. 159–179.

298 Bibliography

Pan, Shan L. and Dorothy E. Leidner (2003), Bridging Communities of Practice with Information Technology in Pursuit of Global Knowledge Sharing, in: Journal of Strategic Information Systems 12/1, p. 71–88.

Perri 6 (2002), Global Digital Communications and the Prospects for Transnational Regulation, in: David Held and Anthony McGrew (Eds.), Governing Globalization. Power, Authority and Global Governance, Cambridge: Polity, p. 145–170.

Perry, Barbara and Patrik Olsson (2009), Cyberhate: the Globalization of Hate, in: Information and Communications Technology Law 18/2, p. 185–199.

Peters, Bernhard (1994), Der Sinn von Öffentlichkeit, in: Friedhelm Neidhardt (Ed.), Öffentlichkeit, öffentliche Meinung, soziale Bewegungen, Opladen: Westdeutscher Verlag, p. 42–76.

Peters, Michael A. (2014), Radical Openness: Towards a Theory of Co(labor)ation, in: Susanne Maria Weber, Michael Göhlich, Andreas Schröer and Jörg Schwarz (Eds.), Organisation und das Neue. Beiträge der Kommission Organisationspädagogik, Wiesbaden: Springer, p. 65–79.

Petersen, Thomas and Clemens Schwender (Eds.) (2009), Visuelle Stereotype, Cologne: Herbert von Halem.

Petit, Jean-François (2008), Reflections on the Global Civil Society, in: Henri-Claude de Bettignies and François Lépineux (Eds.), Business, Globalization, and the Common Good, Oxford: Peter Lang, p. 277–290.

Pettigrew, Thomas (1998), Intergroup Contact Theory, in: Annual Review of Psychology 49/1, p. 65–85.

Pfetsch, Barbara, Silke Adam and Barbara Eschner (2008), The Contribution of the Press to Europeanization of Public Debates: A Comparative Study of Issue Salience and Conflict Lines of European Integration, in: Journalism 9/4, p. 465–492.

Pianta, Mario (2001), Parallel Summits of Global Civil Society, in: Helmut Anheier, Marlies Glasius and Mary Kaldor (Eds.), Global Civil Society, Oxford: Oxford University Press, p. 169–194.

Pichler, Florian (2011), Cosmopolitanism in a Global Perspective: An International Comparison of Open-Minded Orientations and Identity in Relation to Globalization, in: International Sociology 27/1, p. 21–50.

Pickerill, Jenny, Kevin Gillan and Frank Webster (2011), Scales of Activism: New Media and Transnational Connections in Anti-War Movements, in: Simon Cottle and Libby Lester (Eds.), Transnational Protests and the Media, New York, NY: Peter Lang, p. 41–58.

Pietiläinen, Jukka (2006), Foreign News and Foreign Trade: What Kind of Relationship?, in: International Communication Gazette 68/3, p. 217–228.

Pious, Richard M. (2001), The Cuban Missile Crisis and the Limits of Crisis Management, in: Political Science Quarterly 116, p. 85–105.

Pizam, Abraham, Jafar Jafari and Ady Milman (1991), Influence of Tourism on Attitudes. US Students Visiting USSR, in: Tourism Management March, p. 47–54.

Plattner, Michael (2010), Mobile Eliten in der Internationalisierung multinationaler Unternehmensnetzwerke. Die Rolle hybriden sozialen Kapitals bei der Überbrückung kultureller Distanz, in: Markus Gamper and Linda Reschke (Eds.), Knoten und Kanten. Soziale Netzwerkanalyse in Wirtschafts- und Migrationsforschung, Bielefeld: Transcript, p. 221–243.

Plöger, Andrea (2012), Eine andere Welt sichtbar machen. Mediale Repräsentationen, Strategien und Kommunikation im Weltsozialforum, Dissertation Fachbereich Politik- und Sozialwissenschaften, Free University Berlin, http://timecode-ev.org/wp-content/uploads/2015/05/DISS_Ploeger.pdf.

Pomerantsev, Peter (2015), The Kremlin's Information War, in: Journal of Democracy 26/4, p. 40–50.

Poole, Elizabeth and John E. Richardson (Eds.) (2006), Muslims in the News Media, London/New York, NY: I.B. Tauris.

Postmes, Tom and Nancy Baym (2005), Intergroup Dimensions of the Internet, in: Jake Harwood and Howard Giles (Eds.), Intergroup Communication. Multiple Perspectives, New York, NY: Peter Lang, p. 214–238.

Powlick, Philip J. and Andrew Z. Katz (1998), Defining the American Public Opinion/Foreign Policy Nexus, in: Mershon International Studies Review 42 (Issue Supplement 1), p. 29–61.

Prantl, Heribert (2016), In Europa ist Anti-Pfingsten angebrochen, in: Süddeutsche Zeitung, May 13.

Pries, Ludger (2008a), Die Transnationalisierung der sozialen Welt. Sozialräume jenseits von Nationalgesellschaften, Frankfurt: Suhrkamp.

Pries, Ludger (2008b), Transnational Societal Spaces: which Units of Analysis, Reference, Measurement?, in: Ludger Pries (Ed.), Rethinking Transnationalism. The Meso-Link of Organizations, Abingdon/New York, NY: Routledge, p. 1–20.

Pries, Ludger (2015), Transnationalisierung sozialer Ungleichheit und gerechte Migration, in: Steffen Mau and Nadine M. Schöneck-Voß (Eds.), (Un-)Gerechte (Un-)Gleichheiten, Berlin: Suhrkamp, p. 175–182.

Putnam, Robert D. (2000), Bowling Alone. The Collapse and Revival of American Community, New York, NY: Simon & Schuster.

Quandt, Siegfried and Wolfgang Gast (Eds.) (1998), Deutschland im Dialog der Kulturen. Medien – Images – Verständigung, Konstanz: UVK.

Quayson, Ato and Girish Daswani (Eds.) (2013), A Companion to Diaspora and Transnationalism, Chichester: Wiley Blackwell.

Quelch, John A. and Katherine E. Jocz (2012), All Business is Local. Why Place Matters more than ever in a Global, Virtual World, New York, NY: Portfolio/Penguin.

Ramadan, Dunja (2018), Dieselbe Marke, andere Botschaft, in: Süddeutsche Zeitung, February 6.

Ratavaara, Nina (2013), Do We Need Pan-European Media?, Munich: Grin.

Rathje, Stefanie (2008), Von U-Bahn-Helden, Skateboard-Kapitalisten und Partyflüchtern: Fallstudie zur internationalen Werbestandardisierbarkeit, in: Gudrun Held and Sylvia Bendel (Eds.), Werbung grenzenlos. Multimodale Werbetexte im interkulturellen Vergleich, Frankfurt: Peter Lang, p. 37–55.

Rawnsley, Gary (1999), Monitored Broadcasts and Diplomacy, in: Jan Melissen (Ed.), Innovation in Diplomatic Practice, New York, NY: Macmillan, p. 135–150.

Reckwitz, Andreas (2019), Das Ende der Illusionen. Politik, Ökonomie und Kultur in der Spätmoderne, Berlin: Suhrkamp.

Reese, Stephen D. (2015), Globalization of Mediated Spaces: The Case of Transnational Environmentalism in China, in: International Journal of Communication 9, p. 2263–2281.

Reinders, Heinz (2004), Entstehungskontexte interethnischer Freundschaften in der Adoleszenz, in: Zeitschrift für Erziehungswissenschaft 7/1, p. 121–145.

Reitan, Ruth (2013), Theorizing and Engaging the Global Movement: From Anti-Globalization to Global Democratization, in: Ruth Reitan (Ed.), Global Movement, London/New York, NY: Routledge, p. 1–13.

Renneberg, Verena (2011), Auslandskorrespondenz im globalen Zeitalter. Herausforderungen der modernen TV-Auslandsberichterstattung, Wiesbaden: Springer.

300 Bibliography

Requejo, William Hernández and John L. Graham (2008), Global Negotiation. The New Rules, Basingstoke/New York, NY: Palgrave Macmillan.

Rheingold, Howard (2000), The Virtual Community. Homesteading on the Electronic Frontier, Cambridge, MA/London: MIT (revised ed.).

Richter, Emanuel (1990), Weltgesellschaft und Weltgemeinschaft. Begriffsverwirrung und Klärungsversuche, in: Politische Vierteljahresschrift 31/2, p. 275–279.

Richter, Ingo K., Sabine Berking and Ralf Müller-Schmid (2006), Introduction, in: Ingo K. Richter, Sabine Berking and Ralf Müller-Schmid (Eds.), Building a Transnational Civil Society. Global Issues and Actors, London: Palgrave Macmillan, p. 1–28.

Riegert, Kristina (2011), Pondering the Future of Foreign News on National Television, in: International Journal of Communication 5, p. 1567–1585.

Riley, Patricia and Peter R. Monge (1998), Introduction: Communication in the Global Community, in: Communication Research 25/4, p. 355–358.

Rinke, Bernhard and Ulrich Schneckener (2013), Informalisierung der Weltpolitik? Globales Regieren durch Clubs, in: Tobias Diebel, Jochen Hippler, Michèle Roth and Cornelia Ulbert (Eds.), Globale Trends. Frieden, Entwicklung, Umwelt (Stiftung Entwicklung und Frieden), Bonn: Bundeszentrale für politische Bildung, p. 27–42.

Risse, Thomas and Kathryn Sikkink (1999), The Socialization of International Human Rights Norms into Domestic Practices, in: Thomas Risse, Kathryn Sikkink and Stephen C. Ropp (Eds.), The Power of Human Rights: International Norms and Domestic Change, Cambridge: Cambridge University Press, p. 1–38.

Ritzer, George (2010), Globalization: A Basic Text, Malden, MA: Wiley Blackwell.

Robertson, Alexa (2010), Mediated Cosmopolitanism. The World of Television News, Cambridge/Malden, MA: Polity.

Robertson, Alexa (2015), Global News: Reporting Conflicts and Cosmopolitanism, New York, NY: Peter Lang.

Robertson, Roland (1995), Glocalization: Time-Space and Homogeneity and Heterogeneity, in: Mike Featherstone, Scott Lash and Roland Robertson (Eds.), Global Modernities, London/Thousand Oaks, CA: Sage, p. 25–44.

Robins, Kevin (2003), Beyond Imagined Community? Transnational Media and Turkish Migrants in Europe, in: Stig Hjavard (Ed.), Media in a Globalized Society, Copenhagen: Museum Tusculanum Press/University of Copenhagen, p. 187–205.

Robins, Kevin and Asu Aksoy (2015), Transnationalism, Migration and the Challenge to Europe: The Enlargement of Meaning, London/New York, NY: Routledge.

Robinson, Piers (2002), The CNN Effect. The Myth of News, Foreign Policy and Intervention, London/New York, NY: Routledge.

Rodgers, Jayne (2003), Spatializing International Activism. Genetically Modified Foods on the Internet, in: François Debris and Cynthia Weber (Eds.), Rituals of Mediation. International Politics and Social Meaning, Minneapolis, MN/London: University of Minneapolis Press, p. 30–48.

Rofe, J. Simon (2016), Diplomatic Practice, in: Alison R. Holmes and J. Simon Rofe (Eds.), Global Diplomacy: Theories, Types, and Models, Boulder, CL: Westview, p. 19–54.

Rogers, Everett M. (1999), Georg Simmel's Concept of the Stranger and Intercultural Communication Research, in: Communication Theory 9/1, p. 58–74.

Rogers, Everett M. (2003), Diffusion of Innovations, New York, NY: Free Press (5th ed.).

Rojecki, Andrew (2011), Leaderless Crowds, Self-Organizing Publics, and Virtual Masses: The New Media Politics of Dissent, in: Simon Cottle and Libby Lester (Eds.), Transnational Protests and the Media, New York, NY: Peter Lang, p. 87–97.

Roose, Michael (2012), Greenpeace, Social Media, and the Possibility of Global Deliberation on the Environment, in: Indiana Journal of Global Legal Studies 19/1, p. 347–364.

Rosecrance, Richard (1973), International Relations: Peace or War?, New York, NY: McGraw-Hill.

Rosen, Jay (1999), What Are Journalists for?, New Haven, CT/London: Yale University Press.

Rosenau, James N. (1967), Domestic Sources of Foreign Policy, New York, NY: Free Press.

Rosenau, James N. (2007), Three Steps toward a Viable Theory of Globalization, in: Ino Rossi (Ed.), Frontiers of Globalization Research. Theoretical and Methodological Approaches, New York, NY: Springer, p. 307–316.

Rosenberg, Justin (2005), Globalization Theory: A Post Mortem, in: International Politics 42/1, p. 2–74.

Rubin, Jeffrey Z. (1983), Dynamics of Third Party Intervention. Kissinger in the Middle East, New York, NY: Praeger.

Rucht, Dieter (2002a), Herausforderungen für die globalisierungskritischen Bewegungen, in: Forschungsjournal Neue Soziale Bewegungen 15/1, p. 16–21.

Rucht, Dieter (2002b), The EU as a Target of Political Mobilization: Is There a Europeanization of Conflict?, in: Richard Balme, Didier Chabanet and Vincent Wright (Eds.), L'action collective en Europe, Paris: Presses de Sciences Po, p. 163–194.

Rucht, Dieter (2013), Protest Movements and their Media Usages, in: Bart Cammaerts, Alice Mattoni and Patrick McCurdy (Eds.), Mediation and Protest Movements, Bristol/ Chicago, IL: Intellect, p. 251–268.

Rugman, Alan (2002), The End of Globalization, London: Random House.

Rühl, Manfred (1979), Die Zeitungsredaktion als organisiertes soziales System, Fribourg: Universitätsverlag (2nd, extended ed.).

Rühl, Manfred (1980), Journalismus und Gesellschaft. Bestandsaufnahme und Theorie-entwurf, Mainz: von Hase und Koehler.

Rühl, Manfred (2006), Globalisierung der Kommunikationswissenschaft. Denkprämissen – Schlüsselbegriffe – Theoriearchitektur, in: Publizistik 51/3, p. 349–369.

Ruiz, Pollyanna (2005), From the Margins to the Mainstream, in: Wilma de Jong, Martin Shaw and Neil Stammers (Eds.), Global Activism, Global Media, London/Ann Arbor, MI: Pluto, p. 194–207.

Rupp, George (2006), Globalization Challenged. Conviction, Conflict, Community, New York, NY: Columbia University Press.

Russ-Mohl, Stephan (2017), Die informierte Gesellschaft und ihre Feinde. Warum die Digitalisierung unsere Demokratie gefährdet, Cologne: Herbert von Halem.

Sakr, Naomi (2001), Satellite Realms. Transnational Television, Globalization and the Middle East, London/New York, NY: I.B. Tauris.

Samovar, Larry A., Richard E. Porter and Edwin R. McDaniel (2015), Communication between Cultures, Boston, MA: Wadsworth Cengage Learning (9th ed.).

Samuel-Azran, Tal (2009), Counterflows and Counterpublics: The Al-Jazeera Effect on Western Discourse, in: The Journal of International Communication 15/1, p. 56–73.

Saner, Raymond and Lichia Yiu (2008), Business – Government – NGO Relations: Their Impact on Global Economic Governance, in: Andrew F. Cooper and Brian Hocking (Eds.), Global Governance and Diplomacy. Worlds Apart?, Basingstoke/New York, NY: Palgrave Macmillan, p. 85–103.

Sarısakaloğlu, Aynur (2019), Europas Identität und die Türkei. Eine länderübergreifende Framing-Analyse der Mediendebatte über den EU-Beitritt der Türkei, Bielefeld: Transcript.

Sassen, Saskia (2001), The Global City. New York, NY: Princeton University Press.

Sassen, Saskia (Ed.) (2002), Global Networks, Linked Cities, New York, NY: Routledge.

Sassen, Saskia (2004), A Global City, in: Charles Madigan (Ed.), Global Chicago, Urbana, IL: University of Illinois Press, p. 15–34.

302 Bibliography

Sassen, Saskia (2005), Electronic Markets and Activist Networks: The Weight of Social Logics in Digital Formation, in: Robert Latham and Saskia Sassen (Eds.), Digital Formations. IT and New Architectures in the Global Realm, Princeton, NJ/Oxford: Princeton University Press, p. 54–88.

Sassen, Saskia (2007), Theoretical and Empirical Elements in the Study of Globalization, in: Ino Rossi (Ed.), Frontiers of Globalization Research. Theoretical and Methodological Approaches, New York, NY: Springer, p. 287–306.

Saucedo Añez, Carolina (2014), Lateinamerikanische Medien in Deutschland. Medienkonsum und -produktion von Migranten, Berlin: Frank und Timme.

Saunders, Robert A. (2011), Ethnopolitics in Cyberspace. The Internet, Minority Nationalism, and the Web of Identity, Lanham, MD: Rowman and Littlefield.

Schade, Henriette (2018), Soziale Bewegungen in der Mediengesellschaft. Kommunikation als Schlüsselkonzept einer Rahmentheorie sozialer Bewegungen, Wiesbaden: Springer.

Schäfers, Bernhard (Ed.) (1994a), Einführung in die Gruppensoziologie. Geschichte, Theorien, Analysen, Heidelberg/Wiesbaden: Quelle und Meyer (2nd ed.).

Schäfers, Bernhard (1994b), Entwicklung der Gruppensoziologie und Eigenständigkeit der Gruppe als Sozialgebilde, in: Bernhard Schäfers (Ed.), Einführung in die Gruppensoziologie. Geschichte, Theorien, Analysen, Heidelberg/Wiesbaden: Quelle und Meyer, p. 19–36 (2nd ed.).

Schäfers, Bernhard (2013), Felder des Sozialen, in: Bernhard Schäfers (Ed.), Einführung in die Soziologie, Wiesbaden: Springer, p. 95–147.

Scheerer, Lars (2011), Die Ambivalenz des deutschen Kolonialerbes in Namibia aus der Sicht deutscher Reiseunternehmer, Bachelorarbeit, Geographisches Institut, University of Bonn, www.tourism-watch.de/system/files/migrated/Scheerer_Kolonialerbe_Namibia_2011.pdf.

Schejter, Amit, Orit Ben-Harush and Noam Tirosh (2017), The Effect of the Transformation in Digital Media on the Digital Divide, in: Mike Friedrichsen and Yahya Kamalipour (Eds.), Digital Transformation in Journalism and News Media. Media Management, Media Convergence and Globalization, Cham: Springer, p. 235–246.

Schenk, Susan (2009), Das Islambild im internationalen Fernsehen. Ein Vergleich der Nachrichtensender Al Jazeera English, BBC World und CNN International, Berlin: Frank und Timme.

Scheunpflug, Annette (2001), Die globale Perspektive einer Bildung für nachhaltige Entwicklung, in: Otto Herz, Hansjörg Seybold and Gottfried Strobl (Eds.), Bildung für nachhaltige Entwicklung, Wiesbaden: VS Verlag für Sozialwissenschaften, p. 87–99.

Schiffer, Sabine (2005), Die Darstellung des Islam in den Medien. Sprache, Bilder, Suggestionen: Eine Auswahl von Techniken und Beispielen, Würzburg: Ergon.

Schlieker, Christian and Kai Lehmann (2005), Verknüpft, Verknüpfter, Wikis, in: Kai Lehmann and Michael Schetsche (Eds.), Die Google-Gesellschaft. Vom digitalen Wandel des Wissens, Bielefeld: Transcript, p. 253–262.

Schmid, Stefan, Iris Bäurle and Michael Kutschker (1999), Ausländische Tochtergesellschaften als Kompetenzzentren – Ergebnisse einer empirischen Untersuchung, in: Michael Kutschker (Ed.), Management verteilter Kompetenzen in multinationalen Unternehmen, Wiesbaden: Gabler, p. 99–126.

Schmidt, Axel (2004), Doing Peer-Group: Die interaktive Konstitution jugendlicher Gruppenpraxis, Frankfurt: Peter Lang.

Schmidt, Jasmina (2017), Konstruktiver Journalismus – ein Ansatz zur kosmopolitischen Vermittlung fernen Leids?, in: Global Media Journal (Deutsche Edition) 7/2, www.db-thueringen.de/servlets/MCRFileNodeServlet/dbt_derivate_00039841/GMJ14_Schmidt_final.pdf.

Bibliography **303**

Schmidt, Wallace V., Roger N. Conaway, Susan S. Easton and William J. Wardrope (2007), Communicating Globally. Intercultural Communication and International Business, Los Angeles, CA: Sage.

Schmitt, Caroline and Asta Vonderau (Eds.) (2014), Transnationalität und Öffentlichkeit. Interdisziplinäre Perspektiven, Bielefeld: Transcript.

Schmitz, Hans Peter (2001), Menschenrechtswächter: partielle Midlife-Crisis, in: Vereinte Nationen 1, www.dgvn.de/fileadmin/publications/PDFs/Zeitschrift_VN/VN_2001/Heft_1_2001/03_Beitrag_Schmitz_VN_1-01.pdf

Schuldt, Monique (2010), Global Advertising. Internationale Wirtschaftsstrategien im Vergleich, Saarbrücken: VDM.

Schuller, Tom (2007), Reflections on the Use of Social Capital, in: Review of Social Economy 65/1, p. 11–28.

Schultz, Tanjev (2006), Geschwätz oder Diskurs? Die Rationalität politischer Talkshows im Fernsehen, Cologne: Herbert von Halem.

Schumann, Christina, Sven Jöckel and Jens Wolling (2009), Wertorientierungen in Gilden, Clans und Allies. Eine interkulturelle Analyse über den Einfluss jugendlicher Wertvorstellungen auf Spielergemeinschaften in Ungarn und Deutschland, in: Medien Journal 33/2, p. 21–34.

Schuppert, Gunnar Folke (2015), Wege in die moderne Welt. Globalisierung von Staatlichkeit als Kommunikationsgeschichte, Frankfurt/New York, NY: Campus.

Schütz, Alfred (1951), Making Music Together. A Study in Social Relationship, in: Social Research 18/1, p. 76–97.

Schütz, Alfred (1972), Strukturen der Lebenswelt, in: Alfred Schütz and Ilse Schütz (Eds.), Gesammelte Aufsätze III, Dordrecht: Springer, p. 153–170.

Schütz, Alfred and Thomas Luckmann (2003), Strukturen der Lebenswelt, Konstanz: UVK/UTB.

Schützeichel, Rainer (2004), Soziologische Kommunikationstheorien, Konstanz: UVK/UTB.

Schwarz, Andreas and Alexander Fritsch (2014), Communicating on Behalf of Global Civil Society: Management and Coordination of Public Relations in International Nongovernmental Organizations, in: Journal of Public Relations Research 26/2, p. 161–183.

Schwinn, Thomas (2006), Die Vielfalt und die Einheit der Moderne – Perspektiven und Probleme eines Forschungsprogramms, in: Thomas Schwinn (Ed.), Die Vielfalt und die Einheit der Moderne. Kultur- und strukturvergleichende Analysen, Wiesbaden: VS Verlag für Sozialwissenschaften, p. 7–34.

Scott, Martin (2014), The Mediation of Distant Suffering. An Empirical Contribution beyond Television News Texts, in: Media, Culture and Society 36/1, p. 3–19.

Seib, Philip (2012), AJE in the World, in: Philip Seib (Ed.), Al Jazeera English. Global News in a Changing World, New York, NY/Houndmills: Palgrave Macmillan, p. 1–4.

Sengupta, Anasuya, Adele Vrana and Siko Bouterse (2018), Whose Knowledge? Paper presented at Decolonizing the Internet Conference, February 27, https://whoseknowledge.org/decolonizing-the-internet-conference/.

Sezgin, Hilal (Ed.) (2011), Manifest der Vielen. Deutschland erfindet sich neu, Berlin: Blumenbar.

Shaheen, Jack G. (2009), Reel Bad Arabs: How Hollywood Vilifies a People, Northampton, MA: Olive Branch Press.

Shareef, Mahmud Akhter, Yogesh Kumar Dwivedi, Michael D. Williams and Nitish Singh (2009), Proliferation of the Internet Economy: E-Commerce for Global Adoption, Resistance, and Cultural Evolution, Hershey, PA/New York, NY: Information Science Reference.

304 Bibliography

Shipman, Alan (2002), The Globalization Myth, Cambridge: Icon.

Sievert, Holger (1998), Europäischer Journalismus: Theorie und Empirie aktueller Medienkommunikation in der Europäischen Union, Wiesbaden: Springer.

Sikkink, Kathryn (2005), Patterns of Dynamic Multilevel Governance and the Insider-Outsider Coalition, in: Donatella della Porta and Sidney Tarrow (Eds.), Transnational Protest and Global Activism, Lanham, MD: Rowman and Littlefield, p. 151–173.

Silverstone, Roger (1998), Television and Everyday Life: Towards an Anthropology of the Television Audience, in: Roger Dickinson, Ramaswami Harindranath and Olga Linné (Eds.), Approaches to Audiences. A Reader, New York, NY/London: Oxford University Press/Arnold, p. 245–256.

Silverstone, Roger (2007), Media and Morality. On the Rise of the Mediapolis, Cambridge: Polity.

Simonite, Tom (2013), The Decline of Wikipedia, in: MIT Technology Review, October 22, www.technologyreview.com/s/520446/the-decline-of-wikipedia/

Sinclair, John, Elizabeth Jacka and Stuart Cunningham (Eds.) (1996), New Patterns in Global Television. Peripheral Vision, Oxford: Oxford University Press.

Singh, Amritjit (2011), Afterword: Against the Grain. Diaspora Studies at the Crossroads, in: Robert E. Field and Parmita Kapadia (Eds.), Transforming Diaspora. Communities beyond National Boundaries, Madison, WI/Taeneck, NJ: Fairleigh Dickinson University Press, p. 153–166.

Singh, Nitish, Kevin Lehnert and Kathleen Bostick (2012), Global Social Media Usage. Insight into Reaching Consumers Worldwide, in: Thunderbird International Business Review 54/5, p. 683–700.

Sklair, Leslie (1995), Sociology of the Global System, London: Prentice Hall/Harvester Wheatsheaf (2nd ed.).

Skrbis, Zlatko, Ian Woodward and Clive Bean (2014), Seeds of Cosmopolitan Future? Young People and Their Aspirations for Future Mobility, in: Journal of Youth Studies 17/5, p. 614–625.

Smith, Kenwyn and David Berg (1997), Cross-Cultural Groups at Work, in: European Management Journal 15/1, p. 8–15.

Snee, Helen (2016), A Cosmopolitan Journey? Difference, Distinction and Identity Work in Gap Year Travel, London/New York, NY: Routledge.

Snow, Nancy and Philip M. Taylor (Eds.) (2009), Routledge Handbook of Public Diplomacy, New York, NY: Routledge.

Sohn, Yul (2015), Regionalization, Regionalism, and Double-Edged Public Diplomacy in East Asia, in: Jan Melissen and Yul Sohn (Eds.), Understanding Public Diplomacy in East Asia. Middle Powers in a Troubled Region, Basingstoke/New York, NY: Palgrave Macmillan, p. 11–30.

Sommer, Stephanie (2015), Postsozialistische Biografien und globalisierte Lebensentwürfe. Mobile Bildungseliten aus Sibirien, Bielefeld: Transcript.

Sooknanan, Prahalad (2011), Intercultural Communication in the Global Workplace, in: Fay Patel, Mingsheng Li and Prahalad Sooknanan (Eds.), Intercultural Communication. Building a Global Community, Los Angeles, CA: Sage, p. 90–112.

Sparks, Colin (1998), Is There a Global Public Sphere?, in: Daya K. Thussu (Ed.), Electronic Empires. Global Media and Local Resistance, London: Arnold, p. 108–124.

Sparks, Colin (2000), The Global, the Local and the Public Sphere, in: Georgette Wang, Jan Servaes and Anura Goonasekera (Eds.), The New Communications Landscape. Demystifying Media Globalization, London/New York, NY: Routledge, p. 74–95.

Bibliography **305**

Sparks, Colin (2016), Global Integration, State Policy and the Media, in: Terry Flew, Petros Iosifidis and Jeanette Steemers (Eds.), Global Media and National Policies. The Return of the State, Basingstoke/New York, NY: Palgrave Macmillan, p. 49–74.

Spencer, Jennifer W. (2003), Global Gatekeeping, Representation, and Network Structure: a Longitudinal Analysis of Regional and Global Knowledge-Diffusion Networks, in: Journal of International Business Studies 34, p. 428–442.

Spiegel, Albert (2002), Public Diplomacy – the German View, http://media.leeds.ac.uk/papers/vp0101c1.html.

Splichal, Slavko (2012), Transnationalization of the Public Sphere and the Fate of the Public, New York, NY: Hampton.

Springer, Reiner (2007), Globalisierung als Herausforderung für das internationale Marketing, in: Reinhard Moser and Josef Mugler (Eds.), Die Herausforderung der globalen Vernetzung, Wien: Wirtschaftskammer Österreich, p. 20–34.

Sreberny, Annabelle (2000), Feministischer Internationalismus: Zur Imagination und Konstruktion globaler Zivilgesellschaft, in: Hauke Brunkhorst and Matthias Kettner (Eds.), Globalisierung und Demokratie. Wirtschaft, Recht, Medien, Frankfurt: Suhrkamp, p. 289–309.

Sreberny-Mohammadi, Annabelle, Kaarle Nordenstreng, Robert Stevenson and Frank Ugboajah (Eds.) (1985), Foreign News in the Media: International Reporting in 29 Countries. Final Report Undertaken for UNESCO by the International Association for Mass Communication Research, Paris: UNESCO.

Srinivasan, Ramesh (2017), Whose Global Village? Rethinking How Technology Shapes Our World, New York, NY: New York University Press.

Stammers, Neil and Catherine Eschle (2005), Social Movements and Global Activism, in: Wilma de Jong, Martin Shaw and Neil Stammers (Eds.), Global Activism, Global Media, London/Ann Arbor, MI: Pluto, p. 50–67.

Stanley, J. Woody, Christopher Weare and Juliet Musso (2004), Participation, Deliberative Democracy, and the Internet: Lessons from the National Forum on Commercial Vehicle Safety, in: Peter M. Shane (Ed.), Democracy Online. The Prospects for Political Renewal through the Internet, New York, NY/London: Routledge, p. 167–179.

Stanton, Richard C. (2007), All News is Local. The Failure of the Media to Reflect World Events in a Globalized Age, Jefferson, NC/London: McFarland.

[Statistisches Bundesamt (Destatis)] (2019), Bevölkerung und Erwerbstätigkeit. Bevölkerung mit Migrationshintergrund. Ergebnisse des Mikrozensus 2018, Fachserie 1, Reihe 2.2, www.destatis.de/DE/Presse/Pressemitteilungen/2019/08/PD19_314_12511.html.

Steffans, Dagmar (2000), Globalisierung und Informationsgesellschaft, in: Christian Stolorz and Reinhard Göhner (Eds.), Globalisierung und Informationsgesellschaft. Herausforderungen unserer Zeit, Münster: Agenda, p. 9–19.

Stegbauer, Christian (2001), Grenzen virtueller Gemeinschaft. Strukturen internetbasierter Kommunikationsforen, Wiesbaden: Westdeutscher Verlag.

Stegbauer, Christian and Alexander Rausch (2006), Strukturalistische Internetforschung. Netzwerkanalysen internetbasierter Kommunikationsräume, Wiesbaden: VS Verlag für Sozialwissenschaften.

Stegemann, Patrick and Sören Musyal (2020), Die rechte Mobilmachung: Wie radikale Netzaktivisten die Demokratie angreifen, Berlin: Econ.

Stein, Laura (2011), Social Movement Web Use in Theory and Practice, in: Miyase Christensen, André Jansson and Christian Christensen (Eds.), Online Territories. Globalization, Mediated Practice and Social Space, New York, NY: Peter Lang, p. 147–170.

306 Bibliography

Stohl, Cynthia (2001), Globalizing Organizational Communication, in: Fredric M. Jablin and Linda L. Putnam (Eds.), The New Handbook of Organizational Communication. Advances in Theory, Research, and Methods, Thousand Oaks, CA: Sage, p. 323–375.

Stone, John and Polly Rizova (2014), Racial Conflict in Global Society, Cambridge/Malden, MA: Polity.

Stors, Natalie (2014), Explorer-Touristen im Städtetourismus. Ein Charakterisierungsversuch unterschiedlicher Besuchergruppen in Kopenhagen, in: Zeitschrift für Tourismuswissenschaft 6/1, p. 97–105.

Straubhaar, Joseph D. (2003), Choosing National TV: Cultural Capital, Language, and Cultural Proximity in Brazil, in: Michael G. Elasmar (Ed.), The Impact of International Television. A Paradigm Shift, Mahwah, NJ: Erlbaum, p. 77–107.

Straubhaar, Joseph D. (2007), World Television. From Global to Local, Los Angeles, CA: Sage.

Straubhaar, Joseph D. (2014), Mapping "Global" in Global Communication and Media Studies, in: Karin G. Wilkins, Joseph D. Straubhaar and Shanti Kumar (Eds.), Global Communication. New Agendas in Communication, London/New York, NY: Routledge, p. 10–34.

Straubhaar, Joseph D. and Antonio C. La Pastina (2005), Multiple Proximities between Television Genres and Audiences. The Schism between Telenovelas' Global Distribution and Local Consumption, in: Gazette: The International Journal for Communication Studies 67/3, p. 271–288.

Stromer-Galley, Jennifer and Alexis Wichowski (2013), Political Discussion Online, in: Mia Consalvo and Charles Ess (Eds.), The Handbook of Internet Studies, Chichester: Wiley Blackwell, p. 168–187.

Strübel, Michael (2008), Globalisierung und Global Governance: Realität und Mythos, in: Michael Strübel (Ed.), Politische Theorie und Staatswissenschaften, Berlin: De Gruyter, p. 49–66.

Sundermeier, Theo (1996), Den Fremden verstehen. Eine praktische Hermeneutik, Göttingen: Vandenhoeck und Ruprecht.

Szerszynski, Bronislaw and John Urry (2002), Cultures of Cosmopolitanism, in: The Sociological Review 50/4, p. 461–481.

Szyszka, Peter (1996), Kommunikationswissenschaftliche Perspektiven des Dialogbegriffs, in: Günter Bentele, Horst Steinmann and Ansgar Zerfaß (Eds.), Dialogorientierte Unternehmenskommunikation. Grundlagen – Praxiserfahrungen – Perspektiven, Berlin: Vistas, p. 81–106.

Tacke, Veronika (2015), Formalität und Informalität. Zu einer klassischen Unterscheidung der Organisationssoziologie, in: Victoria von Groddeck and Sylvia Marlene Wilz (Eds.), Formalität und Informalität in Organisationen, Wiesbaden: Springer, p. 37–92.

Tajfel, Henri and John C. Turner (1986), The Social Identity Theory of Inter-Group Behavior, in: Stephen Worchel and William G. Austin (Eds.), Psychology of Intergroup Relations, Chicago, IL: Nelson-Hall, p. 7–24 (2nd ed.).

Tanikawa, Miki (2019), Is "Global Journalism" Truly Global?, in: Journalism Studies 20/10, p. 1421–1439.

Tapscott, Don (1996), The Digital Economy. Promise and Peril in the Age of Networked Intelligence, New York, NY: McGraw-Hill.

Tapscott, Don (2012), Succeeding through Radical Openness, in: Harvard Business Review, January 1.

Tarrow, Sidney and Doug McAdam (2005), Scale Shift in Transnational Contention, in: Donatella della Porta and Sidney Tarrow (Eds.), Transnational Protest and Global Activism, Lanham, MD: Rowman and Littlefield, p. 121–147.

Teer-Tomaselli, Ruth (2006), Memory and Markers. Collective Memory and Newsworthiness, in: Ingrid Volkmer (Ed.), News in Public Memory. An International Study of Media Memories across Generations, New York, NY: Peter Lang, p. 225–249.

Tegethoff, Hans Georg (1999), Soziale Gruppen und Individualisierung. Ansätze und Grundlagen einer revidierten Gruppenforschung, Neuwied: Luchterhand.

Tegethoff, Hans Georg (2001), Primärgruppen und Individualisierung. Ein Vorschlag zur Rekonzeptualisierung der Gruppenforschung, in: Zeitschrift für Soziologie der Erziehung und Sozialisation 21/3, p. 279–298.

Teney, Céline and Marc Helbling (2014), How Denationalization Divides Elites and Citizens, in: Zeitschrift für Soziologie 43/4, p. 258–271.

Tepe, Daniela (2012), The Myth about the Global Civil Society. Domestic Politics to Ban Landmines, Basingstoke: Palgrave Macmillan.

Teusch, Ulrich (2003), Die Staatengesellschaft im Globalisierungsprozess. Wege zu einer antizipatorischen Politik, Wiesbaden: Westdeutscher Verlag.

Thiele, Martina (2015), Medien und Stereotype. Konturen eines Forschungsfeldes, Bielefeld: Transcript.

Thiermeyer, Michael (1994), Internationalisierung von Film und Filmwirtschaft, Cologne: Böhlau.

Thussu, Daya (Ed.) (2007), Media on the Move. Global Flow and Contra-Flow, London: Routledge.

Thussu, Daya (2010), Mapping Global Media Flow and Contra-Flow, in: Daya Thussu (Ed.), International Communication: A Reader, Abingdon/New York, NY, p. 221–238.

Thussu, Daya (2019), International Communication. Continuity and Change, London: Bloomsbury (3rd ed.).

Tian, Stella W., Doug Vogel and Felix B. Tan (2012), Continuous Knowledge Sharing in Online Social Network Communities: Service Features, Social Capital Facilitators, and Impact on Motivations, in: Honglei Li (Ed.), Virtual Community Participation and Motivation: Cross-Disciplinary Theories, Hershey, PA: Information Science Reference, p. 228–247.

Tibi, Bassam (1995), Islamic Dream of Semi-Modernity, in: India International Centre Quarterly 22/1, p. 79–87.

Tilly, Charles and Sidney Tarrow (2007), Contentious Politics, Boulder, CO/London: Paradigm.

Tobler, Stefan (2006), Konfliktinduzierte Transnationalisierung, in: Wolfgang R. Langenbucher and Michael Latzer (Eds.) Europäische Öffentlichkeit und medialer Wandel. Eine transdisziplinäre Perspektive, Wiesbaden: VS Verlag für Sozialwissenschaften, p. 107–130.

Tönnies, Ferdinand (2010), Gemeinschaft und Gesellschaft. Grundbegriffe der reinen Soziologie, Darmstadt: Wissenschaftliche Buchgesellschaft (Orig. 1887).

Torjus, Nicole (2014), Kommunikation in Organisationen: Die Bedeutung der Führung für die Qualität der organisationsinternen Kommunikation, Dissertation Fachbereich Erziehungswissenschaft und Psychologie, Free University Berlin, www.deutsche-digitale-bibliothek.de/item/XHEJXNSYTAI245KM7ON7QN5EQV2QLZTV.

Torres, Manuel R., Javier Jordán and Nicola Horsburgh (2006), Analysis and Evolution of the Global Jihadist Movement Propaganda, in: Terrorism and Political Violence 18/3, p. 399–421.

Treml, Alfred K. (2011), Globalisierung als pädagogische Herausforderung: Möglichkeiten und Grenzen einer weltbürgerlichen Erziehung, in: Wolfgang Sander (Ed.), Politische Bildung in der Weltgesellschaft: Herausforderungen, Positionen, Kontroversen. Perspektiven politischer Bildung, Bonn: Bundeszentrale für Politische Bildung, p. 190–203.

308 Bibliography

Tsunokai, Glenn T. and Allison R. McGrath (2012), Virtual Hate Communities in the 21st Century, in: Harrison Hao Yang and Steve Chi-Yin Yuen (Eds.), Handbook of Research on Practices and Outcomes in Virtual Worlds and Environments, Vol. 1, Hershey, PA: IGO Global, p. 34–53.

Tuman, Joseph S. (2003), Communicating Terror: The Rhetorical Dimensions of Terrorism, Thousand Oaks, CA: Sage.

Tumber, Howard and Jerry Palmer (2004), Media at War. The Iraq Crisis, London: Sage.

Turek, Jürgen (2017), Globalisierung im Zwiespalt. Die postglobale Misere und Wege, sie zu bewältigen, Bielefeld: Transcript.

Tzogopoulos, George (2013), The Greek Crisis in the Media. Stereotyping in the International Press, London: Routledge.

Ullmann, Katrin (2017), Generationscapes. Empirie und Theorie einer globalen Generation, Bielefeld: Transcript.

Ulrich, Dirk-Claas (2016), Die Chimäre einer globalen Öffentlichkeit. Internationale Medienberichterstattung und die Legitimationskrise der Vereinten Nationen, Bielefeld: Transcript.

[UN] (2012) List of Global Treaties Deposited with the Secretary-General Close to Universal Participation (status as of April 13, 2012), Vereinte Nationen, https://treaties.un.org/doc/source/events/2012/Treaties/list_global_english.pdf.

[UNCTAD] (2000), Building Confidence. Electronic Commerce and Development, New York, NY: UNCTAD.

[UN DESA and BPB] (2017), Figures and Facts on Globalization: Migration, United Nations Department of Economic and Social Affairs, www.bpb.de/nachschlagen/zahlen-und-fakten/globalisierung/265535/themengrafik-migration.

Urry, John (1988), Cultural Change and Contemporary Holiday-Making, in: Theory, Culture and Society 5/1, p. 35–55.

Urry, John (1990), The Tourist Gaze: Leisure and Travel in Contemporary Societies, London: Sage.

van Aelst, Peter and Stefaan Walgrave (2004), New Media/New Movements? The Role of the Internet in Shaping the 'Anti-Globalization' Movement, in: Wim van den Donk, Brian D. Loader, Paul G. Nixon and Dieter Rucht (Eds.), Cyberprotest. New Media, Citizens and Social Movements, London/New York, NY: Routledge, p. 97–122.

van den Donk, Wim, Brian D. Loader, Paul G. Nixon and Dieter Rucht (2004), Introduction: Social Movements and ICTs, in: Wim van den Donk, Brian D. Loader, Paul G. Nixon and Dieter Rucht (Eds.), Cyberprotest. New Media, Citizens and Social Movements, London/New York, NY: Routledge, p. 1–25.

van Dijk, Jan (2012), The Network Society, London: Sage (3rd ed.).

van Dijk, Teun A. (1988), News as Discourse, Hillsdale, NJ: Lawrence Erlbaum.

van Rekom, Jan and Frank Go (2006), Cultural Identities in a Globalizing World: Conditions for Sustainability of Intercultural Tourism, in: Peter M. Burns and Marina Novelli (Eds.), Tourism and Social Identities. Global Frameworks and Local Realities, Amsterdam: Elsevier, p. 79–90.

Varner, Iris I. (2000), The Theoretical Foundation for Intercultural Business Communication: A Conceptual Model, in: The Journal of Business Communication 37/1, p. 39–57.

Verbik, Line and Veronica Lasanowski (2007), International Student Mobility: Patterns and Trends, London: The Observatory on Borderless Higher Education Dialogue.

Volkmer, Ingrid (Ed.) (2006), News in Public Memory. An International Study of Media Memories across Generations, New York, NY: Peter Lang.

Volkmer, Ingrid (2014), The Global Public Sphere. Public Communication in the Age of Reflective Interdependence, Cambridge/Malden, MA: Polity.

Bibliography   309

von Bassewitz, Susanne (1990), Stereotype und Massenmedien. Zum Deutschlandbild in französischen Tageszeitungen, Wiesbaden: DUV.

von Groddeck, Victoria and Sylvia Marlene Wilz (2015), Auf dem Papier und zwischen den Zeilen. Formalität und Informalität in Organisationen, in: Victoria von Groddeck and Sylvia Marlene Wilz (Eds.), Formalität und Informalität in Organisationen, Wiesbaden: Springer, p. 7–33.

Vowe, Gerhard (2002), Politische Kommunikation. Ein historischer und systematischer Überblick der Forschung, Ilmenau: Diskussionsbeiträge Institut für Medien- und Kommunikationswissenschaft.

Vuorela, Ulla (2002), Transnational Families: Imagined and Real Communities, in: Deborah Bryceson and Ulla Vuorela (Eds.), The Transnational Family: New European Frontiers and Global Networks, Oxford: Berg, p. 63–82.

Waisbord, Silvio (2014), Latin American Media and the Limitations of the Media Globalization Paradigm, in: Manuel Alejandro Guerrero and Mireya Marquez-Ramirez (Eds.), Media Systems and Communication Policies in Latin America, Basingstoke/ New York, NY: Palgrave Macmillan, p. 24–42.

Walls, Jan (1993), Global Networking for Local Development: Task Focus and Relationship Focus in Cross-Cultural Communication, in: Linda M. Harasim (Ed.), Global Networks: Computers and International Communication, Cambridge, MA/London: The MIT Press, p. 153–165.

Walter, Norbert (2002), Globalisierung der Wirtschaft vs. Identifikation durch die Muttersprache, in: Heiner Heseler, Jörg Huffschmid, Norbert Reuter and Axel Troost (Eds.), Gegen die Markt-Orthodoxie. Perspektiven einer demokratischen und solidarischen Wirtschaft, Hamburg: VSA, p. 25–32.

Wang, Xiaopeng (2010), An Exploration of the Determinants of International News Coverage in Australia's Online Media, in: Guy Glam, Thomas Johnson and Wayne Wanta (Eds.), International Media Communication in a Global Age, London: Routledge, p. 261–276.

Wanta, Wayne, Guy Golan and Cheolhan Lee (2004), Agenda Setting and International News: Media Influence on Public Perceptions of Foreign Nations, in: Journalism and Mass Communication Quarterly 81/2, p. 364–377.

Wanta, Wayne and Yu-Wei Hu (1993), The Agenda-Setting Effects of International News Coverage: An Examination of Differing News Frames, in: International Journal of Public Opinion Research 5/3, p. 250–264.

Ward, Stephen J.A. and Herman Wasserman (Eds.) (2010), Media Ethics beyond Borders. A Global Perspective, New York, NY/London: Routledge.

Warf, Barney (2013), Global Geographies of the Internet, Dordrecht: Springer.

Watzlawick, Paul, Janet H. Beavin and Don D. Jackson (1990), Menschliche Kommunikation. Formen, Störungen, Paradoxien, Bern: Hans Huber (8th ed.).

[Web Technology Survey] (2018), https://w3techs.com/technologies/history_overview/content_language.

Weber, Max (1922), Wirtschaft und Gesellschaft. Grundriss der verstehenden Soziologie, Tübingen: Mohr.

Weeks, Michael R. (2012), Toward an Understanding of Offline Community Participation through Narrative Network Analysis, in: Honglei Li (Ed.), Virtual Community Participation and Motivation: Cross-Disciplinary Theories, Hershey, PA: Information Science Reference, p. 90–102.

Weenink, Don (2008), Cosmopolitanism as a Form of Capital. Parents Preparing their Children for a Globalizing World, in: Sociology 42/6, p. 1089–1106.

Weidemann, Doris (2016), Freundschaften auf Distanz durch regionale und globale Mobilität, in: Sina-Mareen Köhler, Heinz-Hermann Krüger and Nicolle Pfaff (Eds.), Handbuch Peerforschung, Opladen: Budrich, p. 223–235.

310 Bibliography

Weiß, Anja (2015), Wie nah ist das Ferne? Gerechtigkeit in Zeiten der Globalisierung, in: Steffen Mau and Nadine M. Schöneck-Voß (Eds.), (Un-)Gerechte (Un-)Gleichheiten, Berlin: Suhrkamp, p. 167–174.

Weiß, Anja (2017), Soziologie globaler Ungleichheiten, Berlin: Suhrkamp

Weiß, Anja (2018), Wodurch wird professionelles Wissen transnational anschlussfähig?, in: Sigrid Quack, Ingo Schulz-Schaeffer, Karen Shire and Anja Weiß (Eds.), Transnationalisierung der Arbeit, Wiesbaden: Springer, p. 129–151.

Weiß, Johannes (2006), Wissenselite, in: Dirk Tänzler, Hubert Knoblauch and Hans-Georg Soeffner (Eds.), Zur Kritik der Wissensgesellschaft, Konstanz: UVK, p. 13–29.

Welge, Martin K. (1999), Informale Steuerungsmechanismen zur Optimierung globaler Geschäfte, in: Michael Kutschker (Ed.), Management verteilter Kompetenzen in multinationalen Unternehmen, Wiesbaden: Gabler, p. 2–24.

Weller, Christoph (2003/4), Internationale Politik und Konstruktivismus. Ein Beipackzettel, in: WeltTrends 41, p. 107–123.

Welsch, Wolfgang (1995), Transkulturalität. Zur veränderten Verfasstheit heutiger Kulturen, in: Zeitschrift für Kulturaustausch 45/1, p. 39–44.

Werbner, Pnina (1999), Global Pathways. Working Class Cosmopolitans and the Creation of Transnational Ethnic Worlds, in: Social Anthropology 7/1, p. 17–35.

Werbner, Pnina (Ed.) (2008a), Anthropology and the New Cosmopolitanism. Rooted, Feminist and Vernacular Perspectives, New York, NY: Berg.

Werbner, Pnina (2008b), Introduction, in: Pnina Werbner (Ed.), Anthropology and the New Cosmopolitanism. Rooted, Feminist and Vernacular Perspectives, New York, NY: Berg, p. 1–29.

Werbner, Pnina (2015), The Dialectics of Urban Cosmopolitanism: Between Tolerance and Intolerance in Cities of Strangers, in: Identities 22/5, p. 569–587.

Werkner, Ines-Jacqueline and Oliver Hidalgo (Eds.) (2014), Religionen – Global Player in der internationalen Politik?, Wiesbaden: Springer.

Werron, Tobias (2010), Media Globalization in Question. Ein soziologischer Blick auf medienhistorische Beiträge zur Globalisierungsforschung (Rezension), in: Zeitschrift für Medienwissenschaft 2/1, p. 140–143.

Wessler, Hartmut and Michael Brüggemann (2012), Transnationale Kommunikation. Eine Einführung, Wiesbaden: Springer.

Wessler, Hartmut, Bernhard Peters, Michael Brüggemann, Katharina Kleinen-von Königslöw and Stefanie Sifft (2008), Transnationalization of Public Spheres, Basingstoke/New York, NY: Palgrave Macmillan.

[Wikipedia Statistics] (n.d.), https://stats.wikimedia.org/DE/.

Wilhelm, Ursula (1993), Gast-Gastgeber-Beziehungen, in: Heinz Hahn and Hans Jürgen Kagelmann (Eds.), Tourismuspsychologie und Tourismussoziologie. Ein Handbuch zur Tourismuswissenschaft, Munich: Quintessenz, p. 263–266.

Wilke, Jürgen, Christine Heimprecht and Youichi Ito (2013), Countries of Location and Countries Involved, in: Akiba A. Cohen (Ed.), Foreign News on Television. Where in the World Is the Global Village?, New York, NY: Peter Lang, p. 63–85.

Williams, Kevin (2011), International Journalism, Los Angeles, CA: Sage.

Willnat, Lars, David Weaver, Agnieszka Stępińska and Ven-hwei Lo (2013), Who Uses News, How Much, and Why?, in: Akiba A. Cohen (Ed.), Foreign News on Television. Where in the World Is the Global Village?, New York, NY: Peter Lang, p. 153–169.

Winseck, Dwayne (2011), The Political Economies of Media and the Transformation of Global Media Industries, in: Dwayne Winseck and Dal Yong Jin (Eds.), The Political Economies of Media and the Transformation of Global Media Industries, New York, NY: Bloomsbury, p. 1–46.

Winter, David G. (2003), Asymmetrical Perceptions of Power in Crises: A Comparison of 1914 and the Cuban Missile Crisis, in: Journal of Peace Research 40/3, p. 251–270.

Winter, Rainer (2010), Widerstand im Netz. Zur Herausbildung einer transnationalen Öffentlichkeit durch netzbasierte Kommunikation, Bielefeld: Transcript.

Witte, Erich H. and James H. Davis (Eds.) (2013), Understanding Group Behavior, vol. 1: Consensual Action by Small Groups, vol. 2: Small Group Processes and Interpersonal Relations, Hoboken, NJ: Taylor and Francis.

Wöhler, Karlheinz (2000), Konstruierte Raumbindungen. Kulturangebote zwischen Authentizität und Inszenierung, in: Tourismus Journal 4/1, p. 103–116.

Wöhler, Karlheinz (2005), Topographie des Erlebens. Zur Verortung touristischer Erlebniswelten, in: Karlheinz Wöhler (Ed.), Erlebniswelten. Herstellung und Nutzung touristischer Welten, Münster: LIT, p. 17–28.

Wöhler, Karlheinz (2011), Touristifizierung von Räumen. Kulturwissenschaftliche und soziologische Studien zur Konstruktion von Räumen, Wiesbaden: VS Verlag für Sozialwissenschaften.

Wolfsfeld, Gadi (1997), Media and Political Conflict. News from the Middle East, Cambridge: Cambridge University Press.

[World Tourism Organization] (2018), UNWTO Tourism Highlights, 2018 Edition, Madrid: UNWTO.

Wright, Steve (2004), Informing, Communicating and ICTs in Contemporary Anti-Capitalist Movements, in: Wim van den Donk, Brian D. Loader, Paul G. Nixon and Dieter Rucht (Eds.), Cyberprotest. New Media, Citizens and Social Movements, London/New York, NY: Routledge, p. 77–93.

Wu, H. Denis (2000), Systemic Determinants of International News Coverage: a Comparison of 38 Countries, in: Journal of Communication 50/2, p. 110–130.

Wu, H. Denis (2003), Homogeneity around the World? Comparing the Systemic Determinants of International News Flow between Developed and Developing Countries, in: International Communication Gazette 65/1, p. 9–24.

Wu, H. Denis (2007), A Brave New World for International News? Exploring the Determinants of the Coverage of Foreign News on US Websites, in: International Communication Gazette 69/6, p. 539–551.

Yeoh, Brenda S.A. and Weiqiang Lin (2018), Cosmopolitanism in Cities and Beyond, in Gerard Delanty (Ed.), Routledge International Handbook of Cosmopolitanism Studies, London/New York, NY: Routledge, p. 299–311 (2nd ed.).

Yilmaz, Aybige and Ruxandra Trandafoiu (2014), Introduction, in: Aybige Yilmaz, Ruxandra Trandafoiu and Aris Mousutzanis (Eds.), Media and Cosmopolitanism, Oxford: Peter Lang.

Yüksel, Ilke Sanlier and Murat Yüksel (2011), Resistanbul: An Analysis of Mediated Communication in Transnational Activism, in: Simon Cottle and Libby Lester (Eds.), Transnational Protests and the Media, New York, NY: Peter Lang, p. 242–254.

Zając, Justyna (2013), Communication in Global Corporations. Successful Project Management via Email, Frankfurt: Peter Lang.

Zerfaß, Ansgar (1996), Dialogkommunikation und strategische Unternehmensführung, in: Günter Bentele, Horst Steinmann and Ansgar Zerfaß (Eds.), Dialogorientierte Unternehmenskommunikation. Grundlagen – Praxiserfahrungen – Perspektiven, Berlin: Vistas, p. 23–58.

Zhao, Shanyang (2006), The Internet and the Transformation of the Reality of Everyday Life. Toward a New Analytic Stance in Sociology, in: Sociological Inquiry 76/4, p. 458–474.

Zhu, Yunxia and Sun Zhu (2004), Communication Barriers to Negotiation: Encountering Chinese in Cross-Cultural Business Meetings, in: Hannah Slavik (Ed.), Intercultural Communication and Diplomacy, Malta/Geneva: DiploFoundation, p. 207–221.

312 Bibliography

Zilg, Antje (2013), Secrets de chez nous: Die Vermittlung von Lokalität in Markennamen, in: Christopher M. Schmidt, Ainars Dimats, Jaakko Lehtonen and Martin Nielsen (Eds.), Kulturspezifik in der europäischen Wirtschaftskommunikation, Wiesbaden: Springer, p. 33–46.

Zöllner, Oliver (Ed.) (2004), Beyond Borders. Research and International Broadcasting 2003, Bonn: CIBAR.

Zuckerman, Ethan (2013), Digital Cosmopolitans. Why We Think the Internet Connects Us, Why It Doesn't, and How to Rewire It, New York, NY/London: Norton.

Zysman, John and Abraham Newman (Eds.) (2006), How Revolutionary Was the Digital Revolution? National Responses, Market Transitions, and Global Technology, Stanford, CA: Stanford University Press.

INDEX

ABX schema 227
actor-network theory 18, 19
Adolphsen, Manuel 154, 265
advertising 96, 128, 129; industry 262;
  style 130; symbolic language of 131
Afghanistan, stereotype 67
Africa, stereotype 68
AIDS/HIV drugs campaign 135
Aksartova, Sada 220
Al-Hurra 103
Al-Jazeera 22, 31, 53, 68, 179
Al-Jazeera English 51, 54, 68
All Business is Local 131
Allport, Gordon W 224, 26
al-Sadat, President Anwar 89
ambassadors: downgrading of 81, 92, 95;
  role of 94
American films 55
American media groups 57
Amnesty International 23, 29, 134, 138, 153
anti-globalist rebellion 3, 245, 258
anti-landmine campaign 252
anti-war movement 145, 148
Appiah, Kwame Anthony 167, 198, 266
Apple 116
Arab diaspora 179
Arab Spring 255
Arab young generation 99–100
association-of-persons-state 77
Attac network 140, 145
audiences 42, 50, 52, 55, 71, 211–14; foreign
  22, 214; target 76, 80, 97; transnational 68
Axford, Barrie 259, 267

Baidu 58
Ball-Rokeach, Sandra 43, 243, 248, 252,
  267
Baptist-Burqa Network 152
Baym, Nancy 193, 231, 267
BBC Monitoring Service (BBCM) 94
BBC World Services 22, 51, 54, 68, 103
Beck, Ulrich 5, 49–50, 218, 245, 246,
  267
Becker, Christian 90, 268
Bennett, W Lance 136, 147, 268
Bercovitch, Jacob 85, 269
Berg, David 117, 119
Bertelsmann 113
Bettermann, Erik 103, 269
Blumer, Herbert 12, 269
Bollywood 54–5, 192
Bolten, Jürgen 111, 129, 269
book culture 14, 15, 43
boomerang effect 141, 154, 251, 253
Brent Spar scandal 155
Brexit 3, 73, 250–1
broadcasting, international 22, 51, 54, 56,
  102–4
Brommesson, Douglas 163
Bryceson, Deborah 202, 270
Bucher, Hans-Jürgen 60, 270
Buddhist Compassion Relief Tzu Chi
  Foundation 138
Bukow, Wolf-Dietrich 202, 270
Burns, Peter 205, 270
Busch, Dominic 184, 193, 271
Bush (George W) administration 98

314 Index

business-to-customer transactions (B2C) 109
Bussemer, Thymian 101, 271

Calhoun, Craig 220, 271
Cambié, Silvia 115, 271
Camp David 85, 89
Carter administration 84, 85, 89
cascade model of online interaction 169
Castells, Manuel 19, 118–19, 121, 122, 125, 271
censorship 101, 141
Chadwick, Andrew 151, 272
chain networks 117, 118, 143
Chandhoke, Neera 143, 272
chat rooms 165, 172–3
"cheap talk" effect 151, 152
Chinese firewall 253
Choi, Junho H 183, 272
Chouliaraki, Lilie 10, 11, 272
Christensen, Christian 174, 176, 272
circular interaction 200–1
circular intergroup communication 209
civil society 133, 134, 138–9, 143
"clash of civilizations" 263
clash of perceptions 199
Clausen, Lisbeth 111, 272
"clictivism" 149
CNN 22, 51, 54, 68; effect 242, 251
coalitions, ability to form 248
Cohen, Akiba A 66, 273
collective information sites 180
communications, formal and informal 33, 122–3
communications modes 14, 35, 38, 46, 121–2, 128
communicative ecology 14, 43
communicative signs, non-verbal and paraverbal 122, 232
communities: characteristics of 91; concept of 160, 161; traditional 24, 162
company structures 117
computer games 175
connectivity 18, 168, 169, 170, 237
constructive ambiguity 92–3
constructivism 161, 162, 163
contact hypothesis 188, 229–30
Conti, Luisa 185, 273
contingency approach 85
co-orientation approach 12
corporate culture 115, 116, 122
corporations, vertical 118
"cosmocrats" 220

cosmopolitan: age 246; attitudes 217; awareness 234, 235; elites 218, 219, 221, 246; marketing 131
cosmopolitanism 9, 10, 207, 218, 219, 225, 253; ethical 240; "pop" 175, 207; rooted 167; as social capital 218–20
cosmopolitans 2, 38, 147, 224
Couldry, Nick 19, 273
couplings: loose 115; tight 117
COVID-19 pandemic 3
crisis situations 10, 60, 250
Croisy, Sophie 183, 273
Cuban Missile Crisis 86, 87
cultural boundaries 171
cultural codes 188
cultural competence 126
cultural essentialism 112
"cultural exile" 174
"cultural imperialism" 249
cultural interpreters 239
cultural policy, foreign 96, 99–101
culture clash 199
culture in economics 111–12
"culture of not knowing" 238
culture stereotypes 117
Curran, James 164, 273
Custard, Holly Ann 148, 274
cyber bullying 184, 185
cyber foreign policy 91
cyber-attacks 150
cybercrime, laws against 185
cyber-diplomacy 91–2
cyber-mobilization 149
cyber-realists 91

Dallas study 213
Danowski, James A 183
"death of distance" 123, 124
DeFleur, Melvin 43, 243, 248, 252
della Porta, Donatella 140, 141, 274, 275
denial-of-service attacks 150
deprivation, relative 223
Deutsch, Karl W 15, 16, 23, 41, 275
Deutsche Welle 51, 103
developing countries 4, 20, 63, 64, 150, 181; knowledge gaps 128; NGOs in 147, 150; power relations 138; technology in 110
dialogic global community 209
"dialogicity" 168, 169
dialogue of cultures 17, 71, 99, 101, 103
diasporas 165–7, 174–9, 220; online communities 165, 176, 177
Diffusion of Innovations 125
digital culture wars 184

"digital divide" 110, 170, 210
digital revolution 91
digital travel 192
Dijkzeul, Dennis 153, 275
diplomacy 22, 28–9, 76, 77, 82, 83–5;
conference 78; cyber-diplomacy
91–2; "hotline" 79, 83, 87; and personal
relationships 88, 89; public and
non-public 91; second-track 78–9
diplomatic communication 249, 262
diplomatic dialogues 230
diplomatic mediation 85–6
diplomatic protocol 86, 90
directive mediation 86
discursive intergroup communication 209
distant suffering 10, 212
Djelic, Marie-Laure 160, 276
document classification 124
domain names 171
domestication 64, 141, 210
Dörner, Andreas 211, 276
dynamic equilibrium 30, 35, 41–2, 45, 50,
244

Earth Summit declaration 151
e-commerce (EC) 129
economic knowledge gaps 124
education 99–100, 196, 201, 218, 225, 263
Elias, Norbert 19
elites 2, 26–7, 249, 263; business 110, 122,
218, 220, 221; cosmopolitan 218, 221,
246; global 56, 127, 218; informational
60, 68, 147, 246; knowledge 155; mobile
46, 56; movement 142, 144; opinions of
71; professional 218
Endruweit, Günter 134, 155, 276
enemy, concepts of 10, 17, 102, 103, 184
English as a link language 171
Enroth, Henrik 163, 276
entertainment communication 235
entertainment sector 41, 54–5, 57–8, 214
episodic interactions 204
epistemic competence 235
essentialism critique 111–12
ethical advertising 129
ethical codes 53
ethical cosmopolitanism 240
ethics: consumer 261; formal 53;
journalistic 53, 261
ethnocentric companies 108, 109, 113, 114,
118
Eurocentrism 6, 181, 182
Euronews 54
Europe, media and politics 72–4

European Union 16, 67, 72, 80, 217;
television directive 56
Eurosports 54
everyday dialogues 210–11, 230, 231
exchange programmes 225
expatriates 204–5, 219
experiential knowledge 13, 36, 121;
not shared 236
extremist online alliances 165, 184

Facebook 57, 58, 170
face-to-face interaction 92, 140, 148
Falklands War coverage 250
family 197, 198, 199, 202, 203–4, 224;
conversations 210–11
fan culture 175, 214–15
"fast subjects" 117
Fletcher, Tom 99, 277
Flew, Terry 58, 277
Flusser, Vilém 14, 278
Fokin, Vladimir Ivanovitch 97, 278
football fans 164
foreign correspondents 42
foreign coverage 21–2, 31, 42, 54, 61–2, 63,
65; and society's attitudes 71
foreign media: access to 31; in Arab
countries 59; online 59–60
foreign news reporting 63
foreign-language learning 225
formality in diplomatic relations 89, 90
formats: global television 59, 213; brand
145; entertainment 213, 214
Fortner, Robert S 35, 176, 278
framing 65, 66, 67, 68, 85, 86
Fraser, Nancy 69, 278
freedom of expression 57, 96
"Fridays for Future" 252
friendship 189, 193, 201, 202, 229; on
Facebook 170
full structure 117, 118
functionalists 20

G7, G8, G20 groups 90, 135
Gambetta, Diego 87, 278
gaming communities 171, 175, 179
gap year travel 191–2
gated communities 191, 205
"gatekeeping" 30, 63, 96
genocide of Herero people 254
geocentric companies 108, 109
geolingistically homogenous areas 55
Georgiou, Myria 203, 220, 279
Gerhards, Jürgen 93, 279
German Federal Foreign Office 99, 100

316 Index

Geser, Hans 123, 280
Giddens, Anthony 5, 6, 280
Giesecke, Michael 14–15, 43, 113, 246, 263, 280
Gladwell, Malcolm 148, 280
global capital 27
"global cities" concept 124, 126, 176
global citizenship 225
"global competence" 235, 238
global governance 79–80, 82, 83, 87–8, 90
global ignorance 234
global interdependence: horizontal 244, 245–8, 250, 251, 253; vertical 244, 250, 252
"global nomads" 224
global players 57–8, 108
global public sphere 8–9, 48, 50, 60; models 69–70
Global South 137–8, 142–4, 150, 181, 185, 190, 225; and North 137–8, 142–4, 150, 181
global teams 117
global village 15, 163, 176
glocalization 25–6, 130, 131
Google 57, 58, 64, 253
Graham, Stephen 165, 280
Granovetter, Mark S 166, 280
Greek crisis 66, 73
Greenpeace 23, 134, 138, 149, 153, 155
"Greenpeace democracy" 147, 155
greeting rituals 229
Gurevitch, Michael 64, 281

Habermas, Jürgen 13, 14, 18, 44, 69, 227, 246, 282
"hacktivism" 150
Hafez, Kai 2, 41, 42, 66, 249, 282–3
Haitian diaspora 177
Hall, Martin 249
Hamas 84
handshakes 86
Hannerz, Ulf 190, 191, 218, 221, 231, 238, 284
Hanrath, Jan 185, 284
"hard power" 98
Harvard Concept of Negotiation 84, 85, 114, 115
"hate speech" 151, 152, 184; combating 185
headscarf wearing 232, 233
hegemonic global community 209
Hellmann-Grobe, Antje 114, 115, 128, 285
Hepp, Andreas 173, 285
Hindu diaspora 174
Hocking, Brian 92, 286

Hofstede, Geert 111
Holbrooke, Richard 99, 286
Hollywood film industry 54, 65, 131
Hong Kong uprisings 255
horizontal corporations 118
horizontal interdependence 46, 47, 253, 254
Hoston, Allison 85
Høy-Petersen, Nina 220, 234, 240, 286
Huck, Simon 131, 286
human capital 111
human issues, basic 198, 199
human lifeways, diversity of 25
human relationships 221
human rights 83, 132, 137; activists 144; reports 153
humanitarian issues 157
hybridization 25–6, 28, 32, 34–5, 75, 130, 131
hyperglobalism 5, 70
hyperlinks 170
hypermediality, extended 60
hyphenated communities 164

Ibn Khaldoun Center 144
Ibrahim, Saad Eddin 144
ICANN regulations 253
ignorance 11, 234, 235–9
imagined community 161, 209
IMF 23, 79
In der Smitten, Susanne 162, 166, 286
indexing 250, 251, 252; hypothesis 242, 249
individual attitudes and behaviour 221–2, 226
individual, autonomy of 216, 255
individual global learning 225
individual processing of knowledge 234
individual's value system 240
individual-collective problem 228
individualization, toxic side effects 217
Indymedia 144
informal communication 38, 88, 89, 90, 120
informality 119–20
information control 43, 262
information, diffusion of 154–5, 181
information gathering 94, 95, 96
information laws 262
information society, key actors 109
"information warfare" 102–3
informational economy 121
Innerarity, Daniel 154, 234, 238
institutionalism 107
integration 204, 247; theorists 15–17; we-feeling 16

inter- and intragroup communication, variants 209
interaction-interpretation problem 228–9
intercultural communication 15, 24, 99, 101, 103, 185, 230; claims to representation 99–100
interdependence 40–2, 46, 243–4, 248, 249, 251; local horizontal: 244; local vertical 244, 250, 251, 252, 253; low 40; negative and positive 40; reflexive 72; technological 253; vertical 46, 47, 248, 253
interdiscourse 61, 211
international broadcasting 22, 51, 54, 56, 102–4, 250
international integration theory 15
International non-governmental organizations (INGOS) 29, 134, 135, 137–8, 139, 140, 143; campaigns 151, 156, 155–6, 157; and the Internet 147
International Red Cross 137
international relations, constructivist school 77
Internet 15, 23, 35, 44, 59, 149; abuse of 151; access to 181; as a combat zone 152, 164; censorship of 57, 253; citizen journalism 66; conferences 148; disputes 168, 178; exclusion from 170–1; foreign content on 170; forums 144, 173; geography 170, 253; and language 121, 171, 172; perpetuation of racism and sexism 193; quality of information on 181; role of 180; traffic, international 170; underuse of 148, 149, 184; users 171; *see also* web
Internet-based business-to-customer (B2C) 129
intertextuality 61
inversion of dependence 252
Iraq War 136, 250, 252
Islam 65, 225, 236
Islamic Relief Foundation 138
Islamic-Western dialogue 17
Islamism 136; jihadist variant of 152, 174
Islamists 84, 128
Islamophobia 223, 225, 255
Israel; negations with the PLO 84; six-day war 93
IT hotspots 127

Japanese anime 235
Jenkins, Henry 175, 287
Jocz, Katherine E 130–1
Jönsson, Christer 91, 249, 287–8
journalistic ethics 53, 261

Kaldor, Mary 153, 288
Kant, Immanuel 13, 102
Karraker, Meg 197, 288
Katz, Elihu 213
Keane, John 143, 288
Keck, Margaret E 142, 144, 153, 157, 288
Kennedy, President J 87
Khrushchev, Premier N 87
Kiel, Christina 151, 289
Kissinger, Henry 84, 85, 89
Klein, Naomi 137, 289
Kleinsteuber, Hans 71, 289
Knoblauch, Hubert 45, 289–90
knowledge capitalism 127
knowledge diffusion 124–6, 127
knowledge management 95–6
knowledge processing 236
"knowledge societies" 127
knowledge, socially constructed 218
Köck, Christoph 205, 290
Kogut, Bruce 253
Korean drama and pop music 175, 235
Korean high-school study 201
Krüger, Uwe 250, 290
Kurdish diaspora 176
Kyoto Protocol 22, 80, 137

labour migration 45, 110, 219
labour movement 138
Laguerre, Michael S 177, 291
Lamont, Michèle 220, 291
landmines 135, 136, 137
Lanier, Jaron 181–2, 291
Latin American diaspora 174
Latour, Bruno 18, 19, 291
Lee, Hyunji 173, 291
Leggewie, Claus 185
Lenz, Ilse 143, 291
Lerner, Daniel 125, 291
Leurs, Koen 203, 220, 292
Levitt, Theodore 130, 292
Levy, Mark R 64
Liebes, Tamar 213, 292
linguistic boundaries 171
"linkage" policy 78–9
local interdependence: horizontal: 244; vertical 244, 250, 251, 252, 253
local-global media-based public spheres 32
London School of Economics (LSE) 19
Luckmann, Benita 36, 37, 292
Luhmann, Niklas 19, 30, 70, 292
lurkers 173

318 Index

Mahmod, Jowan 176, 177, 293
Maletzke, Gerhard 199, 293
Manifesto of the Communist Party 133
marketing 97, 128, 129, 130, 131
marriages, binational 196
mass media 2, 29, 30, 50–2, 65, 82; non-traditional 59–60, 64; patriotism 249; people's dependency on 44; role of 179, 254
Massachusetts Institute of Technology (MIT) 170, 253
Mau, Steffen 196, 294
McAdam, Doug 141, 294
McLuhan, Marshall 53, 104, 176, 294
McQuail, Dennis 243, 245, 249, 294
Mead, George H 12, 294
Meckel, Miriam 163, 165, 294
Médecins Sans Frontières 137
media agenda 61, 62, 63, 104, 211
media dependence 71, 144, 249; theory 43, 242–3, 248
"Media Dialogues with the Arab World" 100
media diplomacy 249
media discourses 48, 53, 68–9, 235
media economics 54, 57–8
media ethics 53
media freedom 57
media giants 58, 59
media and governments 249, 251
media hierarchy 41
media markets 42
media monitoring 94–5
media philosophers 13, 14
media policy 60, 63
media production 30, 54–5, 70, 71
media professionalism 53
media regulations 56, 57, 60
media revolution 91
media systems 10, 22, 50, 70
media technology 249–50
mediatization 85–6, 91, 169
mediators 86, 239
Meerts, Paul W 89, 294
megacities 190
Meir, Golda 89
Melissen Jan 92, 98–9, 294
Merton, Richard K 2, 237, 295
messenger services 122
metatourism 205
methodological connectivism 62
metropolises, diversity of 190
Mexico, land-grabbing in 142
Micklethwait, John 220, 295

Microsoft 58
Middle East conflict 93
migrants 27, 56, 170, 195, 196, 202; communities 165, 205
migration 4, 196, 197, 198, 245
Miike, Yoshitaka 229, 295
Millennium Development Goals 110
modernities, multiple 183
modernization theory 125, 134
Mody, Bella 66, 295
Mohammed cartoons 182
Mongol empire 77
movements: elites of 142, 144; environmental 252; media 144, 145; researchers of 140
Mubarak government 144
multimodality 164, 172, 185
Münch, Richard 2, 3, 258, 296
Munich Security Conference 250
Muslim diaspora 174

narration, monologic 231
Nassehi, Armin 19, 296
nationalism, methodological 177, 178
Nayar, Pramod K 175, 296
Nazi web community 184
negotiations 79, 83, 84–5, 86, 87
Neidhardt, Friedhelm 93, 296–7
neo-institutionalists 20
networking 6, 9, 18, 19
networks 116–17, 118, 120, 143
New World Information Order 52
Newcomb, Theodore 227, 297
news agencies 22, 58, 249
news geographies 63
news management by government 249
"NGOization" 136
non-governmental organizations (NGOs) 23, 79, 134, 143–4, 147
Noack, Paul 250, 297
non-profit organizations 134–5
non-verbal forms of communication 86–7, 232
North-South divide 137–8, 150, 252
Nye, Joseph 98, 297

Obama administration 98
observation 9, 11, 12, 36, 214, 232; intercultural 233; medial 209, 210; of observation 209, 210
Occupy movement 145, 255
OECD 20, 107
office grapevine 33
Ognyanova, Katherine 248, 297

OhmyNews International 66
Olsson, Patrik 184
OneWorld network 149
Ong, Jonathan Corpus 218, 297
online communities 4, 24, 161, 162, 163, 174, 176; communication 173, 184; conflicts and attacks 184; self-regulation 185
online global war 183
online petitions 34, 148, 149, 150, 151
online territories 170, 174, 176
online travels 170
Ooi, Yang-May 115
opinion leaders 236–7, 238
Organization for Security and Cooperation in Europe (OSCE) 79
Oslo peace process 84
Ottawa Treaty 137

Pal, Mahuya 130, 297
Palestinian-Israeli conflict 65
Panama Papers 54
pan-European media 73
Paraguayan émigré study 193
paraverbal signs 122, 232
Parsons, Talcott 19
partnerships 189, 193, 196
Perry, Barbara 184, 298
persuasion 97–9, 102–4; *see also* propaganda
Pettigrew, Thomas 224, 230, 298
Pichler, Florian 217, 298
Plöger, Andrea 143, 298
pluralistic ignorance 11
polycentric companies 108, 109
pop culture 175, 235
post-Fordist knowledge society 114
post-friendships 202
Postmes, Tom 193, 299
power structures of companies 109–10
Prantl, Heribert 132, 299
preconceptions about others 229
prejudices 222
press culture 14, 15
Pries, Ludger 135, 299
procedural mediation 86
production chains 117
propaganda 101; in democratic countries 97; government 250; techniques 101; war 70, 101–2
pseudo-NGOs 134
psychological warfare 103, 184
public diplomacy 80, 96–7, 98, 99–100, 103, 104
public relations (PR) 96, 129, 131, 157

public sphere 10, 69–70
Putnam, Robert D 166, 180, 299

Quack, Sigrid 160
Quelch, John A 130–1, 299

racism 70, 71, 111, 223, 224, 225; extremists 184, 185
"rally-round-the-flag effect" 250
rationality 168, 169
reception gap 55–6
Reckwitz, Andreas 258, 299
recognition 230, 232–4, 241; of ignorance 238; theory 230
refugees 10, 11, 72, 221
relationality 173, 237
relationships: long-distance 15; online 162, 163
Reporters Without Borders 57, 135, 153
"re-tribalization" 162, 255
Reuters 58
Rheingold, Howard 162, 180, 300
Richter, Emanuel 13, 300
Riegert, Kristina 66, 300
right-wing populism 3, 16, 217, 220, 225, 258
rituals and symbolic orders 90
Ritzer, George 18–19, 170, 300
"roadmap" concept 84
Robins, Kevin 176, 300
Roeh, Itzhak 64
Rofe, J Simon 80, 300
Rogers, Everett 125, 300
roles, formal and informal 38
Rosecrance, Richard 40, 83, 301
Rosenau, James N 17, 78–9, 301
RT (Russia Today) 22, 51, 103
Rucht, Dieter 136, 139, 301
Rühl, Manfred 19, 32, 113, 115, 301
Rupp, George 167, 301
Russian diaspora studies 178
Russian domestic broadcasters 103

Sassen, Saskia 18, 153, 301–2
satellite broadcasting 55, 57, 249
scale shift 141
school education 201, 224, 225
Schuldt, Monique 130, 303
Schultz, Tanjev 30, 303
Schütz, Alfred 13, 36, 303
search engines 57, 58, 64
secret services 94, 96, 262
semi-modernity 106, 119, 128, 129
semiotic solidarity 175

320 Index

September 11 2001 aftermath 65, 81, 98, 102
signalling 86–7
Sikkink, Kathryn 141, 142, 144, 153, 157, 304
Silverstone, Roger 19, 210, 304
Six-Day War 93
Skype 122, 172
Smith, Kenwyn 117, 119, 304
social capital theory 167
social co-orientation 12
social co-presence 161
social media 39, 57, 59, 134, 172, 212; bans by states 253; friendships 193; and social movements 148; use of 104, 149, 170
social movement organizations (SMOs) 23, 133, 134
social movements 4, 23, 60, 133, 141, 144, 145; new 135, 136, 137, 138, 144; old 135; on the web 147
social systems 10, 29, 34, 45, 243; non-organized 21, 23, 28, 35–7; organized 21, 28–9, 32–3, 78, 96, 133
sociological communication theory 12
sociologists 2, 19, 49–50, 245, 258
sociospatial delimitation 191
"soft power" 98
solidarity, feelings of 189, 212
Spaces of Identity 174, 176
spatial reference, local 190
speech/text distinction 34, 38
Spiegel, Albert 99, 305
Stanton, Richard C 66, 71, 305
star networks 116–17, 118
state 76, 77; broadcasting 102–4; classification 262; as destructive 105; information policy 81; and social constructivist approaches 77–8; visits 86
Stegbauer, Christian 163, 166, 173, 174, 305
stereotypes 45, 64–5, 67, 206, 222, 223, 224
Stohl, Cynthia 111, 306
stormfront.org 184, 185
Straubhaar, Joseph 213, 306
Strübel, Michael 87, 306
structural-functionalist systems theory 19
structuralists 163; and constructivists debate 247
summit meetings 140
supply chains 109
"swarm intelligence" 180, 182
symbolic interaction 12, 13

symbolic power of civil society 134
synchronous processes 122
system-lifeworld-network approach 18–20, 134, 164, 244, 247–8, 259

talk shows 30, 62
Tanikawa, Miki 66, 306
Tarrow, Sidney 140, 141, 306
team conflicts, spirit 123
techno-functional perspective 56
technological control by states 253
technology, rapid development 110
telecommunications companies 58
Tepe, Daniela 138, 307
terrorism 65, 66, 86, 136
texts 34, 62, 67, 92, 150
text-speech relationships 92
Theories of Mass Communication 243
theory of cognitive dissonance 222
theory of public relations 156
theory of social capital 166
theory of social identity 188, 223
think tanks 95, 262
third culture kids 202, 224
third spaces 76, 77, 80, 89, 246, 247
Tibi, Bassam 106, 119, 128, 307
tolerance, negative and positive 230
Tönnies, Ferdinand 161, 162, 163, 307
totalitarian propaganda 102
totalitarian systems 44–5, 99
tourism 197, 202, 206, 218, 255; "culinary" 219; destinations 192; global 4, 197; "intimate" 201; mass 205; research 192, 205
"tourist gaze" 232
trade 107, 109
trade fairs 126, 127
trade unions 138
transcultural "salons" 177
transnational advocacy networks (TANs) 134, 135–8, 140, 143, 252; campaigns 156, 157; members 151
transnational corporations (TNCs) 23, 107, 108, 109
transnational products 60
transnational socialization 202
travel 28, 194, 206
travellers 239
treaties 92
"trickle-down effect" 249
Trump administration 116, 130, 252
Trump, Donald 3, 86
Turkey, shut down of social media 57
Turkish-language use 176

UN Charter (Article 33) 86
UN Conference on Trade and
  Development (UNCTAD) 110
UN General Assembly, rituals of 90
UN Resolution 242 93
UN World Summit 136
UNESCO 225
urban dwellers 190, 191
US Foreign Broadcast Information Service
  (FBIS) 94
Usenet analysis 183

van Dijk, Jan 18, 308
vertical system-environment-relations 248
video conferences 92
virtual communities 9, 24, 162, 163, 164,
  166, 167
virtual spaces 192
virtuality, excessive 123
Voice of America 22, 51
Volkmer, Ingrid 72, 246, 308
Vowe, Gerhard 75, 309
Vuorela, Ulla 202, 309

war communication 70, 101–2
wars and disasters, reporting on 63, 65
wars in the Middle East 102
weak ties 139
weapons of mass destruction 101
Web 2.0 192
web, functions of 147–8; *see also* Internet
Weenink, Don 224, 309

"we-feeling" 189, 212
Weiß, Anja 225, 310
Welge, Martin K 120, 310
Weller, Christopher 77, 310
Werbner, Pnina 218, 310
wiki communities 168
Wikileaks 135, 262
Wikipedia 181–3, 185
Williams, Kevin 64, 310
Winter, Rainer 149, 311
win-win game in international relations 85
Wöhler, Karlheinz 192, 311
Wolfsfeld, Gadi 251, 311
Woodward, Ian 220, 234, 240
Wooldridge, Adrian 220
World Bank 23, 79
World Social Forum 136
World Summit on the Information Society
  (WSIS) 141
Wright, Steve 148, 311
WTO agreements 127

Y structure networks 117
Yahoo 58, 64
youth cultures 194, 203, 220
YouTube 57

Zapatista movement 142
zero-sum game in international relations
  40, 84, 85, 183
Zoom 122, 172
Zuckerman, Ethan 59, 170, 171, 175

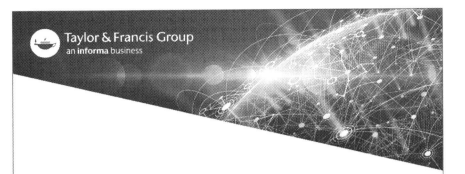

Printed in the United States
by Baker & Taylor Publisher Services